Weltschmerz

Weltschmerz is a study of the pessimism that dominated German philosophy in the second half of the nineteenth century. Pessimism was essentially the theory that life is not worth living. This theory was introduced into German philosophy by Schopenhauer, whose philosophy became very fashionable in the 1860s. Frederick C. Beiser examines the intense and long controversy that arose from Schopenhauer's pessimism, which changed the agenda of philosophy in Germany away from the logic of the sciences and toward an examination of the value of life. He examines the major defenders of pessimism (Philipp Mainländer, Eduard von Hartmann and Julius Bahnsen) and its chief critics, especially Eugen Dühring and the neo-Kantians. The pessimism dispute of the second half of the century has been largely ignored in secondary literature and this book is a first attempt since the 1880s to re-examine it and to analyze the important philosophical issues raised by it. The dispute concerned the most fundamental philosophical issue of them all: whether life is worth living.

Frederick C. Beiser was born and raised in the US, and studied in the UK at Oriel and Wolfson Colleges, Oxford. He also studied in Germany and lived in Berlin for many years, receiving stipends from the Fritz Thyssen Stiftung and the Humboldt Stiftung. He has taught in universities across the US, and is currently Professor of Philosophy at Syracuse University, Syracuse, New York. Beiser is the author of *Schiller as Philosopher* (OUP, 2005), *Diotima's Children* (OUP, 2009), *The German Historicist Tradition* (OUP, 2011), *Late German Idealism* (OUP, 2013), and *The Genesis of Neo-Kantianism, 1796–1880* (OUP, 2014).

Weltschmerz

Pessimism in German Philosophy, 1860–1900

Frederick C. Beiser

OXFORD
UNIVERSITY PRESS

Great Clarendon Street, Oxford, OX2 6DP,
United Kingdom

Oxford University Press is a department of the University of Oxford.
It furthers the University's objective of excellence in research, scholarship,
and education by publishing worldwide. Oxford is a registered trade mark of
Oxford University Press in the UK and in certain other countries

© Frederick C. Beiser 2016

The moral rights of the author have been asserted

First published 2016
First published in paperback 2018

All rights reserved. No part of this publication may be reproduced, stored in
a retrieval system, or transmitted, in any form or by any means, without the
prior permission in writing of Oxford University Press, or as expressly permitted
by law, by licence or under terms agreed with the appropriate reprographics
rights organization. Enquiries concerning reproduction outside the scope of the
above should be sent to the Rights Department, Oxford University Press, at the
address above

You must not circulate this work in any other form
and you must impose this same condition on any acquirer

Published in the United States of America by Oxford University Press
198 Madison Avenue, New York, NY 10016, United States of America

British Library Cataloguing in Publication Data
Data available

Library of Congress Cataloging in Publication Data
Data available

ISBN 978-0-19-876871-5 (Hbk.)
ISBN 978-0-19-882265-3 (Pbk.)

Links to third party websites are provided by Oxford in good faith and
for information only. Oxford disclaims any responsibility for the materials
contained in any third party website referenced in this work.

In memory of Robert C. Beiser (1892–1960).

Preface

This book attempts to explore new territory in the history of philosophy. Its subject matter is the pessimism controversy in 19th-century Germany, the dispute about the value of life or the worth of existence which began in the 1860s with the discovery of Schopenhauer's philosophy. For all its importance for contemporaries, this controversy has been largely forgotten, in Germany and the Anglophone world, since the First World War; if it is known at all, it is mainly through studies of Schopenhauer and Nietzsche. My task has been to sketch the main players in the controversy—Eugen Dühring, Eduard von Hartmann, Philipp Mainländer, Julius Bahnsen—and to explain the major issues that concerned them. Given the vast *dramatis personae* of the controversy and the enormous amount of literature it generated, it has been possible to provide at best an introduction to the controversy. Much work remains to be done on all these figures and the controversy itself.

A special concern of this book has been the influence of Schopenhauer's philosophy upon his age. This is the subject matter of chapters 1 and 5. Chapter 1 deals with the broad significance of Schopenhauer for the neo-Kantian and positivist movements. Chapter 5 treats the neglected figure of Julius Frauenstädt, Schopenhauer's "first apostle", who played a crucial role in the dissemination of Schopenhauer's philosophy.

One thinker treated in this book is, however, very well-known: Arthur Schopenhauer. The second, third and fourth chapters provide a basic outline of his philosophy, whose purpose is to set the context for the later controversy. My main aim in these chapters was to give a sympathetic reconstruction of Schopenhauer's philosophy, to show how its apparent problems disappear when they are understood in the context of his age and his system as a whole. Contemporary Anglophone interpretations of Schopenhauer are too ready to find problems in his philosophy by treating his texts analytically and hermetically. Schopenhauer's philosophy, I argue, tells at least "a likely story", a plausible tale about the universe as a whole. That the world is the manifestation of a cosmic will seems to me to be plausible rather than outlandish.

Because my aim in the Schopenhauer chapters is essentially introductory, it should be obvious that I have not been able to provide a detailed investigation of all the issues pertaining to Schopenhauer's philosophy. For that reason I have also not been able to engage with the increasingly voluminous secondary literature about it. If I have neglected to take into account the interpretations of a recent scholar, I owe him or her my apologies. My main excuse is my historical perspective and concern with historical sources.

I came to the study of pessimism through neo-Kantianism. Anyone who studies the origins of the neo-Kantian movement is struck by the influence Schopenhauer had upon the movement. His philosophy was the greatest threat it faced, partly because of its pessimism, partly because of its revival of metaphysics, and partly because of its claim to the Kantian throne. I soon came to see, however, that the neo-Kantians were only one aspect of a more general reaction against Schopenhauer, and that Schopenhauer too was only one of the many pessimists of his age.

Although the pessimism controversy has been largely forgotten, it has not been totally so. There have been two recent studies of pessimism: Lüdger Lütkehaus, *Nichts* (Frankfurt: Zweitauseneins, 2003) and Michael Pauen, *Pessimismus: Geschichtsphilosophie, Metaphysik und Moderne von Nietzsche bis Spengler* (Berlin: Akademie Verlag, 1997). I have learned much from their work, though I often take issue with them. Their focus is broader than my own and covers more historical ground. It is a pity that neither of these works has been translated.

All parts of this book are new and have not been published before. An earlier version of Chapter 1 was read to the North American Schopenhauer Society at the Meetings of the American Philosophical Association, 1 March 2014.

Syracuse, New York
14 June 2015

Contents

Introduction: The Problem of Pessimism	1
1. Pessimism as *Zeitgeist*	1
2. Intellectual Background	3
3. Philosophy and the Meaning of Life	8
4. Pessimism in the History of Philosophy	10
1. The Schopenhauer Legacy	13
1. Schopenhauer's Influence	13
2. The Puzzle of Existence	16
3. Schopenhauer and the Identity Crisis of Philosophy	18
2. Reconstructing Schopenhauer's Metaphysics	25
1. The Problem of Metaphysics	25
2. The Rehabilitation of Metaphysics	27
3. Self-Knowledge of the Will	30
4. Metaphysics of the Will	35
5. Transcendental Idealism?	38
3. Schopenhauer's Pessimism	43
1. The Dangers of Pessimism	43
2. The Modern Silenus	45
3. Arguments for Pessimism	46
4. Life as Suffering	49
4. The Illusion of Redemption	52
1. The False Promise of Deliverance	52
2. Affirming and Denying the Will	53
3. Practical Reason and Redemption	56
4. Paths to Redemption	60
5. Protestantism without Theism	63
5. Julius Frauenstädt: Apostle and Critic	67
1. An Independent Disciple	67
2. Conversion to Schopenhauer	69
3. Schopenhauer and the Materialism Controversy	74
4. Doubts about Pessimism	79
5. Revisions and Corrections	83
6. The Optimism of Eugen Dühring	87
1. A Positivist and Optimist	87
2. Logical Foundations	91
3. Logic of the Question	95
4. Theory of Value	99

5.	Reckoning with Schopenhauer	101
6.	Death	104
7.	The Political and Economic Dimension	108
8.	A System of Philosophy	111
9.	Replacing Religion	117

7. The Optimistic Pessimism of Eduard von Hartmann — 122
   1. A Fashionable Pessimist — 122
   2. The Unconscious — 126
   3. A New Religion — 129
   4. First Principles — 136
   5. Settling Accounts with Hegel — 142
   6. Foundations of Realism — 146
   7. Eudemonistic Pessimism — 152
   8. Evolutionary Optimism — 156

8. The Pessimism Controversy, 1870–1890 — 162
   1. The Eye of the Storm — 162
   2. Two Classic Objections — 163
   3. Hartmann versus the Neo-Kantians and Dühring — 165
   4. Two Female Allies — 167
   5. The Whip of Cords — 170
   6. A Hyperontology? — 172
   7. The Nature of Pleasure — 176
   8. A Pessimist Counterattack — 182
   9. The Value of Work — 186
   10. Aesthetic Redemption — 190
   11. Love — 195

9. Mainländer's Philosophy of Redemption — 201
   1. The Heroic Pessimist — 201
   2. Life and Philosophical Education — 203
   3. The Gospel of Redemption — 206
   4. Mainländer and the Young Hegelian Tradition — 209
   5. Philosophical Foundations — 211
   6. The Death of God — 215
   7. Ethics — 219
   8. Theory of the State — 223
   9. Communism, Patriotism and Free Love — 225

10. The Pessimistic Worldview of Julius Bahnsen — 229
    1. An Original and Powerful Worldview — 229
    2. The Making of a Pessimist — 232
    3. The Disciple of Schopenhauer — 235
    4. Literary Debut — 238
    5. Foundations of Pessimism — 244
    6. Hartmann's Review of Bahnsen — 246

7. In Defence of Realism	250
8. Philosophy of History	252
9. Hartmann's Offensive against Bahnsen	257
10. A Tragic Worldview	263
11. Prayers of a Pessimist	267
12. Real Dialectic	271
13. Ethics and Politics	276
14. The Pessimist as Tragic Hero	281
Bibliography	285
Index	297

Introduction
The Problem of Pessimism

1. Pessimism as *Zeitgeist*

Beginning in the 1860s, and lasting until the end of the 19th century, the dark cloud of pessimism hung thick over Germany. This bleak and black mood spread far and wide. It was not confined to decadent aristocratic circles; it could also be found in the middle classes, among students at universities, workers in factories, and even pupils in *Gymnasia*.[1] Pessimism soon became fashionable, the talk of the town, the theme of literary salons.[2] There were several anthologies of aphorisms and verse to indulge one's melancholy on any occasion.[3]

The Germans had a word for this mood: *Weltschmerz*. It means literally "worldpain", and it signifies a mood of weariness or sadness about life arising from the acute awareness of evil and suffering. Its origins have been traced back to the 1830s, to the late romantic era, to the works of Jean Paul, Heinrich Heine, N. Lenau, G. Büchner, C. D. Grabbe and K. L. Immermann.[4] By the 1860s the word had an ironic, even derogatory, meaning, implying extreme or affected sensitivity to the evil and suffering in the world. But later in that decade the word also began to acquire a broader more serious meaning: it was no longer just a poet's personal mood; it was a public state of mind, the spirit of the age, the *Zeitgeist*.[5]

The origins of this *Weltschmerz* are puzzling. There seems to be no straightforward social or historical cause for it. Indeed, from a broad historical perspective, the second

---

[1] On the spread of pessimism among all social classes, see Theodor Trautz, *Der Pessimismus* (Karlsruhe: G. Braun'schen Hofbuchhandlung, 1876), pp. 6–7.

[2] On the reception of pessimism in the salons, see Carl Heymons, *Eduard von Hartmann, Erinnerungen aus den Jahren 1868–1881* (Berlin: Carl Duncker, 1882), p. 21. In the social satire by M. Reymond, *Das Buch vom bewußten und unbewußten Herrn Meyer* (Bern: Frobeen & Cie., 1879), Herr Meyer and his wife hold a salon in which the pessimists are invited and hold court.

[3] See Otto Kemmer, ed., *Pessimisten Gesangbuch* (Minden: J. C. C. Brun's Verlag, 1884); Max Seiling, ed., *Perlen der pessimistischen Weltanschauung* (Munich: T. Ackermann, 1886); and Zdenko Fereus, ed., *Stimmen des Weltleids* (Leipzig: Wigand, 1887).

[4] On the etymology of the word, see W. Rasch, 'Weltschmerz', in, *Historisches Wörterbuch der Philosophie*, ed. Joachim Ritter, Karlfried Gründer and Gottfried Gabriel (Basel: Schwabe, 2004), XII. 514–15.

[5] On pessimism as the mood of the age, see Julius Duboc, *Hundert Jahre Zeitgeist in Deutschland* (Leipzig: Otto Wigand, 1889), I. 79–101; and Georg Peter Weygoldt, *Kritik des philosophischen Pessimismus der neuesten Zeit* (Leiden: E. J. Brill, 1875), p. 15.

half of the 19th century in Germany seems a happy age. The horrors of the 20th century lay unknown before it, and the debacles of the early 19th century—the failure of the Revolutions of 1830 and 1848—lay behind it. In September 1870 the Prussians triumphed over the French at Sedan; and in January 1871 the second *Reich* was proclaimed at Versailles. The dream of national unity, so ardently sought for generations, was finally achieved, as if by a miracle. Despite a crash (1873) and a long depression (1874–95), there was great economic and social progress in the second half of the century. Industry and trade expanded exponentially; living standards among the middle and working classes rose; welfare legislation was enacted; universal education had become a reality; great scientific discoveries were made; and transportation (railroads) and communication (telegraph) were greatly improved, far beyond what anyone believed possible. History, it seemed, was on the march, creating national unity and greater prosperity for all.

Whence, then, pessimism? What made *Weltschmerz*, despite the social, political and economic progress of the age, so popular? Contemporaries themselves were perplexed by this phenomenon. Kuno Fischer and Jürgen Bona Meyer, two neo-Kantian philosophers, attributed the rise of pessimism to the widespread disillusionment after the failure of the Revolution of 1848.[6] But other contemporaries were not convinced by their explanation. They pointed out some incontestable facts to refute it: that disillusionment was at its height in the 1850s, but that pessimism became popular only in the decade thereafter. Pessimism had become firmly entrenched in the 1870s, though this decade began with all those impressive achievements, viz., victory over France, the founding of the Second Reich, growing democracy and liberal legislation, which all seem reason to celebrate rather than mope.

There was one important economic development of the 1870s that would seem to be a potent source of *Weltschmerz*: the crash of 1873 and the ensuing "great depression", which lasted more than twenty years (1874–95).[7] Surely, one might think, these events must have had a dampening effect on the public mood. For some, they were indeed the major source of "cultural despair" during this epoch.[8] Nevertheless, however important for the *Zeitgeist*, these events do not account for the *origins* of pessimism. They explain at best the *spread* of pessimism, but not its rise, because we can trace the beginnings of that mood back to the 1860s and early 1870s, before the crash and depression.

---

[6] Kuno Fischer, *Schopenhauers Leben, Werke und Lehre*, Zweite neu bearbeitete und vermehrte Auflage (Heidelberg: Carl Winter, 1898), pp. 100–1; and Jürgen Bona Meyer, *Weltelend und Weltschmerz: Eine Rede gegen Schopenhauer's und Hartmann's Pessimismus* (Bonn: Marcus, 1872), pp. 24–6. The same explanation is given by Julius Duboc, *Hundert Jahre Zeitgeist*, I. 79, 82–4. This explanation still persists. It has been reaffirmed by Georg Lukács, *Die Zerstörung der Vernunft* (Neuwied am Rhein: Luchterhand, 1962), pp. 172–3, 176–7, 183–4, 352–3.

[7] On the "great depression", see Hans Rosenberg, *Große Depression und Bismarckzeit* (Berlin: de Gruyter, 1967).

[8] For the effects of the crash and depression on the culture of the epoch, see Fritz Stern, *The Politics of Cultural Despair* (Berkeley, CA: University of California Press, 1961), pp. xix, 66. See too his 'Money, Morals, and the Pillars of Society', in *The Failure of Illiberalism: Essays on the Political Culture of Modern Germany* (New York: Knopf, 1972), pp. 26–57.

Even if we cannot find any clear connection between pessimism and these political and economic events, one might still think that there is a connection between it and the great political question of the age: the so-called "social question" (*Sozialfrage*). This was the problem about how to deal with the aspirations and needs of the great mass of the population, about how to improve the conditions and alleviate the suffering of the peasantry and working classes.[9] Beginning in the 1830s, this problem had been at the centre of political debate in Germany. It was indeed the cause of the Revolutions of 1830 and 1848, though it had never been resolved by them. After these Revolutions, politicians would constantly debate the issue and divide into parties in their attempt to solve it. Here, it might seem, is one potent source of pessimism. According to this explanation, the pessimist would be someone who thinks that there can be no political solution to the social question, and that human suffering and evil are inherent in human nature and the human condition. By contrast, the optimist would be someone who thinks that there can be such a solution, and that human suffering and evil are surmountable by the proper form of social and political organization.

But this hypothesis too does not work. The division between optimists and pessimists in the late 19th century does not neatly divide into opposing attitudes toward the social question.

Some optimists, viz., Peter Weygoldt, Paul Christ and Theodor Trautz, who very much affirmed the value of life, were political conservatives who questioned whether the state would ever satisfy the aspirations of the working classes. On the other hand, some pessimists believed that there could be a solution to the social question. Eduard von Hartmann, Philipp Mainländer and Julius Bahnsen, for example, believed that social and political reforms, and greater technical progress, could go some way toward alleviating the sources of human suffering; but, in their view, the resolution of the social question was still not sufficient reason for optimism. Even if we relieved all the suffering of the working classes, that could not bring redemption, complete happiness or a meaningful life. After all, how is the meaning and value of life ever determined by material factors alone?

2. Intellectual Background

We cannot explain pessimism, then, simply in terms of a skeptical or cynical attitude toward the social question, still less as a reaction to a specific economic or political crisis, whether that be the failure of the 1848 Revolution or the crash and depression of the 1870s.[10] But even if we could find a satisfactory social, political or economic

---

[9] On the origins of this problem in the early 19th century, see Theodore Hamerow, *Restoration, Revolution, Reaction: Economics and Politics in Germany, 1815–1871* (Princeton: Princeton University Press, 1958), pp. 3–93.

[10] For another critique of the attempt to explain pessimism as a response to specific social and political events, see Michael Pauen, *Pessimismus: Geschichtsphilosophie, Metaphysik und Moderne von Nietzsche bis Spengler* (Berlin: Akademie Verlag, 1997), pp. 8–12, 112–17.

explanation for the rise of pessimism, it would still be far from providing a full account of its meaning and significance. Such an explanation would inform us about its political causes and context, perhaps, but it would do scant justice to its *philosophical* content and significance.

That we must take into account the philosophical dimension of pessimism was recognized and stressed by contemporaries themselves. They held that the distinctive feature of the pessimism of their age was precisely its philosophical aspect. It is striking how contemporaries made a distinction between earlier forms of pessimism and that of their own epoch, which they called "modern pessimism".[11] The distinguishing feature of modern pessimism, they claimed, is that it is philosophical or systematic. They noted that pessimism had been a common mood in many countries and epochs; but they still insisted that, in Germany in the late 19th century, it was more than a mood. Pessimism had now become a philosophy, a whole worldview. What else could one expect of a people who fancied their country "der Land der Dichter und Denker"?

There were, of course, earlier philosophical expressions of pessimism in the history of philosophy. It is only necessary to mention such thinkers as Michel de Montaigne and Giacomo Leopardi, who were profound pessimists and who justified their views philosophically. Nevertheless, there are still good reasons for thinking that Germany in the late 19th century was *the* age of pessimism, *the* epoch of *Weltschmerz*. Never before had so many thinkers thought for so long and so intensely about the problem of pessimism. For nearly a half century, the problem of pessimism would dominate philosophical thinking in Germany.

What was the philosophical meaning of pessimism? If pessimism is more than a mood, more than a passing phase of the *Zeitgeist*, what is the philosophical thesis behind it? The philosophical discussion of pessimism in late 19th-century Germany shows a remarkable unanimity about its central thesis. According to all participants in this discussion, pessimism is the thesis that life is not worth living, that nothingness is better than being, or that it is worse to be than not be. Philosophers often cited the lines from Sophocles' *Oedipus at Kolonos* as the perfect expression of pessimism:

> Never to be born, is by far the best;
> but if you are alive,
> the best is to return quickly from where you came.[12]

For this dark and dire thesis, pessimists gave one of two rationales. Life was held to be not worth living either for *eudemonic* reasons, i.e. because it is filled with more suffering than happiness, or for *idealistic* reasons, i.e. because we cannot achieve, or even progress toward, those moral, political or aesthetic ideals that give our lives meaning.

---

[11] On the term "modern pessimism", see Edmund Pfleiderer, *Der moderne Pessimismus* (Berlin: Carl Habel, 1875), p. 6; Ludwig von Golther, *Der moderne Pessimismus* (Leipzig: Brockhaus, 1878), p. 3; and O. Plümacher, *Der Pessimismus in Vergangenheit und Gegenwart*, zweite Ausgabbe (Heidelberg: Georg Weiss Verlag, 1888), pp. 1–7.

[12] Sophocles, verses 1225ff. Among many others, Schopenhauer and Nietzsche would cite these lines.

Clearly, these rationales are distinct: someone might think that, even though life is filled with suffering, it is still worth living because we make progress toward our ideals. Some pessimists (viz., Schopenhauer, Bahnsen) would combine both rationales; others, however, would carefully distinguish between them, holding one rather than the other (viz., Hartmann, Taubert and Plümacher).

Of course, the fundamental problem of pessimism—the question whether life is worth living or not—is as old as the ancient Greeks. But German philosophers in the 19th century believed that they had rediscovered this problem after it had lain dormant for millennia. Whence this rediscovery? And why had the problem been hidden for so long?

German pessimism in the late 19th century essentially grew out of a rediscovery of the problem of evil.[13] It is not that philosophers had forgotten this problem; they had always known of it; but it was as if they had now finally understood its meaning, the fundamental question behind it. Of course, the problem of evil had been central for philosophers and theologians throughout the Middle Ages and the Christian era. But the problem always took on a religious or theological form: why does evil exist if there is an omnipotent, omniscient and benevolent God? Prima facie, then, it might seem as if there should be no problem of evil if one simply denies the existence of God. There seems to be sufficient causes for the production of evil among human beings and nature for the existence of evil to be no mystery at all.

It is important to see, however, that the problem of evil does not go away even if we deny the existence of God. There was always a deeper question that lay behind that problem. Namely, why should we exist at all? Assume that the world is filled with evil and suffering, as the problem of evil presupposes. Suppose, furthermore, that there is much more evil than good, much more suffering than happiness. We are then confronted with the question whether life is really worth living after all. If I know that life will bring more suffering than happiness, more evil than good, why should I exist at all? We simply cannot assume that being is better than nothingness, that life is better than death. That was just the question that troubled the ancient Greeks, who did not believe in the theist's God, and who still worried and wondered about the worth of life in the face of evil and suffering. Philosophers in the 19th century recovered the ancient Greeks' wonder and perplexity about the value of existence.

Philosophers and theologians in the Middle Ages were always aware of the deeper question behind the problem of evil, of course, but they were convinced they had a compelling answer to it. Although there is much evil and suffering on earth, life is still worth living, they believed, because of the promise of redemption in heaven. Life on earth is a testing ground for the soul before eternal life in heaven; and only he or she who withstands the test will prove worthy of that life. The trials and tribulations of this world are therefore necessary preparation for the salvation of the soul in the world

---

[13] On the general importance of the problem of evil in modern thought, see Susan Neiman, *Evil in Modern Thought: An Alternative History of Philosophy* (Princeton: Princeton University Press, 2002).

hereafter. No matter how miserable someone might be, no one has the right to opt out of life on this earth, to leave it through voluntary death. We have all been created by God, who has made each and every one of us for a reason, even if that reason remains obscure to us. We are all players in his divine drama; and we cannot quit our part without ruining the play; we therefore have to perform our role with courage and conviction, knowing that in the end all pains and labours will be redeemed in heaven. So, however incompatible it seemed with their omniscient, omnipotent and benevolent God, medieval philosophers and theologians never really denied the existence of evil and suffering; they indeed adamantly affirmed their existence because it gave all the more point and power to the doctrine of divine grace and redemption. According to that doctrine, life is worth living, not because of its intrinsic value, but because it is a means to another end, eternal salvation.

This answer to the question of the value of life had lasted for millennia. As long as theism remained a viable form of belief, it would satisfy the heart and capture the imagination of the faithful. But, by the middle of the 19th century in Germany, theism began to falter; it was indeed on the verge of collapse. There were several familiar causes of this crisis, all of which made the demise of theism seem imminent and inevitable. There was Kant's critique of the traditional proofs of the existence of God, which had exposed the weakness of reason in knowing the unconditioned; there was Strauss's, Bauer's and Baer's biblical criticism, which had undermined faith in the sacred status of the Bible; there was Vogt's, Moleschott's and Büchner's materialism, which had attacked the orthodox beliefs regarding the age of the earth, the origin of human beings and the immaterial status of the soul; and there was Feuerbach's anthropology, which explained religion as the hypostasis of human powers. All these developments had taken place by the 1850s. The 1860s brought even more bad tidings for theism. This was the decade when Darwinism was introduced into Germany, where it spread rapidly, far more quickly than in its native England, and where it soon became official science.[14] Darwinism seemed to undermine the last refuge of theism—the mystery of life itself—because it could explain the origin of species on a naturalistic basis. For all these reasons, by the late 19th century, theism seemed doomed. When Nietzsche declared

---

[14] On Darwin's reception and influence in Germany, see Alfred Kelly, *The Descent of Darwin: The Popularization of Darwinism in Germany* 1860-1914 (Chapel Hill, NC: University of North Carolina Press, 1981). See Mario Di Gregario, 'Under Darwin's Banner: Ernst Haeckel, Carl Gegenbaur and Evolutionary Morphology', and Dirk Backenköhler. 'Only Dreams from an Afternoon Nap? Darwin's Theory of Evolution and the Foundation of Biological Anthropology in Germany 1860-75', in *The Reception of Charles Darwin in Europe*, ed. Eve-Marie Engels and Thomas F. Glick (London: Continuum, 2008), I. 79-97, 98-115; Eve-Marie Engels, *Die Rezeption von Evolutionstheorien im 19. Jahrhundert* (Frankfurt: Suhrkamp, 1995); Lynn Nyhart, *Biology Takes Form: Animal Morphology and the German Universities* 1800-1900 (Chicago: University of Chicago Press, 1995), pp. 105-42; William Montgomery, 'Germany', in *Comparative Reception of Darwinism*, ed. Thomas F. Glick (Austin, TX: University of Texas Press, 1972), pp. 81-115; P. J. Weindling, 'Darwinism in Germany', ed. David Kohn (Princeton: Princeton University Press, 1985), pp. 685-98; and Andreas Daum, *Wissenschaftspopularisierung im 19. Jahrhundert* (Munich: Oldenbourg, 2002), pp. 65-84, 300-24, 359-69.

the death of God in the 1880s, he was only drawing attention to an event that had been long in the making.

For the late 19th century, the death of God had the profoundest philosophical consequences. No longer could the problem of evil return in its old theological dress. The existence of evil and suffering impugned no longer the existence of God but the value of existence itself. Now the fundamental question behind it—whether life is worth living—appeared in its full force and it had to be confronted anew. The old theistic answer could satisfy no more: if there is no God, there is no redemption from the evil and suffering of this world. But if there is no deliverance from evil and suffering, why should we live at all? And so Hamlet's old question returned with more power than ever: "To be or not to be?"

Summa summarum, pessimism was the rediscovery of the problem of evil after the collapse of theism. It came from the realization that there is going to be no redemption from all the evil and suffering of life, and from the conviction that, for this reason, life cannot be worth living. The pessimist accepted the traditional Christian emphasis on the evil and suffering of this world; but he rejected the traditional theistic answer to it. He insisted upon two propositions: that (1) there is more evil than good, more suffering than happiness, in this world, and that (2) this evil and suffering will not be redeemed in another world. It followed from these premises, the pessimist argued, that life is not worth living, that non-existence is preferable to existence. The pessimist therefore accepted the negative side of Christian teaching (the evil and suffering of this world) but rejected its positive side (redemption in another world). Pessimism was thus essentially Christianity without theism.

The rediscovery of the ancient Greek question behind the problem of evil was the achievement of a single man: Arthur Schopenhauer. Schopenhauer had stressed how that problem is central to philosophy. We begin to reflect philosophically, he wrote in his masterpiece *Die Welt als Wille und Vorstellung*,[15] when we contemplate the existence of evil. We wonder why the world exists if there is so much suffering, and so we ask ourselves whether nothingness is better than being. No one affirmed more avidly than Schopenhauer the negative side of Christian doctrine (the reality of sin and suffering) but no one denied more decisively its positive side (supernatural deliverance). He was, as Nietzsche once said, "the first confessed and implacable atheist" in German philosophy.[16] Given his denial of theism, and given his affirmation of the evil and suffering of life, Schopenhauer had no choice but to draw his infamous pessimistic conclusions.

So much, very crudely, for the intellectual origins of pessimism. Someone might still ask, though, why the problem of the value of life is really a *philosophical* problem at all. We need to address these doubts.

---

[15] Arthur Schopenhauer, 'Über das metaphysische Bedürfnis', *Die Welt als Wille und Vorstellung*, in *Sämtliche Werke*, ed. Wolfgang Freiherr von Löhneysen (Stuttgart: Insel, 1968), II. 207–8.
[16] Nietzsche, *Die fröhliche Wissenschaft* §357, in *Sämtliche Werke*, ed. G. Colli and M. Montinari (Berlin: de Gruyter, 1980), III. 599.

3. Philosophy and the Meaning of Life

In the 1960s aspiring young philosophy students were told that philosophy has nothing to do with the meaning of life, and that it is essentially a technical discipline about the logic of language. It was held to be a vulgar and naïve error to assume that philosophy has anything to say about the purpose or value of existence. Philosophy had to be a science with its own distinctive method and subject matter, which consists in the analysis of the logic of language. Since questions about the meaning of life did not permit scientific treatment, they were banished from philosophy and relegated to the softer provinces of literature or religion. Although this positivist conception of philosophy has been gradually fading, it is still very much with us. It was crucial in the formation of analytic philosophy, which still dominates the academic establishment in the Anglophone world, and which is now rising to pre-eminence in Germany.

For all those who still cling to the old positivist conception, it is a sobering thought that philosophy has not always been viewed in such a limited way, and that in one epoch in particular such a conception was abandoned—even by its erstwhile staunchest advocates—precisely because it did not allow for reflection on the meaning and value of life. That epoch was the second half of the 19th century in Germany. From the 1860s until the First World War, as a result of the Schopenhauer legacy, philosophers in Germany were deeply concerned with the most basic questions about the value and meaning of life. Their concern is especially evident in the so-called "pessimism controversy", which was the major philosophical dispute in Germany in the last four decades of the 19th century. During that controversy, philosophers from every school intensely discussed and hotly debated the most fundamental question of all: to be or not to be? They asked, in other words, whether life is worth living. It is noteworthy that positivists and neo-Kantians, who had originally defined philosophy in proto-analytic terms as the "logic of science", were compelled to revise their original narrow definition of philosophy, so that philosophy could encompass reflection on the question of the meaning and value of life.

To an unrepentant and hardbitten positivist, the pessimism controversy might still seem like a profound mistake, a prime case in point for how even an entire epoch can get lost in "pseudo-problems". The meaning of life, such a positivist will maintain, is really a "pseudo-problem" because it is about values, and as such it cannot be settled by intellectual or rational means. All questions of value, not least those about the value of life, the positivist holds, depend on an individual's feelings, likes or choices, which no amount of information about the world can determine. While philosophers might have much to say about the nature of the world—so the argument goes—that never logically implies anything about the attitude we should have toward it. For one person, the mere scratching of his finger is a reason not to exist; but for another, the horrors of war are all the more reason to exist. Logically speaking, there is no right or wrong about extreme or even opposing responses to the facts; and if there is no right or wrong, then there are no criteria for meaningful discourse about it. So, whether life is worth living or not depends on an individual's own experience and attitude. Who, after all, is to decide whether we are happy in life other than ourselves?

It is impossible here to discuss the philosophical merits of the positivist's strict distinction of value and fact. Suffice it to point out that the pessimism controversy in late 19th-century Germany stands as a challenge to the claim that such a distinction entails the impossibility or fruitlessness of a philosophical discussion. The fact of the matter is that philosophers of all stripes—positivists as well as non-positivists—argued about the problem of the value of life, and that in doing so they raised all kinds of interesting philosophical issues relevant to its solution. The philosophers who participated in this controversy never doubted that, ultimately, each individual has to decide this question for him or herself, and they readily acknowledged that the answer to it would depend on personal experience and character. Nevertheless, they also recognized that the question raised all kinds of philosophical issues that each individual has to ponder before he or she made a *wise* or *rational* decision about the value of life. How do we measure that value? In moral or eudemonic terms? If in moral terms, what should these be? And if in eudemonic terms, what is happiness? If happiness is pleasure, what is the nature of pleasure? And what is the nature of human desire? Given the nature of human happiness and desire, is there more suffering than happiness in life? These were only the most general questions. All kinds of more specific questions arose concerning those particular aspects of life that are crucial in giving it meaning or happiness. What is the nature of love, of work, of art, of death? How do each of these make life more or less worth living? Although each individual has to make his or her decision about the value of life, he or she still has to make an *informed* decision, one that considers the basic facts, the fundamental values, and the relationship between them.

It is worth noting that many of the philosophers who discussed the value of existence in 19th-century Germany questioned the very distinction between value and fact, 'ought' and 'is', which has been the mainstay of positivism. For Schopenhauer, Hartmann and Dühring, who were the chief antagonists during much of the controversy, there is no hard and fast distinction between value and existence. The value of life very much depends on the nature of life; and the worth of existence very much depends on the structure of existence. Perhaps it was wrong of them to deny the distinction between value and fact; but that distinction cannot be simply taken for granted without begging questions against them.

Recalcitrant positivists who dismiss the philosophical question of the value of life do well to ponder the lesson learned by their 19th-century forebears. Beginning in the late 1870s, positivists and neo-Kantians realized that they could not afford to ignore that question which had aroused so much public interest. To their chagrin, they discovered that their conception of philosophy as "the logic of the sciences" was not very popular, and that, if their own philosophy were not to be an irrelevance, they had to address the question of the meaning of life. As we shall soon see,[17] during the late 1870s

---

[17] See Ch. 1, section 3.

and early 1880s, positivism and neo-Kantianism changed course dramatically in response to the interests of the public and its involvement in the grand questions of the value of life.

4. Pessimism in the History of Philosophy

Despite its great importance in late 19th-century Germany, the pessimism controversy has gone largely unstudied. There have been many studies of Schopenhauer and limitless ones of Nietzsche; but very little has been said about the broader controversy itself as it played out in the last decades of the century.[18] The many thinkers who took part in the dispute, the many issues they were concerned with, and the many contributions they made, have been mainly forgotten, not only in the Anglophone but also in the German-speaking world.

The understanding of pessimism itself, in most recent history of philosophy, has been very limited. If we follow the now prevailing canon, the chief pessimist is Schopenhauer, and his chief critic is Nietzsche. The whole question of the value of life is treated almost exclusively through these two figures, as if they exhaust all that needs to be said, and as if they alone have something interesting to say about it. But any serious historian of philosophy, who should take a broad view of the second half of the 19th century, knows that Schopenhauer was only one pessimist in his age, and that Nietzsche was only one of his critics. There were other important pessimists besides Schopenhauer: Eduard von Hartmann, Philipp Mainländer, Julius Bahnsen, Agnes Taubert and Olga Plümacher. Although they were indeed inspired by Schopenhauer, it would be a mistake to think that they were mere epigones; they depart from Schopenhauer on fundamental issues; and they not only deepen his pessimism but take it to more radical conclusions. Similarly, there were other important optimists and critics of Schopenhauer besides Nietzsche. There were the materialists (Büchner, Duboc), the positivists (Dühring) and a whole host of neo-Kantians (Windelband, Paulsen, Meyer, Vaihinger, Fischer, Rickert, Cohen, Riehl). Although they do not have today the fame of a Nietzsche, they were often cogent critics of Schopenhauer's pessimism, and indeed in some cases more compelling critics than Nietzsche himself. If our interests are philosophical rather than historical—if we are concerned with philosophical insight rather than historical influence—we are indeed better off studying these lesser known critics of pessimism.

The restriction of vision in recent history of philosophy is largely the legacy of one important book: Karl Löwith's *Von Hegel zu Nietzsche*.[19] Löwith's book is a brilliant one, and every student of 19th-century German philosophy should read it. The problem

---

[18] The chief study of the controversy is still that of Olga Plümacher, *Der Pessimius in Vergangenheit und Gegenwart*, Zweite Ausgabe (Heidelberg: Georg Weiss, 1888). We will examine Plümacher's work below Ch. 8, section 6.

[19] Karl Löwith, *Von Hegel zu Nietzsche: Der revolutionäre Bruch im Denken des 19. Jahrhunderts*, Zweite Auflage (Vienna: Europa Verlag, 1949).

with the book lies less in its content than in its reception. It has been taken to be *the* narrative about 19th-century German philosophy, while it should be regarded as really *only* one narrative. Because it has been given so much authority, its cast of thinkers has been made into the canon of 19th-century philosophy. Löwith focused only upon those thinkers who fit his story about 19th-century philosophy as a revolutionary age when humanity freed itself from religious authority and recovered its autonomy. Hence he focused upon Hegel, Marx, Kierkegaard and Nietzsche, who have now become the canonical figures in 19th-century German philosophy. Because he was not an advocate of the new autonomy, Schopenhauer failed to fit into Löwith's narrative, and so he played a mere ancillary role as Nietzsche's catalyst and counterpart.

Löwith's narrative, like all narratives, has its limits, and if we make it canonical we fail to take into account some fundamental developments and problems in 19th-century German philosophy.[20] One shortcoming of Löwith's history has been especially fatal: it neglects the great importance of Schopenhauer's reorientation of philosophy in the second half of the 19th century. It was Schopenhauer who made the question of the value of life so central to German philosophy in the 19th century, and who shifted its interests away from the logic of the sciences and back towards the traditional problems of the meaning and value of life. Once we take into account Schopenhauer's reorientation, the history of philosophy in the 19th century begins to look very different. Schopenhauer becomes central; Marx and the neo-Hegelians fade into the background; and though Nietzsche remains important, he proves to be still one player in a much larger drama, which includes many other pessimists and optimists.

The aim of the present study is to overcome Löwith's shortcoming and to fill a gap in the history of German philosophy in the second half of the 19th century. The narrative begins with a discussion of Schopenhauer's influence on his age, his rehabilitation of metaphysics and his pessimism. It then attempts to reconstruct the pessimism controversy, and to rehabilitate some of the most important optimists and pessimists of the age. This means studying in some detail figures who are almost entirely unknown in the Anglophone world—viz., Hartmann, Mainländer and Bahnsen—but also some almost completely forgotten even in the Germanic world—viz., Frauenstädt and Dühring. What I have attempted to provide here is an introduction to these thinkers, an account of their leading ideas and their intellectual development. I have focused especially on the philosophical foundations of their pessimism, an interest not sufficiently present, I believe, in most recent German literature on these figures.[21]

Some readers will miss in my narrative a figure who looms large in all contemporary discussions of the value of life: Nietzsche. Since, however, he has been so thoroughly studied by so many, I see no reason to add to the already mountainous literature about him. This is not because I regard Nietzsche as a thinker of lesser importance than those

---

[20] I have explained some of these problems in the Introduction to my *After Hegel: German Philosophy 1840–1900* (Princeton: Princeton University Press, 2014), pp. 7–13.

[21] I refer especially here to the work of Pauen, *Pessimismus*, cited above, and Ludger Lütkehaus, *Nichts* (Frankfurt: Zweitausendeins, 2003).

I discuss here. Nietzsche's philosophical and historical significance is a *fait accompli*, and it remains an important task of the history of philosophy to understand his legacy. However, on both historical and philosophical grounds, it is questionable whether the disproportionate emphasis on Nietzsche in recent scholarship is defensible. Nietzsche studies have become a virtual industry, an obsession that has taken attention away from thinkers who were just as interesting philosophically and just as important historically. The enormous emphasis on Nietzsche, compared to the virtual complete neglect of these other thinkers, reveals an astonishing lack of historical sense and philosophical sophistication. It is the task of future scholars to rectify such injustice.

It is indeed arguable that the single-minded focus on Nietzsche has been beneficial for Nietzsche studies themselves. Because many Nietzsche scholars are ignorant of his context, they tend to ascribe an exaggerated originality to him. The ideas of nihilism, the death of God, ressentiment, for example, were not coined by Nietzsche. It remains an outstanding desideratum of Nietzsche scholarship that it should *individuate* Nietzsche, that it determine what is unique and new about him in contrast to his contemporaries, that it be able to identify his precise contribution to controversies and discussions that have been long forgotten. Nietzsche needs to be approached from a new perspective, one that places him in his historical context and one that reconstructs his views in dialogue with his contemporaries and predecessors. Until that it is done it is fair to say that Nietzsche, despite the vast literature about him, will remain largely unknown.

Though most figures studied in this history have been much neglected, the first four chapters focus on a thinker much better known: namely, Schopenhauer. The reason for discussing him here is that he sets the context and background for so much of the pessimism controversy, and I could not take knowledge of him entirely for granted. What I have provided here, therefore, is essentially only an introduction to Schopenhauer's metaphysics and pessimism.[22] Students and scholars who already know their Schopenhauer will find themselves able to skip Chapters 2, 3 and 4. Chapter 1, however, is crucial for the whole narrative, which begins with Schopenhauer's legacy. This aspect of Schopenhauer has been comparatively less studied, and I believe it can be read with profit even by the best informed scholars.[23]

---

[22] There are many good introductions to Schopenhauer's philosophy. See Patrick Gardiner, *Schopenhauer* (Harmondsworth: Penguin, 1963); Christopher Janaway, *Schopenhauer: A Very Short Introduction* (Oxford: OUP, 2002); Julian Young, *Schopenhauer* (London: Routledge, 2005); Dale Jacquette, *The Philosophy of Schopenhauer* (Montreal: McGill-Queen's University Press, 2005); Robert Wicks, *Schopenhauer* (Oxford: Blackwell, 2008); Peter Lewis, *Arthur Schopenhauer* (London: Reaktion Books, 2012); Walter Abendroth, *Schopenhauer* (Hamburg: Rowohlt, 1967); and Wolfgang Weimer, *Schopenhauer* (Darmstadt: Wissenschaftliche Buchgesellschaft, 1982). There are also three important anthologies: Bart Vandenabeele, ed., *A Companion to Schopenhauer* (Chichester: Wiley-Blackwell, 2012); Christopher Janaway, ed., *The Cambridge Companion to Schopenhauer* (Cambridge: CUP, 1999); and by the same editor with Alex Neill, *Better Consciousness: Schopenhauer's Philosophy of Value* (Chichester: Wiley-Blackwell, 2009).

[23] An earlier version of this chapter, 'Re-examining the Schopenhauer Legacy', was read to the North American Schopenhauer Society at the Central Division Meetings of the American Philosophical Association, March 1, 2014.

1

The Schopenhauer Legacy

1. Schopenhauer's Influence

The prevalence of pessimism in Germany after the 1860s was due chiefly to the influence of one man: Arthur Schopenhauer (1788–1860).[1] It was Schopenhauer who made pessimism a systematic philosophy, and who transformed it from a personal attitude into a metaphysics and worldview. To be sure, Schopenhauer was not the only philosophical pessimist of his era; there were many others, among them Eduard von Hartmann, Philipp Mainländer, Julius Bahnsen, Ernst Lindner, Lazar Hellenbach, Paul Deußen, Agnes Talbert, Olga Plümacher and, last but not least, the young Nietzsche. But all these later pessimists were, directly or indirectly, Schopenhauer's progeny. Schopenhauer was the spiritual father of pessimism in the late 19th century, and as such his influence shaped the spirit of his age.

From a contemporary perspective, it is a surprising fact, which is hard to appreciate and explain, that Arthur Schopenhauer was the most famous and influential philosopher in Germany from 1860 until the First World War. This hardly squares with our contemporary image of Schopenhauer, which is that of a maverick and loner, an outsider and recluse.[2] Schopenhauer himself is partly responsible for this image, because he endorsed the description of himself as a "Kaspar Hauser".[3] Many, however, are the facts that testify to Schopenhauer's massive influence on his age: the many editions of his writings;[4] the

---

[1] All references to Schopenhauer's writings are to *Sämtliche Werke*, ed. Wolfgang Freiherr von Löhneysen (Stuttgart: Cotta-Insel, 1968), 5 vols. References to *Die Welt als Wille und Vorstellung* will also include in parentheses the corresponding page numbers of the translation by E. F. J. Payne, *The World as Will and Representation* (New York: Dover, 1969); these references will be indicated by the letter 'P'.

[2] This image of Schopenhauer appears on the back cover of the *Cambridge Companion to Schopenhauer*, ed. Christopher Janaway (Cambridge: CUP, 1999), which describes Schopenhauer as "something of a maverick figure in the history of philosophy".

[3] Kaspar Hauser (1812–33) was a foundling from Nürnberg who spent most of his life in a dark room and who acquired speech only late in his life. He had been the subject of intensive research. Schopenhauer described himself as such in the 'Vorrede' to his *Über den Willen in der Natur*, Werke, II. 303. The metaphor originally came from Friedrich Dorguth, *Grundkritik der Dialektik und des Identitätssystem* (Magdeburg: Heinrichshofen, 1849), p. 9. But, with good humour, Schopenhauer appropriated and exploited it.

[4] There were at least five editions from 1877 to 1911. They were *Sämtliche Werke*, ed. Julius Frauenstädt (Leipzig: Brockhaus, 1877), 6 vols; *Sämtliche Werke*, ed. Eduard Griesbach (Leipzig: Reclam, 1892), 6 vols; *Sämtliche Werke*, ed. Rudolf Steiner (Stuttgart: Cotta, 1923), 12 vols; *Sämtliche Werke*, ed. Paul Deussen (Munich: Piper, 1911), 16 vols; and *Sämtliche Werke*, ed. Max Frischeisen-Köhler (Berlin: Wiechert, 1900), 8 vols. Some of these editions went through several printings.

many copies sold;[5] and the many thinkers that he inspired, among them Friedrich Nietzsche, Richard Wagner, Ludwig Wittgenstein, Sigmund Freud and Thomas Mann.

Schopenhauer's influence on his age is all the more remarkable when we consider his early obscurity and near obsolescence. Though Schopenhauer craved nothing more than literary fame, the sad truth of the matter is that he had been ignored for decades. His rise to fame began in the early 1850s; but the first edition of his masterpiece, *Die Welt als Wille und Vorstellung,* appeared in 1819, three decades earlier. It had sold so poorly that half of the copies had to be pulped. For three decades, then, Schopenhauer languished in obscurity and isolation, leading the life of a bachelor hermit in Frankfurt. He blamed his fate on a conspiracy of academic philosophers, on the dirty work of Schelling, Hegel and Herbart, though the truth of the matter is far less exciting and far more demeaning: the academic philosophers had hardly bothered to notice his existence.[6]

In 1854 Schopenhauer mischievously announced his arrival by declaring, loud and clear, to the academic philosophers who had ignored him: "*Kaspar Hauser ist entsprungen!*" His breakthrough was the result of two factors: first, the success of his two volumes of essays, *Parerga und Paralipomena,* which proved popular for their wit, wisdom and general crankiness; and, second, a small band of devoted admirers, who did much to publicize his philosophy. Among these admirers were Friedrich Dorguth, Julius Frauenstädt, Adam von Doß and Johann August Becker. Due to their efforts, Schopenhauer's major work finally began to sell. There were other significant signs of growing recognition: lectures on Schopenhauer's philosophy in Breslau and Leipzig; essay contests on his work; and textbooks on the history of philosophy that assigned him a modest but solid place.[7] Even better, Wagner had set his philosophy to music; and a wealthy landowner, Carl Ferdinand Wiesike, had built a chapel and shrine for him. Small wonder, then, that in Frankfurt, Schopenhauer had become a veritable tourist attraction. Admirers flocked to his lodgings, sought his autograph and requested tables next to his own at his favourite restaurant. To his delight and surprise, Schopenhauer lived to enjoy his literary fame; and in the last decade of his life he basked in the public admiration which he felt he so deeply deserved, and of which he felt so unjustly deprived.

Though the story of Schopenhauer's rise to fame is fascinating, I have no intention of retelling it here, chiefly because it has already been told so well by others.[8] My task now

---

[5] In 1938 the Schopenhauer scholar Hans Zint wrote to Reclam Verlag to ask how many copies they had sold of their popular edition. The answer was an astounding 750,000–800,000 copies! See his *Schopenhauer als Erlebnis* (Munich: Ernst Reinhardt Verlag, 1954), pp. 188–9.

[6] Herbart, however, had written one of the first substantial reviews of *Die Welt als Wille und Vorstellung* for *Hermes,* Stück 3 (1820), 131–49 (repr. in Johann Friedrich Herbart, *Sämtliche Werke,* ed. Karl Kehrbach and Otto Flügel (Langasalza: Hermann Beyer & Sohne, 1907), XII. 56–75).

[7] Carl Fortlage, *Genetische Geschichte der Philosophie seit Kant* (Leipzig: Brockhaus, 1852), pp. 407–23; and Johann Eduard Erdmann, *Die Entwicklung der deutschen Spekulation seit Kant,* 2nd edn (Leipzig: Vogel, 1853), Zweiter und letzter Theil, §40, 381–412.

[8] Three good accounts of Schopenhauer's rise to fame: Kuno Fischer, *Schopenhauers Leben, Werke und Lehre,* Zweite neu bearbeitete und vermehrte Auflage, Band IX. *Geschichte der neuern Philosophie*

is a very different one: to understand Schopenhauer's influence, especially his philosophical importance for his age. But here too it might seem that there is not much new to say. There have been old studies of that influence, which has been a favourite theme of Schopenhauer scholarship for decades.[9] There are many insightful and informative articles or book chapters on Schopenhauer's impact on Ludwig Wittgenstein, Sigmund Freud, Friedrich Nietzsche, Eduard von Hartmann and Thomas Mann, to name only a few. It might seem, then, that anyone who writes about Schopenhauer's influence will have to pick through old morsels and walk down well-trodden paths.

But, at the risk of impertinence, I would like to say that the study of Schopenhauer's influence has scarcely begun, and that if we are fully to appreciate its depth and breadth, we have to change focus. For all its merits, there has been a basic problem with the study of Schopenhauer's influence: it has committed the proverbial fallacy of missing the forest for the trees. Rather than examining his influence on his entire age, it has focused on later individual thinkers. But we cannot begin to understand the depth and breadth of Schopenhauer's influence if we simply examine the many famous thinkers he inspired; we also need to consider the role he played in the wider crises and controversies of the 19th century.

This is a deep shortcoming, because, ultimately, Schopenhauer's influence lies more on his age than on individual thinkers. In a very important sense Schopenhauer set the intellectual agenda for the second half of the 19th century. He not only posed the chief philosophical problem of his age, but he also addressed, sometimes more effectively than his rivals, its cultural and intellectual crises. For this reason, we can sometimes gauge his influence more from those who *opposed* him than from those who *followed* him. *Incredibile sed verum*: Schopenhauer had a profound influence on two intellectual movements of the late 19th century that were utterly opposed to him: neo-Kantianism and positivism. He forced these movements to address issues they would otherwise have completely ignored, and in doing so he changed them markedly.

My task here is to explain Schopenhauer's influence by showing how his philosophy successfully responded to one fundamental challenge of his age: the identity crisis of philosophy. I also want to demonstrate and explain his often overlooked, and little understood, effect on neo-Kantianism and positivism. Before I do these things, however, I want to consider the basic philosophical problem posed by Schopenhauer, because it, more than anything else, set the agenda for his age.

(Heidelberg: Winter, 1898), pp. 86–97, 103–27; Arthur Hübscher, 'Arthur Schopenhauer: Ein Lebensbild', in *Arthur Schopenhauer, Sämtliche Werke* (Leipzig: Brockhaus, 1937), I. 81–120; and David E. Cartwright, *Schopenhauer: A Biography* (Cambridge: CUP, 2010), pp. 504–17, 624–48.

[9] For recent studies of Schopenhauer's influence, see Wolfgang Weimer, *Schopenhauer* (Darmstadt: Wissenschaftliche Buchgesellschaft, 1982), pp. 149–64; Bryan Magee, *The Philosophy of Schopenhauer*, rev. and enlarged edn (Oxford: OUP, 2009), pp. 271–417; Michael Fox, *Schopenhauer: His Philosophical Achievement* (Totowa, NJ: Barnes & Noble, 1980), pp. 197–254.

2. The Puzzle of Existence

Sometimes the greatest contribution of a philosopher lies less in any theory, argument or idea than in the simple statement of a problem. If that statement is fresh, striking and provocative, it will inspire other philosophers to think about it; and it is even possible that, in rare cases, it will challenge an entire generation. Such was the case with Friedrich Heinrich Jacobi who, at the end of the 18th century, posed the conflict between reason and faith in such a dramatic fashion that no one in his age could ignore it. Something very similar happened with Arthur Schopenhauer, who did for the 19th century very much what Jacobi did for the 18th. Schopenhauer gave a provocative statement of a fundamental philosophical problem, one so clear and compelling that it became impossible to ignore.[10] This problem is a classical one—it has been with us since the Greeks—and it is a problem that we all think about, even if it is not always at the centre of philosophical attention. It was Schopenhauer's great merit to have posed this problem anew, to have insisted upon an answer to it, and to have once again placed it at the heart of philosophy. He called this problem, boldly and strikingly, "the puzzle of existence" (*das Rätsel des Daseins*).

What, precisely, was this puzzle of existence? Schopenhauer sometimes explains it as if it were nothing more than the classical metaphysical conundrum why there is something rather than nothing. He thinks that existence is contingent, that it is logically possible for the universe to be as well as not be, which inevitably raises the question why something exists at all. But there is something misleading about this formulation of his problem, because prima facie it seems like a theoretical or metaphysical problem. But Schopenhauer expressly forbids speculation about the ultimate reasons or causes for existence. He holds that the principle of sufficient reason applies only *within* the realm of experience or nature, and that we cannot extend it beyond that realm to give an explanation of the origin of experience or nature as a whole.

We can understand the meaning of Schopenhauer's puzzle of existence only when we recognize that it has for him an essentially *practical* or *ethical* significance. The radical contingency of existence concerns less the contingency of the world than the fact that we choose to exist rather than not to exist. If we wanted to, we could choose not to exist, to end our lives right here and now through suicide. The puzzle of existence is that we choose to exist in the face of all the evil and suffering of the world. There is so much evil, and so much suffering in the world, that it often seems it would be better if we did not exist at all. This naturally raises the question: what is the *value* of existence? Is life *worth* living or not?

So, ultimately, Schopenhauer's question is more practical then theoretical, more ethical than metaphysical. His puzzle of existence is what we might call "the Hamlet question": "To be or not to be?" That question arises naturally, Schopenhauer thinks,

---

[10] Schopenhauer's best statement of this problem is in ch. 17 of vol. II of *Die Welt als Wille und Vorstellung*, 'Über das metaphysische Bedürfnis', *Sämtliche Werke*, II. 206–43 (P II. 160–87).

whenever we reflect on two fundamental facts of human life: the existence of evil and the omnipresence of suffering.

Although Schopenhauer's problem is as old as the Greeks, it is important to see that, in its 19th-century context, there was something new about it. It was the modern twist that Schopenhauer gave to this problem that proved so challenging for philosophers in the 19th century.

Schopenhauer's problem differs in an important respect from a very similar one that bothered philosophers since the rise of Christianity: namely, what is the meaning or purpose of life? Or, to give the question its most common 18th-century formulation: what is the vocation of man? This question had been posed in the mid-18th century by J. J. Spalding in his famous little book *Die Bestimmung des Menschen,* which was first published in 1748 and which went through no less than thirteen editions.[11] Spalding's question had sparked much discussion in the 18th century, and there had been in the 1760s a famous controversy surrounding it in which Thomas Abbt, Moses Mendelssohn and Johann Gottfried Herder were all participants.[12] Spalding's question was, however, not really new at all, but only a fresh statement of a perennial problem of the Judaeo-Christian tradition. This problem assumes that there is a God who has created nature and humanity according to a plan or design, and that in that divine scheme each individual is assigned his or her proper role and place. The meaning of life, the purpose of existence, is to fulfil one's role in this plan, to play one's allotted part, and so to satisfy our "calling", the purpose of God in creating us. The meaning of life is a mystery for us, however, because God's plan is very obscure, and the only clues about it lie in suggestive passages of the Bible.

Seen from this 18th-century perspective, Schopenhauer's question is new, chiefly because it laid aside the teleological and theological presuppositions of the traditional Christian one. Schopenhauer not only denies theism but he also disputes the teleology behind 18th-century metaphysics. There is for him not only no God, but also no plan or purpose behind our creation and existence. So when Schopenhauer poses the question of the value of life, he does so—for better or worse—from a new secular or atheistic starting point. We can no longer assume that, despite all the suffering, and despite all the evil, there will be divine grace or redemption. If there is no God to redeem suffering, and if there is no God to ensure that good triumphs over evil, the problem of existence poses itself anew. Is life really worth living if it contains more suffering than happiness, more evil than good, and if it promises no reward or redemption in some life to come?

---

[11] Johann Joachim Spalding, *Die Bestimmung des Menschen* (Greifswald: Struck, 1748). See the new edition by Wolfgang Müller (Waltrop: Hartmut Spenner, 1997), which contains the 1st edn of 1748 and the last of 1794.

[12] On this controversy, see my article 'Mendelssohn versus Herder on the Vocation of Man', and George di Giovanni, 'The Year 1786 and *Die Bestimmung des Menschen, or Popularphilosophie* in Crisis', in Reinier Munk (ed.), *Moses Mendelssohn's Metaphysics and Aesthetics* (Dordrecht: Springer, 2011), pp. 217–45.

It was Schopenhauer's great merit to have returned philosophy to this age-old question, but to have done so in a more secular age. He clearly saw that the problem would not go away—that it was indeed more pressing than ever—if we reject the theology and teleology behind its traditional formulations. It is striking how he restates the problem of evil even though he rejects the old theist assumptions behind it. For Schopenhauer, no less than theologians in the Judaeo-Christian tradition, the problem of evil is central to philosophy, and he even goes so far as to say that the origin of philosophy arises from contemplation of the existence of evil.[13] For him too, the existence of evil is the great conundrum; but it is so not because it impugns the existence of God, but because it impugns the value of existence itself. Evil and suffering are for Schopenhauer the great stains upon existence itself—even if that existence is not created by God.

Part of Schopenhauer's merits in restating this problem is that he had raised it to a new philosophical dimension. He had seen that the problem of the value of life raises all kinds of philosophical issues. What is the highest good, the best life for a human being? Can we achieve this good in this life? What is the nature of desire? Do the highest values of life—love, work, art—redeem it or do they involve more suffering than pleasure? Are there some values that justify the suffering and evil in life and make it worth living? By what standards should we measure the value of life? All these questions were posed by Schopenhauer's puzzle of existence, and they deserved, indeed demanded, answers.

In posing the puzzle of existence, and in provoking philosophical reflection about it, Schopenhauer had done something that many of his philosophical contemporaries had called for but never achieved: he had made philosophy relevant to life. Philosophy would now be an essential part of every individual's attempt to answer the most important question of them all: "to be or not to be?"

3. Schopenhauer and the Identity Crisis of Philosophy

To understand Schopenhauer's influence on German philosophy in the second half of the 19th century, it is of the first importance to know something about the so-called "identity crisis of philosophy",[14] and the major attempts to solve it. Schopenhauer's philosophy became so influential chiefly because it offered the most successful solution to that crisis, one more plausible and satisfactory than its competitors. This was so not only in the estimation of Schopenhauerians but even in that of his rivals, whose conception of philosophy became more Schopenhauerian.

What is philosophy? Why should we do it? And how does it differ from the empirical sciences? These were the questions philosophers began to ask themselves in

---

[13] Schopenhauer, *Die Welt als Wille und Vorstellung, Werke*, II. 222 (P II. 171).
[14] The term "identity crisis" was coined by Herbert Schnädelbach, *Philosophy in Germany* 1831–1933 (Cambridge: CUP, 1984), pp. 5, 67. For a survey of the various positions in the identity crisis, see my *After Hegel: German Philosophy* 1840–1900 (Princeton: Princeton University Press, 2014), pp. 15–52.

Germany in the 1840s. They no longer knew how to define themselves or their discipline. Philosophers, it seemed, could no longer justify their existence. The crisis became all the more pressing because some philosophers even declared the death of philosophy. Some materialists and neo-Hegelians, for example, wanted philosophy to disappear, to become one with the natural sciences.

This identity crisis grew out of two recent developments. One was the rapid rise of the new empirical sciences, which had grown enormously in size and prestige since the beginning of the century. These sciences carved up the entire *globus intellectualis* among themselves, so that there seemed nothing left for philosophy to do. Philosophy had given birth to the special sciences; but now that her children had grown up, they scorned the guidance of their mother. As one philosopher described the attitude of the sciences: "It would have been better if the old and cranky mother [philosophy] had laid herself to rest in her grave".[15]

The other development was the collapse of the great idealist systems of Fichte, Schelling and Hegel. By the 1840s, their stature began to decline, and by the 1850s they were generally regarded as intellectually bankrupt, as the flotsam and jetsam of a bygone age. These systems had strived to lead the sciences, to realize the ideal of a first philosophy, and to do so through a priori methods, whether that was rigorous reasoning from a first principle (Reinhold, Fichte), intellectual intuition and construction (Schelling) or the dialectic (Hegel). But these grand ambitions now seemed illusory in comparison to the empirical sciences, whose methods of observation and experiment appeared to be the only way to get solid and sure results. The old a priori methods now seemed suspect; they were illicit attempts to claw content from form, or, as Kant once put it, to squeeze milk from a billy goat. Such, in essence, had been the chorus of some potent critics of the idealist tradition, viz., Adolf Trendelenburg, Hermann Weiße, Hermann Lotze and Ludwig Feuerbach.[16]

The net result of these developments is that philosophy had lost its sense of direction and vocation. It seemed to have no special subject matter, because the empirical sciences covered every sector of reality. But it also seemed to have no unique or characteristic method, because the a priori methods had proven bankrupt, and the a posteriori methods were the possession of the empirical sciences.

One response to this crisis was neo-Kantianism. We can trace the origins of this movement back to the late 18th century, to the criticisms of speculative idealism by Jakob Fries, Johann Friedrich Herbart and Friedrich Beneke; but it came into its own as a self-conscious and organized force only in the 1860s, shortly after Schopenhauer's ascent. What gave this movement its rationale and success was its answer to the identity crisis. In the early 1860s two young neo-Kantians—Kuno Fischer and Eduard

---

[15] See Jürgen Bona Meyer, *Philosophische Zeitfragen* (Bonn: Adolph Marcus, 1870), p. 1.
[16] Four works were crucial in questioning the methodology of the idealist systems: Adolf Trendelenburg's *Logische Untersuchungen* (Berlin: Bethge, 1840); Hermann Weiße's *Über den gegenwärtigen Standpunct der philosophischen Wissenschaften* (Leipzig: Barth, 1829); Hermann Lotze's *Metaphysik* (Leipzig: Hirzel, 1841); and Ludwig Feuerbach's *Grundsätze der Philosophie der Zukunft* (Zurich: Fröbel, 1843).

Zeller—had responded to the crisis by formulating a new conception of philosophy, one that seemed to give philosophy a unique vocation of its own apart from the empirical sciences.[17] Fischer and Zeller saw the fundamental task of philosophy as *epistemology* (*Erkenntnislehre*), as second-order reflection on the *logic* of the empirical sciences, i.e. their aims, methods and presuppositions. Since epistemology is a "transcendental" enterprise, they reasoned, its concern is with the conditions and limits of knowledge rather than with the objects of knowledge themselves. The special interest of the natural scientist, however, is with just these objects, not with the methods and presuppositions by which he acquires knowledge of them. Hence reflection on such methods and presuppositions remains, Fischer and Zeller reasoned, the distinctive task of the philosopher.

At least initially, the neo-Kantian solution to the crisis proved very successful. It not only insured philosophy against obsolescence by the sciences, given that scientists do not investigate the logic of their discipline, but it also made philosophy into something of a science of its own, i.e. a discipline having a strict methodology and standards of knowledge, given that reflection on the logic of the sciences requires technical expertise and rigorous thinking. Admittedly, philosophy had now become a handmaiden of the sciences; but in an age when the new sciences enjoyed enormous prestige, service to them seemed both a virtue and necessity.

For nearly two decades, this definition of philosophy served the neo-Kantians well. Yet, despite its advantages, it suffered from one fatal disadvantage: it left no place for the realm of value. What is the highest good? What is the criterion of morality? What is the value of existence? Since classical times these questions had been the heart and soul of philosophy. Yet they fell outside the neo-Kantian paradigm. Since these questions do not concern the logic of the sciences, the neo-Kantian conception could not accommodate them. Of course, Kant himself had given the greatest importance to these ethical questions; but, because of the prestige and power of the natural sciences in the second half of the 19th century, the neo-Kantians failed to observe their master's precedent in this crucial regard. Such indeed was the neo-Kantian neglect of these issues that, by the early 1870s, their movement had come remarkably close to positivism, which notoriously gave little importance to questions of value. This affinity with positivism became explicit when the neo-Kantians formed an alliance with the positivists in the production of the new positivist journal, *Vierteljahrsschrift für wissenschaftliche Philosophie*.[18] Such prominent neo-Kantians as Friedrich Paulsen, Otto Liebmann, Wilhelm Windelband, Eduard Zeller and Hans Vaihinger were contributors to this journal; and for a short while Alois Riehl even helped with the editing.

---

[17] Kuno Fischer, *Kant's Leben und die Grundlagen seiner Lehre* (Mannheim: Friedrich Bassermann, 1860); and Eduard Zeller, 'Ueber Bedeutung und Aufgabe der Erkenntnistheorie', a lecture first delivered 22 Oct. 1862, in *Vorträge und Abhandlungen* (Leipzig: Fues, 1877), II. 479–96.

[18] *Vierteljahrsschrift für wissenschaftliche Philosophie*, ed. R. Avenarius (Leipzig: Fues, 1877–1901), 24 vols. In 1902 the journal appeared under the new title *Vierteljahrsschrift für wissenschaftliche Philosophie und Soziologie*, ed. Paul Barth (Leipzig: Riesland, 1902–16), 15 vols.

The neo-Kantians would probably have continued down the positivist trail—they would probably have persisted in their "dogmatic slumbers"—if it had not been for one man: the old scrooge of Frankfurt. No one was more effective in arousing the neo-Kantians, in reminding them of the traditional concerns of philosophy, than Arthur Schopenhauer. By the late 1850s, the very years in which neo-Kantians began to coalesce and become a coherent movement, Schopenhauer was quickly becoming the most famous philosopher in Germany. For the neo-Kantians, however, Schopenhauer's rise to fame could only come as a thorn in their side. Although Schopenhauer died in September 1860, well before the neo-Kantians became established professors in German universities, they would have had little difficulty in inferring his attitude toward their up-and-coming movement. University philosophers were Schopenhauer's special *bête noire*, and many neo-Kantians were just that. Schopenhauer had already made well known his dislike of some early neo-Kantians, viz., Friedrich Beneke, Carl Fortlage, Jacob Fries and Johann Friedrich Herbart, whom he dismissed contemptuously as even less important, and even less respectable, than Fichte, Schelling and Hegel.[19] More severe condemnation is scarcely imaginable! Not the least annoying aspect of Schopenhauer's rising fame for the neo-Kantians was his claim to be the sole true heir of Kant. For a movement that legitimated itself by appealing to Kant's name, that pretension was nothing short of provocation. And so Schopenhauer became for the neo-Kantians "the great pretender".

Because of his rising fame, because of his antipathy to the early neo-Kantians, and because of his claim to be Kant's sole legitimate heir, the neo-Kantians became virtually obsessed with "the philosopher king of Frankfurt". Their preoccupation is apparent not least from their many writings about him. From the mid-1860s until the early 1900s, Kuno Fischer, Otto Liebmann, Jürgen Bona Meyer, Friedrich Paulsen, Rudolf Haym, Alois Riehl, Johannes Volkelt and Wihelm Windelband wrote articles, essays, book chapters or even whole books about Schopenhauer. Such, indeed, was their interest that Haym, Meyer, Fischer and Volkelt wrote some of the first monographs on him.[20] By the late 1870s, the pessimism of Schopenhauer had replaced the materialism of Büchner, Moleschott, Czolbe and Vogt as the neo-Kantians' favourite whipping boy.

Despite their many reasons for disliking Schopenhauer, the primary challenge of Schopenhauer for the neo-Kantians came from his conception of philosophy. Schopenhauer stood as a constant warning to the neo-Kantians that their own

---

[19] On Schopenhauer's view of Fries and Herbart, see his famous essay 'Über die Universitätsphilosophie', in *Parerga und Paralipomena*, *Werke*, I. 224. Schopenhauer's contempt for Beneke was boundless, chiefly because Beneke wrote a critical review of *Die Welt als Wille und Vorstellung*. On Schopenhauer's attitude and treatment of Beneke, see his 26 Mar. 1854, letter to Julius Frauenstädt, in *Gesammelte Briefe*, ed. Arthur Hübscher (Bonn: Bouvier, 1978), p. 336. As for Fortlage, *Gesammelte Briefe*, 335, he was "*ein böser Hund, mit einem Maulkorb*".

[20] Rudolf Haym, *Arthur Schopenhauer* (Berlin: Reimer, 1864); Jürgen Bona Meyer, *Arthur Schopenhauer als Mensch und Denker* (Berlin: Carl Habel, 1872); Kuno Fischer, *Schopenhauers Leben, Werke und Lehre*, Zweite Auflage, Band IX of *Geschichte der neuern Philosophie* (Heidelberg: Winter, 1898); and Johannes Volkelt, *Arthur Schopenhauer: Seine Persönlichkeit, seine Lehre, seine Glaube* (Stuttgart: Frommann, 1900).

conception of philosophy as epistemology is much too narrow, much too scholastic, much too removed from the immediate problems of life. That conception could not do justice to the traditional ethical problems of philosophy—"What is the highest good?", "What is the value of life?"—the very problems that give philosophy its enduring relevance and value.

Ultimately, for the general public, Schopenhauer's conception of philosophy proved a more attractive solution to the identity crisis of philosophy than the neo-Kantian one. No less than the neo-Kantian conception, Schopenhauer's conception insured philosophy against obsolescence, given that the natural sciences could not answer questions about the value of life. But, even better than the neo-Kantian conception, Schopenhauer's conception was true to the traditional vocation of philosophy, to what philosophers had been doing since antiquity. And, best of all, Schopenhauer's conception gave philosophy an immediate relevance and importance, because its concern with the value of life was of interest to every human being. To be engaged with its problems, at least as Schopenhauer saw them, one did not have to be an expert on the sciences and their logic, still less a university professor. While the neo-Kantian conception made philosophy a specialized and esoteric discipline, Schopenhauer's made philosophy a public and exoteric concern. No wonder, then, that the neo-Kantian conception remained confined to the universities, whereas Schopenhauer's found favour among the general educated public.

By the late 1870s, the neo-Kantians began to feel Schopenhauer's challenge, even in the halls of the universities. Schopenhauer's philosophy was proving popular among students, who felt more drawn to lectures on the puzzle of existence than those on the logic of the sciences. Faced with dwindling student interest, and concerned to have some social relevance, the neo-Kantians began to broaden their conception of philosophy beyond epistemology so that it could include the problem of value. They now began to distance themselves from their former allies, the positivists. This new more practical, anti-positivist direction of the neo-Kantians is apparent from several developments in the late 1870s and early 1880s. First, some prominent neo-Kantians, especially Windelband, Liebmann and Paulsen, abandoned the positivist *Vierteljahrschrift* and became highly critical of positivism.[21] Second, in 1877, Carl Schaarschmidt, a neo-Kantian, restarted the *Philosophische Monatshefte* by giving it an ethical agenda to counteract the *Vierteljahrschrift*.[22] Third, starting in the late 1870s, there was a great increase in the number of lectures given by neo-Kantians on the topics of practical philosophy and the nature of philosophy.[23]

---

[21] See Wilhelm Windelband, 'Immanuel Kant. Zur Säkularfeier seiner Philosophie. Vortrag' (1881), in *Präludien*, Neunte Auflage (Tübingen: Mohr, 1924), I. 112–45, esp. 123; Friedrich Paulsen, 'Idealismus und Positivismus', *Im neuen Reich*, 10 (1880), 735–42; and Otto Liebmann, *Die Klimax der Theorieen; Eine Untersuchung aus dem Bereich der allgemeinen Wissenschaftslehre* (Straßberg: Trübner, 1884).

[22] See Carl Schaarschmidt, 'Vom rechten und falschen Kriticismus', *Philosophische Monatshefte*, 14 (1878), 1–12. See also Johannes Volkelt, 'Philosophische Monatshefte', *Jenaer Literaturzeitung*, 5 (1878), 95–6.

[23] On these developments, see the data assembled by Klaus Christian Köhnke, *Entstehung und Aufstieg des Neu-Kantianismus* (Frankfurt: Suhrkamp, 1986), pp. 398–9, 404–5, 407, 601–9.

If we look at some signal writings of prominent neo-Kantians in the early 1880s, this shift in direction is fully apparent. In 1881 Wilhelm Windelband, in an influential lecture, sketched a conception of philosophy that made it a "general science of norms", a discipline that would study human values in the widest sense, not only in logic but also in ethics and aesthetics.[24] In 1882 Johannes Volkelt wrote an article that called for a renewal of interest in ethics in the neo-Kantian movement, insisting that the critical philosophy had always been not only an epistemology but also an ethics.[25] And, finally, in 1883 Alois Riehl gave a lecture that divided philosophy into two parts: theoretical or scientific philosophy, which concerns the logic of the sciences; and practical or non-scientific philosophy, which deals with ethics and aesthetics.[26] Although relegating ethics and aesthetics to "non-scientific" philosophy seems to diminish its stature and importance, Riehl insisted he did not intend anything of the kind. He stressed the importance of the practical or "non-scientific" part of philosophy, which became his main concern for the rest of his life.[27]

It was not only the neo-Kantians, though, who were challenged by Schopenhauer's conception of philosophy. Remarkably, even the positivists came under its spell. This is especially apparent in the case of the father of German positivism, Eugen Dühring (1833–1921), who will be the subject of a later chapter. Prima facie one would think that, as a positivist, Dühring would have little interest in a philosopher like Schopenhauer, whose conception of philosophy was an implicit indictment of positivism *avant la lettre*. Nevertheless, in his youth, only one philosopher influenced Dühring more than August Comte: Arthur Schopenhauer. No less than the neo-Kantians, Dühring was especially influenced by Schopenhauer's conception of philosophy. A lifelong *Privatdozent*, whose income depended largely on lecture fees and royalties, Dühring knew all too well that "the logic of the sciences" was not going to be a winner at the box office. And so, beginning in 1865, he published one of the most successful philosophical works of the late 19th century: *Der Werth des Lebens*.[28] This book, which went through no less than eight editions, was an attempt to solve Schopenhauer's "puzzle of existence" and to answer his pessimism. A central contention of Dühring's book is that the question of the value of life is of fundamental importance to philosophy, a point he drove home in edition after edition.

From the positivist and neo-Kantian reconception of philosophy in the late 1870s and early 1880s, then, we can begin to measure Schopenhauer's profound impact on

---

[24] Wilhelm Windelband, 'Immanuel Kant: Zur Säkularfeier seiner Philosophie. Vortrag', *Präludien*, I. 112–46.

[25] Johannes Volkelt, 'Wiedererweckung der kantischen Ethik', *Zeitschrift für Philosophie und philosophische Kritik*, 81 (1882), 37–48.

[26] Alois Riehl, *Ueber wissenschaftliche und nichtwissenschaftliche Philosophie: Eine akademische Antrittsrede* (Tübingen: Mohr, 1883).

[27] See Riehl's later lecture 'The Vocation of Philosophy at the Present Day', in *Lectures Delivered in Connection with the Dedication of the Graduate College of Princeton University* (Princeton: Princeton University Press, 1914), 53–63.

[28] E. Dühring, *Der Werth des Lebens: Eine philosophische Betrachtung* (Breslau: Eduard Trewendt, 1865). On the various editions, see Ch. 5, section 1, n. 2.

German philosophy in the second half of the 19th century.[29] Schopenhauer's legacy affected the very conception of philosophy itself, and it began a shift in interest away from technical problems of logic and epistemology and toward more traditional concerns with ethics and the value of life. We can now see that Schopenhauer's influence was not confined to *Lebensphilosophie* alone, to thinkers like Nietzsche, Dilthey and Simmel, who are seen as his usual heirs; rather, it extended to his opponents, to the positivists and neo-Kantians themselves. It was not least for these reasons that Schopenhauer proved himself to be the most influential philosopher of the late 19th century.

---

[29] It has been said that one of the most difficult problems in understanding neo-Kantianism in the late 1870s and early 1880s is its turn toward the practical. See Köhnke, *Entstehung und Aufstieg*, p. 404. My argument has been that this turn was first and foremost the response to Schopenhauer's challenge. Given the depth and width of that response, this seems the most likely hypothesis. Köhnke's theory that the turn came from a reaction to political events (pp. 421, 427) is highly speculative and at best holds for Windelband and Meyer alone. For a critical assessment of Köhnke's theory, see my *The Genesis of Neo-Kantianism, 1796–1880* (Oxford: OUP, 2014), pp. 525–30.

2

Reconstructing Schopenhauer's Metaphysics

1. The Problem of Metaphysics

Although some aspects of Schopenhauer's idea of philosophy were warmly received in the late 19th century, other aspects proved more controversial. Schopenhauer had convinced his age that philosophy should ponder "the puzzle of existence", that it should be first and foremost a reflection upon the ends of life and the value of existence. He had easily defeated the opposing positivist and neo-Kantian conceptions of philosophy, which had defined it in more scholastic terms as "the logic of the sciences". But Schopenhauer had conceived philosophy as more than just reflection on the meaning of life; he had also understood it to be metaphysics, and indeed metaphysics in the classical sense, i.e. a theory about reality in itself and nature as a whole.[1] Such a conception of philosophy was, to put it mildly, unfashionable. In the second half of the 19th century metaphysics had once again fallen on hard times. The new idealist systems of Fichte, Schelling and Hegel had collapsed just as the old rationalist systems of Spinoza, Leibniz and Wolff had before them. The positivists and neo-Kantians had recently reaffirmed Kant's negative teachings about metaphysics, which made it seem as suspect as ever. In conceiving philosophy as metaphysics, then, Schopenhauer was swimming against the dominant current of his age.

The positivists and neo-Kantians were not slow to challenge Schopenhauer's metaphysics. Eugen Dühring, Wilhelm Windelband, Otto Liebmann, Friedrich Lange, Kuno Fischer, Jürgen Bona Meyer, Hermann Cohen and Alois Riehl were relentless in descrying what they regarded as the wild speculations and metaphysical extravagance of Schopenhauer's philosophy. Schopenhauer's sins were many and they were blatant: he claimed knowledge of the thing-in-itself, insight into Platonic forms and the power to interpret the essence of things. He had even revived *Naturphilosophie* with all its pretentious claims to know the inner core of nature. What, they asked, could be more irresponsibly, more lavishly, metaphysical? The positivists and neo-Kantians deemed Schopenhauer's philosophy as just another metaphysics on par with the now obsolete systems of Fichte, Schelling and Hegel. Just as those systems

---

[1] See *Die Welt als Wille und Vorstellung* (*WWV*), I. 190, §24 (Payne tr. = P 125); *WWV* II. 212 (P 164).

collapsed from within because they could not support their own weight, the same would happen to Schopenhauer's.

However unfashionable, Schopenhauer could neither relent nor retreat from his metaphysics. He was utterly committed to it, and it was vital to his entire philosophy. Fundamental aspects of Schopenhauer's philosophy—his pessimism and ethics—depend on his metaphysics. His pessimism holds that life is suffering because it is the product of an insatiable and incessant cosmic will; and his ethics holds that we achieve redemption only when we recognize our identity with all other things. Schopenhauer insisted that the two aspects of his idea of philosophy—reflection on the value of life and metaphysics—are inseparable. If philosophy were reflection on the value of life, then it also had to be metaphysics. Philosophy could address the puzzle of existence, Schopenhauer held, only if it also pondered basic metaphysical questions about the nature of reality and the cosmos as a whole. Whether life is worth living, he believed, ultimately depends on the nature of life itself, on the place of man in the cosmos. Hence Schopenhauer questioned the positivist and neo-Kantian distinction between value and existence, between 'ought' and 'is', which made it possible to do ethics without metaphysics. From the very beginning, he conceived his philosophy as a unity of metaphysics and ethics.[2]

Although Schopenhauer never lived to learn of the positivist and neo-Kantian polemic against him, he was, even in his own day, fully aware of the objections against his metaphysics. He had pondered the Kantian challenge to metaphysics, and he very much felt the need to respond to it. It is indeed striking that Schopenhauer shared the positivist and neo-Kantian reservations about the metaphysics of Fichte, Schelling and Hegel. He too saw their methods as a relapse into rationalist dogmatism, as a fallacious attempt to reach substantive conclusions from pure thinking alone. Nevertheless, despite such common ground, there was still an irresolvable conflict between Schopenhauer and the Kantian legacy. Namely, Schopenhauer affirmed while the neo-Kantians denied the possibility of metaphysics, and indeed in one and the same sense: knowledge of reality in itself. In the face of this conflict, Schopenhauer remained defiant: "One can lay this down as the necessary credo of all the righteous and good: 'I believe in a metaphysics.'" (*WWV* II. 227; P 175).

All this raises the question: how did Schopenhauer propose to defend his credo? How did he vindicate metaphysics against the heavy charges against it? Schopenhauer turns to this task in many passages of *Die Welt als Wille und Vorstellung*, especially in the 'Anhang über kantische Philosophie' of the first edition, and in chapter 17, 'Über das metaphysische Bedürfnis des Menschen', of the second edition. It is to these texts that we must now turn. After a careful examination, we shall find that Schopenhauer's project is not guilty of the worst charges made against it. Whether or not metaphysics

---

[2] See Arthur Schopenhauer, *Der handschriftlicher Nachlaß*, ed, Arthur Hübscher (Frankfurt: Verlag von Waldemar Kramer, 1966), I. 55.

is ultimately defensible, we will at least attempt to show that it has more plausibility than his positivist and neo-Kantian critics allowed.

2. The Rehabilitation of Metaphysics

An essential part of Schopenhauer's defence of metaphysics was his reformulation of its methods, goals and problems. Such a reformulation was absolutely necessary, he believed, if metaphysics were to have a fresh start and if it were to purge itself of its historical burdens, which came from pre-Kantian rationalism. The main reason Kant had damned metaphysics and declared it impossible, Schopenhauer argued, is that he had a false conception of its methods, goals and problems, a conception that he had inherited from the tradition of Spinoza, Leibniz and Wolff.

Kant had defined metaphysics as knowledge through pure reason of the unconditioned, i.e. the first causes of things, which are God, freedom and the soul. From such a conception, Schopenhauer argued, he easily came to the conclusion that metaphysics is doomed. Since the unconditioned transcends experience, where each thing is conditioned or limited by other things, and since all knowledge is limited to experience, it follows that we cannot have knowledge of the unconditioned. Metaphysics is illegitimate, then, simply because it transcends the limits of experience, from which we acquire all knowledge of existence. Kant also assumed that the method of metaphysics is a priori, i.e. that it must be based on the analysis of concepts and abstract reasoning alone (*WWV* I. 557; P 427). Since he insisted that concepts acquire their content only through experience, he easily concluded that the a priori methods of metaphysics were bankrupt.

Schopenhauer readily agreed with Kant that metaphysics in this sense is impossible. He firmly endorsed Kant's account of the limits of knowledge: that we cannot know anything beyond the limits of possible experience. For just this reason he accepted Kant's teaching that metaphysics, as speculation about an unconditioned object that transcends experience, is impossible. Schopenhauer also concurred with Kant's critique of the *methods* of rationalist metaphysics. No less than Kant, he insisted that the content of knowledge must be given to us in experience, and that it cannot be extracted from the analysis of concepts alone. The foundation of all knowledge, he stressed, lies within experience alone, in the materials given to us in sensation and perception.

Although Schopenhauer believed that Kant's critique of the goals and methods of metaphysical rationalism is successful, he still refused to admit that it destroys metaphysics in general. Schopenhauer defended the possibility of another kind of metaphysics, one that remains strictly within the limits of possible experience, and so one that still complies with the Kantian standards of knowledge. Kant's critique of metaphysics is flawed, Schopenhauer argues, because it begins with a false conception of the goals and problems of metaphysics. Metaphysics need not be *transcendent*, i.e. speculation about the unconditioned beyond experience; rather, it can be entirely and strictly *immanent*, i.e. interpretation of the given in experience. An immanent metaphysics remains strictly within the limits of possible experience, and so it should be beyond suspicion according to the Kantian standard of knowledge.

How, though, can metaphysics be immanent? How can it stay within the limits of possible experience and still be metaphysics? The foundation for Schopenhauer's immanent metaphysics rests on his distinction between two ways of understanding what is given in experience. We can understand *why* something exists or in *what* it consists. Understanding why something exists means knowing its *causes*; understanding in what it consists means knowing its *essence*. While the causes connect one thing with another, and so involve its relations with other things, the essence consists in the thing itself, its intrinsic nature, what it is in itself apart from its relations with other things. Since causal connections are expressible in mathematical terms, knowledge of causes is *quantitative*; since essences exist on their own, apart from any relations, knowledge of them is *qualitative*. Schopenhauer thinks that both forms of understanding are legitimate in their proper sphere. The understanding of causal connections is the province of natural science, while the understanding of essences is the domain of metaphysics.

Though it is simple and basic, this distinction has been confused by traditional metaphysics. It wrongly assumed that its task is to know the first causes of things, and so it extended the principle of sufficient reason *beyond* experience, though its sole legitimate application lies *within* experience (*WWV* I. 377; P 273). But the business of metaphysics, Schopenhauer insisted, is not to know the first causes of things as they lie beyond experience but the essences of things as they are given in experience.

So far, however, Schopenhauer's restatement of the problem of metaphysics seems to beg a basic question. If metaphysics is only the understanding of what is given in experience, then how does it know anything more than appearances? How does it give us knowledge of reality in itself? On Kantian premises this would seem to be a squaring of the circle. To understand Schopenhauer's solution to this problem, we need to consider his account of one very troublesome and notorious Kantian concept: the thing-in-itself.

Schopenhauer's attempt to justify metaphysics lies crucially with his reinterpretation of the concept of the thing-in-itself.[3] The thing-in-itself, he maintains, is not a transcendent entity lying behind appearances, an *ens extra mundanum*. In that sense Schopenhauer is happy to dismiss the thing-in-itself as a mere abstraction or nonentity. An object that is neither representation nor will, he writes in the first section of *Die Welt als Wille und Vorstellung*, is "a dreamed nothing", "an illusion in philosophy" (§2; I. 33). The thing-in-itself is not something that lies beyond appearances,

---

[3] This point is vital but overlooked constantly by commentators, who criticize Schopenhauer for claiming knowledge of an entity that transcends ordinary experience. See, for example the notes below on Hamlyn, Janaway and Magee. The only scholar to see the importance of Schopenhauer's re-interpretation of the concept of the thing-in-itself is Julian Young, *Schopenhauer* (Abingdon: Routledge, 2005), pp. 96–8. Young sees this re-interpretation as a later development in Schopenhauer's thought, though as the citations below make clear, it was perfectly clear from the beginning.

Schopenhauer insists, but it is "that which appears in appearances" (*das in ihr [die Erscheinung] Erscheinende*).[4] Or, to use another of his formulations, it is the *what* that appears as opposed to the *how*, *when* and *where*.[5] Hence the thing-in-itself, properly seen, is simply the *content* or *essence* of appearances. It is not a supernatural object lying beyond appearances, but the inner essence or intrinsic nature of natural objects or appearances themselves.[6]

Following this proposal, Schopenhauer recommends that the distinction between thing-in-itself and appearance should be redrawn in terms of that between form and content.[7] Form is the appearance, content is the thing-in-itself. The form of experience consists in the relations between things, all of which are expressible in mathematical or causal terms. The content of experience, however, consists in the inner nature, quality or essence of appearances, that which stands in the relations between things. We cannot grasp the content or inner nature of experience through its relations alone, Schopenhauer insists. No matter how far our knowledge of relations extends, there will always be some remainder, something which resists analysis into mere relations; the remainder is *that which* stands in these relations, namely, the intrinsic qualities or essence of a thing.[8]

Further along these lines, Schopenhauer warned against interpreting the relationship between thing-in-itself and appearance in causal terms, as if the thing-in-itself were the cause and appearances its effect.[9] He regards the causal relation as one application of the principle of sufficient reason, which is applicable only within appearances alone; we therefore cannot take that principle to explain the origin of experience as a whole. Given that the cause and effect are logically distinct, such an interpretation wrongly separates thing-in-itself from its appearance. Schopenhauer maintains that the relation between thing-in-itself and appearance is much tighter: the appearance is the *objectification*, the *manifestation* of the thing-in-itself, which constitutes and reveals the very nature of the thing-in-itself.[10]

It is in just this context that we must understand another notorious aspect of Schopenhauer's metaphysics: his appropriation of the Platonic distinction between archetype and ectype. No part of Schopenhauer's philosophy seems more wantonly and brazenly metaphysical and mystical than his reintroduction of the Platonic doctrine in book III of *Die Welt als Wille und Vorstellung*.[11] Schopenhauer maintains,

---

[4] Cf. *WWV* I. 379, §53 (P 274) and *WWV* II. 237, ch. 17 (P 183).

[5] See *WWV* I. 185, 187, §24 (P 121–2); 257, §34 (P 178); and 379, §53 (P 274).

[6] Schopenhauer made this interpretation especially clear in his August 1852 letter to Julius Frauenstädt, Aug. 1852, *Gesammelte Briefe*, ed. Arthur Hübscher (Bonn: Bouvier, 1978), p.291.

[7] See *WWV* I. 184, 185, 187, §24 (P 121–2, 123).

[8] *WWV* I. 188, §24 (P 124).

[9] Schopenhauer laid emphasis on this point at the end of his 'Anhang über die kantische Philosophie', *WWV* I. 675, 679 (P 503, 507).

[10] See esp. *WWV* II. 316–17, the beginning of the chapter 'Objektivation des Willens im tierischen Organismus' (P 245).

[11] See, for example, Janaway, *Self and World in Schopenhauer's Philosophy* (Oxford: OUP, 1999), pp. 273, 274, 283.

however, that the Platonic distinction between archetype and ectype mirrors Kant's own distinction between thing-in-itself and appearance. Whatever one makes of that conflation on scholarly grounds, it shows how Schopenhauer construed the Platonic doctrine. For just as he understood the distinction between thing-in-itself and appearance in terms of the content and form of experience, so he understood the distinction between archetype and ectype in similar terms. The archetype is the content of experience, the "whatness", essence or intrinsic nature of things, while the ectype is the form of experience, how one thing stands in relation to others.[12] Understood as a distinction between form and content, the distinction seems less wildly metaphysical, less a distinction between two worlds than two aspects of experience itself. Like the thing-in-itself, the archetype for Schopenhauer is not a transcendent supernatural entity but the intrinsic nature of the object of experience itself.[13]

What should be the method of metaphysics? How should it attempt to know the essences or forms of things given in our experience? Unfortunately, Schopenhauer leaves us with little more than hints and suggestions about the method of metaphysics. This method lies in the *interpretation* (*Deutung*) and *explication* (*Auslegung*) of appearances (*WWV* II. 237–8; P 184). The metaphysician does not engage in conceptual analysis or syllogistic reasoning, and still less in causal explanations of things according to general laws. Rather, his task, as Schopenhauer puts it, is *to decipher* appearances, as if they were texts, or as if they were someone speaking to us.[14] The aim of the metaphysician is therefore to know "the meaning" (*die Bedeutung*) of appearances, not the laws that govern them (*WWV* I. 151, 156; §17). What Schopenhauer needed to explain and justify the method of metaphysics is an account of the logic of interpretation, a theory about how interpretation differs from demonstration and causal explanation. Nowhere, however, does he provide such an account. What he desperately needed, in other words, was "a hemeneutics", a theory of interpretation. That task would fall to the generation succeeding him, to the work of Ranke, Boeckh, Droysen and Dilthey.[15]

3. Self-Knowledge of the Will

So much, if only very crudely, for Schopenhauer's programme to rehabilitate metaphysics. But the question remains: did he remain true to this programme? Did his metaphysics conform to his own immanent ideals? Or did it lapse, as the neo-Kantians insisted, into the speculative and fantastic?

---

[12] See *WWV* I. 257, §34 (P 178); and I. 270, §36 (P 189).

[13] I shall leave aside here the difficult question of the precise relationship between thing-in-itself and idea in Schopenhauer's philosophy. Schopenhauer gives different accounts of that relationship. See *WWV* I. 252, §32 (P 174) and *WWV* II. 469–73 (P 363–6).

[14] See 'Über Philosophie und ihre Methode', in *Parlipomena, Werke*, V. 25; and 'Über das metaphysische Bedürfnis', *WWV* II. 238–40.

[15] On the hermeneutics of these figures, see my *The German Historicist Tradition* (Oxford: OUP, 2011), pp. 253–365.

In the preface to the first edition of *Die Welt als Wille und Vorstellung* Schopenhauer tells us that the entire book is devoted to "a single thought" (I. 7; P xii). This is a very simple yet very bold thought: that the thing-in-itself, or the inner essence of things, is the will. How could Schopenhauer justify such a daring thesis? Let us follow step-by-step his attempt to do so.

Schopenhauer's most concerted and conscientious effort to explain and justify his thesis appears in the opening paragraphs of book II of *Die Welt als Wille und Vorstellung*. His starting point, just as his guidelines require, is a fact of experience. It is a fact of our experience, Schopenhauer assures us, that we are directly aware of our activities, of whatever it is that we are doing. This is an *immediate* experience in the sense that we *directly* know ourselves to be acting, and that we do not have to know this *indirectly* through inference or conjecture. When I know that I am willing something, I just know that I am willing it, and I do not have to guess or infer this. This basic fact of inner experience, the awareness of myself willing, is the beginning of Schopenhauer's metaphysics, which is supposed to be nothing more than an interpretation of this fact.

But Schopenhauer seems to go beyond this simple fact to make an astonishingly bold metaphysical claim: that through this self-awareness I know the inner essence of the world. It is through it, he confidently maintains, that I have "the key to the puzzle", "the solution to the mystery" of the world (I. 157; P 100). My self-awareness is the inner pathway, the secret underground passage, into the fortress of the thing-in-itself, which I can never conquer through all the artifice of an external siege.[16] Schopenhauer thinks that by explaining the full meaning of this original self-awareness, by peeling away its layers of meaning, we will inevitably come to the conclusion that the inner essence of things is nothing less than the will.

Schopenhauer's first step toward that conclusion, which he makes in §18, is a simple distinction between two forms of self-knowledge. I know myself as an individual, he explains, through my body, which makes me just this individual and no other. But I know this body in two ways or from two perspectives (I. 157; P 100). I can view it from an external or third-person perspective, where it appears as one object among others; but I can also view it from an internal or first-person perspective, where it is the single, unique object of my self-consciousness. Schopenhauer stresses that these two modes of knowing ourselves are utterly distinct from one another. They are two incommensurable perspectives upon one and the same thing: namely, my body (I. 161; P 103).

Now this second form of self-knowledge, Schopenhauer maintains, is unique among all forms of knowledge because through it I know the inner essence of something. Through it, I know the inner essence of one determinate thing, which happens to be my own body. But why is it that this is my *inner essence*? This seems to be an extra claim not warranted by the facts of my self-awareness. But here it is important to keep in mind Schopenhauer's distinction between appearance and thing-in-itself, which he

---

[16] 'Von der Erkennbarkeit des Dinges an sich', *WWV* II. 253; P 195.

has already introduced in §17 but then develops in §24.¹⁷ According to this distinction, there are two possible ways of knowing things: in their inner essences, which is in the content of experience; or in their relations to other things, in their external appearances according to the principle of sufficient reason, which is the form of experience. Now it is this distinction which is at play in the two forms of self-consciousness. When I know my body externally, from a third-person perspective according to the principle of sufficient reason, I know its form, its relations to other things, and hence only as an appearance. But when I know it from within, according to a first-person perspective, I know its content, and so as a thing-in-itself. It should be clear from this that when I claim to know myself as a thing-in-itself, it does not mean that I know myself as a noumenon, as some entity transcending my experience; it means only that I know the content of my experience, that I know what appears as opposed to how it appears. There is no claim to metaphysical or transcendent knowledge, a claim to know something beyond experience.¹⁸

When I view myself from a first-person perspective, Schopenhauer goes on to argue,¹⁹ I always see but one thing: the will. This is because, whenever I reflect on myself, I always find myself in some form or other of volition. This volition need not be a conscious act of decision or deliberation; it can be emotions or feelings, sensations of pleasure or pain, which all have their source in the will and thus are only forms of volition.

---

¹⁷ This important point is neglected in some interpretations of Schopenhauer's argument. Both Janaway and Hamlyn, for example, assume that Schopenhauer is trying to know a transcendent entity, and on these grounds argue that his attempt to know the thing-in-itself is indefensible. See Janaway, *Self and World*, pp. 194–9, and D. W. Hamlyn, *Schopenhauer* (London: Routledge, 1980), pp. 92–4.

¹⁸ In a lecture delivered 23 Nov. 1989, in Senate House of the University of London, subsequently reprinted in the 2nd edn of his *The Philosophy of Schopenhauer* (Oxford: Clarendon Press, 2009), pp. 440–53, Bryan Magee argued emphatically that it is a deep misconception of Schopenhauer's philosophy to hold that he maintains we have knowledge of the noumenal will. According to Magee, Schopenhauer thinks that we have no direct knowledge of the thing-in-itself at all, and that we know the will only as a phenomenon. We must distinguish between a direct and indirect knowledge of phenomena, he explains, but not between a knowledge of things-in-themselves as opposed to a knowledge of phenomena. Magee insists that the textual evidence for his reading is massive, and proceeds to cite some of it. To an extent, Magee has a point. Schopenhauer does not think that we have knowledge of the *noumenal self in the specific Kantian sense*, i.e. the purely intellectual or intelligible self that transcends experience. This is the assumption behind Hamlyn's and Janaway's arguments against Schopenhauer (see n. 17), to which Magee is rightly reacting. Magee's thesis is vitiated, however, by his failure to take into account Schopenhauer's own distinction between things-in-themselves and appearances. Taken as the content of inner experience, Schopenhauer does indeed hold that we have knowledge of ourselves in ourselves and not merely as appearances. The textual evidence for this point is no less massive. I refer the reader here, for mere starters, to the many passages in §§18–23 of the second book of *Die Welt als Wille und Vorstellung*, *WWV* I. 157, 161–2, 164, 170, 174, 675, 677. In denying knowledge of the self-in-itself in this more limited sense Magee goes too far and has only sown confusion. Magee's other arguments (*Philosophy of Schopenhauer*, pp. 128–31, 445) for why all self-knowledge is strictly phenomenal are *non-sequiturs*. The most plausible of these is that Schopenhauer maintains that self-knowledge is limited to inner sense, i.e. the a priori form of time, in which case all self-knowledge must be phenomenal. Magee ignores, however, that Schopenhauer thinks that knowledge of inner essences suspends time, that the *nunc stans* holds for this form of experience. See *WWV* I. 253, §32.

¹⁹ Schopenhauer first makes this claim in §40 of *Über den Satz vom Grunde*, *Werke*, III. 168. The argument is made in fullest detail in the later *Über die Freiheit des Willens*, *Sämtliche Werke*, III. 529–31.

The same point becomes clear, Schopenhauer thinks, by reflecting on the content and source of my self-consciousness. Whenever I turn my attention inward, I am aware of myself engaged in some form of activity; but these activities are forms of willing.

The argument so far, then, rests upon three premises: (1) I have an immediate awareness of my own activity; (2) this activity consists in some form of volition; and (3) this self-consciousness is of my inner nature. The first two premises rest upon facts of consciousness; and the third upon Schopenhauer's distinction between thing-in-itself and appearance. All these premises seem plausible or unproblematic enough. Yet they are also extremely controversial, for, famously, Kant argued in the first *Kritik* that I cannot have self-consciousness of my inner self. I cannot know myself as a thing-in-itself, Kant held, any more than I can know something outside me as a thing-in-itself.[20] The same restrictions that hold for knowledge of the world *outside* me—the need to apply the categories and the form of inner sense—also hold for the world *inside* me. Thus Schopenhauer seems to be flying in the face of Kant's constraints on self-knowledge. If he cannot get beyond them, his metaphysical project cannot get off the ground.

It is remarkable, however, that Schopenhauer does not challenge Kant's arguments against self-knowledge. Instead, he endorses and repeats them, though he does so only in one respect.[21] He agrees with Kant that the *knowing* subject cannot know itself, because any such effort would be circular, presupposing exactly what it is trying to know. Nevertheless, he insists that the *willing* subject can know itself, because there is something special and unique about such practical self-knowledge, something that short-circuits the normal restrictions on theoretical self-knowledge. Namely, that in knowing myself as willing, there is an identity between subject and object so that self-knowledge is assured. Why is there such subject-object identity? Because in the case of willing I *create* the very object that I know; that object is my will, which I make, and it is not given to me as if it were some external object.[22] Simply through the act of willing I, the subject, make the object, so that it is transparent to me.[23] But in all *theoretical* knowledge, even self-knowledge, there is a distinction between the subject and object because the object has to be given, and it is not made by me. It was this peculiarity of self-knowledge of myself as willing—the complete identity of its subject and object—that first captured Schopenhauer's attention in his early treatise *Über den Satz vom Grunde*.[24]

Arguably, though, Schopenhauer cannot escape Kant's restrictions on self-knowledge and for one apparently powerful reason: that self-knowledge, like all knowledge,

---

[20] See, for example, *KrV* B152–3, 158, 404.

[21] See *WWV* I. 34, §2; and *Über den Satz vom Grunde*, §41, III. 168–9.

[22] This point is ignored by Janaway, who does not see the Kantian presuppositions behind Schopenhauer's object and who therefore concludes that Schopenhauer has no right to see any peculiarity in knowledge of the will. See his *Self and World*, pp. 194–5.

[23] This does not mean, of course, that the will is *entirely* transparent to me. As Schopenhauer often insists, the will is often very obscure. As Hamlyn notes, *Schopenhauer*, p. 85, what is known is the fact that I am willing, not what I am willing or why.

[24] *Über die vierfache Wurzel des Satzes vom zureichende Grunde*, Werke, III. 171; §42.

requires the application of the form of time, inner sense. Once we apply that form, then on Kant's premises, which Schopenhauer completely accepts, we know ourselves only as appearance. When we apply the form of inner sense to ourselves, we condition what we know, so that we cannot know it in itself, prior to the application of that form. Kant himself rules out self-knowledge on just these grounds.[25] Schopenhauer ponders this objection in the second volume of *Die Welt als Wille und Vorstellung*, and to some extent he even concedes it by minimizing the degree of self-knowledge of the will (II. 255; P 197). Schopenhauer's critics leapt on this concession, noting that the application of the form of inner sense should be sufficient to exclude *all* self-knowledge, which is not a matter of degree. The form of time brings down the veil of Maya, the realm of appearance, either entirely or not at all.

However, this concession is premature. It is remarkable that in making it Schopenhauer seemed to forget another central doctrine from Book III: that when we contemplate something in itself, apart from its relations to other things, this includes temporal as well as spatial relations. In such contemplation time stops and what we perceive lies in the eternal now or present; it is the *nunc stans* of Albertus Magnus (I. 253; P 175). Schopenhauer's point is that when I contemplate something in itself, as if it alone existed in the whole world, its temporal as well as its spatial relations cease to matter. That applies as much to my own self when I contemplate it as it applies to art objects or anything in nature. The same doctrine reappears in Book IV when Schopenhauer maintains that the form of the appearance of the will is the eternal present (354; P 279).

So, in making his claims in behalf of self-consciousness, Schopenhauer seems to be taking issue with Kant after all. For he contends that Kant did not take into account the peculiarities of self-knowledge of the will, and that had he done so he would not have laid down such blanket restrictions on self-knowledge. All Kant's restrictions on self-knowledge were for the *knowing* self, the subject of *theoretical* knowledge, whose object or content is still distinct from itself; but they did not apply to the *willing* self, the subject of *practical* knowledge, whose object or content is identical with itself. It is noteworthy, however, that Schopenhauer did find a Kantian precedent for the claims he made for self-knowledge of the will. "I really assume, though I cannot prove it, that Kant, as often as he spoke of the thing-in-itself, obscurely thought, in the darkest depths of his mind, of the will." (*WWV* I. 677; P 505). Although Kant did not expressly recognize the will as the thing-in-itself, he still took an important step toward such knowledge, Schopenhauer says, by insisting that the moral meaning of human action is very different from, and completely independent of, the laws of appearance.[26]

Although Schopenhauer never accepted Kant's arguments that practical reason, through the moral law, provides a *ratio cognoscendi* of freedom,[27] he could have

---

[25] *KrV* B152–3.   [26] 'Anhang', *WWV* I. 570.

[27] See 'Anhang', *WWV* I. 676. In the 2nd edition of *Über die vierfache Wurzel des Satzes vom zureichenden Grunde*, however, Schopenhauer sees Kant's doctrine of practical reason as encouraging the error,

appealed to another Kantian doctrine that did allow for direct knowledge of our rational activity. In the prefaces to the *Kritik der reinen Vernunft* Kant had declared that what I create according to my own activity is perfectly transparent to myself simply because I create it.[28] Knowledge of the will is a perfect case of such knowledge, however, because my willing is what I create, what I make according to my own activity. What I am trying to do, that I know, and that I know immediately, because I am the source of that very trying. As Schopenhauer himself stressed, knowledge of the will is unlike any other object of knowledge insofar as it is not given to me but created by me.[29]

4. Metaphysics of the Will

Granted that I know myself in myself, Schopenhauer still has to go further to substantiate his central metaphysical thesis. He has established only that there is *one* being in the universe, namely myself, whose intrinsic nature is the will. But he has not shown this to be the case for anyone else. Schopenhauer's next step, which he undertakes in §19, is to generalize what he finds in himself for all other human beings. The knowing subject has to determine whether its double perspective on itself also applies to other beings like itself, i.e. beings with bodies like its own.

The main obstacle against making such a move is what Schopenhauer calls "theoretical egoism", i.e. solipsism, the doctrine that I know only myself to be a self-conscious being. Although he admits that this position is theoretically irrefutable, he dismisses it as a skeptical sophism that cannot be taken seriously, one that stands more in need of a cure than a refutation (I. 163; P 104). Theoretical egoism he likens to "a small border fortification, which is indeed impregnable, but whose occupants never venture outside, so that without danger one can go past it and leave it behind".

Assuming that it is safe to leave that fortification behind, Schopenhauer proceeds to maintain that what holds for my body also holds for all other beings with bodies like mine. Just as I am a self-conscious being whose essence consists in the will, so those creatures with bodies like mine are also self-conscious beings whose essence consists in the will. If we can make this analogical inference, we can assume that there are many self-conscious beings like myself, each of which has a will like mine.

Obviously, though, this is not enough for Schopenhauer to substantiate his more ambitious metaphysical thesis: that there is a *single* cosmic will within the self-consciousness of everyone alike. As it stands his analogical argument is compatible with an ontological pluralism, according to which there are as many wills as there are individuals.

---

so common among post-Kantian idealists, that theoretical reason can provide knowledge of things-in-themselves. *Werke*, III. 145. Cf. *Über die Grundlage der Moral*, *Werke*, III. 678.

[28] See *KrV* Axiv, xx; and Bxiii, xviii.
[29] See 'Von der Erkennbarkeit des Dinges an sich', *WWV* II. 253.

Schopenhauer has, however, an argument up his sleeve that rules out the possibility of such an ontological pluralism, one that provides the basis for his monism, i.e. his thesis that there is one single will within all individuals (I. 174, 193; P 113, 127–8). According to this argument, we cannot individuate the will, assigning one per person, because the *principium individuationis* holds only for things in space and time, for things considered as appearances; when, however, we consider things-in-themselves, we view them apart from the spatial and temporal relations that individuate them. Hence the will must be one, single and indivisible. The will that makes my essence is the same will that makes your essence and that of everyone else.[30]

Even if we admit this argument for monism, we are still far from substantiating Schopenhauer's central thesis: that there is a single cosmic will within the essence of *everything*; that the inner nature of *all* things, and not only self-conscious things, consists in the will. We have established that the will is the inner essence only for self-conscious beings, not for the entire cosmos, for all beings, whether self-conscious or not.

Schopenhauer takes this final bold step in §§21–4. He now encourages the analogical inference that the will I find in my inner nature is the same will that is in the inner nature of everything else, whether animal, plant, mineral or stone. All these things too have an inner nature, and if they were self-conscious, they would find themselves to be willing. As Schopenhauer put it in a humorous vein: "Spinoza said that a stone flying in the air from an external impetus would think, if it were conscious, that it did so out of its own free will. I would only add that the stone would be right." (191; P 126). At least from within, if it could be self-conscious, the stone would be right because its inner nature consists in striving.

Schopenhauer immediately cautions us, though, that attributing will to the inner essence of other things in nature does not mean that they too are self-conscious. The term "will" is only a "*denominatio a posteriori*", i.e. a term that designates the most eminent object in its class, namely self-conscious beings (I. 171; P 110–11). It is perfectly possible for something like the will to occur without self-consciousness or even consciousness, he argues, so that it could appear in plants, minerals and rocks. The will in these beings consists only in a blind striving, a subconscious urge or raw impulse (I. 191; P 126).

It is this last step that seems the most risky and bold, indeed fantastic, well beyond justification according to Schopenhauer's methodological guidelines. The neo-Kantians did not hesitate to censure it as wild and brazen speculation, a massive generalization based on a single instance! Even scholars who are sympathetic to Schopenhauer think that he went too far here, and that by calling the inner essence of things the will he recklessly lapsed into a kind of animistic or vitalistic metaphysics.[31]

---

[30] Georg Simmel pointed out that this argument assumes that space and time are necessary for individuation, an assumption that he questioned. He maintained instead the possibility of non-spatial and non-temporal forms of individuation. See his *Schopenhauer und Nietzsche: Ein Vortragszyklus*, in *Georg Simmepl Gesamtausgabe*, ed. Otthein Rammstedt (Frankfurt: Surkamp, 1995), X. 221.

[31] See, for example, Magee, *Philosophy of Schopenhauer*, pp. 142–4.

But to understand Schopenhauer's self-confidence in making his generalization we have to place him in his intellectual context. When Schopenhauer wrote *Die Welt als Wille und Vorstellung* in the early 1800s, *Naturphilosophie* was in its heyday. Although Schopenhauer was critical of its wild and poetical speculations, he still makes clear in §27 of book II that he endorses some of its fundamental principles; he then proceeds to outline a conception of nature in accord with them. In the early 1800s, it was clear for Schopenhauer, and indeed most of his generation, that the mechanical view of the world had broken down entirely, and that it was no longer possible to explain matter as inert extension. The old Cartesian physics had shown itself to be utterly incapable of explaining the most basic phenomena, viz., magnetism, electricity and action at a distance. To overcome these shortcomings, it was necessary to adopt a dynamic conception of matter, according to which matter consists not in dead extension but in the interrelations of attractive and dynamic force. Even the occupation of space, which seemed primitive to the Cartesians, had to be explained in dynamic terms as the power to resist any body that would occupy the same place. Such was Kant's argument in his *Metaphysische Anfangsgründe der Naturwissenschaften*, which was crucial for the development of romantic *Naturphilosophie*. However, the romantics (viz., Schelling, Baader, Oken, Eschenmeyer), went one significant step beyond Kant. They maintained that matter should be understood not only *dynamically* but also *organically*. A dynamic conception understands matter in terms of the interrelations of its forces; an organic conception conceives it in terms of an internal *nisus*, a spontaneous striving to realize an inner force. Only this organic concept of matter would explain—so it was argued— phenomena like electricity and magnetism, and only it could underpin the continuum of nature ruptured by Cartesian dualism.

If we place Schopenhauer's metaphysics in this context, then it ceases to appear like wild speculation. On the contrary, it was based on scientific orthodoxy, the best normal science of its day. Since it was founded on the latest thinking in the natural sciences, Schopenhauer could claim that his metaphysics is based upon the facts of experience after all. There is indeed nothing extravagant in calling the inner nature of inorganic things the will if we use the term in the broad sense that Schopenhauer recommends. The *nisus* was not simply energy or power, but also a striving, a spontaneous urging and impulse, just as Schopenhauer described it. Schopenhauer's claim that self-consciousness of my willing is consciousness of the thing-in-itself then amounts to the thesis that the awareness I have of my willing is of the same striving, urging and impulse that is found throughout all of nature. The microcosm inside myself reflects the macrocosm outside myself (I. 238; P 162). This is hardly extravagant at all; it is at least a plausible hypothesis.

By the 1830s *Naturphilosophie* ceased to be so popular, coming under the criticism of natural scientists for its a priori theorizing about nature. But Schopenhauer remained an unrepentant believer in *Naturphilosophie*, however much he disliked the excess and extravagance of the Schellingian school. He continued to maintain that the first principles of his own philosophy are in full accord with the latest developments of the natural sciences. In his *Über den Willen in der Natur*, which first appeared in 1836, he provided all kinds of evidence from every field of natural science—physiology, anatomy, botany, astronomy—to show that the will is the ultimate cause of organic and inorganic phenomena. If this were indeed the case, then Schopenhauer could claim that his metaphysics was keeping within his empirical guidelines, and that he was doing nothing more than interpreting and explaining appearances.

Whether the natural sciences were indeed confirming Schopenhauer's doctrine is a point that we cannot investigate here. But even if we lay that issue aside, there still seems a problem in principle with Schopenhauer's appeal to the natural sciences as evidence for his metaphysics. He had argued in depth and detail in §§18, 24 and 25 of Book II that the natural sciences show us only the relations between phenomena, that they cannot grasp their inner meaning. How, then, can they provide evidence for theories about the inner meaning of things? To get metaphysical conclusions from observations and experiments something else seems necessary: namely, an *interpretation* of the phenomena, an *analysis* of their meaning, which is the special task of the philosopher. Here Schopenhauer's whole project seems to founder on a circularity: we need the empirical facts to justify metaphysics; but we need metaphysics to interpret and explain the facts, which do not speak for themselves.

Schopenhauer's response to this circularity is that, though we indeed need metaphysics to interpret the facts, there are still factual constraints on our interpretation (*WWV* II. 238–41; P 184–7). Any decipherment of the text of the world, he explains, finds its confirmation in its power to explain all the phenomena, to understand them as a single coherent whole. This does not mean that any interpretation will be final, in the sense that the solution to the puzzle will be definitively solved; there will always be new phenomena to be understood, new problems to be solved. It was on this more tentative note that Schopenhauer left his metaphysics, which he ultimately concedes to be a hypothesis, though a well-grounded one. We best regard Schopenhauer's metaphysics as "a likely story", as the most plausible account based on the natural sciences in the early 19th century.

5. Transcendental Idealism?

If we were to believe most contemporary accounts,[32] Schopenhauer's philosophy is a system of transcendental idealism, and thus essentially a variant of Kant's philosophy.

---

[32] This is the picture of Schopenhauer's philosophy that emerges from many recent interpretations. See for example, Young, *Schopenhauer*, pp. 17–102; Magee, *Philosophy of Schopenhauer*, pp. 49–104; Patrick Gardiner, *Schopenhauer* (Harmondsworth: Penguin, 1963), pp. 67–123; Frederick Copleston, *Arthur Schopenhauer, Philosopher of Pessimism* (London: Search Press, 1975), pp. 44–71; D. W. Hamlyn, *Schopenhauer* (London: Routledge & Kegan Paul, 1980), pp. 3, 63–79; Dale Jacquette, *The Philosophy of Schopenhauer* (Montreal: McGill-Queens University Press, 2005), pp. 11–39; and Robert Wicks, *Schopenhauer* (Oxford: Blackwell, 2008), pp. 39–81. My own interpretation is anything but novel. It was first put forward by Julius Frauenstädt, *Briefe über die Schopenhauer'sche Philosophie* (Leipzig: Brockhaus, 1854), pp. 76–7, 117–18, 161–3. For a contemporary critique of the idealist interpretation, see Dale and James Snow, 'Was Schopenhauer an

There is certainly some good evidence for this interpretation. Schopenhauer goes to great pains in the first book of volume I of *Die Welt als Wille und Vorstellung*, and in the first four chapters of volume II, to argue that the world is my representation, and that the forms of space, time and causality are true only for appearances. He rails against materialism, declares that true philosophy is idealistic, and maintains that the true form of idealism is transcendental idealism (*WWV* II. 13, 17). So there does not seem to be any more basic and obvious truth about Schopenhauer's philosophy than that it is a system of transcendental idealism.

Still, this truth is only a half-truth. Transcendental idealism is the true philosophy for the world as representation. It is not, however, the true philosophy for the world as will. It is one of the basic principles of Schopenhauer's philosophy that we have to treat the world from both perspectives. But these perspectives are complementary and begin from opposing starting points. When we view the world as representation, we begin from the subject and see the entire world as its objectification or appearance. That is the standpoint of transcendental idealism. But when we view the world as will, we begin from the object, which is the will, and we interpret the entire world as its objectification or appearance. From the standpoint of the world as will, we construct the entirety of nature as so many stages in the self-objectification of the will, and we see the subject as the ultimate stage of its objectification, the point where it reaches self-consciousness as will. What is first from the standpoint of transcendental idealism—the subject—then becomes secondary or derivative. The subject's self-consciousness from the subjective standpoint becomes the will's self-consciousness from the objective standpoint.

This other objective side of Schopenhauer's philosophy, which is far less visible than the subjective or transcendental idealist side, becomes entirely explicit in chapters 20 and 22 of volume II of *Die Welt als Wille und Vorstellung*. Here Schopenhauer makes it perfectly plain that there are two complementary ways of treating the intellect (II. 352–3; P 272–3). One is subjective: it begins from the inside, takes consciousness as its given, and from there shows how the world appears through the mechanism of consciousness. The other is objective: it begins from the outside, takes the world as given, and from there understands the intellect from its place in nature. From this objective standpoint, Schopenhauer explains, representation and thought are seen as the efflorescence of the human brain and the whole organism, which is in turn the product of the will (356–7, 359–60; P 275–6, 277–8). Since self-consciousness is derived from the organism, and the organism from the will, self-consciousness is no longer primary, as Fichte taught, and not even secondary but tertiary (359–60; P 277–8). The unity of apperception, the self-evident starting point of Kant's transcendental idealism, is now seen as the product of the brain and human organism, which is in turn derived from

---

Idealist?', *Journal of the History of Philosophy*, 29 (1991), 633–55. The Snows go too far, however, in the opposite direction by casting doubt on the idealist interpretation, which is at least one half of Schopenhauer's system.

the will (359; P 277). The will has an urge toward self-consciousness, which reaches its highest stage of development in the self-awareness of its own spontaneity, which is the Kantian unity of apperception (359; P 277). According to the objective standpoint, then, the entire world as representation is "only a physiological phenomenon, a function of the brain" (369; P 285).

Commentators have had difficulty in incorporating this objective standpoint within their overall understanding of Schopenhauer's philosophy as a system of transcendental idealism. It seems to be completely at odds with other aspects of his philosophy, such as his critique of materialism, his restriction of knowledge to appearances, and the limitations he imposes on natural and empirical science. One strategy for resolving these apparent contradictions is to interpret the objective standpoint as identical with that of *empirical realism*, which is accommodated within transcendental idealism.[33] In classical Kantian fashion, so we are told, Schopenhauer holds that transcendental idealism involves empirical realism, according to which everything we know in the empirical world is real and conforms to general laws that are instances of the principle of sufficient reason (I. 46; P 15). But this strategy comes to grief against some very firm texts. In chapter 22 Schopenhauer is very explicit that his objective standpoint goes beyond the limits of empirical realism. He tells us that Kant's standpoint is one-sidedly subjective, and that it is "one-sided and insufficient" because it neglects the objective standpoint (II. 353; P 273). It is indeed telling that from his objective standpoint Schopenhauer derives the self-consciousness of the unity of apperception, which is the foundation of Kant's transcendental idealism (II. 359; P 277). Kant's empirical realism takes place *within* the idealistic framework constituted by the unity of apperception, so that it never violates or goes beyond (in Schopenhauer's terms) the world as representation. But it is just this standpoint that Schopenhauer's objective standpoint seeks to transcend. Though it is deeply heretical from the standpoint of transcendental idealism, Schopenhauer's objective standpoint involves a form of *transcendental realism*, i.e. the assumption of the independent reality of the world of experience.

Granted that empirical realism does not work, we are still left with the task of reconciling the apparent contradictions. The objective standpoint seems to make nonsense of Schopenhauer's critique of materialism, and his restriction of scientific explanation to the world of appearances. There is really no contradiction at all, however, provided that we observe the basic differences between the world as representation and the world as will. In the world of representation the basic task is to *explain* the world according to the principle of sufficient reason, which involves knowing laws of cause and effect between appearances. The problem with materialism is that it extends such natural explanation to the transcendental subject, which is the source of the possibility of those laws. It attempts to understand the relationship between subject and object on a causal basis, where the object is understood as the cause of the subject. Schopenhauer

---

[33] See, for example, Wolfgang Weimer, *Schopenhauer* (Darmstadt: Wissenschaftliche Buchgesellschaft, 1982), pp. 77–8.

need not take anything back from that critique in the world of will. For in that world the basic task is not *explaining* but *interpreting* the world; we do not want to know the cause and effect relations between appearances but the *meaning* of things themselves.[34] When the philosopher constructs the world from the objective standpoint, his interest is not in causal relations, but, as Schopenhauer makes clear in chapter 20, in manifestations or objectifications of meaning. These manifestations or objectifications Schopenhauer calls the "self-presentation" (*Sich-Darstellen*) of the will (II. 316–17; P 245). While cause and effect relate to one another as distinct events, there is a closer connection between will and its manifestations and objectification, which make its identity explicit and determinate.

There are not, then, any contradictions between the subjective and objective standpoints, and they should be taken as entirely complementary, having different starting points and methods.[35] We should take both standpoints as necessary parts of Schopenhauer's philosophy, and we should not focus on one, the subjective standpoint of transcendental idealism, at the expense of the other. The reason that scholars have focused so exclusively on the subjective side of Schopenhauer's system has much to do with his own lop-sided exposition. Schopenhauer constantly emphasizes his debts to Kant; and the opening exposition of his philosophy in volume I and volume II stress transcendental idealism as if it were the exclusive truth. There are, however, important hints even in book I of volume I of *Die Welt als Wille und Vorstellung* that transcendental idealism is only half the truth, that it is the philosophy only for the world as representation. Thus Schopenhauer warns us in §1 of book I that the world as representation is only one half of his system, and that on its own it is one-sided, needing to be complemented by another view of the world. And in §17, the first section of book II, which treats the world as will, we are told that we are now interested in the *meaning* behind appearances. In §§27–8 of the first volume he proceeds to construct a system of nature which consists in so many stages of objectification of the will (I. 208–37; P 139–61). This is the very same system that Schopenhauer develops in chapter 20 of volume II. That transcendental idealism cannot be the full truth about the world is most apparent, however, from Schopenhauer's critique of Fichte's subjective idealism in section §7 of Book I and sections §§18 and 24 of Book II. One of the basic problems of subjective idealism, Schopenhauer argues, is that it reduces the world without remainder to the representations of the ego. But this cannot account for one central fact: the reality of the thing-in-itself. That reality is the starting point of the objective standpoint.

That Schopenhauer regarded idealism and realism as complementary standpoints of equal validity is most apparent from the essay 'Über Philosophie und Ihre Methode'

---

[34] Schopenhauer makes this very clear at the beginning of Book II, *WWV* I. 151–6; §17.

[35] Much more could be said about whether and how these standpoints are complementary, but a further examination of this issue goes beyond our compass here. For two interesting explorations of the issue, see Janaway, *Self and World*, pp. 267–70, 295–316; and Robert Wicks, 'Schopenhauer's Naturalization of Kant's A Priori Forms of Empirical Knowledge', *History of Philosophy Quarterly*, 10 (1993), 181–96.

from *Paralipomena*. Here in sections §§13 and 20 Schopenhauer is explicit that we can regard the world from either of two perspectives: we can treat it from an objective standpoint according to which the subject is only one phenomenon in nature; or we can consider it from a subjective standpoint according to which all of nature is only an appearance for the consciousness of the subject. Each perspective on its own—"perfect materialism" or "absolute idealism"—is one-sided and its truth is only relative. The true standpoint, Schopenhauer claims, is one that encompasses both of these partial standpoints in a unity.

In developing a philosophy that attempts to accommodate both a subjective and objective viewpoint toward the world Schopenhauer was only in keeping with the romantic *Zeitgeist*. That Spinoza's naturalism and Kant's transcendental idealism are one-sided viewpoints that need to be combined in the ideal philosophy was a commonplace of the romantic generation. We can find that desideratum expressed in the writings of Schelling, Schlegel, Novalis and Hölderlin. Schopenhauer was a Johnnie-come-lately to this development. In §7 of Book I of *Die Welt als Wille und Vorstellung* Schopenhauer does comment on this development as it appears in Schelling's philosophy of identity, which he rejects because it commits the fallacy common to both idealism and realism in seeing the subject and object as cause and effect of one another (60–1; P 26). But it is noteworthy that Schopenhauer's objection here is against a misplaced application of the principle of sufficient reason to object–subject relations; it is not against the attempt to combine both standpoints. He indeed insists that both realism and idealism are correct, and that the best philosophy is one that combines both (I. 34; P 5). In this respect, as in many others, we do well to play down Schopenhauer's own self-image as a solitary and original genius who stands above his age. Schopenhauer too was a child of his time, and while we should not reduce him down to its aspirations and ideals, we also should not elevate him above them. The task is to locate and determine his individuality among his contemporaries and within his age. With that task, Schopenhauer scholarship has scarcely begun.

3

Schopenhauer's Pessimism

1. The Dangers of Pessimism

The most powerful challenge of Schopenhauer to his age lay not with his conception of philosophy, still less with his metaphysics of will. It came from what was, and still is, regarded as the most salient and notorious characteristic of his philosophy: his pessimism. For most philosophers of his age, and indeed ever since, Schopenhauer has become known as "the philosopher of pessimism".[1] Positivists, idealists, materialists and neo-Kantians alike were troubled by Schopenhauer's pessimism more than any other aspect of his philosophy. Most of their polemics against Schopenhauer's philosophy were motivated by, and directed against, his pessimism.

What was the danger of Schopenhauer's pessimism? Why were these philosophers so alarmed by it? One major reason was political. All these philosophers shared the hope, so common to their age, that there could be progress in history, that we could make the world a better place through science, technology, political reform and public education. Schopenhauer threw cold water on such hopes. There is a deep quietistic message behind his philosophy that makes all human striving to change the world utterly futile. Schopenhauer's teaching in the final chapters of *Die Welt als Wille und Vorstellung* is that we should deny our will and resign ourselves to the evil and suffering of the world. No matter how much we struggle, he seemed to be saying, we will make no progress toward improving the human condition. We are like Sisyphus pushing his rock up the hill, only for it to roll back down again. Rather than striving to create a better world, we should renounce our will to live and attempt to escape the world in religious and aesthetic contemplation.

The demoralizing effect of Schopenhauer's teaching was described in a striking metaphor by Julius Duboc, a materialist critic of pessimism.[2] Pessimism reminded him of the old custom of punishing people by placing them in a pillory. The point of that practice was to humiliate the culprit and to discourage the public from a similar offence. What pessimism did was even more extreme: it put the entire world in the pillory. This was a dangerous practice, Duboc warned, because the spectator himself was part of that world and he saw himself implicated in its punishment. When the

---

[1] To steal the subtitle of a book: Frederick Copleston, *Arthur Schopenhauer: Philosopher of Pessimism* (New York: Barnes & Noble, 1975).
[2] Julius Duboc, *Hundert Jahre Zeitgeist in Deutschland* (Leipzig: Wigand, 1889), I. 96.

spectator saw the whole world punished and humiliated, he went away from the spectacle feeling like that himself. Why, then, should he participate in the foolery of the world? Why struggle and strive if it leads to ridicule and humiliation?

So, although we cannot ascribe political *causes* to the rise and popularity of pessimism in the late 19th century, we can still talk about its (real or apparent) political *consequences*. Because of its alleged quietistic implications, there was an important political dimension to the debate about pessimism. Positivists, neo-Kantians, materialists and idealists argued that pessimism leads to quietism, which undermines the motivation for political action and reform. This is not to say, however, that the debate between optimists and pessimists was between activists and quietists. Some pessimists (viz., Hartmann, Taubert and Plümacher) protested that pessimism had no such quietistic implications; they maintained that it denies only the possibility of achieving happiness in this life; and they insisted that it gave people every reason to strive to make the world a better place because that alone would diminish evil and suffering. It is striking, however, that even these pessimists, for their own political reasons, were motivated to repudiate quietism. They were eager to distinguish their pessimism from Schopenhauer's, which they too believed was guilty as charged.

Another reason for the violent reaction against Schopenhauer's pessimism was moral or ethical. Philosophers of all persuasions, and especially theologians, were convinced that Schopenhauer's philosophy undermined not only the motivation for political change but also the very will to live. The proper practical conclusion of his philosophy, it seemed, is suicide. The Schopenhauerian agent was like a patient suffering from terminal cancer: If life promises only more suffering, why go on living? After all, suicide is painless, as the old adage goes, and death is inevitable anyway. Although Schopenhauer himself preached against suicide, most of his critics viewed his warnings as a mere evasion, an attempt to avoid the inevitable *reductio ad absurdam* of his philosophy. A dispute arose in the 1880s concerning the morality of pessimism, which raised the question of suicide. We will examine that dispute in later chapters.[3]

Much was at stake, then, in the dispute about pessimism. Whether we should be or not be? And if we decide to be, what we should do? How should we react to existence, which is so filled with suffering and evil? Should we resign ourselves to it and withdraw from it in Buddhistic contemplation? Or should we battle against it, striving to make the world a better place so that there is at least less evil and suffering?

We will investigate in later chapters the reactions against Schopenhauer's pessimism. Our task now is to have a better understanding of that pessimism itself, its meaning and justification. Schopenhauer's pessimism provides the fundamental context for the pessimist controversy of the late 19th century. We can understand that controversy only when we have a full grasp of that context.

---

[3] See Ch. 4, section 4; Ch. 8, section 2; Ch. 9, section 7.

2. The Modern Silenus

Although Schopenhauer's philosophy was, and still is, associated with pessimism, it is noteworthy that he did not describe his philosophy as such.[4] "Pessimism" was the term used by his contemporaries and successors. Nevertheless, it is still accurate, and harmlessly anachronistic, to ascribe that term to him. For Schopenhauer not only expressly repudiates "optimism", which he regards as the antithesis of his own philosophy,[5] but he also has a decidedly negative attitude toward life. We have no other word for that antithesis, or for that attitude, than "pessimism".

Even in retrospect, it is easy to sympathize with the dismay of contemporaries about Schopenhauer's pessimism. There is indeed something shocking about it. For Schopenhauer tells us, explicitly and emphatically, that life is *not* worth living, and that non-existence is better than existence. It is as if he were telling us we were better off dead. It sounds like a recommendation of suicide, even if Schopenhauer himself advises against such a drastic remedy.

Schopenhauer's pessimism is best understood as his answer to Hamlet's famous question: "To be or not to be?" Schopenhauer explicitly refers to Hamlet's monologue; and his answer to it could not be more simple and blunt. "The essential meaning of the world famous monologue in *Hamlet*", he writes, "is this: That our life is so miserable that complete non-existence would be preferable to it." (I. 445; P 324). No one at the end of his life, if he were honest and reflective, Schopenhauer wagers, would want to live it over again or would prefer it over nothingness. Existence is a mistake, we are told, and our sole aim should be to grasp that it is a mistake, which means knowing "that it would be better not to exist" (II. 775; P 605).

We should recall the myth of Silenus, which is retold by Nietzsche in *Der Geburt der Tragödie*.[6] King Midas goes in search of Silenus, a satyr, and upon capturing him in a net he asks him what is the best life for man. Laughing hysterically at such a silly question, Silenus sneers back that the best life is never to be born, and the next best life is to die young. Doubtless, in retelling the myth Nietzsche was thinking of Schopenhauer, who had himself cited similar lines from Sophocles.[7]

Schopenhauer is indeed our modern Silenus. It is impossible to surpass his bile and bleakness, which he states with an almost sadistic pleasure. What is the darkest view of life? That which likens it to hell. On several occasions, Schopenhauer did not hesitate

---

[4] As David Cartwright has pointed out: *Schopenhauer* (Cambridge: CUP, 2010), p. 4 n. 11, p. 534 n. 31.
[5] Schopenhauer would often use the term "optimism" for positions he opposed. Among them were Judaism, *Werke*, I. 354; II. 813; IV. 81; V. 366, 447, 450, 459; the belief in progress, V. 663; pantheism, II. 826; IV. 94; V. 121; and enlightened deism, II. 747–50. He insisted that philosophy should not be optimism, II. 222, 788, and that optimism is a fundamental mistake, II. 803. Given his disapproval of optimism, it is hardly a misnomer to describe his own position as pessimism, even if this is only by implication. While Schopenhauer does use the word "pessimism" (*Pessimismus*), it is usually to describe the positions of others. The crucial question is not whether Schopenhauer is a pessimist but what his pessimism means and whether it is true.
[6] *Die Geburt der Tragödie*, §3, *Sämtliche Werke*, I. 35.
[7] Schopenhauer, *Die Welt als Wille und Vorstellung*, II. 752; P 587.

to make that comparison: "The world is *hell*, and humans are in one respect its tormented souls and in another its devils" (V. 354) We do not have to seek hell below the earth, he writes in the second volume of *Die Welt als Wille und Vorstellung*, because we are already living it here and now (II. 744; P 580). He adds that because human beings are devils to one another, their world is even worse than Dante's hell (II. 740; P 578).

Schopenhauer's gloomy views about life have sometimes been taken simply on a *personal* level, as if they were nothing more than expressions of his famously grumpy character.[8] Even worse, they are construed strictly on a *pathological* level, as if they were nothing but symptoms of a sick and sad personality.[9] Some Schopenhauer scholars are even embarrassed by his pessimism, which they regard as the least defensible and most inflated side of his philosophy. To save his intellectual integrity, they make a distinction between his philosophy and his pessimism, insisting that his pessimism is "logically irrelevant to his philosophy" and that it is even "largely irrelevant to a serious consideration of him as a philosopher".[10] The rationale for separating Schopenhauer's philosophy from his pessimism, we are told, is the incontestable distinction between fact and value, according to which his philosophy deals with facts but pessimism with values.

There can be no doubt that Schopenhauer's philosophy is indeed a reflection of his personal attitude toward life. Perhaps too it is the symptom of a deep neurosis. But to take it solely on these levels is reductivist. The problem with such reductivism is that it evades all the important questions. Schopenhauer's pessimism was meant to be first and foremost a *philosophical* standpoint regarding the question of the value of life. For that standpoint Schopenhauer provides arguments or reasons, which we have to take seriously if we are not simply to beg the question against them.

The attempt to excise pessimism from the body of Schopenhauer's philosophy also fails, because the positivist distinction between value and fact is completely alien to his philosophy, which was meant to be from the very beginning a synthesis of metaphysics and ethics.[11] If by "pessimism" we mean the thesis that life is not worth living because it consists in more suffering than happiness, then it was a central aim of his philosophy *to prove* that thesis. To dismiss it simply as a confusion between facts and values is, again, only to beg the question.

3. Arguments for Pessimism

What, then, were Schopenhauer's arguments for pessimism? Why does he think that life is not worth living? What reasons does he give for such an extreme attitude? In

---

[8] See, for example, Eduard von Hartmann's 'Mein Verhältnis zu Schopenhauer', in *Philosophische Fragen der Gegenwart* (Leipzig: Friedrich, 1885), pp. 34–5.

[9] See, for example, Kuno Fischer, *Der Philosoph des Pessimismus: Ein Charakterproblem* (Heidelberg: Winter, 1897). Fischer put forward *ad hominem* arguments against Schopenhauer's pessimism by analysing his neurotic personality. He justified his approach on the grounds that pessimism is more a personal attitude and pathology than a philosophical position.

[10] Magee, *The Philosophy of Schopenhauer* (Oxford: OUP, 2009), pp. 13–14.

[11] See *Der handschriftlicher Nachlaß*, I. 55, #92, Berlin, 1813.

several places in *Die Welt als Wille und Vorstellung* Schopenhauer states various arguments for his pessimism. Chapter 46 of volume II, ominously entitled "Von der Nichtigkeit und dem Leiden des Lebens",[12] is rich with arguments, all of which deserve serious examination.

In one argument Schopenhauer formulates his pessimism as the antithesis of Leibniz's optimism. While Leibniz's optimism states that this is the *best* of all possible worlds, Schopenhauer maintains the very opposite: that this is the *worst* of all possible worlds (II. 747; P 583). To prove his thesis, Schopenhauer reasons as follows:

(1) The worst of all worlds is that which has the maximum amount of evil compatible with existence.
(2) To have the maximal amount of evil compatible with existence means that if we add the slightest evil to the world, the world will cease to exist.
(3) It is a fact that if the slightest evil were added to our world, viz., the temperature of the earth rises ten degrees, the orbit of the planets slightly changes, the chemical constitution of the atmosphere alters, then it would cease to exist.
(4) Therefore, our world is the worst possible.

As it stands, there are obvious problems with this argument. The second premise seems arbitrary because we could also say that the *best* of all possible worlds would be one where adding any evil would destroy its existence. The examples Schopenhauer gives of changes in the world—alterations of temperature, atmosphere, and the orbits of planets—do not seem to be evils at all. While the consequences of any of them happening would be disastrous, these changes are not evil themselves because they are simply natural events. When we think of adding what would be evils in a straightforward sense—the murder of a child—it is hard to imagine that this alone would make the universe cease to exist. We can continue to imagine the universe to exist even if some very great evil had happened—the triumph of the Nazis in World War II—so that this is not the worst of all possible worlds even by Schopenhauer's own criterion. But it is unclear how seriously Schopenhauer intended this argument, so picking holes in it is mere bickering.

Another argument for pessimism in chapter 46 of *Die Welt als Wille und Vorstellung* applies the eudemonic calculus to life, weighing its pleasures against its pains. Measured by such a calculus, Schopenhauer argues, life shows itself to be not worth living simply because its pains vastly outweigh its pleasures, its sufferings greatly overshadow its joys (IV. 343). If we were purely rational beings, who decide strictly according to our advantage, Schopenhauer contends, we would prefer nothingness over being, simply because life creates far more pain than pleasure (II. 742; P 579–80). Hence he compares life to a bad business venture where the losses outweigh the gains, and where we never recover our initial investment (II. 734, 742; P 574, 579–80). Rather than comparing life to a gift, he thinks that we should liken it more to a debt (II. 743;

[12] *WWV* II. 733–54; P 573–88.

P 580). Paying off the interest takes our entire life; and we pay off the principle only with death. The sheer scale, constancy and intensity of human suffering, and the fact that the wicked prosper while the virtuous suffer, makes it necessary to admit, Schopenhauer insists, that it would have been better had the world never existed (II. 738–9; P 576).

As it stands, this argument seems very dogmatic because Schopenhauer writes as if it were a simple fact that suffering greatly outweighs pleasure in life. Many of his critics, as we shall eventually see, contest this apparent fact; they contend that the very opposite is the case: that, on the whole, at least for the great majority of people, pleasure outweighs suffering. We shall see in the next section, however, that Schopenhauer has a strong rationale for his assessment.

Sometimes in chapter 46 Schopenhauer adopts a moral rather than a eudemonic or utilitarian standard to measure the value of life. This becomes clear when he maintains that the existence of *any* evil at all shows that life should not have been (II. 738–9; P 576). In other words, life would be of value only if there were no evil whatsoever. The smallest amount of evil cannot be balanced out, or compensated for, by the greatest amount of good. As Schopenhauer puts it: even if thousands lived in happiness, that would never compensate for the anguish and agony of a single individual.

This argument seems to derive its plausibility from the moral intuition that the suffering of one person cannot be the justification for the happiness of many. This is the intuition behind the old adage: *Floreat justitia, pereat mundi*. There can be no justification for making the entire world happy if it requires committing an injustice against just one person. The problem with this argument is that it rides roughshod over the moral claims of the great majority to be happy. Should we deny such claims just because fulfilling them would deny one person's claim to be happy?

Whatever weight we give to this moral intuition, it does not reflect fully the intention behind Schopenhauer's argument. Schopenhauer's case against pain is meant to apply not only between individuals but also within one individual. Speaking of one individual alone, Schopenhauer cites Petrarch's maxim: *Mille piacer' non vagliono un tormento*.[13] This argument seems to betray, however, an extraordinary sensitivity to pain. After all, most people prefer enduring root canal treatment for the pleasure of eating with their natural teeth.

Thus most of the arguments of chapter 46 prove rather weak. They appear to vindicate those critics of Schopenhauer who think his pessimism rests more on his cranky temperament rather than cool reasoning. Only the utilitarian argument about the preponderance of suffering over happiness has some plausibility. We now need to examine the basis for this argument.

---

[13] "A thousand pleasures are not worth a single torment." See *WWV* II. 737; P 576. Schopenhauer cites Petrarch, *Sonetto* 195.

4. Life as Suffering

Fortunately for Schopenhauer, however, the arguments of chapter 46 are not the heart of his case for pessimism. The most important arguments appear in sections §§57–9 of volume I of *Die Welt als Wille und Vorstellung*. Here Schopenhauer contends that pessimism is the inevitable conclusion of any thorough and accurate examination of the human condition, i.e. of the problems any human being faces in attempting to achieve happiness in this world. Schopenhauer refuses to rest his case on empirical evidence alone, even though he thinks it would provide overwhelming evidence in his favour. In these sections he states what he calls his "a priori" arguments for his pessimism. The intent of these arguments is to prove one central thesis: "that all life is suffering" (*alles Leben Leiden ist*) (I. 426; P 310).

Schopenhauer's arguments in §§57–9 are not modern but classical, coming straight from the playbook of the Epicurean and Stoic traditions. The Epicureans and Stoics had argued that the dynamics of human desire are inherently frustrating, and that they make it impossible to achieve the highest good, which consists in tranquillity, equanimity or peace of mind. Such happiness can be attained, they taught, only through virtue, self-discipline and withdrawal from the world. Schopenhauer borrows much from their arguments, their conception of happiness and even their strategy for attaining it. Where he departs from his forebears is in his skepticism about human virtue, in the power of most human beings to control their desires and to direct their lives toward the good. *Velle non discitur*—the will cannot be taught—is one of Schopenhauer's favourite maxims, which he repeats constantly. If that is true, the highest good of the Epicureans and Stoics will be unattainable in this life.

Schopenhauer's arguments in §§57–9 begin with an analysis of human desire. The very essence of a human being, we are told, consists in willing or striving. We are first and foremost conative rather than cognitive creatures. This willing and striving manifests itself in desire and need, which is some felt deficiency or lack. When we feel this deficiency or lack, we suffer pain (*Schmerz*), Schopenhauer says, by which he means not so much physical pain (pangs, aches, stabs) but something more like discomfort, unease, frustration and yearning. We strive to satisfy these needs (viz., for food or sex), so that the discomfort, yearning or frustration ceases. Although we sometimes satisfy these needs, the pleasure in their satisfaction never lasts very long, and it takes the form of only momentary relief. The needs then regenerate, so that the discomfort, frustration and yearning recur and we again have to chase after the objects of our desire. Since discomfort, frustration and yearning constantly recur, and since they are forms of suffering, we can say that life consists in suffering. Since, furthermore, need is constant and satisfaction brief, we can say that life consists in more pain than pleasure, more suffering than happiness. Here, then, lies the rationale for Schopenhauer's eudemonic argument in chapter 46.

Although this argument brings Schopenhauer close to his conclusion, it is only the beginning of his indictment against life. He adds another novel argument to bolster his case. The suffering of life, he maintains, arises not simply from deprivation, from the feeling of need alone, but it also comes from another potent source: boredom. If need gives rise to an excess of *activity*, which consists in the toil and trouble of striving, boredom comes from an excess of *inactivity*, which consists in the restlessness and discontent of doing nothing at all. Boredom is just as much a source of suffering as need, Schopenhauer insists. For when we are bored, we are desperate. We do not know what to do with ourselves; our very existence is a burden.

Our lives, Schopenhauer contends, constantly oscillate between these two desperate conditions: need and boredom. Whether we feel one or the other depends on how slowly or quickly we satisfy our needs. If we satisfy them too slowly, we feel frustration; if we satisfy them too quickly, we feel boredom. In either case, we suffer, whether from too much or too little activity. These states feed off each other. When we are bored, we long for activity, which brings toil and trouble; but when we are in the midst of toil and trouble, we yearn for rest, which brings boredom. So we are damned whether we act or rest.

Thus our predicament consists in suffering, whether or not we satisfy our needs. If we satisfy them, we suffer boredom; and if we do not satisfy them, we suffer deprivation. But what, one might ask, about those moments when we do satisfy our needs? Surely, someone might object, these are moments of joy or pleasure, however brief, which add to life's value. Schopenhauer, however, has a response to this objection, one that deprives even these moments of any positive worth. In section §59 of *Die Welt als Wille und Vorstellung* he argues, following Epicurus, that pleasure is only a negative quality, i.e. it arises only from the removal of deprivation or need. Pleasure is not a positive quality in itself, one that is distinctive from pain, for the simple reason that it is only the absence of pain. We only feel pleasure, Schopenhauer argues, when we return to our normal condition after feeling need. But once we are in that normal condition, we do not have any special feeling of pleasure. We appreciate what we have only when we lose it.

This analysis of pleasure greatly limits its value and extent. If we feel pleasure only after the removal of pain, or only at the end of suffering, we do not feel it for very long, because as soon as we return to normal, we feel no pleasure at all. So in the calculus of life's costs and benefits, only the pains, which constantly add up, count, because they alone have a positive value; the pleasures, however, are equal to zero.

To appreciate Schopenhauer's arguments for pessimism, it is crucial to consider his views on sex, which he outlines in a famous essay, 'Metaphysik der Geschlechtsliebe', which is chapter 44 of volume II of *Die Welt als Wille und Vorstellung*.[14] These views are an important backdrop to his argument in sections §§57–9. In his essay Schopenhauer makes it clear that sex is the strongest drive in human nature, one even more potent than that for self-preservation, given that people often sacrifice their lives for the sake of love or their progeny. Sex is not only the strongest but also the most pervasive drive, playing a decisive but subconscious role in motivating most of our actions. But this most potent and pervasive of drives, Schopenhauer argues, is blind and irrational, the

---

[14] 'Metaphysik der Geschlechtsliebe', *WWV* II. 678–727.

source of endless suffering that we are powerless to resist. We surrender to it even if it is ruinous for us, and even if its satisfactions are fleeting and momentary. We think that love will bring us the greatest of pleasures; but no sooner do we satisfy its urgings than disillusionment and disappointment begin. Nothing do we flee with greater haste than the bedroom on the morning after! Rather than learning any lessons, though, we persist in our folly because our desires regenerate and we cannot resist them. Although we think that we are the agents behind our quest for love, we are really only the instruments of a higher power that controls us and uses us for its purposes. This higher power is the will to life, and its purpose is nothing more than existence itself, the mere continuation of life. There is no purpose to sex other than procreation; and there is no purpose to procreation other than the survival of the species. The will to life could not care less for the happiness of the individuals who serve it. Each individual procreates for the sake of the species; and once it performs its reproductive task, it is discarded and left to die.

So far Schopenhauer's arguments seem to apply best to what the ancient Epicureans called "natural and necessary desires", more specifically, the desires for food and sex, or nutrition and reproduction. It is these desires that constantly regenerate, and whose frustration lead so quickly to suffering. But Schopenhauer did not limit his argument to these desires alone. In chapter 46 of *Die Welt als Wille und Vorstellung*, in §153 of *Parlipomena*, and in chapter 3 of the *Aphorismen zur Lebensweisheit*,[15] he also considers the so-called "unnatural and unnecessary desires", i.e. those for power, prestige and money. These desires are "unnatural" because they are artificial, the product of culture and education; and they are "unnecessary" because we can survive without them. Nevertheless, because they are so common and such a significant obstacle to the good life, they were the special target of the ancient philosophers. Their argument against these desires is that acting on them inevitably leads to frustration because they have no natural limit or end. The more we have of power, prestige or money, the more we want of them; but the more we want of them, the harder they are to get, and so we become even more frustrated. Schopenhauer accepts this argument. Like Epicurus or Epictetus, he argues that the more wealth and fame we acquire, the more we want them; but the more we want, the harder they are to obtain, so that we are perpetually dissatisfied.

When we consider all these arguments, it is possible to appreciate Schopenhauer's conclusion that life is indeed suffering. Though there are moments of pleasure in life—sexual climaxes, quenched thirsts, sated bellies—they are fleeting, few and far between; and never do they outweigh our usual and common fate: the deprivation of need, the desperation of boredom, and the degradation of sex. During most of our day we struggle to satisfy needs, to stave off boredom or to still sexual urges, only to find that we are doomed to repeat our efforts tomorrow. We know that we are caught in a cycle of torment; but we find it hard, if not impossible, to escape, because we long for the very things that trap us. It is as if we were, as Schopenhauer put it, "lying on the revolving wheel of Ixion...and drawing water from the sieve of the Danaids" (I. 280; P 196). Yes, indeed, there could be no better description of hell.

[15] See *Parerga* in *Sämtliche Werke*, IV. 412–20.

4

The Illusion of Redemption

1. The False Promise of Deliverance

Although Schopenhauer goes to great lengths and pains to prove his pessimism, he does not regard its proof as the sole end of his philosophy. His aim is not only to demonstrate the suffering of life but also to describe the path of redemption from it. Inspired by Christianity and Buddhism, Schopenhauer even regards his philosophy as a *Heilslehre*, a doctrine of salvation, which will deliver its follower from temptation and sin and lead him toward a life of serenity and tranquillity.

It would seem, then, that Schopenhauer's pessimism is not as grim and bleak as it first appears. If Schopenhauer is promising redemption, a path to escape the evil and suffering of the world, then life really cannot be all that bad. There is indeed a striking tension between Schopenhauer's pessimism and his doctrine of salvation: his pessimism tells us that life is not worth living; but his doctrine of salvation tells us that life can be redeemed and made worth living after all. The apparent tension can be resolved if we distinguish between two forms of life: the life not worth living is that which is caught in the cycle of desire and that which affirms the will; the life worth living is one that escapes that cycle and denies that will. But the mere need to make this distinction shows that life in general or as a whole cannot be so bad, at least not if there is one kind of life in which we find redemption and serenity.

It is striking, however, that few of Schopenhauer's contemporaries were impressed by his promises of redemption. They quickly recognized that there are deep problems with Schopenhauer's doctrine of salvation. For one thing, the general principles of his metaphysics seem to forbid the possibility of denial of the will, which is the precondition of redemption. For another thing, even if redemption were compatible with his metaphysics, Schopenhauer limited it to very few people—geniuses and saints—and to very rare and momentary kinds of experience—the epiphanies of mystical experience or the joys of aesthetic contemplation. Last but not least, Schopenhauer always insisted that our moral character is innate and permanent, so that we cannot educate the will or teach virtue. In that case, however, his own prescriptions for a life of redemption would be pointless for anyone whose character is not suitable for it in the first place. That anyone, for reasons we shall soon see, proved to be the great majority of mankind.

Because Schopenhauer's doctrine of redemption seemed illusory, his contemporaries were all the more motivated to challenge his pessimism. As they saw it, Schopenhauer had portrayed a terrible problem for which he really had no solution. He had consigned the great mass of humanity to a life in hell, from which there could be no escape except through death.

Our task in this chapter will be to explain the difficulties with Schopenhauer's doctrine of redemption. These difficulties were the subject and starting point of much discussion and controversy in the second half of the 19th century.

2. Affirming and Denying the Will

For Schopenhauer, the truth of pessimism poses a fundamental choice for every human being: whether he or she should affirm or deny the will to life (I. 393; P 285). To affirm life means to recognize that the world is the objectification of the will, and to make that very fact a *motive* for following the will. To deny life is just the opposite: to recognize that the world is the objectification of the will, but to make that very fact a *quietus* for the will, i.e. a reason for renouncing it. This choice, as Schopenhauer understands it, deals specifically with our physical needs, viz., nourishment and sex (I. 448; P 326-7). Since the will objectifies itself in the body, to affirm the will means attempting to satisfy the body's needs. To negate the will means just the opposite: that a person denies these needs and attempts to lead an ascetic life.

As Schopenhauer explains this choice, both those who affirm and those who deny life know all the horrible facts about the world. They fully realize all the consequences of the will's objectification in the world: a life filled with suffering and sorrow, of endless struggle and striving. But he who affirms life still acts contrary to his better knowledge, realizing that his decision to act on his desires will perpetuate the cycle of desire and suffering (I. 448; P 326). Why, then, does he choose to affirm life? Because, Schopenhauer explains, he acts more according to his desires than his intellect; he still affirms life because he is caught in the service of the will and cannot renounce his desires, especially his need for sex. Although lovers subconsciously recognize that their act, through their progeny, will perpetuate futility and suffering, they still indulge themselves because they cannot resist their desires. Lovers are "traitors", because, though they know they are continuing the cycle of misery, they still act contrary to their better knowledge; hence the shame with which they engage in their acts (II. 718; P 560).

The central question concerning redemption in Schopenhauer's philosophy is whether we really do have, on his general premises, a choice in this matter. How is it possible to deny the will to life if that will is omnipotent, if it manifests itself in everything that we say and do, and if it is bent on eternally reproducing itself? It would seem that to deny the will to life is for the will *per impossible* to negate itself. But if its main urge is to preserve itself, how can it destroy itself?

Schopenhauer's immediate response to this difficulty, of which he is fully aware, is to attribute great powers to the intellect, so that it can turn against the will; in that case, the will does not negate itself but the intellect negates the will (I. 547; P 403). Hence in §§66–8 and §70 of *Die Welt als Wille und Vorstellung* Schopenhauer explains that the intellect has the power to penetrate through the veil of Maya and the *principium individuationis* and to see that there is one cosmic will within all of us whose urgings and strivings are the source of all suffering. It is essentially through this act of insight, through this immediate or intuitive knowledge, that we finally realize what the will is doing to us and so we turn against it (I. 515, 521, 539; P 379, 384, 397). But all this too seems questionable, because Schopenhauer has already stressed the dominance of the will over the intellect, which is only a servant of the will. If this is so, then either the intellect cannot penetrate the veil of Maya at all, because the will sabotages such insight, or we cannot act on that insight because of the strength of our desires. Either way, it appears impossible for the intellect alone to completely change the course of our lives.[1]

Schopenhauer makes several attempts to respond to this difficulty, none of them entirely successful. It is in the penultimate section of *Die Welt als Wille und Vorstellung* (§70) that he addresses this question most explicitly, asking how there can be denial of the will if all actions of the will are determined of necessity (I. 546; P 402). His solution is to apply the distinction between noumena and phenomena: that though all *phenomenal* actions occur of necessity, the *noumenal* will remains free, having the power to do otherwise; and it is through its act of transcendental freedom that it changes its entire phenomenal character. But whence does the noumenal will have this power to turn against its phenomenal self? Schopenhauer replies that the denial of the will to life does not come from the will itself but from its new knowledge (I. 547; P 403). But that still begs the question: How does this new knowledge have the power to change the will when the will has predominance over the intellect?

Schopenhauer seems to have an answer to this difficulty in his distinction between two forms of intellect or two kinds of knowledge (546–7; P 402–3). According to this distinction, which first appears in §§33–4 of Book III of *Die Welt als Wille und Vorstellung*, there is the *discursive* intellect that is subject to the principle of sufficient reason that knows only the relation between things; and there is the *intuitive* intellect that contemplates the forms or ideas of things, their essences or intrinsic natures as opposed to their relations. It is only the former kind of intellect, Schopenhauer maintains, that is the servant of the will; the latter, however, is will-less and attempts to grasp things purely objectively, regardless of the interests of the will. The insights of the wise man are instances of the latter kind of intellect, which alone enables him to renounce the will (I. 393; P 285).

This distinction, however, is still not sufficient to remove the difficulty. For the question still remains: what right does Schopenhauer have to such a distinction in the first place? Why should he be allowed to postulate a second kind of intellect at all? If the will

---

[1] For the dominance of the will over the intellect, see especially Kapitel 19, 'Vom Primat des Willens im Selbstbewußtsein', *WWV* II. 259–315; P 201–44.

is omnipotent, and if it has power over the intellect, as Schopenhauer often tells us, how is it possible for there to be a form of cognition that is will-less, let alone one that has the power to deny the will and to control it?

In his other attempts to address this problem, Schopenhauer vacillates. Sometimes he insists that the will *cannot* deny itself, because such an act would be self-destructive, exercising the very will that is to be denied; so on these grounds he says that the act of self-denial has to originate in the intellect alone.[2] But at other times he admits that the will *must* deny itself, because there is no power higher than it; he then accepts the paradox that the will in denying itself—somehow—affirms itself.[3] There is "a contradiction" in the realm of appearance, he explains, because on the one hand appearances still objectify or express the will even when the will turns against itself in acts of virtue. This contradiction takes visible form when, for example, we see the presence of sex organs in the ascetic.

Sometimes Schopenhauer's attempt to explain self-denial ends in blatant circularity.[4] He insists that the insight by which the will frees itself from its blind striving has to come from the *pure* subject, i.e. the subject who is free from all self-interest and from the blind urgings and promptings of the will. It cannot come from the *empirical* subject, i.e. the subject insofar as it has selfish interests and desires. But then the question arises: how do we become pure subjects? It turns out that we can become pure subjects only through achieving an act of insight, which we can do only if we are already pure subjects.

Despite such vacillation and circularity, it is still possible to provide something of an explanation of the possibility of self-denial on the general principles of Schopenhauer's philosophy. It is important to keep in mind two points. First, although Schopenhauer stresses the dominance of the will over the intellect, he also has a theory, a naturalistic explanation, for how the intellect separates itself from the will and becomes autonomous, free from its domination and control. In chapter 22 of the second volume of *Die Welt als Wille und Vorstellung* Schopenhauer explains how the intellect, in more complex and differentiated stages of organic development, has to grow to serve the organism's greater needs.[5] The more its needs increase, the more the intellect develops to serve them, until eventually the intellect, like many organic functions, becomes autonomous, separating itself from other functions of the organism. But the more we develop our intellect, the more we see the world "objectively", i.e. how it exists independent of our own needs. Eventually, the will disappears entirely in acts of objective contemplation. Second, in his treatment of freedom in §55 of *Die Welt als Wille und Vorstellung* Schopenhauer emphasizes that, though our *character* is indeed unalterable, we can still change our *conduct* through greater knowledge of what we want and how to get it (I. 405–6; P 294–5). We have not only a noumenal and phenomenal

---

[2] See *WWV* I. 514–15; P 378–9; and *WWV* II. 473–4; P 367–8.
[3] See *WWV* I. 393; P 285; I. 397; P 288; I. 546; P 402.
[4] See Kapitel 30, 'Vom reinen Subjekt des Erkennens', *WWV* II. 473–4; P 367–8.
[5] See Kapitel 22, 'Objektive Ansicht des Intellekts', *WWV* II. 361–2, 377–8; P 278–9, 291–2.

character, Schopenhauer reminds us, but also a "third" or "acquired character" that comes from experience, from learning who we are, what we want and how we can satisfy those wants. This acquired character gives people the power to change their conduct in the light of greater knowledge. The same person acting in the same circumstances with the same motives will always do the same thing, Schopenhauer writes, *but not if they have new knowledge that they did not have before.*[6] The addition of new knowledge therefore means that the will has the power to reform itself, to cease past patterns of conduct that are futile or self-destructive. And so, it seems, there is the prospect of redemption. For the new knowledge could come from the insights that the striving of the will is the source of suffering, that I am ultimately the same as everyone else, that there is really no point in competing against others and so on. With these new insights, we should have the power to change our actions, and to cease engaging in futile patterns of conduct.

Neither of these points completely removes the difficulty, however. The first point still leaves the question how the intellect becomes fully autonomous if it is subject to the domination of the will in all the ways Schopenhauer contends. Arguably, the will only *appears* autonomous, and its apparent autonomy is still subject to *subconscious* control. This is a possibility that Schopenhauer cannot discount, given that he argues that the will often dominates the intellect subconsciously.[7] The second point shows only the possibility for a change in *conduct*, which is still not sufficient to provide the complete change in *character* that Schopenhauer thinks is necessary for negation of that the will. If we are to negate the will, he argues, we need a new character which renounces its old ends, and not simply the acquired character that finds new means to old ends. Thus, in the penultimate section of *Die Welt als Wille und Vorstellung* (§70), Schopenhauer describes how the person who negates the will does so in virtue of an act of transcendent freedom that completely changes his character, and in virtue of which he is "reborn" (I. 548; P 403). The acquired character, however, is still in service of the old phenomenal character; it determines new means to its ends but never renounces the ends themselves. But when we ask how this new character arises, we are left with an appeal to the mysterious: an incomprehensible act of transcendent freedom (I. 548–9; P 404–5). It then seems as if redemption is possible only through a *deus ex machina*, an act of transcendent freedom as inexplicable as divine grace.

3. Practical Reason and Redemption

Any adequate treatment of Schopenhauer's theory of redemption has to consider his attitude toward an apparently unrelated topic: Stoicism. Not only does Schopenhauer's

---

[6] See his *Preisschrift über die Freiheit des Willens*, III. 572–3.

[7] In 'Vom Primat des Willens im Selbstbewußtsein', for example, Schopenhauer argues that the will often represses what the intellect should know (II. 268, 280–1; P 208, 217–18).

theory have great debts to ancient Stoicism, but his critical discussion of its merits and limits also contains his clearest account of the powers and limits of practical reason, the faculty upon which redemption ultimately rests. Schopenhauer's main discussion of the practical powers of reason appears in §16 of the first volume of *Die Welt als Wille und Vorstellung* and in chapter 16 of the second volume. Not accidentally, these texts are also his chief discussion of Stoicism. For Schopenhauer, it was the Stoics rather than Kant who made the best case for the powers of practical reason. While Schopenhauer makes important concessions to the Stoics, he makes none at all to Kant, whose case he quickly dismisses.

Schopenhauer's great debts to the Stoics are apparent in his account of the evils of life and in his solution to them. Like the Stoics, Schopenhauer teaches that the common experience of human life consists in suffering, and that the more we attach ourselves to things the more we expose ourselves to misfortune. He also agrees with the Stoics that the pursuit of the unnatural desires—those for fame, wealth and power—is a major source of unhappiness, because these desires are limitless and therefore insatiable. Again like the Stoics, Schopenhauer thinks that the path to true happiness consists in self-control, self-renunciation and withdrawal from the world, where we cultivate an inner indifference to all that happens. Schopenhauer's wise man, much like the Stoics', realizes that he cannot change the world—its suffering, evil and death are eternal and essential features—but he believes that at least he can change his attitude toward it. Achieving the right attitude is a matter of resigning ourselves to the ways of the world, learning to surrender to necessity and then cultivating an indifference to it.

Given such parallels, it should not be surprising that Schopenhauer was an admirer of the Stoic ethic. In §16 he pays it handsome tribute: "The stoic ethic, taken as a whole, is in fact a very valuable and admirable attempt to use reason, the great privilege of humanity, for an important and beneficial end: to elevate it above the suffering and pain that falls to every life ..." (*WWV* I. 145; P 90). In his *Aphorismen zur Lebensweisheit* he endorses the Stoic ideals of self-sufficiency and independence (IV. 407), and he even recommends adopting a Stoic attitude toward life because it teaches us to bear all its insults and injuries with dignity (IV. 564). All this raises the question: why was Schopenhauer not a Stoic?

One's first suspicion is likely to be that Schopenhauer rejected Stoicism because of its too high opinion of the powers of reason. Sure enough, in §55 of *Die Welt als Wille und Vorstellung* Schopenhauer writes that the Stoic ethic makes impossible demands upon reason (I. 405–6; P 294–5). The Stoics wrongly believed that reason has the power to control the will, and so they falsely assumed that it could provide us with tranquillity. Schopenhauer insists that it is impossible to teach virtue, as the Stoics held, and that we can persuade someone of a motive for action only if it already suits his or her character and will, which are fixed and unalterable. We might convince someone through reason to find new means for their ends; but we cannot get them to change the ends themselves. Presumably, then, when Schopenhauer prescribed a Stoic attitude he did so with limited expectations of success, knowing that it would work only for people who already had a disposition and inclination for it.

Although this critique of Stoicism might seem predictable, it turns out that Schopenhauer's attitude toward Stoicism is more complex and nuanced, not least because he has a much more complex and nuanced position on the powers of reason itself. Surprisingly, Schopenhauer ascribes considerable powers to human reason in governing human conduct, something we do not expect from his extreme voluntarism, which appears to give the will complete dominance over reason. While Schopenhauer rejects the Kantian theory that practical reason can determine the principles or ends of human conduct, he accepts the Stoic view that the dignity of human beings lies in learning how to live according to our characteristic powers of reason (II. 190; P 148). If in the realm of theory we should make intuition our standard, Schopenhauer advises, in the realm of practice we should follow reason. Reason shows its power over human life precisely in virtue of its capacity for abstraction, which gives us the ability to take a critical distance on our lives and to view them with detachment. It is thanks to reason that we can see our lives objectively, that we can regard things coolly and calmly, from outside and afar. Once we gain that perspective, we can free ourselves from obsessions, addictions and cravings, so that we are not so prone to all the bruises and humiliations that come with complete immersion in the life of desire. With the power of abstraction, Schopenhauer says, we can see our lives like an actor who, having played his role, now stands among the spectators; he can then see everything that goes on stage with complete equanimity, even if it is his own death (I. 139; P 85).

It is in this context that Schopenhauer pays tribute to Stoicism. The Stoic goal of self-mastery and equanimity is, he writes, "to some extent attainable". What makes it feasible, at least to some degree, is that very power of abstraction of human reason that allows us to take a distance upon our lives and to view them with detachment from a third-person perspective. One product of that power is the Stoic attitude of "letting go", of *Gelassenheit*, which Schopenhauer describes with evident admiration (*WWV* I. 139; P 85). That attitude involves indifference and equanimity, resigning oneself to the necessity of things, letting the world go its own course and not becoming upset by what happens, whatever that might be. Hence the Stoic sage could take all that life threw at him, "suicide, execution, duel, dangerous undertakings of all kinds, and in general things that even his animal nature rebelled against". Impressed by the powers of the Stoic sage, Schopenhauer exclaims: "Here one can really say that reason expresses itself practically" (I. 139; P 86).

Yet, for all his agreement with and admiration of the Stoic, Schopenhauer stops short of complete endorsement. The main problem with the Stoic ethic is not that we cannot follow reason or that reason makes too high demands upon us; it is rather that following reason alone cannot provide redemption. The Stoic ethics takes us as far as we can go with human reason; but that is still not far enough. Assuming that we act fully according to the precepts of reason, that is still not sufficient to achieve the good life. The true basis of human virtue, Schopenhauer teaches in his *Grundlage der Moral*,[8] derives not from reason but from feeling, and from one kind of feeling in particular: sympathy or pity. Having this feeling is a matter of our character and inner nature, and it cannot be commanded or created by following abstract principles or precepts.

Schopenhauer saw his ethic of sympathy and pity as the heart of Christianity, whose great merit, he says, was to have preached *caritas, Menschenliebe*.[9] The Christian sources of Schopenhauer's ethics prove decisive for his judgement of Stoicism, because he endorses the traditional Christian objections against it. In his *Parerga* he affirms one such objection: that the Stoic suffers from hardness of heart (IV. 378). The Stoic tried to be indifferent about everything, even the death of his wife or child. But Schopenhauer makes the telling point: a heart that no longer feels cannot grow. A cold heart is very problematic, Schopenhauer believes, because it shrinks the greatest virtue, which is pity or sympathy. The Christian and Indian wise men were more admirable models for humanity, Schopenhauer argues, because, though they too had the power to withstand misfortune, they never lost their sympathy with the suffering of the world.

Schopenhauer also approves of another famous Christian complaint about Stoic ethics: its recommendation of suicide (I. 146; P 90–1). In Book XIX of *De civitate Dei* Augustine famously argued that the Stoic recommendation is an admission that its ethics is a failure. For it was the goal of the Stoic ethic to lead us to happiness in this life. But then to encourage suicide in certain situations—loss of dignity, illness, old age—is to concede that one's counsel is at an end, and that happiness is really not obtainable on this earth after all. On this score, Schopenhauer agreed with Augustine. In §69 of *Die Welt als Wille und Vorstellung* he makes it plain that those who advise or commit suicide have not really reached the state of redemption that comes with renunciation of the will. Rather than denying the will, the suicide submits to it because he cannot satisfy it under his present circumstances.

Ultimately, then, Schopenhauer parts company with the Stoic ethic because, for all its demands for indifference toward life, it still could not let go of the world. The Stoic's final goal was happiness in this life, and for that his ethic was supposed to provide a complete and fail safe guide. It was only a matter of controlling the will, of directing it according to reason. For Schopenhauer, however, happiness in this life is unattainable, and the only way we can approach anything like the tranquillity and equanimity of the Stoic ideal is not by controlling the will but renouncing it, suffocating it in a complete asceticism. The Christian and Indian mystics and ascetics knew better than the Stoic sage: that there could be no happiness in this world, and that redemption lay not in disciplining but denying the will.[10]

---

[8] *Preisschrift über die Grundlage der Moral*, in *Sämtliche Werke*, III. 740, 742, §16; 763, §18.
[9] Ibid. III. 762, §18.
[10] See Schopenhauer's critique of Stoicism in *Handschriftlicher Nachlaß*, I. 108–9, §197.

4. Paths to Redemption

Admitting, for the sake of argument, that redemption is possible in Schopenhauer's universe, how do we achieve it? What specific paths should we follow? Schopenhauer teaches that there are two paths to escape suffering, two strategies for finding tranquillity in this life. The first lies with aesthetic experience, with the creation and appreciation of beauty and the sublime; and the second rests with a specific kind of virtue, namely, the life of self-sacrifice and asceticism. The artist and the saint are the models for redemption in Schopenhauer's world.

We should examine each path toward redemption, and consider whether it really provides, on Schopenhauer's general principles, redemption.

In §§30–38 of Book III of *Die Welt als Wille und Vorstellung* Schopenhauer gives a decidedly optimistic account of aesthetic experience, one designed to serve as an antidote to his own pessimism. With aesthetic experience, Schopenhauer reassures us, we escape the suffering of life, and for at least a moment we are transported into another world where Ixion's wheel stops. There are two basic features of aesthetic experience that act as an antidote to the suffering of life. First, as Kant taught, aesthetic experience is *disinterested*. When I contemplate a work of art, or the beautiful or sublime in nature, I lay aside my own interests, and I look at the object for its own sake. I do not value the object because it is a means to my ends, a way to satisfy my desires, but I esteem it because it is an end in itself, something that has a value apart from my desires. Aesthetic experience is therefore *will-less*, avoiding the constant urgings and promptings of my will that perpetuate the cycle of suffering. Second, as Kant also taught, aesthetic experience is *impersonal*, concerned not with my individual likes or dislikes but with what would please anyone simply as a human being. When I perceive an aesthetic object, I attempt to judge it from the standpoint of common sense or as a neutral spectator; my own personal feelings and preferences do not factor into its appraisal. Hence the subject of aesthetic experience is, as Schopenhauer put it, "the pure subject", i.e. the subject insofar as he or she abstracts from individual preferences and personal desires and attempts to grasp the qualities of the object itself independent of these preferences and desires. By virtue of the disinterest and impersonality of aesthetic experience, the subject lays aside its own "egoism", i.e. it ceases to put its own desires before everyone else. With art, then, my own individual self no longer appears so important anymore; I can enjoy things for their sakes, not having to care about myself. If, only for a moment, I cease to suffer and the wheel of Ixion stops.

Schopenhauer admits that genuine aesthetic experience is rare and fleeting, offering only temporary relief from the suffering of life (280; P 196). Furthermore, it is not equally accessible to everyone alike. There are great discrepancies between individuals in their aesthetic powers. While all people can enjoy art, at least to some small degree, only the genius can create it and fully appreciate it (278; P 194–5). Between the genius and the ordinary person there is a great difference in the depth, intensity and duration of aesthetic experience. Only the genius has a deep, intense and enduring experience, one which lasts for more than a few moments. Nevertheless, Schopenhauer still stresses that *all* people, even the *populo* and *Pöbel*, have, at least to some small extent, the power to enjoy beauty and the sublime; they can appreciate works of art, even if they do not have the power to create them. At least for a few brief moments, then, everyone can escape from desire and suffering through aesthetic experience (278; P 194–5).

The other path toward redemption in Schopenhauer's universe, which he outlines in §§68–70 of Book IV of *Die Welt als Wille und Vorstellung*, lies in the sphere of morality, and more specifically with one special kind of virtue: self-denial and asceticism. This path to redemption begins with that mystical experience where the individual sees through the veil of Maya and recognizes his identity with all things. The individual who has this transformative experience, Schopenhauer maintains, discovers the basis of all moral virtue: sympathy with the suffering of others. He also sees through the source of human misery—incessant human desire—and the futility of all desire. With these crucial insights, he can acquire the power to renounce his will and to practise self-denial.

This moral path to redemption promises to be less ephemeral than aesthetic experience, because its source lies in a specific kind of moral character, which is a permanent disposition and attitude of mind. Schopenhauer paints in glowing terms the experience of those who achieve self-renunciation and denial of the will. It is "full of inner joy and true heavenly serenity" (I. 529; P 369). The Christian mystics were right to describe it as "ecstasy" and "illumination", "rebirth" and "grace" (I. 548, 556–7; P 403, 410). When we are in this state, Schopenhauer enthuses, we will have conquered the world, because it ceases to bother or affect us; we accept everything that happens with indifference; and we do not even defend ourselves when others assault us (I. 519; P 382).

Yet, even if the experience proves to be more enduring, the moral path to redemption proves to be narrow and perilous. Schopenhauer realizes that it is difficult to remain on the path of virtue, and that the temptations of the world will constantly attract and distract us (I. 531–2; P391–2). But, even more problematically, the path to virtue remains open only to a few because Schopenhauer demands a very rare and nearly superhuman form of it: the saintly or heroic. In §§66–8 Schopenhauer makes a distinction between the merely just man, who has the average moral virtue, and the saint or hero, who does supererogatory deeds. While the just man observes the rights of others and even performs acts of benevolence, the saint or hero is ready to sacrifice his life for others. The just man cannot claim redemption or deliverance because he has not denied the will in himself; he sees others as equal to himself but he does not put others above himself. It is only the saint or hero who breaks his will, who has the power to deny the will in himself, whether by renouncing all his desires or by laying down his life for others (514–15, 516; P 378–9, 380).

Of course, very few of us have what it takes to be saints or heroes. But there is something else that makes the path to heroism or sainthood almost impossible: namely,

Schopenhauer's insistence that virtue cannot be taught. The attempt to improve someone's character he likens to turning lead into gold. To be heroes or saints, what we need is a complete change of character, a new reborn man. But we get that character only through an act of "transcendent freedom", which is completely mysterious to us (I. 548; P 403).

Given that aesthetic experience is so fleeting, and given that true virtue is so rare, it would seem that the more enduring and accessible antidote to Schopenhauer's pessimism lies with suicide. Suicide has the advantages of giving eternal release and being open to everyone alike. It is the obvious and sure remedy against the suffering and pointlessness of life. Yet Schopenhauer is utterly against it. Perhaps fearful of a suicide epidemic like that following Goethe's *Leiden des jungen Werther,* and perhaps mindful of the deep grief caused by his father's own suicide, Schopenhauer went to pains to warn his readers against it. In §69 of *Die Welt als Wille und Vorstellung* he argues that someone who commits suicide has not really triumphed over the will to life but only fallen victim to it (I. 541; P 398). The suicide affirms the value of life, but protests against the circumstances in which he finds himself; just because he cannot achieve happiness in his present circumstances, he kills himself. With his death, not the will itself, but only one manifestation of it, that which appears under his tragic circumstances, is destroyed.

Schopenhauer's prohibition of suicide seems arbitrary. Why should the suicide affirm life itself? Why should he protest only against his own living conditions? Perhaps the suicide has gained insight into the irremediable suffering and meaninglessness of life, and so he hates it under all circumstances? Strangely, Schopenhauer says nothing against the possibility of committing suicide *on principle*, and indeed following the principles of his own philosophy. We shall soon see how one of Schopenhauer's most talented followers—Philipp Mainländer—took his philosophy to its ultimate conclusion.

Whatever the merits of suicide, redemption proves a very rare event in Schopenhauer's universe. Although everyone can have aesthetic experience, its pleasures are for most of us only fleeting and sporadic. Only the genius enjoys it for a long time. And, because virtue, like genius, cannot be taught, only those born with the right disposition can achieve that heroic or saintly virtue that gives serenity. Thus Schopenhauer's therapy against pessimism turns out to be of limited utility. Most of us, most of the time, are doomed to a life of suffering, which we cannot escape except through death.

It was not simply Schopenhauer's pessimism but the ineffective remedies he offered against it that moved so many to write against him. Redemption for an elite few was not an attractive model of life for a new democratic and egalitarian age. Being told that life as it stands is not worth living is bad enough; but then also being told that one cannot do much about it is only a recipe for indignation or despair. This message did not sit well with a Promethean age that believed its strivings could create a new world order, a heaven upon earth.

5. Protestantism without Theism

As if his vision of life were not bleak enough, Schopenhauer adds a cruel twist to it, one that seems almost sadistic. It is not simply a tragic fact that we suffer; we *deserve* to suffer. He expresses this thought on several occasions. "The truth is: we ought to be wretched, and we are so" (*WWV* II. 739; P 577). Alternatively: "Every great pain, be it physical or mental, declares what we deserve: for it would not happen to us if we did not deserve it" (II. 743; P 580). And again: "If we put all misery on one side of the scale, and all guilt on the other side, they will balance one another" (I. 481; P 352). And finally: "If we want to know what human beings in general are worth, morally speaking, then we only have to consider their fate on the whole and in general. This is need, misery, torment and death" (I. 481; P 352).

Why does Schopenhauer harbour this cruel thought? It follows from his adherence to an old religious doctrine: original sin. It is a remarkable feature of Schopenhauer's thought that, despite his atheism, it retains and revives fundamental moral concepts from the Christian tradition. First and foremost among these concepts is original sin. It is because we are all sinners, sons of Adam, that we deserve to suffer. Of course, part of the reason Schopenhauer affirms this doctrine rests with his religious background, his Protestant education.[11] Our concern here, however, lies not with the personal causes of his beliefs but the philosophical rationale for them. That rationale is partly metaphysical, partly moral.

The metaphysical rationale is his fundamental principle that the single universal will exists indivisibly in each one of us (*WWV* I. 454; P 332). This will wants all things for itself; it seeks entirely and only its self-interest; and because its self-interest manifests itself within each individual, that individual is egoistic. The chief source of sin for Schopenhauer lies in this egoism, in this selfishness, which places one's own interests over everyone else. Such egoism is not, however, a sufficient condition of sin. On its own, egoism is not sinful, because sin also requires the violation of some moral or natural law. If there were no moral or natural laws, if all were entirely made by convention, there would be no *original* or *natural* sin. This is where the moral rationale of the doctrine enters. Although most radical voluntarists in the history of philosophy (e.g. Ockham, Hobbes) maintain that all laws are conventional, Schopenhauer, contrary to our expectations, affirms the existence of a natural law, an eternal moral law, according to which we must respect the rights of others and not violate their individual sphere (I. 467; P 341). Our egoistic nature is always violating this natural law, if not in action at least in intention. The moral law demands, however, that we should have the right intentions, that we should act according to the spirit of the law, which is respect for the interests of others; but it is just this of which our selfish nature is incapable. We are all therefore sinful, originally, inevitably and naturally so.

---

[11] On the importance of that background, see Arthur Hübscher, *The Philosophy of Schopenhauer in its Intellectual Context* (Lewiston, NY: Edwin Mellen Press, 1989), pp. 1–33.

Egoism is one of the fundamental reasons for Schopenhauer's pessimism. It is because human beings are selfish that they clash, and it is because they clash that their lives are so miserable. We live in constant fear, never knowing when other individuals will harm us. *Homo homini lupus*, Schopenhauer insists, and for this reason life on earth is worse than Dante's hell (*WWV* II. 740; P 578). The chief rationale for the state is that it enforces laws to prevent one person from harming another; but even the most successful state cannot prevent people from having bad intentions with regard to one another (*WWV* I. 470; P 344). And the weaker the state, the more ready people are to act on those intentions, eager to harm another whenever they fear no penalty. Schopenhauer denies that we can create a state where we educate people to be loyal and patriotic, where its citizens are willing to put the interests of the community over their own personal ends (I. 471; P 345). The fact that the will cannot be taught crushes any hope of creating moral citizens, or the good life, through civil measures.

The old doctrine of sin supported Schopenhauer's pessimism in another important respect. The immediate consequence of this doctrine—if it is affirmed strictly and consistently—is anti-Pelagianism or Augustinianism, i.e. the doctrine that man cannot gain salvation through his own natural powers and efforts. If original sin is true, then these powers and efforts are completely corrupted, so that man cannot know the truth and do good. If we judge his sinful nature strictly according to the standards of the moral law, he deserves only eternal punishment, because his will and actions cannot ever meet such strict standards. The moral law demands that we act for the sake of justice, that we act according not only to the letter but also the spirit of the law; but our egoism means that we act only for our own interests. And so, on moral grounds alone, we deserve nothing less than damnation.

It is striking that Schopenhauer affirms all these implications of the doctrine of original sin. He maintains that Augustine was entirely correct to hold against the Pelagians that works cannot justify us (*WWV* II. 773; P 603). It is his fundamental maxim that our deeds follow our character or nature—*operari sequitur esse*—so that if our nature is sinful, so are all the actions that follow from it. No less than Luther and Calvin, Schopenhauer thinks that man can achieve redemption—freedom from the misery of sin—only if he gains a new character, only if he is reborn. But how can he gain a new character? Surely, not by his own natural efforts and deeds, which are tainted by sin. Schopenhauer thinks that Luther was entirely correct to maintain that we are justified by faith alone, where faith is not just belief but an experience, insight or epiphany.[12] His own version of Luther's faith is that intellectual insight where the veil of Maya falls aside and we realize that we are all one, that we are all interconnected so that we all suffer together. For Schopenhauer, this insight is the epiphany marking the birth of "the new man".

---

[12] On Schopenhauer's retention of Luther's soteriological doctrine, see *Handschriftlicher Nachlaß*, I. 103, §186.

Schopenhauer boasted that it was one of the great values of his philosophy that it preserved the spirit—and demonstrated the rational core of truth—behind traditional religious concepts (*WWV* II. 788; P 615). Hence the concept of sin expresses natural human egoism; the concept of redemption represents freedom from the life of desire; the concept of rebirth symbolizes the new character that gives us the power to renounce the will; and the concept of grace stands for the transformative act of the noumenal will. It is ironic, therefore, that Schopenhauer criticized Kant because his concepts of duty and obligation were too theological, presupposing the idea of a divine lawgiver.[13] What was a merit for his philosophy was apparently a defect in Kant's. Schopenhauer retains so many of the basic concepts of traditional Protestantism that we are justified in regarding his philosophy as Protestantism without theism.

Schopenhauer reckoned, rightly, that his retention of old religious concepts was one reason why his philosophy would be unpopular in his age (II. 788; P 615). For many of his contemporaries, Schopenhauer was relapsing into medieval theology, to the old Augustinian doctrines that had inspired Luther and Calvin centuries ago. These doctrines had apparently been overthrown by the Enlightenment, which began by casting out the old doctrine of original sin. The modern ideas of progress and development had their source in a revived Pelagianism, in the belief that we could redeem ourselves and create a morally better world through our own natural efforts. Schopenhauer's resistance to any form of Pelagianism was one of the chief reasons for his rejection of these modern ideas.

Whatever its merits, Schopenhauer's attempt to rehabilitate old Protestant doctrines is deeply ambiguous in its intentions and implications. It is unclear whether he is secularizing and rationalizing old religious concepts or sacralizing and mystifying traditional moral concepts. Since Shaftesbury, Grotius and Thomasius, the fundamental tendency of modern moral thought had been to secularize and rationalize these concepts, viz., law, obligation, virtue, so that they are free of questionable theological baggage. To some extent, Schopenhauer follows this trend because he intends to rationalize concepts like sin, grace and redemption by giving them a basis independent of theism. Yet, to another extent, Schopenhauer abruptly reverses this trend because he gives these concepts a mystical meaning in the context of his system. Thus he describes redemption and rebirth in terms of the acts of the noumenal will, acts which transcend all the forms of explanation of the phenomenal world. If the ways of God are dark and mysterious, so are the workings of Schopenhauer's will.

It is another token of the depth of Schopenhauer's pessimism, however, that his rehabilitation of these religious concepts destroys the hope behind them. The Christian believer could nurture the hope that his rebirth would bring eternal salvation. Schopenhauer, however, does not accept either personal immortality or the existence of the kingdom of heaven. All that Schopenhauer's saint gets for his feats of self-renunciation and for his supererogatory deeds are a few brief moments of ecstasy on

---

[13] *Preisschrift über die Grundlage der Moral, Sämtliche Werke,* III. 647–8, §4.

this earth. There are passages in Schopenhauer's writings where he holds out the possibility of hope for some kind of life beyond the grave, but he insists that it has nothing to do with personal immortality and that we can know nothing about it. What happens after death he indicates only with an empty space on his page (I. 780; P 609). In the final section of *Die Welt als Wille und Vorstellung* Schopenhauer admits that his philosophy in the end leaves us with nothingness. If we deny the will, we also deny the entire world that depends on it, so that we are left with nothing. And so he passes this sentence on his own philosophy: "For us, there remains only nothingness" (I. 557; P 411). A chilling and grim pronouncement! Yet it was an honest and fair summary of all his philosophy had to offer. No wonder so many of his contemporaries felt obliged to attack it.

5
Julius Frauenstädt
Apostle and Critic

1. An Independent Disciple

The first notable critic of Schopenhauer's philosophy also happened to be his most famous apologist: Julius Frauenstädt (1813–79). No one did more to champion and publicize Schopenhauer's philosophy in the 1850s than Frauenstädt, who proved himself to be Schopenhauer's chief advocate. Schopenhauer was fully aware of his debt, calling Frauenstädt "Apostole primarie" and praising him as "the most strident and active pioneer of my philosophy".[1] Frauenstädt's services to Schopenhauer's philosophy were indeed considerable. He wrote several books publicizing its cause; he constantly supplied Schopenhauer with notices and reviews of his work; and he arranged publishing deals and contracts. For two decades, he served as Schopenhauer's secretary and virtual lieutenant. His services even extended beyond his master's lifetime. After Schopenhauer's death in 1860, Frauenstädt published the first edition of his collected works and a Schopenhauer lexicon.[2]

Not surprisingly, Frauenstädt has gone down in history as Schopenhauer's disciple and dogsbody, and he has been remembered for little more than that. Yet this picture of Frauenstädt does him a grave injustice. He was always an independent thinker in his own right, both before and after his association with Schopenhauer. Before that association, he had published no less than three books on philosophy, which concerned the problem of freedom and the relationship between faith and reason.[3] While these early works are broadly in the Hegelian tradition, Frauenstädt was also no uncritical devotee of Hegel. It was indeed his criticisms of Hegel that eventually drove him toward Schopenhauer. After his temporary break with Schopenhauer in 1856, Frauenstädt continued to write works of his own, which deviated from Schopenhauer's philosophy

---

[1] Schopenhauer to Frauenstädt, 26 Sept. 1851, in *Arthur Schopenhauer, Gesammelte Briefe*, ed. Arthur Hübscher (Bonn: Bouvier, 1978), p. 265.

[2] Julius Frauenstädt, *Arthur Schopenhauers Sämtliche Werke* (Leipzig: Brockhaus, 1873–8), 6 vols; and *Schopenhauer-Lexikon: Ein philosophisches Wörterbuch, nach Arthur Schopenhauers sämmtlichen Schriften und handschriftlichen Nachlass* (Leipzig: Brockhaus, 1871).

[3] J. Frauenstädt, *Die Freiheit des Menschen und die Persönlichkeit Gottes* (Berlin: Hirschwald, 1838); *Die Menschwerdung Gottes, nach ihrer Möglichkeit, Wirklichkeit und Nothwendigkeit. Mit Rücksicht auf Strauss, Schaller und Göschel* (Berlin: Voß, 1839); and *Studien und Kritiken zur Theologie und Philosophie* (Berlin: Voß, 1840).

on fundamental points.[4] Although his writings in the materialism controversy of the 1850s were publicity for Schopenhauer's cause, they are still original and important contributions in their own right, anticipating the later arguments of Friedrich Lange and the neo-Kantians.

It was a token of Frauenstädt's independence of mind that he was unremittingly critical of Schopenhauer. Never did he accept Schopenhauer's views in blind faith, and always he would constantly test them by seeing whether they could withstand his objections. He believed that he served Schopenhauer best in playing the role of adversary, a point that Schopenhauer grudgingly acknowledged. Frauenstädt's tireless criticisms would sometimes try Schopenhauer's patience. Indeed, he so hounded the old man with objections, and so harried him with questions, that Schopenhauer would often lose patience and berate him.[5] Frauenstädt's relentless questioning, he declared, had made his life a misery.[6] For these reasons, on several occasions Schopenhauer was on the verge of breaking with Frauenstädt; and a rupture finally came in 1856, when Schopenhauer upbraided Frauenstädt for appearing to endorse a materialist morality.[7] Ultimately, though, Schopenhauer relented, and gave Frauenstädt what he deserved for his many services to his philosophy: the rights to his literary estate.

Frauenstädt's first exposition of Schopenhauer's philosophy was his *Briefe über die Schopenhauer'sche Philosophie*,[8] which appeared in 1854. This work was modelled on Reinhold's famous *Briefe über die kantische Philosophie*, which was vital to the reception of Kant's philosophy in the 1780s.[9] What Reinhold had done for Kant, Frauenstädt hoped to do for Schopenhauer. And in this he did not fail. The *Briefe* proved very successful. The public, as the critic Ludwig Börne put it, sometimes likes to read more a book about a book than the book itself.[10] The *Briefe* is fundamentally a work of exposition rather than criticism, and its aim is simply to explain the rationale of Schopenhauer's position. We must not confuse, however, Frauenstädt's exposition and defence of Schopenhauer's philosophy with his own beliefs and positions. He felt obliged to give the best statement of Schopenhauer's philosophy to his contemporaries, so he would conscientiously reply to objections, answer troubling questions and explain basic premises; but it is important to see that he did not always share those premises. His own views were often hidden in the background. When Frauenstädt did

---

[4] J. Frauenstädt, *Das sittliche Leben. Ethische Studien* (Leipzig: Brockhaus, 1866); and *Briefe über natürliche Religion* (Leipzig: Brockhaus, 1858).
[5] See Schopenhauer to Frauenstädt, 24 Aug. 1852, and 12 Sept. 1852, in *Gesammelte Briefe*, pp. 290, 293–4. Frauenstädt had sent Schopenhauer a set of objections under the title 'Anti-Schopenhauer', which Schopenhauer sent back unanswered.
[6] Schopenhauer to Frauenstädt, 12 Sept. 1852, *Briefe*, pp. 293–4.
[7] Schopenhauer to Frauenstädt, 31 Oct. 1856, *Briefe*, p. 403.
[8] Julius Frauenstädt, *Briefe über die Schopenhauer'sche Philosophie* (Leipzig: Brockhaus, 1854).
[9] Schopenhauer himself noted the Reinholdian precedent. See Schopenhauer to Frauenstädt, 19 Sept. 1853, *Briefe*, p. 321.
[10] As cited in Kuno Fischer, *Schopenhauers Leben, Werke und Lehre*, Zweite und vermehrte Auflage (Heidelberg: Winter, 1898), p. 107.

accept and endorse Schopenhauer's philosophy, it was only because he saw it as the best solution to his own problems.

After Schopenhauer's death in 1860, Frauenstädt was more forthright in stating his own position and criticizing Schopenhauer. The new, more independent and critical tone is apparent from the successor to the *Briefe*, his *Neue Briefe über die Schopenhauer'sche Philosophie*, which was first published in 1876.[11] If the *Briefe* intended to provide a summary exposition of Schopenhauer's philosophy, the *Neue Briefe* was meant to be a critique. In the foreword Frauenstädt explained that his new work was partly expository, partly apologetic, but also partly corrective, attempting to modify and revise the faulty parts of Schopenhauer's system. "To a certain extent", Frauenstädt explains in his first letter, "I belong among his opponents" (1). The *Neue Briefe*, it must be added, are still very much worth reading today. The criticisms, replies to objections and explanations of difficulties—too many of which are ignored or forgotten by contemporary scholars—take the reader into the very heart of Schopenhauer's system. It was Frauenstädt who first saw the weakness of the transcendental idealist interpretation of Schopenhauer, an interpretation still advanced by many Schopenhauer scholars today. It has to be said: no one understood Schopenhauer better than Julius Frauenstädt.

Ultimately, Frauenstädt had a very different attitude toward life than Schopenhauer. Although he initially endorsed Schopenhauer's pessimism, he eventually grew out of it and made basic objections against it. Frauenstädt believed that Schopenhauer's bleak attitude toward life was much too extreme, and that we have to balance his emphasis on its evil and suffering with an appreciation of its good and pleasures. On Frauenstädt's final reckoning, life, for all its sorrows, was still very much worth living.

Our task in this chapter will be to reconsider and resurrect this long forgotten but remarkable figure in the history of philosophy, an author whose work marks one of the most important contributions to German philosophy in the age of *Weltschmerz*. We will examine Frauenstädt's criticisms of Schopenhauer, especially his reaction to Schopenhauer's pessimism. But we will also consider Frauenstädt's contributions to the materialism and pessimism controversy. Before we turn to these tasks, however, we have to engage in some preliminary business: we have to explain Frauenstädt's discovery of and conversion to Schopenhauer. This experience has not been properly examined, and myths about it prevail to this day.

2. Conversion to Schopenhauer

How did Frauenstädt first discover Schopenhauer? And why did be become a convert to his philosophy? Given Frauenstädt's major role in the reception and dissemination of Schopenhauer's philosophy, these questions are of no small significance.

---

[11] Julius Frauenstädt, *Neue Briefe über die Schopenhauer'sche Philosophie* (Leipzig: Brockhaus, 1876).

In a retrospective account written in 1863,[12] Frauenstädt himself tells us the story of his discovery of Schopenhauer. In 1836 he had been a student of philosophy and theology in Berlin for three years without ever hearing a word about Schopenhauer, who was then a recluse living in Frankfurt. Frauenstädt was doing research for an essay competition on the relationship of psychology to metaphysics when he ran across a mention of Schopenhauer in an article on idealism in Ersch and Gruber's *Enzyklopädie*.[13] The author of the article, C. F. Bachmann, praised Schopenhauer's system of idealism as "ingenious and original", though he went into no details about how or why. That was enough to pique Frauenstädt's curiosity. He borrowed the copy of *Die Welt als Wille und Vorstellung* from the Royal Library, and read it intensely, day and night. After finishing it, he was convinced that ten pages of Schopenhauer were worth more than ten volumes of Hegel! *Voilà!* A convert was born.

The truth, however, was not so simple. Frauenstädt's story makes it seem as if he became a convert to Schopenhauer virtually overnight, or at least after a week of sleepless nights and feverish reading. It is as if, all of a sudden, he realized that he was wasting his time reading Hegel. Yet in 1836 Frauenstädt was still very much immersed in Hegel's philosophy, and he would remain so for at least the next five years. This is not to say, however, that he was a disciple of Hegel. At the end of the decade he published two works discussing Hegel's philosophy—*Die Freiheit des Menschen und die Persönlichkeit Gottes* (1838) and *Die Menschwerdung Gottes* (1839)—that reach highly critical conclusions about it.[14] Hegel's philosophy, Frauenstädt argues, leaves us with an irresolvable conflict between reason and faith because its fundamental principles cannot explain either human freedom or the Christian trinity. Understanding human freedom and the trinity requires grasping the unity of divine self-consciousness and human self-consciousness. But this, Frauenstädt argues, is impossible.[15] If God attains self-awareness in human beings, such that he maintains his self-identity, he destroys the plurality and independence of human selves, which are only his appearances or modes; but if human beings attain self-awareness in God, such that their plurality and independence is preserved, then the unity of God is destroyed. This fundamental dilemma Hegel's philosophy cannot solve, Frauenstädt maintains. As a result, those who want to believe in freedom and the trinity have to abandon his philosophy.

Nevertheless, despite such criticisms, Frauenstädt had still not broken entirely with Hegel. This is apparent from a book he published in 1840, *Studien und Kritiken zur*

---

[12] Julius Frauenstädt, *Arthur Schopenhauer: Von ihm. Ueber ihn* (Berlin: A. W. Hayn, 1863), pp. 133–4.

[13] C. F. Bachmann, 'Idealismus', in Johann Samuel Ersch and Johann Gottfried Gruber, *Allgemeine Encyclopädie der Wissenschaften und Künste* (Leipzig: Brockhaus, 1838), Section H-N, Theil 15. 113–18, esp. 118. Bachmann writes: "*Geistreich und originell ausgeführt ist das idealische Thema…in Arthur Schopenhauer.*"

[14] J. Frauenstädt, *Die Freiheit des Menschen und die Persönlichkeit Gottes* (Berlin: Hirschwald, 1838); *Die Menschwerdung Gottes, nach ihrer Möglichkeit, Wirklichkeit und Nothwendigkeit: Mit Rücksicht auf Strauss, Schaller und Göschel* (Berlin: Voß, 1839).

[15] Cf. *Die Freiheit des Menschen*, pp. 117–20; and *Die Menschwerdung Gottes*, pp. 128–45.

Theologie und Philosophie.¹⁶ Here again Frauenstädt is very critical of Hegel. He aligns himself with Feuerbach and other left Hegelians in thinking that Hegel has not gone far enough in the critical direction of his philosophy, and that he has compromised too much with theological dogma (vii). Philosophy and theology, reason and faith, are at odds, Frauenstädt contends, and there is no point in saving theology or faith when in conflict with philosophy or reason (xi–xiv). Nevertheless, despite these criticisms, Frauenstädt, unlike other radical Hegelians, never took radical criticism so far that it went beyond the bounds of Hegel's system. Against Feuerbach's criticisms, he defends the possibility of philosophy as a science of the absolute (3–18). And he insists, as all good Hegelians should: "The idea of the universe, of the infinite, of the absolute, is the beginning and end of philosophy" (vi).

So before Frauenstädt could become a Schopenhauerian, he had to cease to be a Hegelian, even if a nominal or half-hearted one. How did that happen? Frauenstädt offers some interesting clues in a work he published in 1842, *Schelling's Vorlesungen in Berlin*.¹⁷ This was Frauenstädt's account of Schelling's famous 1840 Berlin lectures, the basis of his famous "positive philosophy" and his late critique of Hegel. In the first chapter Frauenstädt reveals that, even before hearing Schelling's lectures, he had become very critical of both theism and pantheism (3). On classical Kantian grounds, he had come to regard both theories of the divine nature as illegitimate metaphysics (23, 33–43). Both are guilty of extending concepts which have only an empirical validity beyond possible experience. In making God the creator of the universe, theism took the concept of *cause* beyond possible experience; and in making God the single universal substance, pantheism extended the concept of *substance* beyond empirical bounds. Furthermore, Frauenstädt held that neither theism nor pantheism could resolve the problem of evil (53–4). Theism makes God the cause of evil, whether by omission or commission, while pantheism makes evil part of the divine nature. This disenchantment with pantheism is telling about Frauenstädt's changing attitude toward Hegel. For the idea of the absolute, to which he was utterly committed in 1840, is essentially a form of pantheism. The absolute is the infinite, the single divine substance. So, in criticizing pantheism, Frauenstädt was moving away from Hegel. No longer is the absolute for him the beginning and end of philosophy.

But how did this move away from Hegel turn Frauenstädt toward Schopenhauer? Frauenstädt himself tells the rest of the story in a later work he published in 1848, his *Ueber das wahre Verhältniß der Vernunft zur Offenbarung*.¹⁸ After his critique of theism and pantheism, Frauenstädt informs us, he planned to write a new system of philosophy, one that avoids the errors and preserves the truth of both theism and pantheism. Schelling himself wanted to construct just such a system in his lectures on positive

---

¹⁶ J. Frauenstädt, *Studien und Kritiken zur Theologie und Philosophie* (Berlin: Voss, 1840).
¹⁷ J. Frauenstädt, *Schelling's Vorlesungen in Berlin. Darstellung und Kritik der Hauptpunkte derselben* (Berlin: August Hirschwald, 1842).
¹⁸ J. Frauenstädt, *Ueber das wahre Verhältniß der Vernunft zur Offenbarung: Prolegomena zu jeder künftigten Philosophie des Christenthums* (Darmstadt: Carl Wilhelm Leske, 1848), pp. 89–90.

philosophy; but his efforts were a miserable failure, a metaphysics of pure fantasy. Frauenstädt thought he could succeed where Schelling had failed. But then, in 1844, he had an epiphany: he remembered that such a system already existed in the philosophy of Arthur Schopenhauer (90). Frauenstädt was reminded of Schopenhauer, whom he had otherwise nearly forgotten, because it just so happened in that year Schopenhauer published the second volume of *Die Welt als Wille und Vorstellung*. As Frauenstädt describes it, then, there was no need to construct a new system of his own; it already existed in the system of Schopenhauer.

So, as Frauenstädt later tells his story, his conversion to Schopenhauer really came in 1844, after his break with Hegel and only after the publication of the second volume of *Die Welt als Wille und Vorstellung*. The decisive turn to Schopenhauer came some eight years after his initial acquaintance with him. Furthermore, disillusionment with Hegel was more the condition than consequence of his conversion to Schopenhauer.

But there are still some strange incongruities in the story as Frauenstädt tells it. The new system he sought was to be a synthesis of theism and pantheism,[19] and it still clung to the idea of God, which Frauenstädt saw as essential to all religion.[20] Schopenhauer's system, however, was atheistic, dropping the idea of God entirely. So the transition from Hegel to Schopenhauer was not as smooth and easy as Frauenstädt makes it appear. It was not that Schopenhauer had already found and constructed the very system Frauenstädt was seeking. There was something more in Schopenhauer that attracted Frauenstädt to him, something that Frauenstädt had not fully explained but that went beyond his plans for a new system of theism and pantheism.

So our story cannot end here. We still have to explain what it was that Frauenstädt saw in Schopenhauer. The solution to the mystery is somewhat paradoxical: Frauenstädt saw Schopenhauer's atheism as the only means of saving religion. Although Frauenstädt was convinced that neither theism nor pantheism are tenable, although he rejected both predominant theories about the nature of God, he was still not ready to abandon religion itself. For all his left Hegelianism, for all his radical criticism, Frauenstädt was never ready to drop his Christian faith. The reason for this is remarkable. Frauenstädt had converted from Judaism to Christianity in 1833, a conversion he took very seriously. It was no mere formality, a passport for social acceptance and success, but a very personal matter, one where his own moral integrity was on the line. It was all well and good for Feuerbach, Strauss and Bauer to declare that Christianity is dead; they had been born and baptized Christians. But, for Frauenstädt, Christianity came from a later profession of faith, which he could not so easily renounce, without invoking charges of hypocrisy or social climbing.

Ultimately, then, it was Frauenstädt's abiding adherence to Christianity that moved him away from the left Hegelians and toward Schopenhauer. What Frauenstädt was

---

[19] Frauenstädt offers only the sketchiest hints about the shape of his new system. See *Schelling's Vorlesungen*, pp. 53, 66, 159.

[20] Ibid., p. 11.

searching for in the early 1840s was something unique and rare: a philosophy that was still Christian yet neither theistic nor pantheistic. What other philosophy satisfied such strange desiderata than that of Arthur Schopenhauer?

Exactly what Schopenhauer meant for Frauenstädt becomes clear when we take a closer look at the argument of his 1848 tract *Ueber das wahre Verhältniß der Vernunft zur Offenbarung*. As soon as we open the book, its debt to Schopenhauer stares us in the face: it is dedicated to the old scrooge, who is addressed as "Grosse Meister". From Frauenstädt's opening exposition it quickly becomes clear that he could not accept the positions of either the orthodox Christians or the radical Hegelians. While the orthodox Christians insisted on the literal meaning of their faith, which made it vulnerable to criticism, the radical Hegelians were eradicating faith entirely, which pushed them in the direction of materialism. From this perspective, Schopenhauer must have seemed very appealing indeed, because he was neither theist nor materialist. He offered a middle path between these warring extremes, a way of saving faith and upholding criticism.

What was this middle path? Faith, Frauenstädt explains, is not based upon the understanding but the will, with how we feel and act in the world (13, 17, 18). If it were founded on the understanding, on the attempt to acquire knowledge of the world, it would be entirely appropriate to criticize it; but such criticism is completely inappropriate because knowledge is not the aim of religion. The true goal of religion is not theoretical but practical: to reconcile us to the evil and suffering of the world, to comfort us in the face of tragedy, to teach us the road to salvation. Appreciating this as the true goal of religion saves it from so much needless criticism, Frauenstädt argues. Feuerbach could expose religion as hypostasis; Strauss could regard it as mythology; and Bauer could make it into poetry; but all these criticisms did not matter in the end and they were really beside the point. For they all shared the same false premise: that religion is more about theory than practice, more about the understanding than the will.

Frauenstädt could advocate such a practical conception of faith because he was now convinced, thanks to Schopenhauer, that the beliefs in the existence of God and immortality are not essential to religion. These beliefs are indeed subject to rational criticism; but if they are not necessary to religion, faith is all the more spared criticism and can stand on its own. Following Schopenhauer, Frauenstädt now holds that religion is essentially a doctrine of salvation, i.e. a guide to renouncing sin, to rising above evil and suffering, to achieving peace of mind (47, 48). Salvation has nothing to do with divine grace, with immortality, or with an eternal life in heaven, still less with faith in a merciful God; but it has everything to do with gaining insight into the source of suffering, with denying the will to life and with finding inner serenity. Following Schopenhauer, Frauenstädt insists that asceticism and pessimism, not optimism and theism, are the defining characteristics of Christianity (49, 66, 69). Since we can achieve redemption without them, the beliefs in the existence of a personal God and an immortal soul play no essential role in Christianity (71). All that we need for salvation, for redemption from the corruption of the world, is renunciation of the will to life, which is the source of all sin and suffering. Hence Frauenstädt's confidence that the criticism of theism cannot affect the inner core of Christianity. Even if God does not exist, even if there is no immortal soul, the message of Christianity about salvation still stands.

Far from implicit in his early Hegelianism, Frauenstädt's new practical conception of faith was a *volte face* from his old Hegelian position. In *Schelling's Vorlesungen* Frauenstädt was still convinced that there must be some point of unity between reason and faith, a conceptual space where reason could still provide a *theoretical* rationale for faith (v, 14). There could still be some kind of metaphysics, some kind of demonstration of the beliefs in the existence of God and immortality. That was the hope behind his new system, his planned synthesis of theism and pantheism. But Schopenhauer had taught him to abandon these hopes. He now adopts a dualism between the spheres of reason and faith: while reason rules in the realm of theory, faith prevails in the realm of practice. Schopenhauer himself had advised clearly separating the realms of religion and philosophy,[21] a policy that Frauenstädt now accepts.

Frauenstädt's early reaction to Schopenhauer's philosophy, though very personal, was not without historical repercussions. Its central theme—that Schopenhauer's philosophy saves the content of religion and provides a middle path between theism and materialism—would resonate among the wider public, becoming one of the major attractions of Schopenhauer's philosophy.[22] The message would not be lost or forgotten because Frauenstädt would replay it constantly in the 1850s, in his *Briefe über die Schopenhauer'sche Philosophie* and in his writings on the materialism controversy.

We must keep in mind, however, that Frauenstädt's stance on Schopenhauer's philosophy would not always remain the same, and that it would go through major shifts in the course of the next decades. Indeed, what first attracted Frauenstädt to Schopenhauer would later repel him. The early tract on revelation praises Schopenhauer's pessimism and stresses the importance of his doctrine of the renunciation of the will. But, as we shall soon see, Frauenstädt would later distance himself from those elements of Schopenhauer's philosophy. As early as 1858 he formulates an "ethical pantheism" as the only philosophy of religion and criticizes Schopenhauer's pessimism as well as his asceticism.[23]

3. Schopenhauer and the Materialism Controversy

Frauenstädt's conversion to Schopenhauer's philosophy was essentially complete by the mid-1840s. In July 1846 Frauenstädt made his great pilgrimage to Frankfurt to

---

[21] Schopenhauer, 'Über das metaphysische Bedürfnis des Menschen', *WWV* II. 217 (P 168).

[22] The importance of the religious message of Schopenhauer's philosophy—Protestantism without theism—is especially clear from the work of Otto Busch, *Arthur Schopenhauer: Beitrag zu einer Dogmatik der Religionslosen* (Heildelberg: Bassermann, 1877), esp. pp. 139–76.

[23] See Julius Frauenstädt, *Briefe über natürliche Religion* (Leipzig: Brockhaus, 1858), pp. 110, 132, 151, 153, 164–72.

meet his master in person. For days, they walked and talked, and quickly a friendship formed, which was not between equals, though it was based on mutual need. The friendship was essentially an alliance formed for the sake of literary fame. Schopenhauer needed Frauenstädt as his protagonist, who, he wagered correctly, might supply him with the recognition he so desperately desired and so deeply deserved. Frauenstädt too craved literary fame, which had not come to him in Berlin despite his three books and many articles. If he could not get recognition from his own philosophy, Frauenstädt rightly reckoned, he could perhaps get it by supporting a greater philosophy than his own. Just as there could be no Faust without a Wagner, so there could be no Schopenhauer without a Frauenstädt.

Frauenstädt's conversion to Schopenhauer gave birth to a literary campaign on behalf of his philosophy, which lasted for the next seven years. It began in 1848 with his *Ueber das wahre Verhältniß der Vernunft zur Offenbarung*, where Schopenhauer's philosophy is championed as the only way to save religion from rational criticism. In the following years a steady stream of propaganda appeared: in 1849 a long article on Schopenhauer's philosophy for the *Blätter für literarische Unterhaltung*;[24] in 1852, in the same journal, a favourable review of *Parerga und Paralipomena*;[25] in 1853 a whole book explaining Schopenhauer's aesthetics, *Aesthetische Fragen*;[26] and, finally and most importantly, in 1854 the *Briefe über die Schopenhauer'sche Philosophie*, which gave a clear and popular exposition of Schopenhauer's whole system. With all these efforts, Schopenhauer was mightily pleased, as he well should have been. Frauenstädt had well-earned his title: *Apostole primarie*. The break with Schopenhauer in 1856 would stop the propaganda; but by then it did not matter: Schopenhauer was becoming famous.

As helpful as all these writings were, they were still not Frauenstädt's most important efforts in behalf of Schopenhauer's philosophy. These contributions came in response to one decisive intellectual event: the materialism controversy, which began in 1854.[27] Although the controversy began small—a quarrel between the theist Rudolph Wagner and the materialist Karl Vogt—it soon became big, so that eventually every major philosopher of the day got involved in it. The dispute revolved around one fundamental question: whether natural science is leading of necessity to materialism? At stake were some fundamental moral and religious beliefs: the beliefs in freedom, the immortality of the soul and the existence of God. All of these beliefs appeared threatened by a growing naturalism, which seemed to many the worldview of science itself. Thus the materialism controversy raised again the old conflict between reason and

---

[24] 'Stimmen über Arthur Schopenhauer', *Blätter für literarische Unterhaltung*, 277–81 (19–23 Nov. 1849), 1105–22.
[25] *Blätter für literarische Unterhaltung*, 9 (28 Feb. 1852), 196–202.
[26] J. Frauenstädt, *Aesthetische Fragen* (Dessau: Gebrüder Katz, 1853).
[27] On the materialism controversy, see my *Late German Idealism: Trendelenburg and Lotze* (Oxford: OUP, 2013), pp. 239–49.

faith, though reason now played the role of natural science rather than demonstrative or syllogistic reasoning.

Frauenstädt seized upon the materialism controversy as his best opportunity to advance Schopenhauer's cause. If he could explain effectively that only his master's philosophy solved the fundamental problem posed by the controversy, then he would have truly succeeded in putting it on the intellectual map. The great advantage of Schopenhauer's philosophy, Frauenstädt argued, is that it alone avoids the dilemma between theism and materialism. It alone provides a middle path between these extremes, one that justifies our essential moral and religious beliefs without having to make the supernaturalistic and archaic assumptions of theism. Furthermore, Schopenhauer's philosophy provides a metaphysical rationale for science, for the naturalistic investigation of the world, though it also shows the essential limitations of materialism and the implausibility of its reductivist mechanism.

Frauenstädt wrote two books discussing the materialism controversy and advocating Schopenhauer's role in it. His first book is his *Die Naturwissenschaft in ihren Einfluß auf Poesie, Religion, Moral und Philosophie*,[28] which appeared in 1855. This work is a critique of the views on reason and faith of Rudolph Wagner, who was the chief defender of theism in the early years of the controversy. Frauenstädt's second book, *Der Materialismus*,[29] which appeared in 1856, is essentially a critique of "the materialist's bible", Ludwig Büchner's *Kraft und Stoff*.[30]

In both these works Frauenstädt's essential concern was to address the conflict between reason and faith that had been at the centre of the materialism controversy. Frauenstädt agreed with the materialists, Karl Vogt and Ludwig Büchner, that the progress of natural science had falsified some old theistic beliefs: creation *ex nihilo*; the descent of man from a single original pair (Adam and Eve); and the existence of an immortal soul that could survive the death of the body. Frauenstädt still could not accept, however, a complete mechanistic explanation of human life, the reduction of the mind and organism down to the combination of its material components. Such mechanism was in his view incompatible with some indispensable moral and religious beliefs: the belief in freedom, the need to take responsibility for our actions; and the purposive structure of the cosmos. The incompatibility of mechanism with these beliefs did not imply, however, that there is an insuperable conflict between science and faith. That apparent conflict arose because so many had conflated science with materialism. Frauenstädt sternly warned against such a conflation, insisting that materialism is not science itself but a philosophy or metaphysics claiming to be based upon,

---

[28] Julius Frauenstädt, *Die Naturwissenschaft in ihrem Einfluß auf Poesie, Religion, Moral und Philosophie* (Leipzig: Brockhaus, 1855).

[29] Julius Frauenstädt, *Der Materialismus: Seine Wahrheit und sein Irrthum. Eine Erwiderung auf Dr. Louis Büchner's "Kraft und Stoff"* (Leipzig: Brockhaus, 1856).

[30] Ludwig Büchner, *Kraft und Stoff: Empirisch-naturphilosophische Studien* (Frankfurt: Meidiger, 1855). Frauenstädt refers to the 3rd edn of the work, which appeared with the same publisher in 1856. From 1855 until 1904 *Kraft und Stoff* went through no less than 21 editions.

but actually going beyond, the evidence uncovered and amassed by science. Natural science is perfectly compatible with morality and religion, Frauenstädt argued, provided that we do not confuse science with materialism, and provided that we do not define morality and religion by the old theism, whose beliefs in the supernatural (miracles, creation *ex nihilo*) violate the principles of naturalism of empirical science.

In his introduction to *Der Materialismus* Frauenstädt advises a completely new approach and attitude toward materialism from that prevailing in the controversy so far. Too many critics of materialism had dismissed it on moral and theological grounds, though in doing so they had only begged the question against it. They also write as if the materialist *denies* the existence of consciousness and conscience, though he only *interprets* them differently. Materialism has to be examined strictly and fairly on theoretical grounds alone, Frauenstädt insists, and that means that we interpret it from within, judging it according to its own standards and ideals.

In accord with that policy, Frauenstädt was very careful to distinguish the truth from the errors of materialism. For all his resistance to materialism, he still believes that it has some fundamental strengths, both "formal" and "material". Its *formal* strengths concern its discourse, its method and way of doing philosophy. These are threefold: (1) its empiricism, its insistence on basing theories upon the evidence of sense experience; (2) its clear and distinct language, which make it intelligible and accessible to the general public; and (3) its determination to know the truth, regardless of the consequences for our moral and religious beliefs. All these formal strengths, Frauenstädt insisted, gave materialism a great advantage over the tradition of speculative idealism, the philosophy of Fichte, Schelling and Hegel, which he, following Schopenhauer, saw as a defence of the moral and religious status quo. The *material* strengths of materialism concern the content or general principles of its metaphysics. These are twofold: (1) its monism, its insistence on explaining everything within the world according to a single principle; and (2) its naturalism, its demand that we explain everything in nature according to natural laws, avoiding all reference to the supernatural.

Despite all these strengths, Frauenstädt insists that materialism suffers from some very basic shortcomings. The most serious of these, he argues in *Der Materialismus*, is its *realism* and *dogmatism*, i.e. its naïve acceptance of the reality of the external world (43–5). The materialists write as if Kant's critical philosophy never appeared, as if there were no need to investigate the faculty of knowledge. Materialism is a species of naïve or (as Kant called it) "transcendental" realism, i.e. it assumes that the world that we perceive through our senses is the world as it exists in itself, apart from and prior to our perception of it. Its belief in the reality of matter is based on this naïve realism, because it assumes that the spatial and temporal objects of our ordinary experience are things-in-themselves, i.e. that they continue to exist as we perceive them even when we do not perceive them. In making this assumption, however, it completely ignores Kant's critical teaching about the a priori conditions for knowledge: that the object we perceive in our sense experience is only an appearance, determined by the conditions under which we perceive it. If we take this teaching into account, it then becomes clear that matter is not a thing-in-itself, a reality that exists independent of our consciousness, but that it is really only an appearance for us. Frauenstädt then goes on to add that this critical teaching has been vindicated by the latest empirical research on sense perception, by the work of Hermann Helmholtz and Johannes Müller. Their work has shown that what we perceive very much depends on our nervous apparatus and intellectual activity, that the objects of perception do not just float unchanged into the mind.

Frauenstädt explains the materialists' basic error thus: they wrongly assume that matter is something given to us, as if its reality were complete in itself before we perceive it (64–70). All that we are given in sense perception, however, are mere sensations, viz., intensive magnitudes of different qualia. We make these sensations into an object by applying the intuition of space and the category of causality to them, i.e. by assuming that there is something external to us that is the cause of these sensations. But this apparent external object causing our sensations, Frauenstädt insists, is not an objective entity but simply the construction of the mind, the product of our a priori intuition of space and the category of causality. The materialist therefore hypostasizes the object of perception, treating a creation of the mind as if it were an entity.

Another serious mistake of materialism, Frauenstädt maintains, is its belief in the eternity and permanence of the laws of nature. It assumes that the combination and groupings of matter that we see now will be the same forever, and that they have been always the same, because the laws operating upon matter are eternal and essentially one with matter itself (94). But Frauenstädt finds this assumption at odds with natural history, which shows that there are different laws and powers in operation in the early stages of earth (92). If we accept the materialist views about the eternity of matter, we then find ourselves incapable of explaining natural change and development. The materialists, Frauenstädt says, are like small-town dwellers who assume that the entire world follows the customs of their town (82). We have no a priori reason to assume, however, that the laws governing matter now will forever be the same, or that the laws holding on earth will also be the same on other planets. As Frauenstädt expounds his argument, however, it suffers from a grave ambiguity: whether the laws of nature themselves change, or whether they operate differently under different conditions, where only the conditions change. He is also very unclear about the degree of change, whether it applies to general laws or only their specific instances.

Most of the argument in *Der Materialismus* is a critique of mechanism, the materialist programme for accounting for all the phenomena of life on the basis of efficient causality and its material elements. Frauenstädt agrees with the materialists that life has to be explained according to mechanical and chemical powers, but he insists that it cannot be fully explained according to them alone (95, 98–9). While these powers are necessary, they are still not a sufficient condition for the explanation of life. It is also necessary to have recourse to final causes and some form-giving principle or *Bildungstrieb* (109, 115). The problem with materialism is that it does not see how and why all the elements of an organism come together and combine in the first place (111, 167–8). The materialist indeed reverses the proper order of explanation. He reasons:

because there is matter combined in such and such a way, there is life; but the very opposite is the case: because there is the will to life, matter becomes combined in such and such a way (152). Without ears we cannot hear, and without eyes we cannot see; but it does not follow from this that we hear only because we have ears and that we see only because we have eyes. Ears and eyes presuppose a purpose, a will in nature itself (153). Without such a will, there would be no seeing and no hearing (153). Seeing and hearing will emerge on their own in nature no more than a house or a ship will appear without a builder and designer.

As much as Frauenstädt is opposed to materialism, he is careful in his judgement about which arguments to use against it. He finds no weight in the classical objection that the material and the mental are so heterogeneous and too unlike for there to be interaction between them (165–6). The materialist could reply to this argument: although thoughts are indeed different from nerve vibrations, the forces in the nerve vibrations are themselves capable of creating thought. Where we should press the materialist, Frauenstädt advises, is with not with regard to the apparent heterogeneity of mind and matter but with regard to the status of forces themselves. Because we cannot have a direct experience of these forces, they are not themselves material (178).

It is precisely with regard to the heterogeneous appearance of mind and matter that Frauenstädt finds one of the major advantages of Schopenhauer's philosophy.[31] He does not give too much weight to that appearance chiefly because he thinks he has a better way of explaining it. If we assume, as is traditionally done, that mind and matter are distinct substances, then it becomes hard to explain the interaction between them. We then have to postulate some immaterial forces within matter itself. But Schopenhauer's philosophy, following a line of thought already developed by Kant, regards the material and mental not as distinct substances but only as different forms of representation. The material is constituted and constructed by our forms of representation and does not exist independent of them. The distinction between the mental and physical then falls within the realm of the ideal or representation itself. The question how they interact with one another is then only how one and the same thing can be represented in such different ways. The materialists and idealists attempt to derive mind from matter, or conversely, because they assume that matter or mind exists on its own. The basic question of philosophy should be not how mind and body, two distinct substances, interact but how the ideal and real, appearance and thing-in-itself, relate to one another.

4. Doubts about Pessimism

No point of Schopenhauer's philosophy more troubled Frauenstädt than his pessimism. In *Ueber das wahre Verhältniß der Vernunft zur Offenbarung* he was content to

---

[31] This line of argument is developed in *Briefe über die Schopenhauer'sche Philosophie*, Zwölfter Brief, pp. 114–20.

reaffirm Schopenhauer's pessimism because it seemed so central to the doctrines of renunciation and redemption in which he located the heart of religion.[32] It is striking, however, that in his *Briefe* Frauenstädt hardly discusses Schopenhauer's dark doctrine. It is as if he knew that it was no selling point of his philosophy, and that it would gain it few adherents. He went as far as to say that the doctrine was not based on Schopenhauer's pathology and that there were objective grounds for it (327); but, tellingly, he did not expound Schopenhauer's arguments for it.

This failure to discuss Schopenhauer's pessimism, and the attempt to qualify its meaning, probably had its source in Frauenstädt's deeper misgivings about the doctrine itself. From the earliest days of his acquaintance with Schopenhauer he had wondered and worried about the possibility of redemption on the basic principles of his philosophy. In his first meeting and afternoon walk with Schopenhauer, which took place in July 1846, he caught the old man off-guard with a thorny question: if the will dominates the intellect, which is its mere servant, how is it that the intellect raises itself above the will and negates it?[33] This was essentially to ask about the possibility of redemption on Schopenhauer's premises. The question made the old grouch pause and ponder. His answer was cryptic and metaphoric: the will, carrying a lantern, which is the intellect, comes to an abyss; seeing that it can go no further, it turns around and goes back. Schopenhauer's metaphor implies that the will's blind striving is self-destructive, and that the intellect only illuminates this for the sake of the will. Whatever the meaning of Schopenhauer's metaphor, Frauenstädt was not satisfied with the answer. How is it, he asked himself, that the lantern, which is meant only to serve the will, elevates the will above the world?

In later years Frauenstädt came to regard Schopenhauer's theory of redemption as "the Achilles heel" of his philosophy.[34] The doubts that he had expressed in his first walk with Schopenhauer grew in his mind to the point that he broke utterly with the old man's ethics. He later complained that Schopenhauer had made redemption rest upon the complete denial of the will, a total turning away from the world; but this was much too drastic, much too dramatic. It was a harsh either/or: either we are completely caught in the selfish striving of the world; or we turn our backs on it and lead an ascetic life. But, asked Frauenstädt, why cannot I affirm aspects of the temporal without losing sight of the eternal? Was it not possible to renounce the *selfish* striving of the will alone, and to recognize that there are good aspects of the will to life, such as the will to truth, beauty and justice? The crucial question is not whether we affirm or deny life altogether, he insisted, but whether we affirm and deny it in the right way. We should affirm it insofar as it is compatible with justice and virtue, and deny it insofar as it is incompatible with them. Schopenhauer's ideal of a complete denial of life, his total asceticism, was an abstraction, an unrealistic ideal beyond the true goal of ethics. We must

---

[32] *Ueber das wahre Verhältniß der Vernunft zur Offenbarung*, p. 69.
[33] Frauenstädt, *Arthur Schopenhauer: Von Ihm, Ueber ihm*, p. 152.
[34] Ibid., pp. 316–20.

break not the will to life as such, Frauenstädt advises, but only the egoistic will. Furthermore, we should not surrender individuality as such, but individuality only insofar as it is egoistic. Individual character, Frauenstädt insisted, reaffirming an old romantic theme, remains one of the main values of ethics.

Frauenstädt's turn away from Schopenhauer's ethics is clear from a treatise he published in the 1860s, *Das sittliche Leben*.[35] Here he puts forward a perfectionist ethic along the lines of the *Aufklärung*, and even cites approvingly from the ethics of Christian Garve, one of the foremost *Aufklärer* and champions of such an ethic.[36] The goal of ethical action, Frauenstädt explains, consists in promoting the true welfare of a being, in acting according to its inner nature. True welfare consists not in satisfying the creature's immediate needs or desires, which often might be harmful for it, but in helping to promote its intrinsic and individual nature, in aiding its efforts to develop the perfection characteristic of its kind. *Aptitudo rerum*, i.e. fitting the nature of things, is then the guiding principle of ethics. Such an ethic marks a radical departure from Schopenhauer's own ethics. It was scarcely compatible with Schopenhauer's own rehabilitation of the doctrine of sin, still less his insistence that the will could not be taught or educated.

In the *Neue Briefe*, written after Schopenhauer's death and more than twenty years after the *Briefe*, Frauenstädt was finally ready not only to reinterpret Schopenhauer's pessimism but to criticize it. He first attempts to soften and moderate Schopenhauer's bleak doctrine. He maintains that Schopenhauer is not "a pessimist in the strict sense of the term" because he still believed in "redeemability from this worst of all worlds and this hell" (288). Schopenhauer is "not an absolute but a relative pessimist", because even though he holds that evil and suffering are a necessary consequence of the will to life, he still makes it possible to deny this will (287). In other passages, Frauenstädt goes on to criticize Schopenhauer's pessimism. He now develops his point about Schopenhauer's extremism.[37] Though he accepts the Schopenhauerian doctrine that "the world principle" is a hungry and suffering will, and that the entire world arises from the striving of the will, he insists that this principle alone does not entail pessimism (98–9). While it does imply that there cannot be any enduring satisfaction, it does not imply that the world is filled with suffering alone (99). "Every breath in pure fresh air is a satisfied will, every satisfied hunger or thirst is a satisfied will, every coitus is a satisfied will. A satisfied will, as long as the satisfaction lasts, is not suffering but joy" (99). It is therefore one-sided, Frauenstädt concludes, to make the will the source of suffering alone. It is also just as much the source of joy. The essence of life consists neither in the satisfied nor in the frustrated will alone but in the interplay between

---

[35] Julius Frauenstädt, *Das sittliche Leben: Ethische Studien* (Leipzig: Brockhaus, 1866).
[36] Frauenstädt cites both Christian Garve, *Uebersicht über die verschiedenen Principe der Sittenlehre von dem Zeitalter Aristoteles bis auf unsere Zeiten* (Breslau: Korn, 1798); and *Eigene Betrachtungen über die allgemeinsten Grundsätze der Sittenlehre* (Breslau: Korn, 1798).
[37] 'Neunzehnter Brief', pp. 97–9.

them. It was only because he was so extreme, because he ignored the satisfaction of the will, Frauenstädt implies, that Schopenhauer became a pessimist in the first place.

There is another insuperable problem with Schopenhauer's pessimism, one which goes to the very heart of his metaphysics, Frauenstädt contends.[38] In the final analysis, Schopenhauer cannot explain the origin of evil and suffering any better than the theist or pantheist. He assumes that evil and suffering are a consequence of egoism, of the conflict between individuals, and he explains the origin of egoism from the manifestation of the will in disparate individuals. The striving and insatiable universal will appears entirely and indivisibly in each of its manifestations, so that each of them acts like the will itself and sees itself as the centre of the universe. This is the origin of conflict between wills, from which springs evil and suffering. But how, Frauenstädt asks, does the single universal will, which exists in *every* individual, so lose itself in *each* that it thinks it exists in each alone and separately? Why should a single universal will divide itself into a multiplicity of individual wills, each of which regards itself alone as the whole universe? Why does it not simply recognize itself in all individuals, leading to greater harmony and sympathy? Thus Schopenhauer does not explain the origin of the illusion by which the will becomes individuated and appears to exist in one individual alone. He faces not only the classic problem of evil but also accounting for how the one becomes many. This puzzle Schopenhauer, his boasting notwithstanding, has not resolved any more than other monists.

Given this critique of Schopenhauer's pessimism, it is surprising to find Frauenstädt defending it elsewhere in the *Neue Briefe*. He is critical of Eduard von Hartmann's attempt to combine pessimism with optimism, to adopt Schopenhauer's ethics regarding the pursuit of happiness but to qualify it regarding the possibility of achieving cultural and moral perfection.[39] This eclectic doctrine is scarcely consistent, Frauenstädt argues. If life is really not worth living, as Schopenhauer says and Hartmann agrees, then there is really no point in striving to make the world a better place culturally and morally. "Would a prisoner strive to liberate himself from prison... if he held freedom to be something worthless?" Rather than Hartmann's preposterous combination of pessimism and optimism, Frauenstädt thinks that pessimism is best left neat and straight. If existence is not worthwhile, it's best to get redemption immediately by turning away from the world rather than by struggling vainly to improve it.

But in criticizing Hartmann, Frauenstädt was letting his old loyalties to Schopenhauer overtake him and conceal his own viewpoint. He did not really want his pessimism neat and straight, because, no less than Hartmann, he wanted it moderated and balanced by a heavy dose of optimism, the recognition that there is as much pleasure and pain, as much joy as suffering, in the world. It is also noteworthy that in the 1850s Frauenstädt had already espoused an ethic very like Hartmann's and very unlike

---

[38] 'Dreiundvierzigster Brief' pp. 265–70.
[39] 'Sechsundvierzigster Brief', *Neue Briefe*, pp. 290–6. On Hartmann's attempt to combine "eudemonic pessimism" with "evolutionary optimism", see below, Ch. 7, sections 7–8.

Schopenhauer's. In his *Die Naturwissenschaft* he had argued that natural science is compatible with the belief in the teleology of nature, and that we need to believe that nature and history are directed by ends, that our own individual actions will make a difference in the world.[40] Frauenstädt then argued that the ends we should pursue in history should be not greater happiness, because Schopenhauer had shown that to be impossible, but the development of intellectual and moral culture. This was just the doctrine, the very combination of eudemonic pessimism and moral optimism, that Hartmann would put forward some fifteen years later.[41] But expressing agreement with Hartmann's apparent improvement on Schopenhauer would have been far too much for Frauenstädt, for whom Schopenhauer remained the master.

5. Revisions and Corrections

After his break with Schopenhauer in 1856, Frauenstädt became more openly critical of him. He had always been critical; but now he was so in print. In his 1858 *Briefe über die natürliche Religion* he rejects Schopenhauer's pessimism and asceticism and develops an "ethical teleological pantheism", according to which the single universal substance has to be understood as a purposive system.[42] Doubtless, his master would have regarded this as a relapse into the bad old ways of Hegelian "*Wischi-Waschi*".[43]

Frauenstädt's final settling of accounts with Schopenhauer is his *Neue Briefe über die Schopenhauer'sche Philosophie*, which appeared in 1876. The *Neue Briefe* breaks entirely with Schopenhauer on some points; but it is also an attempt "to revise" or "correct" him on others. Frauenstädt's goal is not to develop his own system but to reformulate Schopenhauer's, so that it is more consistent and plausible. The net result of these "revisions" or "corrections" is a reinterpretation of Schopenhauer, a new perspective on his philosophy.

The most important respect in which Frauenstädt attempts to correct Schopenhauer's philosophy concerns its persistent dualisms (100). Frauenstädt always saw unity as one of the foremost demands of reason, insisting that the only satisfying metaphysics would have to be monistic.[44] He regarded monism as indeed one of the central advantages of Schopenhauer's system, because it made the will the source of all reality. Nevertheless, there were still troublesome dualisms remaining in Schopenhauer's system, dualisms that clashed with its ideal of unity. One of these was Kant's dualism between thing-in-itself and appearance. Frauenstädt does not dispute that, in many passages, Schopenhauer expressly intends to uphold Kant's dualism, and that he even stresses its importance for his philosophy. But he also maintains that there

---

[40] *Naturwissenschaft*, pp. 97–8.   [41] See Ch. 7, section 8 below.
[42] *Briefe über natürliche Religion*, pp. 165, 164–72, 198–9.
[43] Schopenhauer's actual reaction to it is unknown. He refers to a review of it in the *Blätter für literarische Unterhaltung* in a letter to David Asher, 31 Aug. 1858, *Gesammelte Briefe*, p. 434. As usual, though, he is interested in the review more for its opinion of himself than Frauenstädt.
[44] *Der Materialismus*, pp. 14–15.

are aspects of Schopenhauer's thinking which undermine this dualism and which imply a close connection between thing-in-itself and appearance. One such aspect appears in Schopenhauer's insistence that the will, the thing-in-itself, *objectifies* or *manifests* itself in nature. This concept of "objectification" or "manifestation" is omnipresent in Schopenhauer's philosophy, and it breaks down the wall between thing-in-itself and appearance (90). There are in fact two concepts of appearance in Schopenhauer's philosophy, one idealistic and another realistic (111, 114). In the idealistic sense, appearance is only a representation in the consciousness of the perceiver; but in the realistic sense, it is the manifestation or objectification of the thing-in-itself, the thing-in-itself revealing and realizing itself in its appearances.

Frauenstädt's emphasis on this realistic aspect of the concept of appearance was part and parcel of his more general realistic interpretation of Schopenhauer's philosophy. Frauenstädt was the first—and virtually the last—Schopenhauer scholar to emphasize, rightly, the realistic as well as idealistic aspects of his system. Unlike some later scholars, he realized that Schopenhauer's philosophy is not simply a system of transcendental idealism, according to which appearances are only representations in consciousness, but that it is also a system of transcendental realism, according to which appearances are objectifications of the thing-in-itself. This interpretation of Schopenhauer's philosophy is already laid down expressly in the *Briefe*,[45] and it is defended more resolutely in the *Neue Briefe*. There are passages in the *Neue Briefe*, however, where Frauenstädt goes so far as to say that Schopenhauer's philosophy is primarily realistic, as if developing its theory of intuition and appearance would imply an abandonment of transcendental idealism (113, 114, 177).[46]

Another persistent dualism in Schopenhauer's philosophy, which is based on that between thing-in-itself and appearance though not identical with it, is that between will and representation. Schopenhauer drastically separates the will from representation by insisting that the will alone belongs to the realm of reality in itself whereas representation belongs to the realm of appearances. But Frauenstädt finds something wrong with such a strict separation. If we must universalize the will as the inner source of all phenomena, we should do the same for representation. We cannot separate will from representation because the will must have an object, which it has only through representation, the conception of what we will (36–7). Futhermore, purposive activity in nature becomes intelligible only if we attribute to it some awareness, however subconscious, of its actions and the stimuli of the environment acting upon it (183). So just as there are subconscious forms of the will, so there should be subconscious forms of representation. There are many passages in Schopenhauer, Frauenstädt finds, where he acknowledges the existence of subconscious representations, so this is a line of thought already implicit in Schopenhauer (36–8). In making this point Frauenstädt

---

[45] See *Briefe*, pp. 76–7, 117–18, 161–3, 319–20.
[46] There are other passages where he continues to say that it is both idealistic and realistic. See, for example, *Neue Briefe*, p. 104.

was attempting to undercut one of Eduard von Hartmann's major criticisms of Schopenhauer: that he failed to recognize subconscious representations. Schopenhauer not only anticipated their reality, Frauenstädt argues, but he also did not lapse into Hartmann's error of separating subconscious will and representations. Schopenhauer always saw, as Hartmann did not, that the realm of will is dominant over that of representation, whether in the subconscious or conscious realm (38).

Still another questionable dualism in Schopenhauer's philosophy for Frauenstädt was that between philosophy and natural science. Schopenhauer had made a sharp distinction between philosophy and natural science that followed his dualism between thing-in-itself and appearance. According to that distinction, philosophy deals with the "what" of the world, whereas natural science deals with its "how" and "why". While the "what" of the world concerns the thing-in-itself, the inner essences of things, the "how" and "why" deal with appearances, the relations between them according to the principle of sufficient reason. Since Frauenstädt questions the dualism between thing-in-itself and appearance, since he thinks that the thing-in-itself appears in its phenomena, he also doubts the distinction between philosophy and natural science. He maintains that the natural sciences too deal with the "what" of the world, the essences of things (21). Their concern is not simply with the law-like relations between phenomena or appearances but also with the forces or powers that make up their very essence. The only difference between philosophy and empirical science, Frauenstädt therefore holds, is the level of their generality. Philosophy deals with the "what" or essence of the world on the most general level, whereas science deals with specific essences according to its special subject matter.

One of the weakest sides of Schopenhauer's philosophy, Frauenstädt argues, is its contempt for history (195). Notoriously, in the second volume of *Die Welt als Wille und Vorstellung*,[47] Schopenhauer had deprecated history, both the philosophy of history and history itself. He could see no progress or development in history, which consists only in recurrent cycles. The only lesson to be learned from history is that there is nothing new under the sun, and that people learn nothing from it; it is a story about humanity's constant self-inflicted woe and suffering, for which there is no redemption. There is also no point in attempting a philosophy of history, Schopenhauer argued, because history is just one damn fact after another, each of them unique and particular, so that it lacks the universality and necessity required of science. This polemic against history was inspired by Schopenhauer's contempt for Hegel, who had made the philosophy of history such a central part of his system. But Frauenstädt was still enough of a Hegelian to take exception to Schopenhauer's drastic stance. Schopenhauer would have thought better of history, he argues, if he had abandoned his rigid dualism between thing-in-itself and appearance, which had consigned the realm of time, and therefore history, to the realm of appearance alone (205). Once we recognize that the thing-in-itself appears in history, that history is its objectification or manifestation,

[47] Kapitel 38, 'Über Geschichte', II. 563–73; P 439–46.

then we have to grant it a more important role in the system of philosophy (206). History, Frauenstädt declares in some Hegelian lines, is still the sphere in which a nation achieves self-consciousness, and it would not be worth studying if it were only "a long, troubled and confused dream" (210–11), as Schopenhauer describes it. More significantly, Frauenstädt objects to Schopenhauer's conception of history as only a tale about evil and suffering, as if it were evidence for his pessimism. Neither the optimistic nor the pessimistic view of history is entirely correct, Frauenstädt contends. History is neither all good nor all bad, but it is very much about a struggle between good and evil. We should not accept or reject it entirely, but accept and reject parts of it on their merits (212).

The more we consider Frauenstädt's attempts to revise Schopenhauer, the more it becomes clear that he was still something of a late Hegelian. The emphasis on a close connection between thing-in-itself and appearance, the insistence on the realism of space and time, the lack of an essential distinction between philosophy and empirical science, and the recognition of the role of history—these are all Hegelian themes. When we add to this the "ethical-teleological pantheism" of *Briefe über die natürliche Religion,* it becomes necessary to admit that Frauenstädt was really more a lingering and late Hegelian than a Schopenhauerian. All the more reason to assume, then, that Frauenstädt was not simply the officious and servile disciple of Schopenhauer. In fact, Schopenhauer's first apostle was really a covert Hegelian.

6

The Optimism of Eugen Dühring

1. A Positivist and Optimist

The first thinker to mount a systematic response to Schopenhauer's pessimism, and to address in a rigorous philosophical manner all the issues surrounding the question of the value of life, was Eugen Dühring (1833–1921). As early as 1865 he wrote an entire book on the topic, *Der Werth des Lebens*,[1] which was widely read in its day, and which eventually went through eight editions.[2] One careful reader of the book was Nietzsche, who took copious notes on it in the summer of 1875.[3] Dühring's book was meant to be the antidote to Schopenhauer's pessimism, a cheerful affirmation of life in the face of Schopenhauer's grim denial of it. Although there would be many other opponents of pessimism in the second half of the 19th century, Dühring still stands out as the most effective and profound spokesman for optimism.

As a young man Dühring read Schopenhauer, who deeply impressed him. He admired his clarity, rigour and bluntness, and especially his stand against university philosophy. In his opinion, in breadth and depth, Schopenhauer stood head and shoulders above all the post-Kantians. It was Schopenhauer's great merit, Dühring believed, to have dragged philosophy out of its scholastic cocoon and to have made it confront the greatest question of them all: to be or not to be. That question was for Dühring nothing less than "the chief theme of philosophy".[4]

Despite his great admiration for Schopenhauer, Dühring was greatly challenged by his pessimism, which he regarded as utterly dangerous, indeed as "the greatest evil of all".[5] The danger of his pessimism was its quietism, its message of renunciation and withdrawal in the face of the evils of life. The primary purpose of *Der Werth des Lebens* was to combat such quietism, to defend an activism that gave people reason and motivation to face and fight the problems of the world.

---

[1] Eugen Dühring, *Der Werth des Lebens: Eine philosophische Betrachtung.* (Breslau: Eduard Trewendt, 1865).
[2] The 2nd edn appeared in 1877 with Fues Verlag in Leipzig. The later editions appeared in 1881, 1891, 1894, 1902, 1916 and 1922 with O. R. Reisland, which had taken over Fues Verlag.
[3] Friedrich Nietzsche, *Sämtliche Werke,* VIII. 131–85. These notes are a careful paraphrase of Dühring's text, with occasional critical remarks. They were written while Nietzsche was still under the influence of Schopenhauer. One can find many anticipations of Nietzsche's later philosophy in Dühring's book.
[4] *Der Werth des Lebens* (1865), p. 1.
[5] *Der Werth des Lebens,* Zweite auflage (Leipzig: Fues, 1877), pp. 219–20.

Today, Dühring is very much forgotten. If he is remembered at all, it is as the hapless target of Engel's *Anti-Dühring*.[6] But it was not for nothing that Engels chose to attack Dühring, who was one of the most controversial figures of German intellectual life in the late 19th century. Starting in the mid-1860s, Dühring became involved in a protracted and bitter dispute with his colleagues at the University of Berlin, chiefly because of his outspoken and controversial views on several topics, viz., the originality of Helmholtz's discovery of the law of conservation of energy, the values and limits of university philosophy and the rights of women.[7] When, in 1877, he was removed from his lectureship, he accused his enemies of violating his academic freedom. The dispute then went public in a dramatic fashion, with articles in newspapers taking sides for and against him, and with massive protests by students against his dismissal. Despite the outcry, Dühring never regained his position, and for the rest of his life he had to eke out a scanty living as an independent writer. Fittingly enough, he cast himself in Schopenhauer's old role: the solitary, independent and persecuted thinker who had the courage to blow the whistle on university philosophers. For the remainder of his long life, he nurtured and vented his grudges against a host of enemies, whether they were university philosophers, reactionary politicians, radical socialists or, worst of all, the Jews. Along with Heinrich von Treitschke, Adolf Stöcker and Wilhelm Marr, Dühring has the dubious distinction of being a founder of the anti-Semitic movement in the late 19th century.[8]

However disgraceful, Dühring's reputation should not overshadow his important place in the history of 19th-century philosophy. Despite his prejudices and pettiness, Dühring redeemed himself through a singular accomplishment. For he was the founder of German positivism, the grandfather of Moritz Schlick, Rudolf Carnap, Otto Neurath and Hans Reichenbach. The foundational text of German positivism is one of his early works, his *Natürliche Dialektik*, which was published in 1865. Many of the signal themes of logical positivism make their first appearance in this work: faith in the unity of science; rejection of speculative metaphysics; the orientation of philosophy around the sciences, especially mathematics and physics; the defence of empiricism and the rejection of the synthetic a priori; the quantitative and mathematical paradigm of reasoning; the concept of a pseudo-problem; and so on. Dühring's attitude toward the value of life was also fundamental for later positivism. It was no accident that Dühring was a great admirer of Auguste Comte, the French founder of

---

[6] Friedrich Engels, *Herrn Eugen Dührings Umwälzung der Wissenschaft* (Leipzig: Genossenschaftsbuchdruckerei, 1878).

[7] Dühring discusses the controversy at great length in his autobiography, *Sache, Leben und Feinde* (Leipzig: H. Reuther, 1882). A second expanded edition appeared in 1902 with Thomas Verlag, Leipzig.

[8] Dühring wrote three anti-Semitic tracts: *Die Judenfrage als Frage der Racenschädlichkeit für Existenz, Sitte und Cultur der Völker* (Karlsruhe: Reuther, 1881); *Der Ersatz der Religion durch Vollkommeneres und die Ausscheidung alles Judäerthums durch den Modernen Völkergeist* (Karlsruhe: Reuther, 1881); and *Die Ueberschätzung Lessings und dessen Anwaltsschaft für die Juden* (Karlsruhe: Reuther, 1883). In *Sache, Leben und Feinde* the Jews are a pathological obsession for Dühring, who blames them for every misfortune and criticism.

positivism, whose works he had read in his youth.⁹ In his opinion, there were two great philosophers who paved the way for modernity: Feuerbach and Comte.¹⁰

Though often critical of Comte,¹¹ Dühring never broke with the main direction and spirit of his thought. While he described his own system as "the philosophy of reality" (*Wirklichkeitsphilosophie*), partly to distinguish it from positivism, it was really only a more radical form of positivism. Dühring's chief criticism of Comte was that he had not taken his scientific rationalism far enough, that he had insisted on limits to knowledge only to leave an unknowable realm as the last refuge for religion and pessimism. The philosophy of reality was so-called because it emphasized a realistic attitude toward the world (just like positivism), and because it refused to acknowledge the existence of any world beyond that explicable by science (more positivist than positivism). The philosophy of reality was therefore positivism (i.e. scientific rationalism) taken to its ultimate limits. What the methods of the sciences could not explain simply did not exist.

What, one might ask, does Dühring's positivism have to do with his views on the value of life? *Prima facie* the abstract epistemological doctrines of the *Natürliche Dialektik* have no obvious connection with them. But when we place these doctrines in the context of Dühring's authorship as a whole, it becomes clear that they reflect his entire attitude toward life. Positivism meant for Dühring having a positive attitude toward life, an affirmative stance toward existence. The positivist sees the facts of this life as the ultimate reality, as the sole form of existence, so that we should not trouble ourselves about some other kind of reality above or beyond them. We should seek redemption in this life because there is no life hereafter. The highest good therefore must be sought in the here and now.

Dühring regarded his philosophy as a guide to life, as a strategy for making life worth living.¹² Of all such guides or strategies, positivism is the most effective, he maintained, because it alone adopts a realistic and practical attitude toward the suffering and evil of life. While the optimist turned a blind eye to these problems, and while the pessimist saw them but advised withdrawal from them, the positivist alone squarely faced them and did everything in his power to conquer them, so that we could live in a better world. So, for Dühring, positivism does not mean, contrary to its popular image and its critics, just endorsing the facts of this life, accepting them as they are given and now exist; rather, it means the readiness to change these facts, the courage and effort to refashion reality so that it comes closer to our ideals.¹³

---

⁹ See *Sache, Leben und Feinde* (1902), pp. 77, 109. Dühring's chief discussion of Comte is in his *Kritische Geschichte der Philosophie*, Vierte, verbesserte und vermehrte Auflage (Leipzig: O. R. Reisland, 1894), pp. 505–25.

¹⁰ E. Dühring, *Cursus der Philosophie als streng wissenschaftlicher Weltanschauung und Lebensgestaltung* (Leipzig: Eric Koschny, 1875), p. 486.

¹¹ For Dühring's many criticisms of Comte, see his *Cursus der Philosophie*, pp. 42, 59, 75, 135, 298, 410.

¹² *Cursus der Philosophie*, p. 546: "Meine Philosophie ist nun...kein blosses Wissenssystem, sondern vor allen Dingen die Vertretung einer auf die edlere Menschlichkeit gerichteten Gesinnung."

¹³ Ibid., p. 14.

The positivist attitude toward life was also decisive for Dühring's politics, which were decidedly left-wing and socialist. Formulating a distinction later usurped and transformed by Friedrich Engels, Dühring explains that the positivist is not a *utopian* socialist, who wants to destroy existing institutions for the sake of some ideal, but a *scientific* socialist, who uses existing institutions as the basis for reform. The more Dühring wrote about the value of existence, the more he would stress its political dimension.[14] Life could have little value, he taught, if it were lived under political oppression, and if a person had to struggle to earn the mere means of subsistence. Dühring saw the value of existence as more a practical than theoretical problem, where the solution to the practical problem lay with political action. For Dühring, no less than Marx, all the mysteries of theory are to be dissolved through practice.

Seen from a broad historical perspective, Dühring's philosophy appears to be a modern Epicureanism. It shares some chief tenets of that classical tradition: materialism, hostility to religion, the denial of personal immortality, the central role of feeling and the senses in epistemology and ethics, the uniqueness and value of life, and the role of freedom as the means to create a worthy existence. It is indeed revealing that, in the ancient conflict between Epicureanism and Stoicism, Dühring sided with the Epicureans. For all their virtues, the Stoics wrongly condemned the passions and gave a paltry value to life; and for all their flaws, the Epicureans rightly recognized the value of life and the passions. Nevertheless, despite these affinities, Dühring stopped short of a full and explicit endorsement of Epicureanism. He disapproved of its individualism, elitism, primitive metaphysics and lack of commitment to social and political life.[15]

Our main task in this chapter will be to analyse and appraise Dühring's position regarding the value of life. This will involve examining the metaphysical foundation for that position outlined in his *Natürliche Dialektik* and in his later *Cursus der Philosophie*. But it will also require taking a close look at the arguments of *Der Werth des Lebens*, which is Dühring's most sustained reflection on the meaning of life.

Unfortunately, this latter task is not as simple and straightforward as it might seem. Dühring's *Der Werth des Lebens* is a philologist's nightmare. There are eight editions, some very different than others. *Der Werth des Lebens* is indeed not really one book but several depending on the extent of the revisions. Dühring claimed to have made major changes in the second, seventh and eighth editions.[16] The second 1877 edition is indeed virtually a new book. It introduces new topics; it deletes old ones; it revises all that it retains; and it adds nearly one hundred pages. In the face of this problem, our policy will be to focus mainly on the first edition. We do so for two reasons. First, it is the most

---

[14] Ibid., pp. 369–70, 539.   [15] *Der Ersatz der Religion,* pp. 88–90.

[16] According to the title-page of the second edition, the book was "completely rewritten and significantly enlarged" (*völlig umgearbeitete und bedeutend vermehrte*). The seventh edition was completely revised (*durchgearbeitet*), while the eighth was "heavily rewritten" (*stark umgearbeitet*). Even the subtitle changed. The first edition is described as *"Eine philosophische Betrachtung".* The second and third editions appeared with the subtitle *"Populär Dargestellt";* the remaining editions had the subtitle *"Eine Denkerbetrachtung im Sinne heroischer Lebensauffassung".*

philosophical, discussing in depth the problem of the value of life. Second, it is also the most historically influential, the one read by Nietzsche and contemporaries. Still, we cannot neglect later editions, which often have crucial chapters and passages not in the first edition. We will be careful to mark the difference between editions by noting in parentheses its publication date.

2. Logical Foundations

The basis for Dühring's views on the value of life lay in his chief work on logic and epistemology, his *Natürliche Dialektik*, which he published in January 1865,[17] only months before *Der Werth des Lebens*. Dühring himself stressed the close connection between these works. They relate to one another, he later wrote, "as head and heart".[18] Any theory about the value of life, Dühring believed, requires a logical and epistemological foundation. The task of *Natürliche Dialektik* was to provide just that foundation.

What does Dühring mean by a "natural dialectic"? His entire conception of logic is packed in this phrase. He describes his dialectic as "a higher logic", i.e. one which would deal with the basic principles of logic rather than their application and results. The term "dialectic" he intends in its original and ancient sense: namely, the logic of our ordinary thinking and reasoning (1–2).[19] He explicitly spurns the narrow and negative sense given to the term by Kant, who saw the dialectic only as "the logic of illusion", i.e. the critique of the fallacies of metaphysics. Dühring calls his dialectic "natural" because it attempts to uncover the principles of reasoning involved in common sense and ordinary discourse. The term "natural" is also intended to distinguish his dialectic from Kant's allegedly artificial and arbitrary dialectic, which lays down unnecessary restrictions on the understanding. Kant's dialectic, Dühring complains, bows and bends to religious prejudices by placing the ideas of God and immortality in a noumenal realm beyond all criticism (12, 174). The natural dialectic makes the understanding completely sovereign; nothing will be immune to its criticism (159–60).

Dühring intends his natural dialectic to be both the completion of and replacement for Kant's critical philosophy. Although Dühring regards Kant's critique as a great step forward, he insists that it is necessary to take it a step further and complete the task Kant had begun. There are three reasons Kant had not gone far enough. First, he was too uncritical of the traditional logic, which he regarded as a complete and perfect science. Second, he did not investigate the concept of the infinite itself, its source in logic and mathematics, but limited himself to its application in the concepts of space and time (6–7, 12). And, third, in his attempt to deny knowledge to make room for faith,

---

[17] Eugen Dühring, *Natürliche Dialektik* (Berlin: Mittler, 1865). The preface is dated Jan. 1865, while the preface to the 1st edn of *Der Werth des Lebens* is dated Apr. 1865. The publication of two major works in such a short time is remarkable; but Dühring explained in his autobiography that both were the product of a decade of thought. See *Sache, Leben und Feinde* (1902), p. 111.
[18] *Sache, Leben und Feinde* (1902), p. 115.
[19] All references in parentheses are to the first and only edition, cited above (n. 17).

Kant placed the ideas of the infinite in a sacred moral and practical realm where they were immune from criticism (12, 160). His critique of hypostasis should have made him suspicious of the whole concept of the unconditioned; but rather than banishing it, he reintroduced it through the backdoor with his doctrine of practical faith, which made the unconditioned an object of faith rather than reason (12, 124). It is especially in this third respect that we can see the ethical purport of Dühring's dialectic, which will sweep away the ideas of God and immortality.[20]

Fundamental for Dühring's natural dialectic is his treatment of the problem of the infinite. The central task of dialectic is "how to conceive the infinite" (7). All the conundrums and confusions of metaphysics, Dühring is convinced, ultimately revolve around this thorny problem (7, 109). There is nothing wrong in principle with the idea of the infinite, he assures us, if it is taken as the simple idea of repeating a quantity without limit (112). The idea of an infinite series, which we construct with the idea of a number greater than any given number, is not self-contradictory. All the problems with the concept of the infinite arise, however, when one assumes that the entire series of infinite things *exists*, or that there is *some definite thing* that is infinite (114–15). Both assumptions are problematic because they are hypostases, reifications of a rule of understanding. The infinite is not an existing endless series of things, still less a special kind of thing, Dühring insists, but solely a *method* of counting things (115, 117). More exactly, it is that *procedure* that allows us to construct a new quantity by adding to any given quantity. Or, in mathematical terms, the infinite is not a number but the *rule* that allows us create a new number by adding another number to any given one (123). The concept of a *definite* infinite number is indeed contradictory, because if it were a definite number we could still conceive one greater than it, so that it would no longer be infinite at all (121).

It is from this simple logical point that Dühring draws weighty conclusions against metaphysics. Central to metaphysics since classical times, he points out, was its concept of the unconditioned, which attempts to complete the series of conditioned things by postulating the existence of something unconditioned. But, however venerable, this concept commits, Dühring argues, the same kind of fallacy that we find with the infinite in pure mathematics (125–6). It is like assuming that there is an infinite number. The concept postulates the existence of some thing that is infinite, when the infinite is not a thing but simply the procedure for constructing a series of things. We have to realize, Dühring teaches, that the urge to explain the whole of experience by postulating the existence of something beyond it arises from an illusion: the hypostasis of rules of explanation. We explain definite things in experience by other definite things which are their causes, where there is no limit to this procedure for anything in experience; but we then take this rule and apply it to experience in general, as if there were some

---

[20] Toward the idea of freedom Dühring had an altogether more tender attitude. He maintains that the principle of sufficient reason has a strictly logical meaning, and that it does not imply a strict necessity of natural events. See *Natürliche Dialektik*, pp. 180, 188.

general thing to explain all of experience, just as there is always a specific thing to explain other specific things in experience. But we cannot get beyond our experience to grasp the cause of experience as a whole: "We are lacking an Archimedean point to lift the world from its axis" (144). The assumption that there is some general thing unifying the world is the hypostasis of a purely formal rule of explanation, one that demands systematic unity in our conception of the world (83–4, 137–8). Because we must provide a unified explanation of the world does not entail, however, that there is some thing that unifies everything.

Having exposed the illusion inherent in metaphysics, Dühring saw himself in a position to debunk Schopenhauer's programme for its revival (141). All Schopenhauer's talk about "the riddle of existence" or "the puzzle of the world", he argues, is pure mystification and obfuscation. There is really no riddle or puzzle at all, because the question is based on a false assumption. It assumes that there is something outside the world—the will or the thing-in-itself—that can explain the entire world, even though we have no reason to assume that there is any such thing at all. The confusion or mystification comes from nothing more than hypostasis, the reification of a rule of the understanding that demands unity in explanation. We shall see later, however, how Dühring learned to appreciate Schopenhauer's call for a metaphysics.[21]

Dühring's positivist programme grew directly out of his critique of metaphysics. This programme is essentially Kant's critique of metaphysics taken to its ultimate limit: the elimination of the noumenal or otherworldly as hypostasis. The central principle of the positive philosophy, as Dühring first announces it in *Natürliche Dialektik*, states that "Factuality (*Tatsächlichkeit*) is the ultimate basis of all positing; it is the simple form upon which all knowledge has to be led back in the final instance" (57–8). To say that factuality is the ultimate basis of all positing means that facts of experience should be taken as simple and primitive, that they should not be explained by some transcendent principle beyond or behind experience. This principle is for Dühring not simply epistemological, a verificationist thesis that limits knowledge to experience. Rather, it is more fundamentally ethical or existential, because it is a principle of immanence, according to which all meaning or value comes from within human life itself; it contains the implicit injunction that we not make meaning or value dependent upon another world beyond this life. Hence, for Dühring, positivism is first and foremost a philosophy about the value or meaning of life. Its central doctrine, as he later put it in the second edition of *Der Werth des Lebens,* is that "human existence is a complete and sufficient reality in itself" (61).

Though the critique of hypostasis is fundamental to Dühring's positivism, it is remarkable that, in the final analysis, he could not entirely eliminate the transcendent from his philosophy. It obtrudes in the least likely place: in the very foundations of logic itself. The transcendent reappears because, in many passages in *Natürliche Dialektik*, Dühring finds it necessary to postulate an ultimate ground for all thinking, a

---

[21] See below, section 7.

ground that transcends thinking itself.[22] This ground cannot be an object of thinking, he reasons, because it is the necessary condition of thinking itself (34–5, 39, 222). Any attempt to think it will presuppose it, and so be circular. Dühring postulates this ground primarily because he has to explain truth, the correspondence between thinking and reality (59, 79). Truth presupposes that there is some overriding unity between our thinking about things and things themselves. This unity Dühring identifies with the concept of being (*Sein*), which is so general and abstract that it applies as much to our thinking about things as things themselves.

Dühring swithered about the precise logical status of this ultimate ground of thinking. There are passages where he seems to insist that it should have a purely regulative status, i.e. it is an idea we have to postulate to explain the truth of our thinking about the world but we have no reason to assume that there is some thing answering to it (40, 76, 84). Thus he states that the concept is purely formal, and that we should not make any definite inferences from it (40, 192). There are other passages, however, where Dühring clearly gives the idea more than a merely regulative status. The necessity of thinking according to the pure concepts of the understanding, we are told, lies in a constraint (*Zwang*) coming from a force or power, which lies beyond thought itself (59). The basic principles behind all logical thinking, he explicitly maintains, are not formulable as axioms, and do not appear in any conceptual form, because they are "driving forces" and "shaping powers" behind all thinking (225–7). Indeed, the very role that Dühring assigns to the concept of being as a mediator between subject and object, thinking and reality, requires its constitutive status. For unless this ground designates some existing unity, it cannot mediate these realms; a merely regulative concept does not ensure that there is an *actual* connection, only that we must think that there is one. So far is Dühring from giving this concept a merely regulative status that he explicitly refuses to call it an "idea" (226), and later he even describes it as the object of feeling or sensation.[23]

This lingering element of the transcendent in Dühring's thinking also has important implications for his theory about the value of life. For in the first edition of *Der Werth des Lebens* Dühring would invoke his postulate of the ground of thinking to argue that thinking alone cannot justify human existence (178–80). It turns out that there is a higher transcendent sphere to life after all, a realm that excludes all conceptual thinking and that has to be felt and sensed alone. It is ironic that this transcendent sphere is not the product of religious mystification but the result of hard logical analysis: to explain the very possibility of truth, the basis of all thinking, it is necessary to postulate—so the argument goes—a sphere that transcends all thinking. Kant himself had pointed to this terrain when he insisted that the 'I' that accompanies all thinking cannot itself be an object of thinking. Now Dühring found himself bumping up against the same limits.

---

[22] See *Natürliche Dialektik*, pp. 34–5, 39, 59, 67, 79, 84.
[23] Namely, in the first edition of *Der Werth des Lebens*, pp. 178–80.

Dühring's postulate of a transcendent ground of all thinking raises the question whether he really has a coherent theory about the value of life after all. Dühring, it seems, both affirms and denies a transcendent dimension to life. We will see in later sections how Dühring came to deal with this thorny problem.

3. Logic of the Question

Having laid down his fundamental principles in *Natürliche Dialektik*, Dühring was ready to apply them to the question of the value of life in his *Der Werth des Lebens*.[24] The critique of metaphysics, and the principle of immanence, had set the basic parameters for his theory of the value of life. The critique of hypostasis had eliminated the classical ideas of the unconditioned—viz., God and immortality—which had been the pillars of the traditional Christian view about the meaning of existence. Now there was no providential order in which the individual could find his place; and there was no eternal soul to find redemption in another world. Somehow, then, Dühring had to show that this life, despite all its suffering and sorrow, is still worth living. Since there is no life beyond this one, we have to prove that there is value and meaning here and now.

It was in just this respect, though, that Schopenhauer would prove such a challenge for Dühring. For Schopenhauer too had rejected the traditional Christian view; but he also held that the traumas and troubles of life put it beyond redemption. It was no accident, then, that Dühring, in the preface to the first edition of *Der Werth des Lebens*, would declare his total opposition to Schopenhauer's views about the value of life (vi). That opposition will appear constantly in Dühring's book in its many criticisms of Schopenhauer's pessimism.

Before engaging Schopenhauer, though, Dühring thinks it necessary to examine the logic of the question about the value of life. What kind of question is this? What does it presuppose? To what extent can a philosopher answer it? And to what degree must the response to it be personal and individual? All these questions Dühring attempts to answer in the preface, introduction and chapter VIII of the first edition, all of which were deleted in the second edition. It is only from these early deleted texts, though, that we can fully appreciate the logic of Dühring's position.

In his preface Dühring states that in treating his question he will follow Kant's critical method. This means that rather than answering the question directly, he will first examine our *judgements* about it (vi). Dühring immediately notes something significant and peculiar about these judgements, something that will prove decisive for his entire theory. Namely, these judgements are not theoretical but practical, i.e. they are not about what *is* but what *ought to be* the case. In other words, the value of life is not a matter of fact, some objective state of affairs about which we can make true or false judgements; rather, it is a matter of acting on norms or ideals about what we want life to be. What makes life worth living, Dühring was saying, is the ideals and goals we set for it and

---

[24] All references in parentheses in this section are, unless otherwise noted, to the 1st edn.

nothing intrinsic about life itself. In making this point Dühring was simply applying the critique of hypostasis from his *Natürliche Dialektik*. Just as we should not hypostasize the idea of the unconditioned, so we should not do that to the value of life. This idea is not a reality given to us but an ideal that we should strive to achieve. This reading of the question reflects Dühring's general theory of value, according to which values arise from the human will and are not objective properties of things themselves (7).

From this analysis of the question, Dühring draws an important general conclusion: that we human beings determine the criteria by which we measure the value of life. We should not defer to some higher transcendent standpoint, which would determine our criteria for us. Dühring much stresses this point: "We ourselves are the measure of the value of life; we cannot make a decision for or against it without taking the constitution of our strivings as our norm" (6). The problem with metaphysics, he argues, is that it conspires to rob us of our human autonomy; it attempts to determine the value of life from some standpoint beyond it, though it can be meaningfully determined only from within human experience itself (4). Once we see through these hypostases, Dühring claims much like Feuerbach before him, we can reclaim our human freedom and recreate the world according to our own ideals.

On these grounds Dühring criticizes two eminent metaphysicians: Spinoza and Schopenhauer. Both want to settle the issue of the value of life from an abstract metaphysical standpoint, as if it could be decided entirely *sub specie aeternitatis* or from a theoretical perspective. Spinoza demands too much of us: that we lose ourselves in the infinite, that we become one with the universe; but if were we to do that, Dühring argues, we would surrender the very desires that make our lives valuable to us (6). Schopenhauer thinks that we can see through the futility of human striving by an act of insight, that we can get beyond suffering through disinterested contemplation (6, 164). But he too fails to see that we can never completely disengage from our desires, that our practical interests constantly determine our theorizing. Both Spinoza and Schopenhauer demand that, in determining the value of life, we abstract from desires and feelings, though they alone provide the criteria to determine its value.

Neither optimism nor pessimism, Dühring maintains, have understood the practical dimension of the value of life (1, 2–3). Although they are antithetical, these worldviews still have something in common: they intend to reconcile us to life, to make us accept the world as it stands. They are simply attitudes toward life rather than strategies for changing it. The optimist advises celebrating life because of its many pleasures and goods; the pessimist enjoins renouncing life because of its many pains and evils. Both go astray because they do not realize that the task is to change the world rather than our attitudes toward it.

The deficiencies of optimism and pessimism show us, Dühring believes, the desiderata for an adequate theory of the value of life. Such a theory should recognize the reality of evil and suffering, but it should also encourage us to confront and combat them rather than deny (optimism) or flee from (pessimism) them. Dühring would sometimes call this activist attitude a more profound optimism, one differing from the blind optimism that refuses to recognize the reality of evil and suffering as it now exists in the world. This attitude was not a Nietzschean affirmation of life as it is, has been or will be, but an idealist affirmation of a life as it can and should be.

As stated so far, there is a serious difficulty with Dühring's account of the question. Having stressed its practical dimension, having cast aside all metaphysics, and having emphasized the role of the will, it seems as if the question is not really philosophical at all. From all that Dühring has said, it seems to follow that each person should decide the value of life for him- or herself, simply from his or her own experience and according to his or her own desires. All that people need to do is ask whether life, by and large, has satisfied their personal preferences and aspirations. We then get very different answers about the value of life depending on each individual's experience and desires. This is indeed just what we should expect as a result of Dühring's own analysis, which maintains that each individual forms his own world, that he or she has a unique measure of the value of life. Each subject, he writes in chapter II, forms "his own system of experience", where these systems vary with age, sex and temperament (37–8).

However inevitable this conclusion seems to be, it is noteworthy that Dühring stoutly resists it. He refuses to dissolve the question into a mere matter of personal experience and preference. If theoretical satisfaction were not a goal of his investigation, he writes in the introduction to the first edition, then the whole question of the value of life would not have the great importance he gives to it as "the chief theme of philosophy" (1). Whether or not life is worth living, he further explains, depends on not only our essential human needs but also the general nature of things. The question then proves to be theoretical after all: whether there is a general correspondence between essential human needs and desires and the nature of things (4, 9). Dühring later analyses the question into two main elements: a practical and theoretical one (190). While the practical element concerns our desires and aspirations, the theoretical one considers the general facts of experience and whether our desires and aspirations are satisfied or frustrated by the world.

So far, so good. Dühring seems to have provided sufficient space for the theoretical, so that philosophy can play a significant role in determining the value of life after all. This is not, however, the end of the matter, which becomes much more compromised and complicated. For in the penultimate chapter of the first edition,[25] Dühring comes to a very different account of his question, one which drastically restricts the power of philosophy. Here that transcendent realm that Dühring first wrote about in *Natürliche Dialektik* creeps into his analysis and reshapes his whole conception of the question. In no uncertain terms Dühring now tells us that there is something more to the nature of things than what we grasp through the understanding or intellect (177). The chief activity of the intellect is analysis; but all analysis rests upon an ultimate synthesis, which is indivisible and therefore escapes the intellect. This final ground of the understanding

---

[25] See chapter VIII: 'Die Erkenntnis', pp. 163–80.

relates to the understanding itself as the indeterminate to the determinate, between which there is a great gulf (177). We can have some sense of this ultimate ground of things, this final synthesis, Dühring explains, only through immediate feeling and sensation. For all these reasons, Dühring claims that the intellect alone, because it cannot grasp the ultimate ground of things on which all existence depends, can never justify our existence (179–80). Hence philosophy too, which has its *modus operandi* in the intellect, cannot make a final determination about the worth of existence. Here, in these remarkable passages, Dühring took his *salto mortale* into the realm of the ineffable, renouncing the very intellect that he had made the sovereign authority in his epistemology.

Proceeding from these considerations, Dühring comes to another conclusion that even more drastically restricts the role of the intellect and theory in determining the value of life. Since we cannot know the ultimate ground of things through the intellect, and since we cannot provide an explanation or justification of our intuitions about it, it follows, Dühring concludes, that all we can have in the end is a *faith* in the value of life (190–2). We cannot claim that the nature of things really does correspond to the essential desires and needs of human beings; all that we can do is state, on the basis of our own individual experience so far, that we *believe* life worth living. We cannot generalize beyond our own experience about that of everyone else, because any such generalization would be, as Hume states, an act of faith, an inference resting on the unjustifiable premise that the unknown is like the known. All that we can know about the value of life, Dühring then suggests, is whether things, at a particular time and place and under particular circumstances, match our expectations for life (182). Only in that very limited respect can we decide whether to have faith in the value of life. It seems, then, that the value of life is determined not only by a particular person but also by his particular moods at a particular time and place.

So, although Dühring recognizes this theoretical side of the question, he ends up greatly restricting it, limiting it to determining whether circumstances at a particular time and place match a particular person's expectations of life. He has so stressed the practical aspect of the question, and so confined its theoretical aspect, that it seems as if the answer to the question about the value of life is going to depend on individual decision and experience at a particular moment. Since people have different experiences and conflicting moral views, and since we cannot generalize beyond our own experience, it seems that we cannot generalize about the value of life itself. Thus the dissolution of the question into an anarchy of individual answers, which Dühring at first resists, he ultimately seems forced to accept. What was to be a philosophy about the value of life is ultimately reduced to a mere act of faith depending on the individual's own experience.

Fortunately, Dühring did not follow through with all these self-defeating reflections. Most of his book is precisely what he abandons in his penultimate chapter: a philosophical reflection on the value of life. Not surprisingly, the penultimate chapter was deleted in the second edition; its content never reappears in later editions.

4. Theory of Value

Crucial for Dühring's views on the value of life is his general theory of value. This theory is set forth primarily, if only in a very crude and rudimentary way, in chapters 1 to 3 of the first edition of *Der Werth des Lebens*.[26] Heavily revised, in exposition if not content, these chapters were condensed into a single chapter for the second edition.[27]

Regarding the basis of value, Dühring is a straightforward empiricist. The source of value lies for him not in the principles or ideals of reason, but in the feelings and sensations of experience. To know whether something is of value, we must be able to sense or feel it (13). We approve what gives us positive feelings, we disapprove what gives us negative ones. Reason alone cannot give normative force to moral principles or ideals, Dühring argues, because they must receive their content from sensation and feeling (20). Not only the reason or justification for a moral principle, but also the incentive or motive to act on one, comes from feeling or sensation (16). If a person felt nothing, he would have no motive to act, and so he would do nothing.

Dühring offers no argument for his ethical empiricism.[28] We are served bald statements and bold assertions. Part of the reason for his position rests on his general empiricism, which he had already defended in his *Natürliche Dialektik*. According to that work, *all* principles, not only moral ones, receive their content from experience. There are no synthetic a priori principles, whether moral or metaphysical. In *Der Werth des Lebens* Dühring also affirms the classical empiricist tenet that feelings or sensations cannot err. Like a true Epicurean, he maintains that feelings or sensations cannot be mistaken, for the simple reason that they do not judge. Since sensations and feelings refer to nothing beyond themselves, they have no cognitive component, and so cannot be right or wrong (110). If they sometimes seem to lead us astray, that is only because of the ideas or beliefs that accompany them, not because of the feelings themselves. No sensation as such is illusory: "it is what it is, entirely and complete" (38).

Since feeling or sensation (*Empfindung*) is the sole source of value, Dühring makes it the criterion to judge the value of life. "Existence has its charm and worth through the totality of affections in which it develops" (13). It might seem from such empiricism that Dühring must be a eudemonist, holding in classical fashion that the highest good depends on happiness and that happiness consists in pleasure. It is striking, however, that Dühring does not take this position, at least not in the first edition of *Der Werth*

---

[26] *Der Werth des Lebens* (1865): Capitel I: 'Das Leben als Inbegriff von Empfindungen und Gemüthsbewegungen', pp. 13–27; Capitel II: 'Der Unterschied als der eigentliche Gegenstand des Gefühls', pp. 28–39; and Capitel III: 'Die Grundgestalt in der Abfolge der Lebenserregungen', pp. 40–51.

[27] *Der Werth des Lebens* (1877), pp. 61–85. This chapter bears the title of the first chapter of the first edition.

[28] At least not in the first or second editions of *Der Werth des Lebens*. His chapter on Kant in his *Kritische Geschichte der Philosophie*, pp. 399–437, criticizes the emptiness of the categorical imperative (pp. 412–13).

des Lebens.²⁹ He holds that the value of life depends not only on our pleasant feelings but on the whole life of feeling, which includes pain as well as pleasure. What makes for a worthwhile existence, Dühring maintains, is the total play of passions, which comprises not only pleasant but also painful sensations (16). Not only the heights but also the depths of sensation or feeling are essential for vitality, the intensity and fullness of living, upon which all well-being depends. Likening the life of feeling to the rising and falling of a wave, Dühring stresses that the entire movement is important for a complete life (30). "Take away our love and our hate and you make existence itself into a barren desert" (17).

To explain exactly how and why the value of life depends on the whole play of feeling, Dühring set forth a general theory of feeling in the second and third chapters of *Der Werth des Lebens*.³⁰ The fundamental principle of this theory is what Dühring calls "the principle of difference". According to this principle, feelings arise from, and are in proportion to, change or difference in stimulus. If the stimuli in life are constant, or if they change in a strictly regular way, then they do not give rise to a new feeling. Hence to have a valuable life, one rich and intense in new feelings, one must have change and variety in their stimuli. In a nutshell: "The multiplicity of risings and fallings of feeling is the indispensable requirement for a valuable existence" (30).

From this theory, Dühring drew important conclusions about the value of existence. First, we should value not only pleasure itself, conceived as the end or reward of activity, but also the activity of trying to achieve it. We could never value constant, uninterrupted pleasure, which would quickly prove dull and enervating; we also need the stimulus and excitement involved in striving and struggle. Ironically, then, the resistance to the enjoyment of life, and the attempt to overcome it, are a crucial value of life itself. As Dühring later formulated this point: the evaluation of life has to proceed from the principle that the natural resistance opposed to the enjoyment of life is not something evil but a necessity, without which an enjoyable life is impossible.³¹ Second, that we enjoy certain experiences and situations only once, and that we should not strive to repeat them.³² We value experiences and situations, though we are not self-conscious of it at the time, because they are unique and unrepeatable. The problem with repetition has nothing to do with the content of the experiences themselves, Dühring insists, but simply the fact of repetition itself. What is the case for individual experiences can then be generalized for life itself, so that we value it for its uniqueness and brevity; so from this perspective, death itself becomes a necessity. We find true self-satisfaction with existence only when we recognize how all its valuable moments are unique,

---

²⁹ In the second 1877 edition, there is a passage where Dühring seems to affirm the classical eudemonist position. He states (p. 192) that the source of all privation (*Ungemach*) lies in pain (*Schmerz*). In the *Cursus der Philosophie*, however, Dühring reaffirms his theory of feeling and draws the non-eudemonist conclusions from it. See pp. 361–6.

³⁰ *Der Werth des Lebens* (1865): Capitel II: 'Der Unterschied als der eigentliche Gegenstand des Gefühls', pp. 28–39; and Capitel III: 'Die Grundgestalt in der Abfolge der Lebenserregungen', pp. 40–51.

³¹ *Cursus der Philosophie*, p. 361.

³² Dühring drew this conclusion most explicitly in his *Cursus der Philosophie*, p. 366.

unrepeatable, irreplaceable and short. Hence Dühring implicitly excluded something like Nietzsche's eternal recurrence as a test for the value of life.

To appreciate the novelty of Dühring's theory, it is important to place it in a broad historical perspective. In stressing the importance of vitality, the whole play of passions, Dühring was breaking with not only eudemonism but also the entire classical tradition. Both the Epicureans and Stoics had placed the greatest value on equanimity, or peace of mind, which rests upon regulation of the passions. Dühring questions, however, not only our power to control the passions but also the value of equanimity itself. A completely peaceful life, where we are never distressed or dissatisfied, would be, in his view, a complete torment (16).

It is noteworthy that, when Dühring discusses the classical dispute about the highest good, he sides with neither Epicurean nor Stoic. Both schools are mistaken, he maintains (14). While the Epicureans place too much value on physical sensation and feeling, neglecting the higher pleasures of the intellect, the Stoics exaggerate the value of abstract ideals and general principles, ignoring the importance of sensation and feeling. If the Epicureans *degrade* human nature by reducing it to physical sensation and feeling, the Stoics *sacrifice* it by repressing all sensation and feeling. Ultimately, though, true to his empiricism, Dühring's greater sympathy lies with the Epicurean tradition. He declares that, if one had to make the choice, it would be better to be an Epicurean than a Stoic. Better to have one half of our human nature than to sacrifice the whole on the altar of moral ideals (18). With Schopenhauer's asceticism, then, Dühring has no sympathy whatsoever. Compared to the ascetic warfare against human nature, he avers, even suicide and murder appear innocent (18).

Although Dühring stresses the fundamental role of feeling and sensation in determining the value of life, he recognizes that people often value life according to their ideals and principles, and that their moral views, not their feelings, are one of the chief sources of their satisfaction or dissatisfaction with life (169). He warns, however, against having strict or narrow moral views, because they all too readily come into conflict with life itself (169–70). The great objection against moralism, against having rigid principles and unswerving ideals, is that they can diminish the worth of life. All too often life fails to meet the expectations created by these principles and ideals, which then leads to bitterness and disappointment. Rather than judging life according to preconceived principles, Dühring recommends that we should derive our principles from life itself. Ideals and principles have no worth in themselves, and never should we sacrifice our lives for them. In short, life should not be for the sake of morals and ideals; morals and ideals should be for the sake of life (171).

5. Reckoning with Schopenhauer

Having adopted feeling and sensation as his criterion of value, Dühring again had to face the challenge of Schopenhauer, who had also adopted such a criterion in advancing his pessimism. Fully aware of this threat, Dühring duly examines Schopenhauer's theory of feeling and desire in several chapters of *Der Werth des Lebens*.[33]

Dühring agrees with Schopenhauer that the gap or tension between subjective need and the objective world is fundamental to our existence (50), and that there is an element of need and dissatisfaction involved in all human striving (93). Still, he thinks that Schopenhauer fails to appreciate the intrinsic value of striving and the necessity for that gap or tension, which is a *sine qua non* for a valuable existence. Schopenhauer sometimes writes as if the sole measure of the value of life were pleasure, the moment when we satisfy our desires; but he then fails to see the importance of the entire play of feeling, how both pleasure and pain, make for the worth of existence.

Even if we leave aside the whole play of feeling, even if we measure the value of life by a hedonic calculus alone, Dühring contends, Schopenhauer reckons wrongly. Schopenhauer overstates the amount and duration of pain involved in need. He assumes that pain is constantly present throughout the striving to satisfy need, while it is usually present only at the onset. Need arises only slowly and gradually, so that its first stirrings are only slightly painful (94). And if Schopenhauer overrates the pain of human striving, he underrates its pleasure. Sometimes the pleasure from satisfying a need, and from striving to satisfy it, is much longer and more intense than the pain that arises from first feeling the need. Schopenhauer writes as if the normal life of feeling were the movement from pleasure to pain but the very opposite is the case (95). In any case, pleasure does not have a strictly negative significance as freedom from pain, as Schopenhauer assumes, because it often has a positive quality of its own. It is necessary to postulate a state of indifference between pleasure and pain (95).

No less than Schopenhauer, Dühring recognizes that one of the greatest challenges to the quality of life is posed by boredom. According to his theory of feeling, the value of life rests on the entire play of feeling, not simply on pleasure, and it depends on our interest in and engagement with things, even if that happens to result in pain. If this is so, then there is no greater danger than boredom, which undermines this play, interest and engagement. Hence the more boredom prevails, the less life can be worthwhile.

Boredom, Dühring maintains, comes from two sources: the lack of stimuli or the homogeneity of stimuli (33). Because we need to be active, because we seek new and intense feelings, we want neither constancy nor uniformity in our lives. We need change, but not only the same kind of change; we also need variety, different kinds of change. If we have neither, we do not feel alive. The most important and urgent task in educating a child, Dühring notes, is keeping it from boredom, which is the chief source of unrest and dissatisfaction (62). There are three forms of activity—play, learning and work—and all of them, Dühring contends, are forms of keeping us engaged and holding boredom at bay. Where Dühring takes issue with Schopenhauer is in seeing the

---

[33] *Der Werth des Lebens* (1865): Capitel II: 'Der Unterschied als der eigentliche Gegenstand des Gefühls', pp. 28–39; Capitel V: 'Die Liebe', pp. 87–124; and Capitel VI: 'Der Tod', pp. 125–74. Dühring's explicit references to Schopenhauer are sporadic and intermittent in these texts, though Schopenhauer is constantly in mind.

value of boredom within the whole life of feeling. Placed in the context of a whole life, boredom serves the purpose of rest and recuperation before we engage in new activities. While Schopenhauer thinks that boredom immobilizes us, freezing us in a state of inactivity, Dühring thinks that it can be a stimulus for new activity (34).

The most important feelings to give value to life, Dühring maintains, are not physical but social. This was a point overlooked by Schopenhauer, who focuses too much on physical pleasure and pain and on a person's private life. But physical pleasure and pain are virtually nothing to us compared to the joy and suffering that comes from our relations to others (69). There is an enormous leap, Dühring claims, from the physical pain we suffer from some wound to the mental pain caused us by humiliation or dishonour (24).

Of the social feelings, Dühring thinks that two are especially important in giving value to life: honour and love. Both feelings are in need of revaluation from their current reputation, he thinks. Honour is our feeling of self-worth as it depends on the approval of others (81). Rather than a source of injustice, a form of competition or *amour propre* that strives to outdo others, honour is only the claim of the self for justice, the demand that one receives the recognition one deserves. It is only because of its power, the need to feel self-worth, that someone is inspired to great achievements (83). In insisting that honour is "a motive of moral action that cannot be prized enough", Dühring was breaking with the Epicurean tradition, which had seen the drive for honour as one of the unnatural and unnecessary passions.

Love, Dühring argues, is no less important than honour in giving value to life, and it too stands in need of revaluation. Schopenhauer has exaggerated the pains of love, as if erotic desire were an affliction. But, Dühring replies, love does not consist chiefly in pain, or even in a mixture of pleasure and pain, but essentially in pleasure. The only pain of love is "the soft draft of a slight unease". Nature has made the yearning of love such an intense pleasure that we hardly detect the element of pain contained in it (92). Schopenhauer also gave love a mainly instrumental value, the means toward reproduction. But this only goes to show, Dühring claims, that Schopenhauer fails to understand its intrinsic value (94). He has no conception of erotic love, which is a pleasure in itself. Love works for its own sake, and it is not merely a means to an end (124). Of course, there is often the terrible disappointment of love; but this is not an argument against the feeling itself so much as the romantic notions and high expectations that surround it (120–1).

In stressing the importance of the whole play of passions for the value of life, and in calling for a revaluation of passions such as hate and honour, Dühring clearly anticipates Nietzsche's later revaluation of all values in the 1880s. The foreshadowings of Nietzsche are most apparent of all, however, in Dühring's analysis of justice, which he traces back to the feeling of revenge. Justice, he explains, arises from the life of feeling, and more specifically when someone's honour is injured. That injury gives rise to the demand for retribution and restitution, which alone restores what has been taken away (72). In his 1875 notes on *Der Werth des Lebens* Nietzsche paid careful attention to

Dühring's theory, remarking that it was reason to question Schopenhauer's own theory of justice.[34] Famously, in his *Zur Genealogie der Moral* Nietzsche would expound a theory of the origin of justice very similar to Dühring, whom he called the "*Berliner Rache-Apostel*".[35] Though Nietzsche would later draw very different conclusions from a similar concept of justice, we should not let this obscure what he had perhaps once learned from Dühring.

6. Death

Any discussion of the value of life inevitably poses the topic of death. We cannot determine the value of life, it would seem, without some knowledge of its opposite. All kinds of questions arise about death. Is it annihilation? Or is there life after it? And what about the experience of death? Is it horror or release, torment or deliverance? The experience of death concerns not only those who are dying but also those who are left behind. And for the latter the question arises: how, or whether, one can reconcile oneself to the loss of one's nearest and dearest? It is to Dühring's credit that he did not shirk these questions, which he tackles in chapter VI of *Der Werth des Lebens*.[36]

Any treatment of these issues immediately bumps up against a paradox: if the living cannot experience death, they cannot know anything about death. Attempting to answer the question about the value of life then seems to transcend the limits of knowledge, which lie within experience. Dühring, however, did not trouble himself with the paradox. We should not worry, he thinks, about what lies beyond life. Death is the end of life, utter annihilation.[37] That is the end of the story. We do not have to concern ourselves about what lies beyond life, then, for the simple reason that there is nothing there. All knowledge depends on experience, on feeling and sensation; but the destruction of the body means that there is no feeling or sensation, and so there is nothing to know.

Nothing, however, seems more frightening than nothingness. So, in preaching annihilation Dühring, it seems, does not dissolve the problem of death but only makes it all the more apparent and frightening. The nihilist, whose views Dühring strongly condemns, is precisely that character who wants to scare us with the prospect of nothingness, that vast and spooky realm that lies before and after our short existence. But if death is annihilation, as Dühring tells us, how are his views any different from the nihilist? To this question Dühring's reply would be that the crucial issue concerns not whether one affirms nothingness but how one responds to it, i.e. it is a matter of one's attitude toward nothingness. The nihilist wants to frighten us and does so by playing

---

[34] See Nietzsche, *Sämtliche Werke*, VIII. 152–3, 176–8.
[35] See Nietzsche, *Zur Genealogie der Moral*, *Sämtliche Werke*, V. 370, §14.
[36] See *Der Werth des Lebens* (1865), 'Der Tod', pp. 125–47.
[37] This is more explicit in the second edition, where Dühring declares his materialism. See *Der Werth des Lebens* (1877), p. 165: "Für die gereifete Einsicht des Geschlechts ist der Tod nichts als das Ende des individuellen Lebens."

on our old prejudices about life after death. Nothingness seems terrible to him only because he cannot easily relinquish old Judaeo-Christian habits, which cling to the idea of an eternal soul. But if we learn to abandon these habits, Dühring believes, we can then see nothingness with new eyes. Precisely because death is the end, we should accept it as deliverance, "the last refuge", "the final harbor against tormenting feelings" (138).

It should be obvious by now that Dühring has no sympathy for the idea of a life after death, which for him is only an *Ersatz* for a better life on earth. Such an idea, he argues, simply transports the desires and feelings we have in this life to another world, as if what we experience now we will also experience there, only in a more constant and purer form (125–6). But this idea is illusory, Dühring believes, because these desires and feelings, which are the source of all value, will cease with our natural existence. When we hope that they will continue in another form of existence, we thereby only tacitly reaffirm the value of life itself, given that these desires and feelings have their meaning and existence only within this life. Hence another world will not bring redemption from the sorrows and sufferings of this life; it is only an expression of regret that we have not lived better in this life.

It is striking, however, that Dühring was not always so dogmatic or self-assured in his dealings with death. To the first edition of *Der Werth des Lebens* he added an appendix which reconsiders the question of another world.[38] Rather than dismissing ideas of life after death as a mere projection of feelings and desires, he now engages in philosophical argument. At first he excludes the existence of another world beyond this one because it violates the principle of the unity of existence, the thesis that the universe forms a systematic whole (212–13). But he then realizes that affirming this principle only begs the question. Why should a dualist who believes in another world accept a principle of the unity of existence? And so Dühring admits that a world beyond this one—even a life after death—is a logical possibility after all (216). Yet he limits the force of this concession by insisting that such a beyond, precisely because we cannot know anything about it, should not interest us (218). This purely pragmatic point was not likely to sway, however, someone anxious to know what happens to their departed loved ones.

Death, the grim prospect of utter annihilation, had always been a heavy weapon in the pessimist's arsenal. Rather than attempting to remove the fear of death, Schopenhauer did everything to increase it, attempting by that means to build his case against life. He portrayed death as the most horrific experience of all, the final horrible end for a lifetime of sorrow and struggle. Death was the last trauma and torment, the inevitable fate that overshadowed all of life.[39] For Dühring, however, that portrait is all too melodramatic. There is nothing to fear in death precisely because it is nothingness.

---

[38] *Der Werth des Lebens* (1865), Anhang: 'Der theoretische Idealismus und die Einheit des Systems der Dinge', pp. 193–218. This appendix is a critique of neo-Kantianism.
[39] Schopenhauer, *Die Welt als Wille und Vorstellung*, *Werke*, I. 429.

He would have agreed with the classic Epicurean maxim: "While we are, death is not; and when death comes, we are not."[40] Like a good Epicurean, he teaches that death means the end of sensation, and therefore the end of pain and suffering itself.

But, granted that death is nothingness, what about the process of dying? Is that not dreadful? Dühring thinks that this too is overblown. What makes the prospect of dying so horrific for us, he maintains, is simply the fears that we have about it (132–3). The pains of dying are of the same kind and no worse than those we have within life itself (132). Assume, for example, that someone dies suddenly with no suspicion of his impending death. What he will experience will be the same as any pain he has felt within life itself (132). We have no reason, therefore, to fear that the pain of death will be especially horrific, a trauma beyond our normal experience. A natural death is the result of a gradual weakening of our powers, and so is not really painful for us but only "a peaceful and gentle fading away" (131). Although Dühring admits that dying is often accompanied with great pain, he still thinks that the prospect of such pain should not blacken our views about life. Most people, he thinks, would accept a painful death as the price for a meaningful and eventful life (132). It would certainly be strange for someone to shirk from the pain of death, he adds, when they go through so many pains for the sake of a better life.

We can best reconcile ourselves to death, Dühring advises, when we come to regard dying as another event within life itself (136). That event can be something that happens according to the laws of nature, as when a person's life comes to an end because of a natural decline of his or her powers; but it can also be the result of someone's voluntary decision, when a person does something risky or dangerous (viz., mountain climbing).[41] In this latter case we regret less death itself than a premature or early death, so that we should blame not death itself but fortune. *Fortuna* is the great goddess of human affairs, and no one escapes her fickle rule. But we should not judge her too harshly, Dühring urges. She is part of the very fabric of life, because it is the very nature of life to contain within itself unpredictability and indeterminacy. We have to live with the prospect that our life might end before our time. But it is precisely this which gives our life its piquancy and intensity. "Life would be not life if it did not include indeterminacy. Under certain circumstances man loves to play with life and death ... Chance is the law of the world, and it is not an unhappy law" (137).

Pursuing further this line of thought, Dühring maintains that the meaning of death has to be judged by life itself. Since death is annihilation, we measure its significance by what it annihilates (135, 145). When a youth dies, he loses the prospect of a full and rich life; and when a man dies at the height of his powers, he loses his work and career; but when an older person dies, someone who has lived a rich and rewarding life, he loses nothing. We are indeed ready to depart from life when we know that we have

---

[40] Epicurus, 'Letter to Menoeceus', in *The Epicurean Philosophers*, ed. John Gaskin (London: Dent, 1995), p. 43.

[41] This is my example. Dühring's argument here, *Der Werth des Lebens* (1865), pp. 135–6, is very abstract and he does not provide examples of his own.

played our role, that we have done our part, and that there is nothing more for us to do. All this goes to show, Dühring concludes, that dying is an event within life itself and that it has its meaning strictly in relation to the kind of existence we have had (136).

But Dühring also proposes that we reverse the equation. We should not only judge death by life but life by death (145–6). We must learn to value death itself, precisely because it gives life itself all its value. The great value of existence becomes apparent to us, Dühring maintains, only against the background assumption of death itself. We cherish life, and feel it in its greatest intensity, only because we know that these moments will not last forever, or only because we realize that they are unique and will not repeat themselves. What gives pathos to life, what arouses our deepest passions, is the awareness of its temporality and finality. Such pathos and passion is the subject matter of the highest form of art, which is tragedy. In some lines that anticipate Nietzsche, Dühring declares that the meaning of life becomes fully apparent only in tragedy, because it raises life to those heights where it borders with death (146).

The hardest aspect of death, Dühring concedes, comes not for those who suffer it but for those who are left behind (138–9). There is no more difficult experience in life, and none harder to endure and overcome, than the loss of a loved one. Grief seems an indictment of life itself. But here again Dühring thinks that we should learn to make death the measure of life. We learn to treasure life more, to cherish its uniqueness and preciousness, through death. It is only because of death that we realize the great value of what we once had. It is precisely through their death that we appreciate their lives all the more.

What, though, should we think of suicide? This seems an even harsher indictment of life. A person can be so unhappy about life that he or she is willing to annihilate it in their own person. What could be a greater demonstration of the cruelty and futility of life? But Dühring does not see suicide in this light. A person who commits suicide does not protest against life itself but against his or her fate and the demeaning or debilitating conditions under which he or she lives. He or she loves life so much that they are not willing to accept a lesser form of it. So it is the very love of life itself that makes someone decide to end a life that seems less worthy or happy (141).

As much as he believes in the value of life, Dühring is not prepared to condemn those who voluntarily end their lives (143–4). We need to realize that suicide is the result of extreme and unusual circumstances that afflict a small minority of individuals. It is difficult for us to understand fully their feelings and desperation, and all too often we simply read our feelings into their situations. Those who condemn suicide, like Schopenhauer, lack the imagination needed to understand what people go through in desperate circumstances. Schopenhauer, Dühring complains, never really abandoned the old Christian idea that suicide is contemptible because it takes away the life given by the creator (143).[42]

---

[42] This is an entirely unfair criticism on Dühring's part. Schopenhauer was not only sympathetic to those who took their own lives, but he was also highly critical of religious dogma for condemning them. See his 'Über den Selbstmord' in *Paralipomena*, §§157–60, *Sämtliche Werke*, V. 361–7. Dühring seems not to have read this essay.

7. The Political and Economic Dimension

Dühring thought that the most original and novel feature of *Der Werth des Lebens* was his application of economic theory to the question of the value of life. In the preface to the first edition he inveighs against those "school philosophers" who deny the relevance of economics and decry it as a form of materialism (v). Economists have done more to illuminate this question, he counters, than "a whole era of more narrow philosophy". His only regret, however, is that he devotes but one chapter to economics when it is so important for the issues (vi).[43]

Dühring's belief in the importance of economics brought together the two sides of his authorship. He was not only a philosopher who wrote on epistemology and ethics, but also a social theorist who wrote on economics and politics. In the 1860s he had made his name in both disciplines. What joined these apparently very different fields together in his mind was the question of the value of life, which was for him "the chief theme of philosophy".[44] Just as he applied his epistemology to this question, so he applied his economics to it.

Why, though, conceive this question in economic terms? Why should economics be relevant at all? Those "school philosophers", whom Dühring mentions in his preface, would have strongly objected to such an approach. They saw the problem of the value of life in essentially metaphysical or ethical terms. The meaning of existence, in their view, depends upon a person's attitude toward such spiritual issues as love and death, which hardly permit quantitative treatment. Economics is concerned with human beings as consumers and producers of goods, which are material issues that should not affect their attitude toward existence in general. The old school feared that an economic approach would be much too reductive, even materialistic, an undertaking sanctioned by Feuerbach's noxious dictum "*Ein Mensch ist was er ißt*".

Yet Dühring questions the entire metaphysical approach. In his view, this approach was simply too abstract, failing to appreciate the importance of particular facts. It saw the value of life chiefly as a universal and existential problem, whose solution is independent of particular forms of human organization or the specific kind of society and economy in which someone lives. But this perspective, Dühring believed, failed to see that the quality of life depends upon, and varies with, specific forms of state, society and economy.

The errors of the old metaphysical approach were for Dühring especially apparent in the case of Schopenhauer.[45] His pessimism was based on the belief that the chief evils afflicting human life are eternal and inescapable, having their roots in existence itself rather than in any specific form of human organization. Dühring notes that, in making his case for pessimism, Schopenhauer chiefly focuses on instances of physical evil and only occasionally on cases of individual moral evil. He overlooks two crucial facts:

---

[43] This is chapter VII, 'Das Gemeinleben', pp. 148–62. Despite his regrets, Dühring did not expand but shrank the economic treatment of his problem in the second edition, which drops chapter VII entirely.
[44] *Der Werth des Lebens* (1865), p. 1.   [45] *Der Werth des Lebens* (1877), p. 214.

first, that moral evil is much worse for human beings than physical evil, that physical pain does not compare with the moral suffering created by oppression and humiliation; and, second, that the chief source of moral evil comes from not individual crimes but from social and political injustice.

In the first edition of *Der Werth des Lebens* Dühring says very little about the social and political dimension of his problem. However, there is a passage in the introduction where he unmistakably alludes to it. He says that the value of life is not a theoretical but a practical problem, and that the practical problem is one of removing evil and the major obstacles to justice (12). These evils and obstacles lie first and foremost, Dühring then intimates, in "social misformations" (*sociale Mißbildungen*). He clearly means by this problematic social, political and economic institutions, though he does not elaborate further on them or how they are obstacles to the value of life.

The relevance of economics to Dühring's problem becomes clear when he eventually identifies these "social misformations". Although he does not write about them in *Der Werth des Lebens*, he elaborates on them in great detail in his two early writings on economics, *Carey's Umwälzung der Volkswirthschaftslehre* and *Capital und Arbeit*.[46] These works make it clear that Dühring thinks that the question of the value of life is connected with the main problem of economics, which is indeed the "problem of the century".[47] This problem is what Dühring and his contemporaries called "the worker question" (*die Arbeiterfrage*) or more broadly "the social question" (*die soziale Frage*). This question referred to the disturbing fact that the great mass of the population, viz., the urban working classes and rural peasantry, lived in dire poverty and had to struggle to earn the mere means of subsistence. The relevance of this problem to the question of the value of life is immediate and obvious: how can life be worth living if the overwhelming majority of people in modern society live in great deprivation?

The source of this deprivation, Dühring believes, lies primarily in the capitalist economic system, which has given rise to great inequalities in wealth. It is an illusion, he argues, to think that this economic system is a creation of nature, a product of natural laws, which work on their own independent of all human intervention.[48] Rather, the capitalist system has been created and enforced by the modern state. While economists preach laissez-faire, the truth of the matter is that they use this doctrine to disguise the capitalist's power over the government and control over legislation.

Given that the state serves capitalism, and that capitalism makes life not worth living, the only solution to the problem of the value of life must then lie with political action. But what form should this action take? Dühring believed that it should take two forms: unions, which advocate political reform and engage in bargaining for the workers; and co-operatives, which help workers save, purchase and produce.[49] These

---

[46] Eugen Dühring, *Carey's Umwälzung der Volkswirthschaftslehre und Socialwissenschaft* (Munich: E. A. Fleischmann, 1865); and *Capital und Arbeit: Neue Antworten auf alte Fragen* (Berlin: Eichhoff, 1865).
[47] Dühring, *Carey's Umwälzung*, p. 26.
[48] Ibid., pp. 91–2; and *Capital und Arbeit*, pp. 1, 29–30.
[49] See *Capital und Arbeit*, pp. 22–5, 227.

workers' organizations should also be supported by "social organizations", which would be led by intellectuals and politicians who could articulate and advocate workers' interests.[50] Dühring was largely sympathetic with the "self-help" movement formed by Hermann Schulze-Delitzsch, though he believed it was not radical enough and had been contaminated by bourgeois interests.[51] The goals of these associations would be achieved if factories were run and owned by the workers themselves and their managers received wages like everyone else.[52]

Although Dühring was sympathetic with socialism, he distanced himself from its more radical wing, especially the communism of Marx and Engels. He criticized radical socialism for several reasons: for enlarging the power of the state, which would endanger individual liberty; for its naïve idealism, which did not recognize the inherent human need for acquisition; and for its demand for revolution, which would overthrow all social and political institutions. As if to protest against the radical socialists, Dühring affirmed the value of private property, individual liberty and the ultimate separation of society and state. It was Dühring who first made a distinction between utopian and scientific socialism, which he had cast in just the opposite way from Engels.[53] While a utopian socialism is revolutionary, striving to overthrow and destroy the entire existing order, scientific socialism studies the laws of society and adapts its reforms to them. While the utopian socialist is a dreamy idealist who would destroy the machinery of society, the scientific socialist learns how to make that machinery serve his own ends.

The relevance of Dühring's economic theory to the question of the value of life becomes even more apparent when we consider his reaction to classical economic theory, especially the works of Malthus, Ricardo and Mill. To defend the possibility of having a worthy existence, Dühring believed, one has to oppose this theory. For in the hands of these authors economics had indeed become "the dismal science", the foundation for a pessimism no less depressing than that of Schopenhauer. According to Dühring, the classical British economists saw the economic order as governed by natural laws that doomed the great mass of the population to ever increasing hunger, poverty and conflict. They viewed all civil society as a conflict between individuals seeking to maximize their self-interest at the expense of others. There was competition between capitalists for markets and between workers for employment. One party could win only at the expense of their rivals. Even worse, there was Malthus's law, also adopted by Mill and Ricardo, according to which human population increases beyond the means of agriculture to produce the foods necessary for its subsistence. While the population increases "geometrically", i.e. by the multiplication of the original number, the production of agriculture increases only "arithmetically", i.e. by the addition of the original number. So even assuming an arithmetical increase, which is an optimistic assumption

---

[50] Ibid., pp. 225–7.   [51] Ibid., p. 7. Cf. *Carey's Umwälzung*, p. 90.
[52] *Carey's Umwälzung*, p. 90.
[53] See Dühring, *Capital und Arbeit*, pp. 95–6, 101–2. Engels's famous *Socialism: Utopian and Scientific* was a response to Dühring's own distinction.

given droughts and crop failures, there will be continually less food available for the population.

To combat such pessimism, Dühring championed the economic theory of the American Henry Carey (1793–1879),[54] who was highly critical of the classical British tradition. The reasons for Dühring's advocacy of Carey become clear from the first letter of his *Carey's Umwälzung der Volkswirtschaftslehre*, where he praises Carey's "optimism" because it affirms "the value of life" and the potential for change (13). Carey's critique of classical economic theory, Dühring stresses, is essentially a critique of its pessimism and quietism. It gives the masses reason to believe that they can achieve economic justice through their own efforts, and reason to doubt that hunger and competition are inevitable. Contrary to the classical economists, Carey taught that the interests of workers and capitalists can harmonize, and that the conflict between them is not inevitable but only a temporary and passing phase of economic development. Higher wages for the workers are also in the interests of capitalists, Carey argued, because if the workers' wages increase, so do demand and consumption, which creates the need for more goods and services. The real source of wealth does not lie in the profits, savings and interests of the capitalist, Carey held, but in human productivity itself, so that we should do everything necessary to ensure employment, even if that means imposing protective tariffs. Dühring also credited Carey with exposing the fundamental flaw of Malthus's theory: its failure to take into account the growth of agricultural technology, which could increase the amount of new arable land as well as yields on old cultivated lands.[55]

8. A System of Philosophy

It was part of the Schopenhauer legacy that metaphysics, despite Kantian critique, is necessary, a fundamental and indispensable field of philosophy. The Frankfurt pessimist had taught that we cannot settle the riddle of existence—whether to be or not to be—unless we first know our place and purpose in the universe, which is the task of metaphysics.

On this score, Dühring eventually agreed with his old nemesis. Without a metaphysics, he came to believe, the question of the value of life could not be definitively resolved. If we stay within the limits of experience, and if we refuse to make general statements about the nature of being as such, as the neo-Kantians and positivists insist, we cannot refute pessimism. For it is then still possible that behind experience there lies that impersonal, insatiable and incessant will to life that is the source of all suffering and evil. Against that dreadful possibility, the neo-Kantians and positivists could

---

[54] Carey's main work is his *Principles of Social Science* (Philadelphia: J. B. Lippincott & Co., 1858–60), 3 vols. Dühring used the translation of 'Dr. Adler', *Prinzipien der Socialwissenschaft* (Munich: E. A. Fleischmann, 1863–4).

[55] *Capital und Arbeit*, pp. 188–91; *Carey's Umwälzung*, pp. 62–7.

only affect indifference; they could only shrug their shoulders and declare "*je ne sais pas*". This prospect was for Dühring, however, a nightmare, an intolerable limit to enquiry. It was his aim to formulate a competing metaphysics to Schopenhauer's, one that would not only finally settle the issue that Schopenhauer had raised but also give reason for the affirmation rather than the denial of life.

In his call for the elimination of the transcendent Dühring was reacting against not only Schopenhauer but also his own earlier work. For, as we have seen, in his *Natürliche Dialektik* and the first edition of *Der Werth des Lebens* he had postulated a transcendent realm of being behind and beyond all thinking and experience, a realm for which we could have only a feeling or intuition but no discursive knowledge. The effect of that postulate was to undermine his own attempt to provide a complete immanent philosophy about the value of life, one based on reason alone. Dühring's move toward metaphysics was an attempt to put his own philosophical house in order and to rectify the deep inconsistency in his worldview.

At first blush Dühring's call for a metaphysics seems surprising. Had he not, like a true positivist, expressed his hostility toward metaphysics in *Natürliche Dialektik* and *Der Werth des Lebens?* He had indeed. But Dühring, over the years, came to distinguish between two kinds of metaphysics: speculation about the supersensible; and enquiry into our most basic concepts about the world.[56] While he rejected metaphysics in the former sense, he accepted it in the latter. In this latter sense metaphysics would eliminate all mysterious transcendent entities by arguing that being as such, the world in general, is rational or comprehensible in principle. This affirmation of metaphysics eventually became one of Dühring's major points of departure from his positivist brethren, who, he believed, had failed to see the importance of having a general worldview.[57] In his opinion, this was a responsibility that philosophy simply could not shirk.

As important as a worldview was for Dühring, he had not formulated one in either his *Natürliche Dialektik* or the first edition of *Der Werth des Lebens*. Here and there he would state his metaphysical principles; but he did not engage in a general exposition of his worldview. Although much of his argument rested on monistic and materialist assumptions, he still provided no defence of them. Dühring made up for these shortcomings in his major work of the 1870s, his *Cursus der Philosophie*, which appeared in 1875.[58] Here Dühring restates his views about the value of life; but he now places them in the context of a general metaphysics. The longer version of the title—*Cursus der Philosophie als streng wissenschaftliche Weltanschauung und Lebensgestaltung*—shows the crucial importance that Dühring still gave to the question of the value of life. The aim of the book is twofold: to provide the reader with a worldview (*Weltanschauung*), i.e. an attitude toward life, and to help him shape his

---

[56] On this distinction, see *Cursus der Philosophie*, pp. 11–12.
[57] Ibid., pp. 59, 79.
[58] E. Dühring, *Cursus der Philosophie als streng wissenschaftliche Weltanschauung und Lebensgestaltung* (Leipzig: E. Koschny, 1875). All references in parentheses are to this edition, which is the only one.

life accordingly (*Lebensgestaltung*). Dühring himself later said the book was meant to be "*ein Program des Lebens*".[59]

The worldview that Dühring expounds in his *Cursus der Philosophie* has three salient characteristics: it is monistic, materialistic and rationalist. It is therefore the perfect antithesis of Schopenhauer's worldview, which is dualistic, idealistic and irrationalist. Since these adjectives are too abstract as they stand, we need to examine the meaning of each in more detail, all the while keeping in mind its implications for the value of life.

Dühring begins his book with a bald statement of his monism: "All comprehensive being is one" (16). Since it includes everything, being has nothing beyond it. Nothing escapes its all encompassing nature. If we try to think of something outside being, we still tacitly think of it inside being insofar as we assume that it can or does exist. As just stated, such a monism seems harmless and empty because it is so abstract, capable of including all kinds of difference within itself. But the thrust and point of Dühring's monism becomes clear when he declares a little later, firmly and explicitly, that everything exists within nature (62). The realm of being and that of nature turn out to be coextensive. We are told that all reality, even all possibility, must conform to the laws of nature. Thus Dühring's monism means naturalism.

The importance of this naturalistic monism for Dühring's views about the value of life should be obvious enough. It means that there cannot be any higher reality above and beyond nature itself, so that it is pointless trying to find redemption in another world than this one. "There can be only a single reality", as Dühring put it.[60] If this is so, we have to make our peace with this world; and should this world be filled with sorrow and suffering, we have to change it.

Although the universe is one, a single unified whole, Dühring insists that it is not static and homogeneous (22). Being is not empty, deprived of all determination, and still less is it unchanging. Rather, as the whole of all that exists, being contains difference and change within itself. There is not only the permanent unity of things, but also the flowing multiplicity of things (21).

From this metaphysical principle too Dühring draws important implications for the value of life. It is only the realm of becoming, of birth and decay, creation and destruction, he avers, that makes "the stage of existence" meaningful for us. A universe that is the same in every moment would mean "the paralysis and nothingness of life" (21). Only constant movement and change satisfies the requirements of a rich and intense life of feeling (362–3).

But now an old problem arises. If being in itself is one and unchanging, what is the source of difference and change? Somehow, difference and change have to be within being, which encompasses everything; but the one and many, the permanent and changing, contradict one another. This was the classic problem for Spinoza and the German idealists, which now Dühring faces too. He admits its difficulty (24),

---

[59] *Sache, Leben und Feinde* (1902), p. 179.   [60] *Der Werth des Lebens* (1865), p. 3.

and criticizes the positivists and neo-Kantians for not facing it (79). Yet he does not pretend to have a solution for it and limits himself to pointing out the difficulties. We cannot grasp the origin of difference and becoming from the standpoint of contemporary physics, he points out, because there is no transition from a mechanical to a dynamical system (80). Many contemporary accounts of the origin of things claim that the primal homogeneous mass differentiates itself through the transformation of mass movements into atomic ones; but this does not explain the origin of the mass movements themselves (81). The Kantian-Laplacian hypothesis explains the origin of the solar system by assuming a mass of gases revolving in a single direction around a core; but it cannot explain why there is a core and why the mass moves around it (92). These admissions on Dühring's part are somewhat embarrassing because it was on just these grounds that the positivists and neo-Kantians refused to speculate in the first place. But Dühring replied that they were making artificial and arbitrary epistemic limits out of the temporary state of research; we would be better advised to wait and see the results of future research.

After its monism, the second basic characteristic of Dühring's universe is its materialism. There is nothing in the *Natürliche Dialektik* or the first edition of *Der Werth des Lebens* that prepares us for this doctrine. Indeed, in the latter work, Dühring went to pains to avoid the charge of materialism that some believed tainted his economics. But now in *Cursus der Philosophie* Dühring's materialism could not be more explicit and emphatic. "Without the guiding thread of materiality", he writes, "one relapses into illusory dreaming and baseless fictions" (62). His materialist principles are clear: "Being in general is co-extensive with material and mechanical being" (62). Or, again: "Nature is to be treated as the universal connection of matter" (62).

"What is matter?", Dühring asks. His answer is simple and straightforward: matter is the support (*Träger*) of everything actual (73). This means that matter is the permanent, the bearer of all change. It is only if we regard matter as the permanent in space, Dühring says, that we have reason to identify it with absolute being (75). We must not identify matter with its attractive and repulsive forces alone, as Schelling once did, because these forces cannot exist on their own but still have to inhere in something, which is matter. Rather than the product of its forces, matter is the basis of its forces, which are only its states (75).

Regarding the great stumbling block of materialism, the phenomena of consciousness, Dühring is remarkably uncertain and evasive. Although he admits that these phenomena are not simply matter in motion or mechanical forces, he states that their occurrence is still explicable only "through the mediation of material and mechanical events" (62). A proper psychology denies the existence of the psyche as a substance or thing, and it focuses instead on its mechanical and physiological causes alone (134). Nevertheless, Dühring still regards the realm of inner experience as a legitimate field of observation, as if pace Comte we could still have an introspective psychology after all (134). It is simply wrong, he contends, to deny the realm of consciousness, which consists in "subjective occurrences as such and their felt innerness" (135). Comte is then duly reproved for failing to recognize the need for a "theory of consciousness" (*Bewusstseinslehre*). However far we push our mechanical explanations, there will always be a gap, a difference in kind, between sensation and its material explanans (142). All things considered, Dühring's view seems to be a kind of epiphenomenalism: "Of everything that happens, the phenomena of consciousness form only an extremely limited part, and they are at first much more effect than working cause" (137). But even this position is not consistent and firm. Note that consciousness is only *more* effect than cause, implying that sometimes it is a cause.

Although Dühring admits the reality of a *sui generis* realm of consciousness, he is determined to limit its role in constituting experience and the perception of our world. Never does he allow consciousness to assume such a role that it would undermine his realism, his thesis that we have direct knowledge of objective reality. The neo-Kantians have overstated their case, he argues, when they assume that our ways of perceiving the world actually determine the content of sensation (145). The fact that we must learn to perceive the world, that we have to use inferences to perceive it correctly, does not alter the content of sensation itself, the images of intuition (*Anschauungsbilder*), which are an accurate reflection of reality itself (138, 145). The thesis that space is simply a construction of consciousness, an a priori form of intuition, is false because it alone cannot explain the perception of particular spatial relations between things (146). While the general concept of an absolute mathematical space is indeed a construction, we develop it only after the experience of particular distances between things.

Departing from his early non-cognitivist position on sensation in *Der Werth des Lebens*,[61] Dühring now maintains that sensation is a cognitive state, and that through it we have an immediate cognition of the relations between real things (138). Sensation is now declared to be "the interpreter of objective relations" (146). The basis for this realist theory of sensation is Dühring's claim that all sensation consists in the feeling of resistance (147–8). All sensations, not only tactual but also visual, arise from immediate contact with external reality, which gives rise to a feeling of resistance. We know that there is something external to our inner states because there is something that resists our activity, something that refuses to be the mere product of will and imagination. It is this feeling of resistance that integrates our consciousness into the mechanical system of nature, and shows how it is the product of external forces (147).

Only in the second edition of *Der Werth des Lebens*, which was published two years after *Cursus*, does Dühring spell out the meaning of materialism for his theory of the value of life. Materialism is for him the doctrine that liberates mankind from all forms of religious superstition. It consists in three denials: (1) the denial of the existence of the soul; (2) the denial of the existence of immortality; and (3) the denial of the existence of God.[62] Dühring was convinced that the modern age would be completely

---

[61] See section 4 of this chapter. Cf. *Der Werth des Lebens* (1865), p. 38, and *Cursus der Philosophie*, p. 138.
[62] *Der Werth des Lebens* (1877), pp. 46–7.

secular: "In fact the new spirit can rise only to the degree that religions fall" (440–1). The basis and mark of that new secular mentality would be, of course, materialism.

The third chief characteristic of Dühring's system—its rationalism—is apparent from his principle of the sovereignty of reason. Though they are not distinguished by Dühring himself, this principle involves three central theses. First, that philosophy and science, whose principles and methods are the embodiment of reason, are the ultimate arbiters or standards of knowledge (6–7). The beliefs of religion, morality and the state fall under their tribunal, and they have no appeal against it. Second, that the principles of logic and mathematics are laws of being itself; they are not mere laws of thought, or rules for ordering our thinking about reality, because they represent the structure of reality itself (11, 30–1). Third, there are, in principle, no limits to scientific knowledge; in other words, there is nothing that exists that is unknowable, viz., the Kantian thing-in-itself. As Dühring put it: "What is nothing for thought exactly corresponds to nothing in the world and reality" (14).

The confidence and vehemence with which Dühring puts forward such a radical rationalism is astonishing and in direct proportion to his inability to demonstrate it. Yet it is on its basis that he distinguishes his own philosophy, quite correctly, from that of the neo-Kantians and positivists. Dühring agrees with the neo-Kantians and positivists insofar as they too affirm the first thesis; but he disagrees with them sharply insofar as they deny the third. Both the neo-Kantians and positivists think that there are limits to scientific knowledge, which are circumscribed by possible experience. Dühring bluntly rejects such epistemic modesty, such "self-denial of the intellect". He chastens the neo-Kantians for their fantasy of an unknowable thing-in-itself (38); and he castigates the positivists for committing the worst sin of all, "high treason against science" (59).

Dühring's radical rationalism seems to have an unlikely ally in the absolute idealism of Schelling and Hegel, who also affirmed the second and third theses with their principle of subject-object identity.[63] But this similarity is really only apparent. Dühring's rationalism is not idealistic but realistic. We are not allowed to identify reality with thought, as the absolute idealists did, because there is really only a correspondence between them (42). Our concept of the world is not the same as the world in its existence but only in its formal structure. To think that thought is the structure of the world itself is a fallacy, Dühring claims, because all thought presupposes some subject or thinker whereas the world itself is in its existence distinct from the thought about it (17–18). The problems of a too close identification of thought with reality are apparent, Dühring contends, in the Hegelian system, whose dialectic confuses logical contradiction with the real opposition of the forces in nature (31–2).

The radical rationalism of Dühring's *Cursus der Philosophie* marks an important advance over his earlier position in the *Natürliche Dialektik*. For it is with this rationalism

---

[63] The comparison was made by Hans Vaihinger, *Hartmann, Dühring und Lange: Zur Geschichte der deutschen Philosophie im XIX Jahrhundert* (Iserlohn: Baedeker, 1876), pp. 50, 99.

that Dühring finally eliminates that transcendent realm of being which blocked his aspiration to develop a completely immanent philosophy. Gone in the *Cursus* is all reference to the transcendent, to the unthinkable ground of all being and thinking, which stubbornly remained in the earlier work. After explicitly raising the question whether the ground of all thinking and being transcends thinking about it, Dühring now explicitly concludes that it does not: "That which makes conscious thought possible cannot lie deeper than the complete product itself" (50). The powers behind our thinking, we are now told, "in fact lie this side of the ideal sphere". With these simple lines, Dühring had finally eliminated all trace of hypostasis from his system.

However important it was for Dühring to remove this inconsistency, the ultimate motive behind his radical rationalism lay with his animus against Schopenhauer. The importance and power of this animus becomes clear when Dühring declares that, if our thought did not correspond with being, then all knowledge would be "ein nichtiger Schein", which is exactly what "a mystically inclined philosophy wants it to be" (40). Though he is not named, the allusion to Schopenhauer is plain. Here the reason for Dühring's vehement rejection of the neo-Kantian and positivist limits of knowledge becomes all too plain: it leaves a conceptual space open for Schopenhauer's pessimism. Behind and beyond these limits of knowledge there could lie that horrible Schopenhauerian will, whose blind and ceaseless urgings make life a spectacle of misery and despair. Dühring would later find the weakest point in positivism in its leaving itself vulnerable to this horrible possibility, which could be eliminated only through a more thoroughgoing rationalism.[64]

9. Replacing Religion

The driving force behind Dühring's philosophy had always been fundamentally anti-religious. His so-called "philosophy of reality" was first and foremost motivated by the urge to dispel all forms of transcendence, by the demand to seek redemption in this world alone. The aim behind his early logic and epistemology had been to expose all forms of hypostasis, the reification that is the very source of religion. Mankind had enslaved itself through hypostasis, by inventing supernatural things and forces to which it had subjugated itself. The task was then to expose that hypostasis, so that mankind would become self-conscious of its autonomy. Life on earth would be finally worth living once mankind reclaimed the energies and powers it had once squandered on heaven.

Dühring was convinced that, in the modern era, the decline of religion is inevitable. The mechanism behind its demise was clear and simple. If the source of religion lies in fear and superstition, in the assumption that gods or spirits are the causes of extraordinary natural events (thunder, famine and plagues), then it will disappear once science discovers the natural causes of such events. Hence the more science advances, the

[64] Dühring, *Kritische Geschichte der Philosophie*, p. 517.

more religion retreats. And so the modern age, which expands and rests its case with science, will be necessarily a secular one: "In fact the new spirit can rise only to that degree that the religions sink."[65] A world rid of divine domination—the realm of spirits—was then ripe and ready for human domination.

Yet the imminent end of religion posed a problem. The banishment of the gods from the face of the earth left a vacuum. Now that religion would disappear, what would replace it? People needed some kind of worldview, some system of beliefs, to give meaning to their lives, to find their place within the whole of things. Morality alone was not enough; although its principles were valid independent of religion, they did not help the individual to face death. Sooner or later, each individual had to reconcile himself with the order of the cosmos, which would destroy him just as it created him.

By the late 1870s this problem began to trouble Dühring. His first effort to address it appears in the final chapter of the second edition of *Der Werth des Lebens*, which first appeared in 1877.[66] It was one of Dühring's most important departures from Comte's positivism that he believed in the necessity of a metaphysics, a general worldview, the impotence of science alone to answer all questions about the meaning of life. Although Comte too felt that there needed to be a system of belief to fill the gap left by the disappearance of religion, his own solution to the problem—a new scientific cult and catechism—only revealed how little he had freed himself from old religious habits and superstitions. While his new cult addressed the heart, it compromised the mind. What was needed was a completely new worldview, one that satisfied heart and mind while still making no concessions to old superstitions and rites.

Which philosophy would be the new worldview? Dühring's own, of course. It would be that monistic, materialistic and rationalist metaphysics that he had just expounded in his *Cursus der Philosophie*. He had always intended that philosophy to be a worldview, i.e. not only a system or theory but also a guide to life. At the close of the work he wrote: "My philosophy is no mere system of knowledge, but above all things a plea for a new attitude or disposition (*Gesinnung*) toward a more noble humanity."[67] This "new attitude" or "disposition" involves not only a whole new way of thinking about the world, but also the willingness to live by it and the effort to change the world according to it.

Dühring especially stresses the practical side of his new worldview. If it were to replace religion, the new worldview would have to include an ethic, just like all religions. He cautioned that the good life could not be found in the realm of theory alone (267–8). To make life worth living, it is not enough to think about the world; it is also necessary to change it, to make it conform to our ideals. Hence Dühring is highly critical of the classical philosophical tradition because it saw the highest good in the realm of contemplation alone. The German idealists, he argued, had never really

---

[65] *Cursus der Philosophie*, pp. 440–1.
[66] *Der Werth des Lebens* (1877), 'Zehntes Capitel: Ausgleichung mit der Weltordnung in Gesinnung und That', pp. 267–301.
[67] *Cursus der Philosophie*, p. 547.

broken with this tradition. The romantics too had followed it, though they gave it an aesthetic twist by seeing contemplation as artistic insight.

Dühring states that the aim behind his new worldview is to create in the reader a new "Gesinnung". This is an untranslatable term which refers to not only a person's intentions but also their dispositions to act on them. He defines "Gesinnung" as "the light of thinking and research with the warmth of a noble and reflective willing" (279). This new attitude would involve a whole way of thinking and acting, a readiness to change the world according to the basic mandates of economic justice and human perfection.

What exact form should this new worldview take? Dühring did not expect the general public to read his *Cursus der Philosophie*, which was written for university students and professional philosophers. He realized that his philosophy, if it were to replace religion, would have to be more popular. It was the great advantage of religion that it reached the hearts and minds of the general public, so that any philosophy replacing it would somehow have to do the same. On this score Dühring criticized David Friedrich Strauss for his "egoism", because his proposed replacement for religion was only a form of aestheticism inaccessible to the great mass of the public (270).[68]

Granted that philosophy should be popular, how could it become so? What form should its exposition take? In the second edition of *Der Werth des Lebens* Dühring envisaged a series of popular writings (*Volksschriften*) that would consist in simplified summaries of the latest science and plain expositions of the philosophy based upon them. These writings would teach "the laws of nature... good and ennobled morals... and correct thinking about the whole of things" (277). But on no account, Dühring insisted, should these popular writings be poetic or mythological. That would be to lapse into the old religious ways. The attempt by the romantics to create a new mythology for the modern age shows how little they had freed themselves from religious ways of thinking. For similar reasons, these popular writings could not be anything like catechisms *à la* Comte. They would eschew any attempt to be authoritative, and they would instead encourage readers to think for themselves.

Although Dühring clearly wanted his worldview to replace religion, he would often complain about the phrase "replacement for religion" (275). Too many replacements for religion tended to satisfy religious impulses when the real task was to eradicate them. The problem was not to find freedom in religion but freedom from religion (276, 280). But there is one aspect of Dühring's new worldview that shows that the old religious impulse never really left him. This is his insistence that the individual needs to find reconciliation (*Ausgleichung*) with the universe as a whole (281). The object of a new worldview should not just be humanity, as Feuerbach thought, but also the whole cosmos, the universe as a whole (281, 286). We reach such reconciliation, Dühring explains,

---

[68] Dühring takes issue with David Friedrich Strauss's *Der Alte und der neue Glaube*, Zweite Auflage (Leipzig: Hirzel, 1872). Strauss proposed cultivating literary and musical classics as a substitute for religion.

only when we identify with the cosmos as a whole and only when we sense our oneness with all things (281). There is even something reminiscent of Schleiermacher's "intuition of the universe" in Dühring's claim that the individual needs to identify with the universe. Hence he stresses the etymological connection of *Gesinnung* with *Sinn*, suggesting, like Schleiermacher, that having the proper attitude and disposition to things involves a way of perceiving things.

Dühring's demand for reconciliation with the universe, plus his monistic, naturalistic and rationalist metaphysics, is reminiscent of no one more than Spinoza. There is indeed nothing wrong at all with calling Dühring's worldview Spinozistic—at least if we keep in mind Dühring's own interpretation of Spinoza. The chapter on Spinoza in his *Kritische Geschichte der Philosophie* is highly sympathetic to the Jewish philosopher.[69] Spinoza's life was the very model of "philosophische Gesinnung" (289). Dühring admired Spinoza's intellectual independence, his refusal to belong to any form of institutional religion after his banishment from the Jewish community. The spirit of Spinoza's system Dühring finds in its monism and naturalism, in its abolition of everything supernatural, religious and mental. If Spinoza were consistent, he argues, he would not have made thought an attribute of God and would have accepted a complete materialism (298, 302). The pantheism of Spinoza's system is for Dühring a mere poetic colouring, which has nothing to do with its real naturalistic content (293, 315–16).

Throughout the late 1870s and early 1880s Dühring continued to think about the question of the replacement for religion in the new world order. In 1881 he published an entire book devoted to the issue, his *Der Ersatz der Religion durch Vollkommeneres*.[70] This book marks a significant shift from Dühring's earlier position. Gone entirely is the sympathy with Spinoza, the victim of Dühring's increasingly virulent anti-Semitism. Spinoza's metaphysics and ethics are dismissed as a "Jewish worldview" which is completely unsuitable for the Aryan culture of the future.[71] The discrepancy with the earlier work is most apparent, however, in Dühring's new metaphysics. Dühring now insists that man can find value in his life, and that he can reconcile himself with death, only if he finds goodness and justice in "the ground and basis of all things" or "the whole and deepest foundation of things" (159–60, 161–2). In his earlier works Dühring held that human beings create all the value in the world, which comes solely from their will; the worth of existence is not inherent in it but created by us. This was the very core of Dühring's "heroic conception of life". Now, however, he maintains that value must be something objective in the very nature of things, because only that will answer to our deepest longing for reconciliation with the universe. Dühring goes on to insist that this objective good and justice in the world is perceivable only by "Gemüth", i.e. by one's

---

[69] *Kritische Geschichte* (1894), pp. 283–321.
[70] *Der Ersatz der Religion durch Vollkommeneres und die Ausscheidung alles Judenthums durch den modernen Völkergeist*, Zweite Auflage (Berlin: P. Kufahl, 1897). The first edition appeared in 1881. Here we cite the second edition.
[71] Ibid., pp. 53, 78–9, 155, 172, 201.

whole soul, which comprises "the entirety of noble feelings and motives" (174). He stresses especially the role of feeling in perceiving the good, because "Gemüth" means "a unique and better kind of character from the side of feeling" (*Empfindung*) (174). The emphasis on feeling as the instrument of cognition marks a clear departure from Dühring's rationalism in the *Cursus der Philosophie*.

By 1883, then, Dühring's development had come full circle. That dimension of being that transcends all thinking and that is accessible only to feeling now returns to its honoured place in Dühring's philosophy. He had originally postulated it in his *Natürliche Dialektik* and the first edition of *Der Werth des Lebens*; but he had all but eliminated it in his *Cursus der Philosophie*, where his rationalism is most explicit and excessive. But now it returns in *Der Ersatz der Religion* to reassure the individual that the world is not a meaningless realm barren of moral value. The recrudescence of this dimension within the topography of Dühring's philosophy shows how far he was from completely disavowing the religious legacy. For that dimension of being is really the moral world order of the Judaeo-Christian tradition. Despite his hostility to Judaism and Christianity, Dühring could not bring himself to abjure it. Positivism, it turned out, was too hard an ethic even for so heartless and fearless a man as Eugen Dühring.

7
The Optimistic Pessimism of Eduard von Hartmann

1. A Fashionable Pessimist

The most famous pessimist in the age of *Weltschmerz* was neither Schopenhauer nor Nietzsche but someone who has nearly passed into oblivion: Eduard von Hartmann (1842–1906).[1] But if he is almost forgotten today, Hartmann was a celebrity in his age. When his *Philosophie des Unbewussten* first appeared in 1869,[2] it created a sensation and became a philosophical bestseller. The first edition rapidly sold out, and in the next decade the book went through no less than eight editions.[3] Hartmann's philosophy became the hot topic in literary circles, and droves of articles, reviews, pamphlets and whole books appeared, either attacking or defending it. Such was the fuss raised by Hartmann's work that a bibliography published in 1881 of all the "Hartmann Literatur" from 1869 to 1880 listed some 750 items.[4] According to one reviewer writing in 1880, Hartmann was "the best known, the most important, and the most discussed among the German philosophers of the present".[5]

Why was Hartmann so famous? Why was his book so important for his contemporaries? It is very difficult today to understand all the hubbub surrounding Hartmann's book. The *Philosophie des Unbewussten* is a hefty tome whose aims are obscure, whose arguments are intricate and whose style, while clear and straightforward, is flat, dry and boring. There were few in its day who understood, and even fewer willing to discuss, the details of its metaphysics. What did catch the attention of the public, however, was Hartmann's pessimism, which he expounded at some length in the final chapters

---

[1] For recent literature on Hartmann, see Michael Pauen, *Pessimismus: Geschichtsphilosophie, Metaphysik und Moderne von Nietzsche bis Spengler* (Berlin: Akademie Verlag, 1997), pp.118–30; Ludger Lütkehaus, *Nichts: Abschied vom Sein, Ende der Angst* (Frankfurt: Zweitausendeins, 2002), pp. 223–42; and Jean-Claude Wolf, *Eduard von Hartmann: Ein Philosoph der Gründerzeit* (Würzburg: Königshusen & Nemann, 2006).

[2] Eduard von Hartmann, *Philosophie des Unbewussten: Versuch einer Weltanschauung* (Berlin: Duncker, 1869).

[3] For all the editions and copies printed, see Carl Heymons, *Eduard von Hartmann, Erinnerungen aus den Jahren 1868–1881* (Berlin: Duncker, 1882), p. 60. For many years Heymons was Hartmann's publisher.

[4] See Olga Plümacher, 'Chronologisches Verzeichniss der Hartmann Literatur von 1869–1880', in *Der Kampf um's Unbewusste* (Berlin: Duncker, 1881), pp. 115–50.

[5] According to an anonymous opinion in *Das Buch für Alle*, Heft1 (1880), p. 7.

of his book.⁶ To many, Hartmann seemed to offer not only a more rigorous and systematic pessimism than Schopenhauer, but also a kinder and gentler version, one which combines pessimism about human happiness with optimism about cultural progress.⁷ Even if we could not be happy in this life, Hartmann taught, we could still create, through constant striving and conscientious effort, a morally and culturally better world. It was an attractive message, an appealing selling point. Hartmann's book showed the citizen of the new Reich how he or she could achieve redemption without having to practise a Christian or Buddhistic ethic of renunciation. One could have all the savvy and sophistication of pessimism—all the airs and graces of worldly wisdom—and still have confidence in the progress promised by the new Reich.

For a younger generation of pessimists, for Nietzsche, Bahnsen and Mainländer, Hartmann's pessimism was a philistine betrayal of Schopenhauer's message. To them, Hartmann represented the new establishment—the authoritarian Bismarckian state allied with nationalism—and he had twisted Schopenhauer's philosophy to serve its ends. To what extent their charges were justified I will consider in a later section.⁸

Because he had formulated a more popular and systematic version of pessimism, Hartmann's philosophy—not Schopenhauer's—became the centre of the controversy surrounding pessimism. Most discussion of the topic in the 1870s and 1880s would focus on his book. For better or worse, Bahnsen's, Mainländer's and Nietzsche's writings would be pushed into the background.

Although Hartmann became famous chiefly from his central role in the pessimism controversy, it would be a mistake to see his historical importance in these terms alone. As a philosopher, Hartmann was greater than that controversy, and he deserves recognition for his wider place in German intellectual history. That place is firm and clear: Hartmann was the last great representative of the metaphysical idealist tradition.⁹ He very much falls into the same late idealist tradition as Trendelenburg and Lotze, who self-consciously upheld the idealist legacy after Hegel.¹⁰ There is in Hartmann the same circle of ideas that we find in these late idealists: a concern to preserve the idealist heritage in an age of scientific specialization; a commitment to a teleological metaphysics, to "the organic view of the world", in opposition to materialism and atheism; and an attempt to found that old metaphysics on a new method, a more empirical inductive approach instead of the a priori procedures of the past. As the years wore on, Hartmann

---

⁶ See *Philosophie des Unbewussten*, Zweite vermehrte Auflage (Berlin: Duncker, 1870), CXI–XIII, pp. 552–681. Unless otherwise indicated, all references to Hartmann's work will be to the second edition.
⁷ See the *Prospect* (Berlin: Duncker, 1881), pp.2–4, which cites many current reviews and opinions about Hartmann's pessimism.
⁸ See section 8 below.
⁹ I say expressly "metaphysical" idealist tradition to distinguish this idealist tradition from its neo-Kantian counterpart, which would continue into the 20th century in the work of Hermann Cohen and Ernst Cassirer.
¹⁰ See my *Late German Idealism: Trendelenburg and Lotze* (Oxford: OUP, 2013). The omission of Hartmann from this work, I now realize, was a mistake. It was only after the book was in print, in spring 2013, that I began a detailed study of Hartmann.

became more self-conscious of his role as a defender of the idealist tradition, and he realized that his views were becoming unfashionable and incomprehensible to the young. All the same, however, he stood his ground, insisting that nothing was more important for the culture of his age than the revival of the idealist tradition.[11]

It is in Hartmann's attempt to preserve the legacy of idealism that we can understand another aspect of his success and appeal to his age. The idealist tradition had always proffered a middle path between the extremes of a materialist atheism and an antiquated theism; it had promised a rational justification, through its metaphysics, of the beliefs in God and providence. There was still such a thing, the idealists held, as rational religious belief. No one defended this conviction more systematically and fervently than Eduard von Hartmann. For an age which had not outgrown its need for religion, but which also insisted on reason and science, Hartmann seemed to have something to offer. He was for many the last great hope for a rational religion.

Who was Eduard von Hartmann? As the "von" in his name indicates, Hartmann had an aristocratic background.[12] He was born 23 February 1842, the son of a Prussian army officer who was stationed in Berlin, the city where Hartmann would spend all his childhood and almost all his adult life. Though his family was not wealthy, Hartmann inherited sufficient means to live independently, which gave him the time and energy to write his many books and articles.[13] In his youth he showed great interest in music and drawing; but not regarding himself as sufficiently talented in either, he resolved to follow family tradition and try a military career. A knee injury forced him to resign, however, and he soon found himself crippled and unemployed. The only resource he had after his resignation from the military was, he later said, "his ideas". While in bed or a wheelchair he began reading intensively and writing down his thoughts, which eventually coalesced into the plan for the *Philosophie des Unbewussten*. The composition of the book lasted three years, from 1864 to 1867, after which it was abandoned in a desk drawer for a year before it was rescued by a publisher. After the enormous success of the book, Hartmann was offered academic positions—in Leipzig, Tübingen and Berlin—but he turned them all down. His knee injury prevented lectures from a podium; but, in any case, he preferred his status as an independent writer. Hartmann would spend the rest of his life reading and writing in Berlin, living in isolation from the academic world, though constantly engaged in intellectual controversies. He never repeated the success of his first book; but then again he did not need to; his fame was already firmly established.

---

[11] Alma von Hartmann, his second wife, fully conscious of his position in history, gave a series of lectures in Berlin under the title: *Zurück zum Idealismus: Zehn Vorträge* (Berlin: Schwetschke & Sohn, 1902).

[12] All the details of this account come from Hartmann's autobiographical essay 'Mein Entwickelungsgang', which covers his life to 1874 and which appears in his *Gesammelte Studien und Aufsätze* (Berlin: Duncker, 1876), pp. 11–41. Another useful account of Hartmann's life appears in Arthur Drews, *Eduard von Hartmanns philosophisches System im Grundriss*, Weite Ausgabe (Heidelberg: Winter, 1906), pp. 1–70. Though Drews's account is based on Hartmann's, it also includes other important details.

[13] For a full bibliography, see Alma von Hartmann, 'Chronologische Übersicht der Schriften von Eduard von Hartmann', *Kant-Studien*, 17 (1912), 501–20.

No less than Dühring, Hartmann was a political writer, convinced that the philosopher had to take a stand on the main issues of his day. Though he wrote no systematic treatise on political philosophy, he published over the decades scores of articles on politics.[14] Hartmann's political convictions were very conservative, standing firmly and fully on the right wing of the political spectrum of his day. An admirer of Kaiser Wilhelm I and Bismarck,[15] he was a believer in the old Prussian monarchy as well as the values of the military that sustained it. He celebrated the creation of the new German *Reich*, though he greatly feared the growing democratic forces it had unleashed.[16] His two great enemies were the chief threats to the new *Reich*: social democracy and the ultramontanism of the Roman Catholic Church.[17] On two issues Hartmann was very liberal: the need to separate church and state; and the rights of religious minorities. His one book on political issues, *Das Judenthum in Gegenwart und Zukunft*,[18] concerned the Jewish question. Hartmann advocates the complete assimilation of Jews into the new *Reich*, though at the price of surrendering their separate identity.[19] Though no liberal, Hartmann's greater sympathy toward the Jews contrasts markedly with Dühring's unremitting hostility.

In his social and economic independence, in his reservations about the academic world and in his conservative social and political views, Hartmann reminds us of no one more than Schopenhauer. The resemblance was not accidental. Like Dühring, Hartmann was deeply influenced by Schopenhauer from an early age. His reading of Schopenhauer goes back to the autumn of 1863, his first year after retirement from the military.[20] Hartmann's theory of the will, his pessimism and his attitude toward Christianity all reveal his debts to Schopenhauer. It would be a mistake, however, to see Hartmann as a Schopenhauerian, as many of his critics, and some of Schopenhauer's disciples, first viewed him. He rightly protested against this conflation, and he constantly took issue with Schopenhauer. His own philosophy is best described as a

---

[14] The articles were collected in three anthologies: *Zwei Jahrzehnte deutscher Politik* (Leipzig: Friedrich, 1889); *Tagesfragen* (Leipzig: Hermann Haacke, 1896); and *Zur Zeitgeschichte. Neue Tagesfragen.* (Leipzig: Hermann Haacke, 1900). After Hartmann's death, Alma von Hartmann published a miscellany of his political views, *Eduard von Hartmann: Gedanken über Staat, Politik und Sozialismus* (Leipzig: Kröner Verlag, 1923).

[15] See his 'Kaiser Wilhelm I: Ein Nachruf', in *Zwei Jahrzehnte*, pp. 328–40.

[16] See his 'Die Gefahr der Demokratie' and 'Unsre Verfassung', in *Tagesfragen*, pp. 25–44, 45–57. Hartmann supported Bismarck's legislation against the socialists; see his 'Für das Socialistengesetz', in *Zwei Jahrzehnte*, pp. 170–3.

[17] See 'Die Gegner und die Stützen des Reichs', in *Zwei Jahrzehnte*, pp. 97–106.

[18] Eduard von Hartmann, *Das Judenthum in Gegenwart und Zukunft* (Leipzig: Friedrich, 1884).

[19] Hartmann's uncompromising insistence on "*Friede durch Verschmelzung*", the slogan for his position, was not consistent with his own liberal stance toward religious minorities. It is a mistake, however, to regard Hartmann as "an anti-Semite". His book was written against the anti-Semitic movement, and is in many places sympathetic to the Jews, whose national character is held up as a model for the Germans to emulate. See *Das Judenthum in Gegenwart und Zukunft*, pp. 17, 23. For a more critical assessment of Hartmann's attitude, see Wolf, *Eduard von Hartmann*, pp. 203–14.

[20] Drews, *Hartmanns System*, p. 15.

Schellingian synthesis of Schopenhauer with Hegel. Exactly how—and whether—such a strange concoction holds together we will consider in later sections.[21]

Our main task in this chapter is to provide an exposition of Hartmann's pessimism, a necessity if we are to have a clear idea of the doctrine that became the chief subject of discussion in the 1870s and 1880s. In treating Hartmann's pessimism, we will have to go the long and slow route, which is the path through his metaphysics. Like Schopenhauer's pessimism and Dühring's optimism, Hartmann's attitude toward life is deeply embedded in his metaphysics, which provides it with both its foundation and context. In his later years, under pressure from criticism, Hartmann attempted to separate his pessimism from his metaphysics, and conversely, as if each could stand on its own without the other.[22] But this polemical ploy does not represent his abiding attitude and his deeper convictions: that ethics without metaphysics has no foundation and "hangs in mid air".[23]

2. The Unconscious

Hartmann's chief work, *Philosophie des Unbewussten*, is devoted entirely to the theme indicated in its title: the unconscious. Hartmann spends almost all his time and energy in his massive book attempting to demonstrate, with all the latest results of the natural sciences, the existence of a single unconscious force throughout all of nature. We are shown the existence of this force in instinct, nerves, reflex movements, muscle contractions, organic growth, sexual love, feeling, the origin of language, sense perception, mysticism and history. A chapter is devoted to each of these phenomena. But why all the toil and trouble? Why is it so important to demonstrate the existence of the unconscious in all these spheres? Hartmann scarcely explains. His fundamental concept seems unmotivated and pointless. After reading more than 700 pages (in the second edition), the reader is no wiser about why he has been taken on such a long and arduous journey.

To understand why the concept of the unconscious was so important for Hartmann, we have to go back in history, back to the late 1860s, the years when Hartmann first conceived his philosophy. That decade still stood under the shadow of the social and political struggles of the 1840s, which had left behind a profound ideological schism. There were two competing worldviews: the materialism of the far left and the theism of the far right. For the young Hartmann, neither extreme was acceptable. Materialism reduces the world down to a machine without meaning, value or purpose; and theism is an anthropomorphic, anthropocentric anachronism which is scarcely credible in

---

[21] See sections 4–6 of this chapter.
[22] See Eduard Hartmann, 'Die Stellung des Pessimismus in meinem philosophischen System', in *Zur Geschichte und Begründung des Pessimismus*, Zweite, erweiter Auflage (Leipzig: Hermann Haacke, 1891), pp. 18–28, p. 25. This important article appears only in the second edition of this work.
[23] See Hartmann's comment in *Phänomenologie des sittlichen Bewußtseins* (Berlin: Wegweiser Verlag, 1924), p. 610.

the modern world. Hartmann accepted the results of Strauss's historical criticism of the Bible, and of Feuerbach's humanist analysis of religious belief. He rejected, however, their atheism. Though he advocated jettisoning theism in the future, he believed, unlike Dühring, that some form of religion is still essential in the modern world. However autonomous the modern individual might be, Hartmann felt, he or she still needs some sense of meaning in life, some feeling of belonging to a larger whole; and that sense and that feeling can be provided only by religion. A world in which individuals seek only their own self-interest will result in complete anarchy, a war of all against all, a result undesired by even the most selfish individual.

So if materialism and theism are unsatisfactory, what worldview should replace them? Hartmann's answer was what he called "pantheism" or "monistic spiritualism".[24] According to this worldview, at least as Hartmann vaguely defines it, there is a single, universal "substance or subject" which exists throughout all of nature, and which is rational and purposive. Since this substance is intelligent and acts for ends, it is not material and not a mere machine; and since it is an impersonal being immanent in and co-extensive with the whole of nature, it is not anthropocentric or anthropomorphic. If we assume that there is such a universal subject or substance, Hartmann reasons, we will be able to give the individual some sense of meaning and feeling of belonging. The individual will find purpose in his life when he understands that his actions help to fulfil the plan of the universe; and he will gain a feeling of belonging when he recognizes that he is an integral part of the universal whole.

Granted that such pantheism or spiritual monism avoids the problems of materialism and atheism, the problem remains why we should assume it in the first place. Obviously, it was not enough for Hartmann simply to postulate the possibility of such a substance or subject; it was also necessary for him to demonstrate its reality. But, to do that, he first had to remove a weighty obstacle that stood in his way: the prejudice that all subjectivity, purposiveness or intelligence involves consciousness. It was no accident that this widespread conviction of modern philosophy was a common premise of both theism and materialism. The materialist denies that there is purposiveness in nature because he holds that all intelligence is limited to the realm of human consciousness; and the theist denies that the divine is in nature because he maintains that only God is intelligent and self-conscious and not his creation. The materialist and theist were therefore uncommon bedfellows, committed to limiting intelligence to the realm of human or divine consciousness, which they refused to locate in the totality or whole of nature itself. Hartmann could clear the path for his pantheism or spiritual monism, then, only if he first contested this crucial premise, i.e. only if he first undermined the view that subjectivity or intelligence requires consciousness. The realm of the unconscious would be that sphere of subjectivity,

---

[24] Hartmann first explains the importance of this doctrine in his *Die Selbstzersetzung des Christenthums und die Religion der Zukunft* (Berlin: Duncker, 1874), pp. 99–121.

purposiveness or intelligence that existed throughout all of nature but that does not necessarily appear as consciousness.

It should now be clear why Hartmann went to all that toil and trouble to prove the existence of the unconscious. He was attempting to demonstrate that there is purposiveness and intelligence in nature. That had been a classic thesis of Schelling's and Hegel's *Naturphilosophie*. But it was a risky and controversial business for Hartmann to revive it in the 1860s, and for two reasons: first, because *Naturphilosophie* had become discredited; and, second, because this was the breakthrough decade for Darwinism in Germany, which for many spelled the end of the teleological worldview. Darwin throws a long shadow over the *Philosophie des Unbewussten,* and it was not least because of him that Hartmann laboured so mightily to build his case for the unconscious.[25]

Prima facie it might seem that Hartmann had a mighty precedent for his theory of the unconscious: namely, Schopenhauer. For Schopenhauer had made the will the essence of reality in itself, and he had conceived it as a blind striving and restless urge underneath the realm of consciousness. As much as Hartmann derived great inspiration and sustenance from Schopenhauer's philosophy in the 1860s, he still found Schopenhauer's theory of the will more a challenge than an aid. Schopenhauer, it turns out, was a third strange bedfellow in that odd materialist-theist liaison, for he too limited subjectivity or intelligence to the realm of consciousness. Subjectivity or intelligence belongs for Schopenhauer to the realm of representation, which is for him co-extensive with that of consciousness. Because Schopenhauer conceives the will in itself as a *blind* striving or *aimless* urge, and because he so clearly separates the realms of will and representation, he refuses to attribute intelligence or design to nature itself. This is especially clear from his *Über den Willen in der Natur* where he expressly rejects the old teleological conception of nature, according to which its order is the product of intelligence or design.[26] Although Schopenhauer attributes a kind of purposiveness to nature, he insists that it has to be explained as the product of the will alone; what might seem to be the work of design is really the work of a blind drive.[27]

So Hartmann had to expand the concept of the unconscious beyond its limits in Schopenhauer's philosophy. The unconscious would have to involve not only volition but also cognition, not only the realm of the will but also that of the idea or representation. A will makes sense, Hartmann argued,[28] only if we can attribute purposes or ends

---

[25] Hartmann takes issue with Darwin in several places in *Philosophie des Unbewussten* (1870), pp. 192, 237, 521, 531. He would discuss Darwin more fully in *Wahrheit und Irrtum im Darwinismus* (Berlin: Duncker, 1875). In *Das Unbewusste vom Standpukt der Physiologie und Descendenztheorie* (Berlin: Duncker, 1872), Hartmann provided an anonymous self-critique from the standpoint of his positivist critics, who were much embarrassed when he eventually revealed his authorship. On this episode, see Drews, *Hartmanns System im Grundriss*, pp. 35–7.

[26] *Über den Willen in der Natur,* in *Sämtliche Werke,* ed. Freiherr von Löhneysen (Stuttgart: Insel, 1968), III. 358.

[27] Ibid. III. 360–1.

[28] See the 'Einleitung' to *Philosophie des Unbewussten* (1870), pp. 19–21. See also AIV, pp. 90–2.

to it; and we can do that only if we also attribute representations, ideas or intelligence to it, because a creature acts for the sake of ends only if it has some representation or idea of them.

There were, of course, other precedents for Hartmann's concept of the unconscious; if Schopenhauer was far from it, other philosophers were much closer to it. In the introduction to *Philosophie des Unbewusstens* Hartmann duly discusses and gratefully acknowledges his historical precedents. First and foremost among them was Leibniz, who affirmed the existence of subconscious *petites perceptions*. Even closer to Hartmann was the early Schelling, who in his *Naturphilosophie* assumed the existence of subconscious and purposive activity throughout all of nature. Hartmann saw his own philosophy as in fundamental respects a revival of Schelling's *Naturphilosophie*, though he stressed the importance of following a more cautious empirical method and of avoiding the speculative fantasies that had marred the work of his glorious predecessor.

It is now possible to understand Hartmann's attitude toward his great idealist forebears, Schelling and Hegel. Hartmann saw himself as a preserver and reviver of the idealist tradition, the memory of which was rapidly fading in Germany. The great value of that tradition, he believed, is that it provides a sustainable metaphysics for a future religion, one that avoids the pitfalls of modern materialism and traditional theism.[29] But that tradition can be revived, Hartmann stressed, only by reforming its methodology, by dropping its methods of speculative construction and a priori deduction, and by adopting a more inductive and analytic approach which is based upon the observation and experiment of the new sciences.[30] Hence the motto of the *Philosophie des Unbewussten*—placed on the title-page of every edition—became "speculative results according to an inductive-natural scientific method". Making this programme credible required, of course, a thorough and extensive examination of the evidence from many scientific fields, from biology, physiology, physics, anthropology, linguistics and history. But Hartmann did his best to fulfil these high standards. Hence his long and arduous labours, through hundreds of pages, milling and sifting through myriads of empirical results and attempting to glean the meaning of them all. It was all much toil and trouble; but nothing less would do; it was the only way to fulfil his own demanding methodological precepts.

3. A New Religion

We have seen that religion was a powerful force behind Hartmann's philosophy of the unconscious. The whole point of that philosophy was to vindicate the central thesis of his spiritual pantheism: that there is a single intelligent subject throughout all of

---

[29] *Selbstzersetzung des Christenthums*, pp. 110, 111.
[30] See Hartmann's 'Naturforschung und Philosophie: Eine Unterhaltung in zwei Briefen', *Philosophische Monatshefte*, 8 (1871), 49–58, 97–105.

nature, which acts purposively and intelligently yet subconsciously. That spiritual pantheism was to be the religion of the modern world, the sole alternative to a bankrupt theism and a soulless materialism. The contrast with Dühring's atheism and materialism could not be starker.

The great importance of Hartmann's religious concerns in the formation of his philosophy makes it worthwhile to investigate them more fully. What, more exactly, were these concerns? And how, more precisely, did they influence Hartmann's metaphysics?

Hartmann's religious interests go back to his early school days. In a later autobiographical essay,[31] Hartmann informs us that the director of his *Seminarschule*, "*Stadtsschulrath Fürbringer*", imparted religious instruction with such clarity and rigour that it made a lasting impression upon him. Hartmann later said that Fürbringer gave his own metaphysical interests their "first powerful impetus". Already in the *Gymnasium* Hartmann acquired a reputation for his "*kühne Freidenkerei und Pietätslosigkeit*", which awed his schoolmates.[32]

These concerns, as they stood in the late 1860s, could be formulated in three core beliefs: that religion is irreplaceable and an eternal need; that it is in danger of becoming neglected and oppressed in the modern world; and that nothing less is necessary to serve this need, and to avoid this danger, than a new religion. It would not do, the young Hartmann believed, to revive Christianity, which now lay in its grave. Hardly anyone believed anymore in the dogmas of Protestantism, at least not in their original intended sense as formulated by Luther and Calvin. Because repairing the old religion would no longer work, it was necessary to create a new one. Not "*Umbildung*" but "*Neubildung*" was the order of the day. The aim of Hartmann's metaphysics was to justify this new religion, to demonstrate its central doctrines, its value and necessity in the modern world.

All this raises a new set of questions. What was this new religion? Why was it necessary? And what had gone so wrong with the old one that it could not be repaired? Hartmann's answer to these questions came in two remarkable books of the early 1870s: the pseudonymous *Briefe über die christliche Religion*,[33] which appeared in 1870, and *Die Selbstzersetzung des Christenthums*,[34] which was first published in 1874. Both works are critiques of Christianity, especially liberal Protestant theology. Both make the case for a new religion and the retirement of Christianity. We can no longer rationalize or reconstruct Christianity, whose fundamental dogmas are beyond redemption,

---

[31] Eduard von Hartmann, 'Mein Entwickelungsgang', in *Gesammelte Studien und Aufsätze*, p. 12.

[32] Ibid., pp. 18–19.

[33] F. A. Müller, *Briefe über die christliche Religion* (Stuttgart: Verlag von J. G. Kötzle, 1870). Hartmann published this book under his own name in 1905 as *Das Christentum des neuen Testaments* (Sachsa: Hermann Haacke, 1905). He explains in the 'Vorwort zur zweiten Auflage', p. vii, that he first published it pseudonymously to avoid distraction from the controversy surrounding *Philosophie des Unbewussten*. Apparently, Hartmann feared fighting a war on two fronts.

[34] Eduard von Hartmann, *Die Selbstzersetzung des Christenthums und die Religion der Zukunft* (Berlin: Duncker, 1874).

rescue and repair, Hartmann argues, because they are incompatible with the fundamental values of the modern world. Since, however, we still have a need for religion, we must create a new religion, one more in accord with the values and beliefs of the present age.

Hartmann's *Briefe* is a *tour de force*, a compelling critique of traditional Christianity on the basis of a thorough and exacting knowledge of its scriptural sources. It is Hartmann's best book on the philosophy of religion, but also his least known because of its pseudonymity.[35] The *Briefe* is in the tradition of the biblical criticism of Strauss, Bauer and Baur—a debt fully acknowledged—but it goes beyond them in drawing general negative conclusions about the incoherence of Christian doctrine. Carefully and methodically, Hartmann sifts his way through the New Testament, demonstrating how the doctrines of Jesus, Paul and John are hardly credible in the modern age. We learn that Jesus was not "an ultraliberal non-Jew", as most Protestants would like him to be, and that his aim was not to bring salvation to the Gentile masses (75, 77).[36] Jesus was "through and through a Jew...and felt and thought of himself only as a Jew" (77). He never had any intention of creating a new religion, and he wanted to do nothing more than teach Jewish doctrine (74). His central and characteristic doctrine was the imminent coming of the kingdom of God, which he prophesied would be within his own time (69–72). But because that prophecy proved to be false, and because he suffered an ignominious death on the cross, his followers devised all kinds of rationalizations to uphold his authority (135). One of these followers was Paul, who invented the doctrine of the atonement, i.e. Christ's propitiatory sacrifice for the sins of mankind. But this doctrine, Hartmann complains, is "a horrible web of barbaric-oriental views of law and logical nonsense" (184). It involves the conception of God as a bloodthirsty tyrant who demands sacrifices in his honour, even if it be own son; it also assumes that it is morally permissible for an innocent person to suffer for the sins of others (148–9, 184). Paul's God is morally repellent, Hartmann finds, because he creates masses of human beings only to condemn them, and because he leaves his creatures with no rights against him (151). Behind all this theorizing about God lay "the old Jehovah, who thought of nothing but the honour of his own name and the propagation of his fame" (148–9). Paul's moral doctrines also lead to complete irresponsibility, even "libertinage", Hartmann argues, because a person can perform moral actions only due to divine grace, where the only criterion for the possession of grace is inner feeling (201, 203).

The gospel of John is no more acceptable for the modern age than that of Paul, in Hartmann's view. The ethic of love seems so sublime and admirable, yet it is meant only for Christians and excludes the rest of mankind, who are condemned to eternal

---

[35] Hartmann informs us that the book was passed over in silence. See the 'Vorwort' to *Die Krisis des Christenthums in der modernen Theologie* (Berlin: Duncker, 1880), p. v.
[36] All references are to the original 1870 edition (as cited in n. 33 above).

perdition (249, 250, 251). It is utterly absurd to love a God who would save only those who believe in him, and who would destroy everyone else.

Although Hartmann believed, on the basis of these criticisms, that the imminent collapse of Christianity would be a blessing, he still insists that there is a need for religion. He defends the free community movement in Germany, which was experimenting with new forms of belief and ritual; and he attacks the legal establishment for requiring that every individual belong to some officially recognized church (271–4).

His book ends with the ringing declaration: "Die Religion ist in Gefahr! Nieder mit Dogma und Hierarchie! Es lebe die Religion!" (280).

The publication of Hartmann's *Die Selbstzersetzung des Christenthums* in 1874 raised a storm of protest and indignation. It was not only Hartmann's critique of Christianity but also the occasion and context of its publication that proved so controversial. Hartmann wrote the book in the midst of the *Kulturkampf*,[37] the battle between the Prussian state and the Roman Catholic Church regarding the rights of the church in the new Prussian state. The Prussian and Protestant establishment became alarmed in the early 1870s by electoral victories of Catholic candidates, and by the papal declaration of infallibility by Pius IX. These developments seemed to encourage Catholic resistance to Prussian rule, and to endanger the privileged position of the Protestant church. The Protestants denounced Hartmann's book as a betrayal of their cause, and somewhat understandably. For Hartmann had contended not only that there is no life left anymore in Protestantism, but also that the only genuine representative of old Christian doctrine was the Catholic Church! Hartmann was not writing, of course, on behalf of the ultramontanism of the Catholic Church, which he opposed as staunchly as the old Protestants. But he was using the *Kulturkampf* for his own agenda: to show the necessity of his new religion to fight Catholicism. The proper source of resistance to ultramontanism, Hartmann was saying, should be not materialism, still less a decrepit Protestantism, but a new religion in tune with the spirit of the modern world.

The *Selbstzersetzung* begins and ends with an apology for religion. Hartmann's defence of religious faith distinguishes him from his great contemporary, David Friedrich Strauss, who, in his *Der alte und der neue Glaube*,[38] had argued that we should completely abandon religion and accept materialism as the only tenable worldview in the modern world. It was partly in reaction to Strauss that Hartmann wrote his book,[39] which endorses Strauss's critique of Christianity while attempting to avoid his atheist conclusions. Remarkably, in defending the need for religion, Hartmann goes back to Schopenhauer. Like the great sage of Frankfurt, he was convinced that there is a deep

---

[37] On the *Kulturkampf*, see James Sheehan, *German Liberalism in the 19th Century* (Chicago: University of Chicago Press, 1978), pp. 135–7.

[38] See David Friedrich Strauss, *Der alte und der neue Glaube*. Zweite Auflage (Leipzig: Hirzel, 1872).

[39] In the 'Vorwort zur zweiten Auflage' of *Selbstzersetzung*, pp. ii–iv, Hartmann says that he intended to avoid the controversy surrounding Strauss's work; but in the 'Vorwort' to *Krisis des Christenthums*, pp. vi–vii, he makes it clear that he was taking issue with Strauss, especially his advocacy of materialism as the substitute for Christianity.

need for religion in the human heart, a need which can be neglected or repressed for a while, but which can never be entirely extinguished or extirpated. Man is for Hartmann a religious animal because he naturally asks the question why we exist in face of all the evil and suffering of the world.[40] We need to know why we are here, and what value to give our existence, if we are to get through all the turmoil, traumas and terrors of life. These religious questions then give birth to philosophy, which is nothing more than a metaphysical attempt to answer them. Religion and philosophy are for Hartmann continuous, both attempts to answer questions about the meaning and value of life. They differ only in their form of exposition: religion is the *poetic* form of philosophy, philosophy the *discursive* form of religion.

But if the need for religion is eternal and universal, it is still under threat, indeed on the verge of disappearing, in the modern world. Modern Christianity, Hartmann contends in the *Selbstzersetzung*,[41] is facing a crisis. Why is this? It is chiefly because the orthodox form of Christian belief is theism, the belief in an extramundane personal creator (28). Both the Catholic and Protestant churches have clung to theism, which they see as the only proper form of religious belief. But that belief, Hartmann argues, has shown itself to be untenable, because it is incompatible with two basic principles of the modern world: moral autonomy, i.e. the right of every individual to lead his life according to his own volition and values; and free enquiry or criticism, i.e. the right of every individual to investigate the truth according to reason alone. The demand for moral autonomy has undercut theism because its ethics is essentially heteronomous, based on the belief that we should follow ethical precepts simply because they are commands of God (30). Free enquiry or criticism has undermined theism in two ways: first, it has questioned the belief in the authority of the Bible, which has been the main source of evidence for theism; and, second, it has shown that the personal attributes of God are anthropomorphic projections, hypostasizations of forms of human consciousness.

Although Hartmann thinks that the principles of criticism and autonomy are central to the modern age, he also recognizes their religious origins. Both principles arose, he explains, during the Reformation. But the great reformers, Luther and Calvin, failed to see that, if taken to their limits, these principles erode the authority of scripture itself (9). The Catholics always warned against the consequences of criticism and autonomy, insisting to this day on the need for religious authority. But that authority, Hartmann believes, is not acceptable to the average modern individual, who has liberated himself from all the shackles of the past, both political and religious. He wants to lead his life according to his own ideas, and to examine all beliefs in the light of his own conscience. Now that he has been set free, he will never return to the cages of the past. Because the traditional churches, both Catholic and Protestant, have clung so firmly to theism, and

---

[40] Cf. *Selbstzersetzung*, p. 87; and *Briefe*, p. 272.
[41] All references in parentheses in the following paragraphs are to the first edition of the *Selbstzersetung* (1874), whose pagination is identical with the second edition.

because theism has proven so untenable, it now seems as if the only alternative is atheism. Such, in sum, is the crisis of modern religion. Strauss's solution to it was to embrace materialism. But that, Hartmann insists, threw the baby of religion out with the bathwater of theism (29).

Hartmann is convinced that there is a better solution to the crisis, a middle path between the dilemma of atheism or theism: spiritual pantheism.[42] Pantheism avoids the anthropomorphisms of theism because its God is an impersonal universal substance; and it escapes materialist naturalism because it sees nature not as matter in motion but as a purposive organic whole. Pantheism not only fulfils the dreams of the mystics but it is also a strictly rational religion (116). Unlike theism, which believes in miracles and the supernatural, there is nothing irrational or supernatural about pantheism, which identifies the divine with the single universal substance that manifests itself in the laws of nature.

It is another great advantage of pantheism, Hartmann contends, that it can provide a foundation for ethics. Ethics, he insists, cannot be separated from metaphysics. An ethics without metaphysics simply "hangs in mid air" (84). Moral principles require that we surrender the claims of egoism, that an individual cease to put self-interest first, and that he or she recognize the equal claims of others. Pantheism satisfies this requirement, Hartmann argues, because it is a form of monism, according to which the identity of each individual is connected with that of everyone else, and according to which all particular individuals are really only one self (84, 116–17). One individual cannot harm another, then, without also harming his deeper and better self. Egoism rests upon a faulty ontology, which holds that we can somehow separate personal identity from the cosmic whole; but metaphysics, through its demonstration of monism, shows us how this is a mistake. Hartmann will develop this metaphysical ethics only later in the 1870s and early 1880s, where it finds its mature formulation in his 1879 *Phänomenologie des sittlichen Bewusstseins* and in his 1881 works, *Die Religion des Geistes* and *Das religiöse Bewusstsein der Menschheit*.[43] However, its roots are already clear in his earlier religious writings, especially the *Selbstzersetzung*.

In calling for a revival of pantheism Hartmann, of course, was following a well-trodden path. He knew all too well that pantheism had been, as Heine once put it, "the secret religion of Germany",[44] and that it had inspired virtually every major thinker of the *Goethezeit*. Such, however, had been the resistance against pantheism from the side of the orthodox churches, Hartmann believed, that the doctrine had never been given

---

[42] Hartmann's argument for pantheism appears mainly in the final chapter of *Selbstzersetzung*, pp. 99–122, esp. 101, 107–8, 112.

[43] See Eduard von Hartmann, *Phänomenologie des sittlichen Bewusstseins* (Berlin: Duncker, 1879), especially sections CI and II; *Die Religion des Geistes* (Berlin: Duncker, 1882); and *Das religiöse Bewußtsein der Menschheit im Stufengang seiner Entwicklung* (Berlin: Duncker, 1882). For a detailed analysis of the latter two works, which cannot be undertaken here, see Wolf, *Hartmann*, pp. 179–202.

[44] See Heinrich Heine, *Religion und Philosophie in Deutschland*, in *Sämtliche Schriften*, ed. Klaus Briegleb (Munich: Hanser, 1976), V. 571. Hartmann cites Heine's lines approvingly, *Selbstzersetzung*, p. 112.

a fair hearing.⁴⁵ All too often it was equated with Spinoza's naturalism, and there was no attempt to grasp it in its proper "spiritual sense". It was crucial to revive, reformulate and reassert pantheism in this "spiritual sense", Hartmann urged, before cultivated nations turned against religion itself.

Hartmann did not advocate any attempt to save and explain the old Christian doctrines in a pantheist sense. This would be only to distort the historical sense and meaning of these doctrines. The new religion should not limit itself to Western sources alone, he advised, but it should be a synthesis of the best of the occident and orient. The monistic and immanent metaphysics of Brahmanism and Buddhism are indeed closer to pantheism than Christian theism or deism, and they therefore deserve a vital role in the new religion.

Now that we have examined Hartmann's new religion, it should be clear how it was a guiding force behind his metaphysics. The purpose of his philosophy of the unconscious was to provide a metaphysical foundation for his new religion, nothing more, nothing less. But it is crucial to note that there is another aspect of Hartmann's philosophy that has its sources in his early religious concerns: his pessimism. All religion, Hartmann declares, must have a pessimistic starting point, with reflection on the origins of evil and suffering (87, 115). The gospels of Jesus, Paul and John, Hartmann remarked repeatedly in his *Briefe*,⁴⁶ all arose from pessimism, from a belief that man's true happiness and highest good lay beyond the earth, which was a vale of tears and a tale of woe. In their view, life on earth was a pilgrimage on the way to heaven, which was our true resting place and the only source of peace. The same pessimistic starting point, Hartmann notes, also appears in Buddhism, in its recognition of the suffering of this life. The religious origins of Hartmann's pessimism are not apparent in his *Philosophie des Unbewussten*, where he makes his chief statement of pessimism, though they are fully apparent from his *Briefe* and *Selbstzersetzung*.

Not only Hartmann's pessimism, but also his reflections on the limits of pessimism, the general structure of his own theory of the value of life, derive from his early religious concerns. As much as Hartmann was inspired by the pessimism of early Christianity, he could not accept what he called its "supernatural optimism", i.e. its belief that the sufferings in this world would be redeemed in another life hereafter. Such optimism is no longer tenable in the modern world, he argued, because the beliefs in personal immortality, and in a heaven beyond this world, have lost all credibility among the educated public. However, the rejection of this supernatural optimism should not mean, Hartmann insisted in the *Selbstzersetzung*, the complete acceptance of Schopenhauer's pessimism, which gives the individual no reason whatsoever to find value in this life. Even if we cannot be happy in this life, Hartmann held, we can still find value in it through striving for cultural achievement and moral improvement. Meaning in life should come not from the belief in personal happiness in the hereafter,

---

⁴⁵ See the 'Vorwort zur zweiten Auflage' of *Selbstzersetzung* (Berlin: Duncker, 1874), p. ix.
⁴⁶ See, for example, *Briefe über die christliche Religion*, pp. 102–3, 162, 220–1, 261.

which is only a form of egoism, but from the belief that one's efforts to improve the world really do matter and that they ultimately do make a difference.

The proper form of religious belief—and the best theory of the value of life—should therefore be a synthesis of what Hartmann calls "eudemonic pessimism" and "evolutionary optimism", where the former is the thesis that happiness is unattainable in this life, and where the latter is the thesis that we can make moral and cultural progress in history. It is the belief in evolutionary optimism, in progress in history, that Hartmann saw as characteristic of the Western world, and as having no place in any of the oriental religions (Judaism, Islam and Buddhism). But it is just this belief, he insisted, that we must defend if we are to have a sense for the value and meaning of life in the modern world.

We shall examine below these two sides of Hartmann's philosophy—its eudemonic pessimism and its evolutionary optimism—but suffice it to say for now that Hartmann saw both as prerequisites of his new religion. Hence not only Hartmann's pessimism, but his syncretic theory of the value of life arose from his religious concerns.

4. First Principles

It was one thing to call for a new religion, to show the need for it in the modern age; but it was quite another thing to provide it with a philosophical foundation. Hartmann turned to this arduous task in his *Philosophie des Unbewussten*. Here we are less interested in the details of Hartmann's argument than in his first principles and basic concepts. Nowhere does Hartmann state them more clearly and explicitly than in the final retrospective chapter of *Philosophie des Unbewussten*, appropriately entitled 'Die letzten Principien'.[47] *Prima facie* it is odd to find his first principles laid down only at the end of his book. But Hartmann believed this expositional oddity to be a methodological necessity. First principles should be the result, not the starting point, of his new inductive and empirical methodology.

Though Hartmann insisted that first principles must be a posteriori, he also recognized that they presuppose more basic concepts. There must be, he realized, fundamental concepts even to formulate the first principles and to construct a system. Such concepts explain all others, but they are inexplicable themselves. Hartmann then reveals that his system presupposes two such concepts: will and representation.

These two concepts remind us of Schopenhauer, who divided the world into will and representation, and who constructed his own philosophy around them. This impression seems to support the common assumption that Hartmann's philosophy is essentially only a variation of Schopenhauer's. Yet Hartmann quickly corrects this impression. It becomes obvious to even the most casual reader that he understands these concepts in a very different way from his predecessor. In Schopenhauer, the

---

[47] Kapitel CXIV: 'Die letzten Principien', pp. 682–723. All references in parentheses above are to the second edition of 1870.

distinction between will and representation coincides with that between thing-in-itself and appearance; in Hartmann, it coincides with that between real and ideal, existence and essence. To understand why Hartmann explains the distinction in just these terms, we have to return to an unexpected source: the late Schelling. The chief inspiration behind Hartmann's metaphysics, it turns out, was not Schopenhauer but the late Schelling.

The decisive role of the late Schelling for the young Hartmann becomes clear from one of his first writings, a short tract which he published in 1869, his *Schelling's positive Philosophie als Einheit von Hegel und Schopenhauer*.[48] As the title suggests, Hartmann saw Schelling's late philosophy as the means for reconciling the conflict between the two great metaphysical systems of his age: Hegel's panlogicism and Schopenhauer's voluntarism. Each philosophy represented one of Hartmann's basic concepts; each had taken one concept to extremes, making it the sole principle to explain the world. Schopenhauer's voluntarism held that reality in itself, the essence of the world, consists in the will alone. Hegel's philosophy held that reality in itself, the essence of the world, consists in the idea (one form of representation) alone. The problem was to recognize and explain how reality in itself consists in *both* elements, will and idea.

Now the great value of Schelling's positive philosophy, Hartmann tells us, is that it explains not only why neither extreme works, but also how it is possible to combine them. Though Schelling himself never embarked on such a syncretic project, he gave Hartmann the inspiration and conceptual means for carrying it out. Those means lay in a distinction crucial to Schelling's positive philosophy, a distinction fundamental to his critique of Hegel's panlogicism and his system as a whole. We must distinguish, Schelling argued, between the realms of existence and essence, between reality and possibility, or between the "that" and the "what" of things.[49] While we can use concepts, ideas or representations to explain the essence or what of things, we can never use them to prove the existence or "that" of things, which remains irreducible, given, something we learn from experience alone. The realm of concepts, ideas or representations is that of possibility; its truths concern only the *relations* between essences; but these truths are only *hypothetical*, i.e. they tell us only *if* X, then Y, leaving it undetermined whether or not there is an X. It was this very basic distinction, Schelling held, that had been ignored by Hegel's absolute idealism. However valid Hegel's logic might be as an account of the realm of essence, he could never demonstrate that his system held for reality itself. Notoriously, Hegel had great difficulty in explaining the transition from his logic to nature, because the truths of his logic hold for "pure essences", so

---

[48] Eduard von Hartmann, *Schelling's positive Philosophie als Einheit von Hegel und Schopenhauer* (Berlin: Löwenstein, 1869). Reprinted in *Gesammelte Studien und Aufsätze* (Berlin: Duncker, 1876), 650–720. Alma von Hartmann's bibliography, p. 501, places this writing in the year 1868, though the title-page clearly states 1869.
[49] F. W. J. Schelling, *Einleitung in die Philosophie der Offenbarung*, in *Sämtliche Werke*, ed. K. F. A. Schelling (Stuttgart: Cotta, 1856–61), II/3. 57–8, 70–1. References to Schelling's *Werke* will be first to the Abtheilung, indicated by a Roman numeral, and then the volume, indicated by an Arabic numeral.

that there is no guarantee that they also hold for nature or existence itself. Rather than deriving the realm of existence from essence, Hegel was forced to resort to metaphors, saying that the idea "alienated" or "dismissed" nature from itself. But how, Schelling asked, could the purely logical and rational become the non-logical and non-rational? These metaphors were only desperate devices to conceal Hegel's fundamental weakness: his inability to leap the gap between essence and existence, possibility and reality.

Schelling's argument against Hegel had demonstrated for Hartmann that the concept of representation by itself could not explain the existence or reality of things, and that it had to be complemented with the concept of the will. While the concept of representation stood for the realm of the ideal or essence, the concept of the will stood for the realm of the real or existence. But why this odd pairing, this strange coupling, of the concept of will with that of reality and existence? Here again Schelling provided Hartmann with the explanation. According to the late Schelling, we can explain the transition from possibility to reality, from essence to existence, only through the concept of the will. It is the will alone that explains the act of creation that brings us from possibility to reality, essence to existence. This point had been made by the great Leibniz himself, who held that the divine understanding reigns over the realm of essence while the divine will rules over that of existence.[50] Schelling went a step further in ascribing even more importance to the will. An act of will is necessary to explain not only creation, he maintained, but also the preservation or maintenance of existence, the permanence of things once they have been created. What makes something continue to exist is that it asserts itself; it resists other things that attempt to take over its existence; but resistance lies only in some act of will.[51]

It was Schelling, then, who fathered Hartmann's distinction between will and representation, which Hartmann then put to use for his syncretic project. Following Schelling, Hartmann saw the distinction between will and representation as a distinction between real and ideal, existence and essence. While the will is the principle of the real realm or existence, representation is the principle of the ideal realm or essence. The ideal realm consists in the "what" of the world, whereas the real realm consists in its "that". Ideas or representations have no reality on their own; they are only possibilities and cannot do anything. It is only the will that acts, and that brings ideas into existence. We can now see why both Schopenhauer and Hegel were correct, though only partially and not entirely so. Schopenhauer was right about the realm of reality or existence—that only the will creates things and brings them into existence—while Hegel was right about the realm of ideality or essence—that it consists in eternal forms and fixed structures, which cannot be altered by the will and to which it must conform. Hence the following schema was active in Hartmann's mind: will = realm of existence = Schopenhauer's philosophy; representation = realm of essence = Hegel's philosophy.

---

[50] See, for example, Leibniz, *Monadologie*, §46.
[51] Schelling, *Sämtliche Werke*, II/3. 67–8, 70, 205–6.

As much as Hartmann insisted on keeping a firm distinction between these realms, he also made it a desideratum of philosophy to unite them, to synthesize the ideal and the real, the logical and the illogical.[52] Although these principles are distinct, for all the reasons Schelling made clear, they still have to be joined. After all, there is but one universe, one world of which the ideal and real are only aspects. Without argument, Hartmann simply made monism a prerequisite of any satisfactory worldview. Accepting that requirement, it was necessary to bring Schopenhauer and Hegel together to form a single system.

How is it possible to unite such opposing systems? How can one join the real and ideal realms? There are three ways in which this can be done, Hartmann later explained.[53] Either one makes the real a moment of the ideal, the will a product of representation, as Hegel had done; or one makes the ideal a moment of the real, representation a product of the will, as Schopenhauer had done; or, finally, one makes the ideal and real equal moments of a single absolute substance or subject. It is this last alternative that Hartmann saw as his own. His philosophy gives the ideal and real, the logical and illogical, equal but separate status as independent aspects, appearances or attributes of a single reality.

What brings together real and ideal, will and representation, for Hartmann is a simple fact about the logic of willing. The will by its very nature must have an object; it must will something; it must have some goal or purpose. But this object or purpose, because it does not yet exist, has a strictly ideal status; it is present to the will only as an idea or representation. Hence will and representation, real and ideal, belong together in virtue of the very nature of willing. It was the great flaw of Schopenhauer's theory of the will, Hartmann contended, that it conceived the will as a blind striving, a crude urge, a formless impulse, having no object or goal; but a will without a goal, without some end, is not really a will at all.[54] We must always conceive the will as having some end or purpose, which is its ideal content.

Hartmann's way of joining the ideal and real through the intentionality of willing seems to slant more to voluntarism than idealism. The ideal is united to the real, the representation to the will, because the ideal or representation is only an object for the will. It is important to emphasize, however, that Hartmann does not think that the essence of ideas depends on the will, only their existence. The ideas still have a distinct logical structure or identity of their own, which is independent of the will. Thus Hartmann stresses that there is a Platonic dimension to his philosophy where the ideas have an independent status (685). It was one of the great inconsistencies of Schopenhauer's philosophy, he contends, that it introduced a realm of ideas into reality in itself. If all reality were only an irrational will, how could it manifest or objectify itself in ideas, in purely rational or intelligible objects? Once, however, we admit the realm of ideas, then we cannot maintain, as Schopenhauer did, that the will is entirely

---

[52] See his *Erläuterungen zur Metaphysik des Unbewussten* (Berlin: Duncker, 1874), p. 14.
[53] Ibid. [54] *Philosophie des Unbewussten* (1870), pp. 20, 90–2.

irrational; for these ideas are necessary for the will to have an object, and they have a rational or intelligible structure all their own independent of the will. Hence there is an important element of rationalism in Hartmann's philosophy, one that is entirely missing in Schopenhauer's.

Hartmann admits that he does not know how to describe the ontological status of the ideas on their own. While he insists that they have no *existence*, which is conferred on them entirely by the will, he does assume that they have some kind of *being* or *subsistence*, whatever that might be. In trying to describe their ontological status we bump up against the limits of language, he confesses (708, 711–12).

Hartmann, we have seen, wanted to join the ideal and real in a single thing that gave independent reality to each. What, though, is this, this single subject or substance of which will and representation are different aspects? Hartmann was remarkably silent about this point, which concerns the very foundation of his metaphysics. He confronted the issue in an addition to a later edition of *Philosophie des Unbewussten*.[55] Here he explained that the will and idea should be seen, much like in Spinoza's theory, as different attributes of a single substance. Hartmann's substance would have as its attributes, however, not thought and extension but idea and will. Only the attributes—will and representation—are different; but the single substance—that which wills and represents—is one and the same. Because will and representation are characteristic of mind, Hartmann calls his substance "mind" or "spirit" (*Geist*). It is only if we make will and representation attributes of a single thing, he argues, that we can explain the interconnection between them. Willing alone is irrational, and the idea alone does not exist; but that which wills is rational because it is also idea, and that which represents exists because it is also a will. Hartmann did not see the irony in appealing to Spinoza, for whom idea and reality belong together in the single infinite substance only because essence involves existence—a thesis that violates Schelling's crucial distinction. Hartmann left the whole issue unresolved because he held that why something exists rather than nothing is a complete mystery, the end of all enquiry.

Hartmann's careful efforts to distinguish yet unify the ideal and real realms eventually came to grief, trapping him in a labyrinth of reasoning from which he could not escape. He notes a circularity in his position: the will exists only through having a representation; but a representation comes into existence only through the will (696). To resolve this circularity, Hartmann postulates a middle position between the will as a pure potentiality, which has no object, and the will as actuality, which has an object; this middle position is the will understood as pure activity, the act of pure willing. This will is in a middle position because it is actual with respect to the will as pure potentiality, and because it is potential with respect to the will as actuality (696). Hartmann calls this act of pure willing "empty willing" or "formal willing" because it is a mere willing

---

[55] See chapter CXIV, 'Die identische Substanz beider Attribute', in *Philosophie des Unbewussten*, Zehnte erweiterte Auflage in drei Theilen (Leipzig: Hermann Haacke, 1900), I. 451–60.

without a specific content or goal. It is a willing that wills only itself, which wills to will rather than not to will.

We will leave aside here Hartmann's subtle explorations of this act of pure willing. The basic problems with his theory are obvious enough. How do we move from the will in itself, the purely potential will, to active willing? And how do we describe the ontological status of this act of willing, which is neither purely potential nor actual? The problem of moving from possibility to actuality has only been thrown back another step.

The problems of Hartmann's solution to this difficulty are less interesting than the conclusions he draws from it. For it is in describing this primal act of will that we can see clearly—only at the finale of Hartmann's vast system—the metaphysical aspect of his pessimism. Hartmann describes this act of willing by which it moves from nothingness into being as an act of "struggle", "torment" and "misery" (698). It is as if the will prefers pure nothingness to being, as if it never wants to will anything at all, because this would mean moving into existence and leaving behind the serenity of nothingness. "The state of empty willing, before its satisfaction, is an eternal pining for satisfaction, which is given to it by representation, i.e., it is absolute misery (*Unseligkeit*), torment without pleasure, even without pause" (698). The act of willing can never be satisfied, Hartmann further explains, because it is infinite while any particular goal is only finite (699). So, for Hartmann, the primal act of will that brings the world into existence is an act of trauma, a fall from the paradise of pure nothingness into the wretchedness of existence. Having begun in trauma, it only seemed appropriate for the rest of the creation to be one dramatic, interminable act of suffering.

These pessimistic reflections on the origin of things also seem to have been inspired by Schelling, who was driven to similar conclusions in his later philosophy. In his *Philosophische Untersuchungen über das Wesen der menschlichen Freiheit*, which had appeared in 1809, a decade before Schopenhauer's *Welt als Wille und Vorstellung*, Schelling had already insisted that "willing is primal being" (*Ursein*), and that "in the final and highest sense there is no other being than will".[56] But, even more strikingly, Schelling described the act by which the will creates itself, by which it moves from possibility into actuality, as a "torment", as "a path of pain".[57] Furthermore, Schelling regarded pain as "universal and necessary in all life", insisting that "all pain comes from being itself".[58] Willing is an infinite insatiable striving; its ultimate goal is to will nothing; but the more it strives for it, the further away it is from it.[59] All this suggests that it was not only Schopenhauer but also Schelling who was the precedent for Hartmann's own pessimism. It is at least noteworthy that Hartmann, in his *Schelling's positive Philosophie als Einheit von Hegel und Schopenhauer*, pointed out the close affinities between Schelling's and Schopenhauer's philosophy, and that he stressed

---

[56] Schelling, *Philosophische Untersuchungen über das Wesen der menschlichen Freiheit*, Werke, I/7. 350.
[57] Schelling, *Darstellung des philosophischen Empirismus*, Werke, I/10. 266.
[58] Schelling, *Die Weltalter*, Werke, I/8. 335.   [59] Ibid., pp. 235–6.

how Schelling came first to many doctrines that had been seen as characteristic of Schopenhauer.[60]

5. Settling Accounts with Hegel

No account of Hartmann's metaphysics is complete, or even adequate, without an analysis of his complex relationship to Hegel, who, along with Schopenhauer, made up the other half of his system. Hartmann's stance toward Hegel is not only intricate but also shifting, changing in tone and attitude (if not content) over the years. At first Hartmann had been very hostile to Hegel, especially his dialectic.[61] But the more he began to distance himself from Schopenhauer, the more he began to approach Hegel, who seemed less repellent as the years moved on. He once described himself as a "Hegelianer von 1870";[62] and in a later statement about the historical position of his philosophy, he stressed the Hegelian over the Schopenhauerian side of his system: "Should the position of my system of philosophy be characterized in a few words, one could say: it is a synthesis of Hegel's and Schopenhauer's systems with a decisive preponderance of the former".[63] All this, inevitably, leads us to the question: what did Hartmann adopt, and what did he repudiate, from Hegel?

In going back to Hegel, Hartmann knew that he was in danger of appearing an anachronism. By the late 1860s the owl of Minerva had long flown from German lands; the once illustrious Hegelian system, and its many squabbling disciples, were rapidly fading from memory. Writing in 1885,[64] Hartmann noted that the Hegelian system was more forgotten than the other systems of his age. While scholars were investigating the pre-Socratics with greater zeal and intensity, Hegel's books were lying untouched on library shelves, even though their spirit had penetrated modern history, theology and public life. Nowadays people only read Kant, and they had little knowledge of the philosophical development that led from him to Fichte, Schelling and Hegel. Hence Hegel's system seemed like "a book with seven seals". Hartmann believed that it was his duty to rescue Hegel from oblivion, not least because his ideas addressed contemporary

---

[60] Hartmann, *Schelling's Positive Philosophie*, pp. 21–31. In suggesting this, Hartmann probably was unaware that Schopenhauer's originality had already been called into question by others. Some of the first reviews of Schopenhauer's work stressed his dependence on Schelling. See, for example, 'Frei Mittheilungen eines Literaturfreundes', in *Literarisches Wochenblatt*, IV, No. 30 (October 1819), 234-6. In 1859 Ludwig Noack argued that Schopenhauer's philosophy was a stolen reformulation of Schelling's. See his *Schelling und die Philosophie der Romantik* (Berlin: Mittler, 1859), II. 360-75. On Schopenhauer's response to this charge, see 'Fragmente zur Geschichte der Philosophie', in *Parerga, Sämtliche Werke*, IV. 165-70.

[61] See 'Mein Entwickelungsgang', in *Gesammelte Studien und Aufsätze*, p. 37.

[62] See Eduard von Hartmann, 'Ueber die nothwendige Umbildung der Hegelschen Philosophie', in *Gesammelte philosophische Abhandlungen zur Philosophie des Unbewussten* (Berlin: Duncker, 1872), p. 56. First published in *Philosophische Monatshefte*, 5 (1870), 388–416. All references here are to the later edition.

[63] See Eduard von Hartmann, 'Vorwort zur zehnten Auflage', *Philosophie des Unbewussten*, I, p. xiii.

[64] See Eduard von Hartmann, *Philosophische Fragen der Gegenwart* (Leipzig: Wilhelm Friedrich, 1885), pp. 3–4.

interests and needs. He would do his best, therefore, to present Hegel's philosophical relevance in an exoteric language.

Following Kuno Fischer,[65] Hartmann described the central principle of Hegel's philosophy as the idea of development. He said that Hegel's philosophy could be summarized in the following sentence: "The world-process is development, development is logical; what develops is the logical and beyond it there is nothing."[66] What Hartmann wanted to adopt from Hegel's philosophy was precisely its principle of development; and given the importance he assigns to that principle in Hegel's philosophy, it is easy to understand why he would then describe himself as a Hegelian. What Hartmann especially admired in Hegel's principle of development is its teleology. Hegel rightly understood the world-process as a progression from lower to higher, where progress is measured in terms of the realization of some purpose or end. For Hartmann, this was an advance over the mechanism of Spinozism and materialism, which banished all purposes from nature and placed all reality on the same level.

It was not only the teleology of Hegel's principle of development that Hartmann admired. This principle was for him not only a counter against materialism, but also a check against complete pessimism. If Schopenhauer represents the pessimistic side of Hartmann's system, Hegel represents its optimistic side. As much as Hartmann borrows from Schopenhauer's pessimism, he never wanted to give it an unconditional validity, so that it became a source of quietism or fatalism. Hegel's concept of development—if properly purged of its purely logical meaning—could give reason for optimism, for it gives hope that history is moving in a new and progressive direction, and that it is not simply a repetition of the same damn old thing, as Schopenhauer said.

In his later *Phänomenologie des sittlichen Bewusstseins*,[67] Hartmann gave an interesting explanation for why the ethics of Schopenhauer had to be complemented with that of Hegel. Schopenhauer's ethics culminated in the idea that all individuals are identical in the single cosmic will, that we are all one and the same being and that egoism is pointless because to act against others is to act against oneself. But that idea on its own, Hartmann argues, encourages a complete quietism, a contemplative approach to life where there is no reason for action. For why strive to change the world if total contentment can be found simply by contemplating the absolute that already exists within me? Hartmann accepted Schopenhauer's monistic metaphysics; but he deplored his quietism. To avoid that doctrine, he insisted that we must conceive the absolute in dynamic and teleological terms, as not something already existing but as something gradually developing in history. It is the vocation of each individual to

---

[65] See Kuno Fischer, *Logik und Metaphysik oder Wissenschaftslehre* (Stuttgart: Scheitlin, 1852), §§23–24, pp. 42–6; and *System der Logik und Metaphysik oder Wissenschaftslehre* (Heidelberg: Bassermann, 1865), §§68–72, pp. 186–202.

[66] Hartmann, *Philosophische Fragen der Gegenwart*, p. 25.

[67] Eduard von Hartmann, *Phänomenologie des sittlichen Bewußtseins*, Dritte Auflage (Berlin: Wegweiser Verlag, 1924), pp. 651, 655–60. This work first appeared in 1879 with Duncker Verlag, Berlin. The second edition appeared under the title *Das sittliche Bewusstsein*.

participate in this evolutionary process and to help make the absolute come into existence through one's own actions. The absolute could realize itself only in and through the actions of all finite individuals, not above or apart from them. In acting in the world, then, we aid the absolute in realizing itself, so that one's individual actions take on a cosmic importance and play a definite role in creating the moral world order; our actions then make a difference, even if a very small one, to the world. Hence the importance of Hegel's idea of development for Hartmann. That idea served a vital purpose in overcoming the quietism of Schopenhauer's pessimism and in giving each individual meaning and purpose in life.

As much as Hartmann embraced Hegel's principle of development for these reasons, he still could not endorse it entirely or unconditionally. Hegel had given the principle an additional meaning that he wanted to repudiate. This additional meaning came from Hegel's "panlogicism". Hartmann described Hegel's philosophy as "panlogicism", because it maintains that the *sole* substance and subject of development is "the logical". In other words, Hegel saw development in strictly rational terms, as if it were nothing more than the unfolding of the concept or reason. As important as the idea of development was for Hartmann, he did not want it to be understood *strictly* or *entirely* in rational or logical terms. The great truth of Hegel's philosophy is that it understood the world-process as development; but its great falsehood is that it understood development *only* in logical terms.[68]

What, exactly, did Hartmann reject in Hegel's panlogicism? Why is it impossible to understand development entirely in logical terms? Hartmann gave three different reasons, which he did not precisely distinguish. First, development could not be understood as a logically necessary movement from potentiality to actuality, from essence into existence, because, as Schelling said, the realm of potentiality or essence is logically distinct from that of actuality or existence. The realm of reason is that of possibility and essence, and it cannot move itself into reality and existence. What makes that movement must be some extra-logical principle, which is the will. Second, development takes place in time, having earlier and later moments; but logical relationships are eternal and do not take place in time. Hegel often wrote about the development of the concept, as if it unfolds in time; but this is impossible, because logic concerns only eternal relationships between concepts. He made this mistake because he had confused our *thinking* about these relationships, which does take place in time, with the *relationships themselves*, which are not temporal at all. Third, development cannot be understood as a conceptual movement from the indeterminate to the determinate, from the general to the particular, because there is no such movement. The whole realm of concrete content—this or that particular thing with all its properties—falls outside the realm of the idea. There is a gap, then, not only between essence and existence, but also between the indeterminate and determinate, the universal and particular, within the realm of essence itself.

---

[68] 'Umbildung der Hegelschen Philosophie', p. 25.

If we subtract all these elements from Hegel's concept of development, we are left with little more than the idea of purposiveness. Development will be purposive, the realization of goals or an end; but it will not be logical, at least not in the sense of a *logically necessary* movement from essence to existence or from general to particular. Existence and particularity are for Hartmann realms beyond the strictly logical, and as such they have to be given to us.

It is important to see, however, that though Hartmann denies that development is a logical process, he still conceives of the structure of the world itself as logical. How the world comes into existence has an extra-logical source in the will; but the structure of the world itself is rational. This structure consists in the realm of universal and necessary laws, which compose the realm of eternal essences. Hartmann makes no distinction between natural and rational necessity: the necessity by which events follow one another in nature is a manifestation of a rational or logical necessity.[69] Of course, these laws seem contingent from our finite human perspective; we can affirm their causes and deny their effects without contradiction. But that is only because we, with our limited intellects, cannot fully reconstruct or understand the logical necessity behind natural laws.[70] For the divine intellect, which has unlimited powers, all the laws of nature are necessities of reason; it can derive all laws from a few general ones, because its powers are intuitive rather than discursive. It is at least to this extent, then, that Hartmann is willing to give some validity to Hegel's panlogicism or objective idealism.

A crucial part of Hartmann's critique of Hegel was his refutation of his dialectic.[71] Hegel had seen development in strictly logical or rational terms because of his dialectic, which attributes "movement" and "life" to logic. The dialectic is supposed to reveal concepts in their "movement" or "development" because it shows how they, by virtue of their own content, "move outside themselves" by creating and resolving contradictions. If we can attribute such "life" and "movement" to concepts, there will be no need to assume some principle outside them, such as the will, to make them move. Hartmann's appeal to the will as the source of movement and creation would then be superfluous.

It is not surprising to find, then, that Hartmann had already settled his accounts with Hegel's dialectic in the late 1860s, the very period he first conceived his syncretic system. In the summer of 1867 he wrote a critique of Hegel's dialectic, his *Ueber die dialektische Methode*, which appeared in April 1868.[72] In this polemical tract Hartmann

---

[69] See *Philosophie des Unbewussten* (1870), p. 710; and 'Ueber die notwendige Umbildung der Hegelschen Philosophie', p. 31.

[70] 'Ueber die notwendige Umbildung der Hegelschen Philosophie', p. 35.

[71] Hartmann explains this point in his later 1874 *Erläuterung zur Metaphysik des Unbewussten*, pp. 12–16.

[72] Eduard von Hartmann, *Ueber die dialektische Methode* (Berlin: Duncker, 1868). All references in parentheses above are to this edition, which is the only one. There are obvious problems with Hartmann's objections to Hegel, which we cannot pursue here. Not surprisingly, Hartmann was later forced to defend his critique of Hegel's dialectic against the Hegelians, especially Karl Michelet. See Hartmann's 'Erwiderung

makes a slew of objections against Hegel's method. Three of them deserve special mention in the present context. First, in affirming the existence and necessity of contradictions, Hegel violates the laws of identity and contradiction, which are indispensable to all reasoning (41, 45, 92, 98–9). Second, the dialectic cannot be justified by any external standards, such as common sense or ordinary experience, because it denies the very principles by which they operate (66–75). Third, because the dialectic involves discovering contradictions in our ordinary concepts, and because these concepts are necessary for all communication, the thinking of the dialectic becomes incommunicable and mystical (63, 65). For all these reasons, and more like them, Hartmann rejected the dialectic, leaving space for some extra-logical or extra-rational principle to be the source of movement and development. That principle, as we have seen, would be the will, which is for Hartmann the source of all movement and creation.

In his polemic against Hegel, Hartmann made some sharp comments on Hegel's ideal of the absolute (71). He endorsed Schopenhauer's complaint that the absolute is just another word for God, and he complained that Hegel had presupposed the absolute without having really demonstrated its existence. It is precisely with regard to the absolute that we can detect an important change in Hartmann's attitude toward Hegel. For in his later writings Hartmann not only has no qualms about retaining the idea of the absolute, but he also describes it in very Hegelian terms. We should conceive the single universal substance or absolute, he later wrote,[73] in terms of spirit, because the concept of spirit unites the concepts of will and idea. Though Hartmann does not make it explicit, the association with Hegel is inescapable. Who, if anyone, was the philosopher of spirit if not Hegel? It was most probably because Hartmann borrowed Hegel's spirit that he later called his system more Hegelian than Schopenhauerian.

6. Foundations of Realism

Hartmann's philosophy, like Schopenhauer's, is a metaphysics in the grand style, a complete worldview claiming knowledge of the universe as a whole. But it was no easy business in the 1860s to legitimate and sustain such an ambitious enterprise. Hartmann faced the same imposing challenge as Schopenhauer: how to vindicate metaphysics in the face of the Kantian critique of knowledge? This challenge was even more potent in the 1860s than in the 1810s when Schopenhauer first stared it in the face. Since the start of the 1860s, the neo-Kantian movement began to dominate the philosophical scene in Germany. The neo-Kantians did not slacken but only tightened the Kantian screws on metaphysics, holding it to be a bankrupt enterprise discredited by their master's critique of the rationalist tradition. As a result, metaphysics was much more suspect in the 1860s than ever before.

---

auf Herrn Professor Michelets Kritik meiner Schrift Ueber die dialektische Methode', in *Philosophische Monatshefte*, I (1868), 502–5.

[73] 'Die identische Substanz beider Attribute', in *Philosophie des Unbewussten*, I. 451–60.

Hartmann knew metaphysics to be unpopular, and he was especially concerned to defend his against the neo-Kantians. Part of his response to the neo-Kantian challenge was his methodology, which renounced the discredited deductive methods of speculative idealism (viz., dialectic and construction), and which recommended the proven inductive methods used in the natural sciences. In this respect Hartmann's response to the Kantian challenge was much like Schopenhauer's: metaphysics could not rely on a priori reasoning but would have to be founded on experience and inferences from it. But this methodological response, though necessary, was still not sufficient. For however reliable such an inductive method might be, the neo-Kantians insisted that it could provide knowledge only of appearances and not reality in itself or as a whole. The realm of experience, the neo-Kantians held, consists entirely in appearances, from which we cannot make inferences about things-in-themselves. But that flatly contradicted Hartmann's metaphysics, which, no less than Schopenhauer's, claims to give knowledge of things-in-themselves and reality as a whole.

Hartmann saw the issue this way: his metaphysics, in claiming knowledge of reality in itself, is committed to a kind of realism. This realism would assume that the knowledge we have of the world somehow conforms to reality itself, i.e. to the world as it exists apart from and prior to our knowing it. This brought his metaphysics into conflict with Kant's transcendental idealism, according to which we know only the appearances of things, i.e. things only as they appear to our faculty of cognition and not as they are independent of it. Prima facie Hartmann's realism seems to contradict his "idealism", a term that Hartmann himself used to describe his own philosophy. It is important to see, however, that Hartmann's "idealism" is a very special kind: absolute idealism, according to which nature is "ideal" not in the sense that it exists only in some consciousness, but "ideal" in the sense that it conforms to ideas or prototypes, which are ends or purposes. Such teleological idealism is opposed, therefore, not to realism (in the above sense), but to mechanism or materialism. Like many in his generation,[74] Hartmann used the term "idealism" in this specific teleological sense. He believed that his own idealism is not only compatible with, but presupposes realism, because it claims to be true not only of our representations of nature but of nature itself, i.e. nature as it exists independent of and prior to our consciousness of it. But it was just this realism, of course, that brought Hartmann into conflict with the neo-Kantians, who, one and all, were loyal to Kant's transcendental idealism, according to which we have knowledge of appearances alone and not things-in-themselves.

The disagreement between Hartmann and the neo-Kantians might be formulated along more Kantian lines: Hartmann's metaphysics affirms *transcendental realism* and denies *transcendental idealism*, whereas the neo-Kantians deny transcendental realism and affirm transcendental idealism. Here "transcendental realism" is the doctrine

---

[74] This sense of "idealism" was formulated explicitly by Adolf Trendelenburg in his 'Über den letzten Unterschied der philosophischen Systeme', *Philologische und historische Abhandlungen der königlichen Akademie der Wissenschaften zu Berlin* (Berlin: Dümmler, 1847), 241–62.

that the knowledge we have of how things appear to us in experience gives us knowledge of things-in-themselves, i.e. of how things exist apart from our experience of them; "transcendental idealism", on the other hand, is the doctrine that we have to distinguish between appearances and things-in-themselves, so that no amount of knowledge of appearances gives us knowledge of things-in-themselves.[75]

No one was more acutely conscious of his disagreement with the neo-Kantians on this score than Hartmann himself, who vowed to fight out the issues between them. This he duly did in a short tract he first published in 1870, *Das Ding an sich und seine Beschaffenheit*,[76] but then expanded and republished in 1875 under the new but no less provocative title *Kritische Grundlegung des transcendentalen Realismus*.[77] In the introduction Hartmann stressed that it was "urgently necessary" to give a foundation for the "decisive realistic view" on which his own philosophy was founded (2). He explained the issues dividing him from the neo-Kantians in just the terms I have set out. The basic aim of his tract was to demonstrate "transcendental realism", which assumes that the contents of our consciousness give us knowledge of things-in-themselves, i.e. of how things exist independent of and prior to our consciousness of them. Hartmann gave his transcendental realism an extra meaning, though, beyond its strict Kantian sense. He distinguished it from "naïve realism" in this way: where the naïve realist simply identifies his representations with things-in-themselves, the transcendental realist recognizes that there is a difference between them but still holds that they give knowledge of things-in-themselves, because, though they are not identical with things-in-themselves, they still correspond to them (6). Transcendental realism and transcendental idealism are still opposed, however, because the transcendental realist permits, while the transcendental idealist prohibits, inferences from appearances to things-in-themselves (6).

Hartmann's method in his *Kritische Grundlegung* is to begin from within Kant's transcendental idealism and to show how its own assumptions about the limits of knowledge lead to a *reductio ad absurdam*. Having shown the absurdities and inconsistencies of transcendental idealism, he then proceeds to show how the problem of explaining the possibility of knowledge is resolvable only if we remove Kantian assumptions about the limits of knowledge and replace them with transcendental realist ones.

Hartmann's critique of Kant in *Kritische Grundlegung* maintains that Kant's transcendental idealism, if it is only consistent and follows its critical limits upon knowledge, ends in "absolute illusionism", i.e. the thesis that we know only our own

---

[75] See Kant, *KrV* A369, A490–1.

[76] Eduard von Hartmann, *Das Ding an sich und seine Beschaffenheit: Kantische Studien zur Erkenntnistheorie und Metaphysik* (Berlin: Duncker, 1870).

[77] Eduard von Hartmann, *Kritische Grundlegung des transcendentalen Realismus* (Berlin: Duncker, 1875). Under the same title an expanded third edition appeared in 1885 as volume I of *Eduard von Hartmann's Ausgewählte Werke* (Leipzig: Verlag von Wilhelm Friedrich, 1885). All references in parentheses above are to this third edition.

representations and nothing beyond them. Kant's thesis that we know only appearances, Hartmann argues, is equivalent to the thesis that we know only our own representations, simply because Kant himself so often identifies appearances with representations (17). Kant explicitly states that if we remove representations, then the entire world of physical reality also disappears.[78] Hartmann has little patience for the thesis put forward by some neo-Kantians that appearances are aspects of things-in-themselves, because he cannot see what justifies attaching appearances to things-in-themselves if, as Kant insists, we cannot have knowledge of things-in-themselves. Hartmann also gives short shrift to Kant's empirical realism, i.e. the thesis that transcendental idealism justifies knowledge of the existence of bodies in space outside us (19). The problem with empirical realism is that transcendental idealism makes space itself a representation within us, so that we cannot claim that in knowing things in space we have knowledge of reality independent of our representations. Kant's argument in the Second Analogy also makes no impression on Hartmann, who insists that it comes no closer to giving objective knowledge of the world (23). In the Second Analogy Kant had famously argued that we distinguish the *objective* order of events in experience from the *subjective* order of their appearance in consciousness by applying the principle of causality, according to which the order of our representations conforms to a universal and necessary rule (23). Hartmann responds: even that rule is nothing but a representation, a second-order representation of representations, so that even if the representations follow a rule they are still, strictly speaking, within the realm of consciousness. When all is said and done, Hartmann concludes, Kant must admit that we have knowledge only of our own representations, and that we cannot know if they represent anything. Any attempt to get outside these representations to things-in-themselves infringes the critical limits upon knowledge, which restrict it to possible experience, which consists in nothing but representations. On the whole, Hartmann's critique of Kant is a reassertion of Jacobi's famous argument that Kantian-Fichtean idealism ends in "nihilism", i.e. the doctrine that our representations represent nothing, and that we know nothing beyond them.[79] Hartmann's "absolute illusionism" was simply Jacobi's "nihilism" without the melodramatic afflatus.

Having pushed Kant into a corner, Hartmann then suggests a way out of it. We can avoid absolute illusionism, he argues, if we drop Kant's restrictions upon knowledge, more specifically, his limitation of the categories and forms of intuition to mere appearances. There were always tendencies toward transcendental realism in Kant's philosophy—for example, his belief in the existence of things-in-themselves and in the givenness of sensation—and it is only a matter of liberating these tendencies from needless constraints, Hartmann assures us, to get a consistent philosophy of transcendental realism. There is one point in Kant's philosophy where we can begin to ground

---

[78] *KrV* A376, A390.
[79] The *locus classicus* for this charge is Jacobi's *Brief an Fichte*, in *Werke* (Leipzig: Fleischer, 1816), III. 1–57.

that realism, where we can move outside the immanent realm of consciousness and make contact with a transcendent reality beyond it. What is that point? It consists in sensation (55). The intensity and quality of our sensations do not derive from consciousness alone but from something outside them, namely, the thing-in-itself which is their cause. Affection, as Hartmann puts it, is "the bridge between the immanent and transcendent", that point where the contents of consciousness connect with a reality independent of them (56). The positive content that we give the transcendent is now clear: it is the cause of sensation (57). Kant himself wanted to say this, because he stated in several places that things-in-themselves affect sensibility; but his limitations upon the categories prohibited him from making this point more explicitly. But once we admit things-in-themselves as causes of sensation, Hartmann argues, we have to accept that a whole slew of categories also are valid beyond experience. For if the thing-in-itself is the cause of the quality and intensity of sensation, we have to apply not only the category of causality, but also the categories of substance, quality and quantity to it (58–9, 80). Furthermore, we must also assume that the thing-in-itself is in time, because it causes this sensation just now, and that it is in space, because there are many other things acting at the same time (96–7).

The necessity of a realist interpretation of experience becomes especially apparent, Hartmann contends, whenever we attempt to explain the order of events on the principles of transcendental idealism. It immediately becomes apparent that we have to go outside the order of representations in our consciousness and to assume an independent order in things-in-themselves. To make this point clear, Hartmann asks us to undertake a thought experiment. Assume that I am in my study turning the pages of a book and then, suddenly, I am startled by the sound of a gunshot beneath my window (79). I cannot explain the sound of the gunshot from the order of my representations alone; if I were left solely to the order of my representations, there would be only another page of the book. But I cannot claim that my representation of the page of the book somehow creates the sound of the gunshot. Similarly, suppose that I am again in my study and hear two men arguing on the street outside; I then look out my window and see them fighting. While there is some connection between my audio and visual sensations, no one would say that the audio sensation is the cause of the visual sensation (78). To say that, I must go outside the order of my own sensations and assume something about things-in-themselves, viz., that the anger between the two men is the cause of their fighting and then my seeing them do so. So the moral of the story is clear: that to explain what we see, we have to go beyond the order of our own representations. The order of things in the world is continuous and permanent, whereas the order of our representation of the world is often interrupted and changing.

Hartmann's tract was controversial, and intentionally so, for it would often take issue with the leading neo-Kantians of his day (viz., Hermann Cohen, Friedrich Lange, Jürgen Bona Meyer, Kuno Fischer). Given the context in which he was writing, controversy was as inevitable as it was intentional, because the first edition of Hartmann's tract appeared in the midst of the famous controversy between Kuno

Fischer and Adolf Trendelenburg concerning Kant's Transcendental Aesthetic.[80] Since its beginning in the mid-1860s, that controversy had aroused enormous public interest, and it was impossible for anyone to avoid it. Hence it was *de rigueur* for Hartmann to take sides, which he did, coming down firmly on Trendelenburg's side.[81] The fundamental issue in the dispute between Fischer and Trendelenburg concerned the so-called "third alternative" to Kant's argument in the Transcendental Aesthetic. As Kant saw it, there were only two alternatives: either our representations conform to objects, with transcendental realism, or objects conform to our representations, with transcendental idealism. Kant held that the a priori status of our intuitions of space and time serve as proof of transcendental idealism. If these intuitions are a priori, he argued, they arise from our mental activity, and they do not therefore derive from things-in-themselves; but if they do not derive from things-in-themselves, Kant reasoned, they also cannot conform to them. Trendelenburg, however, held that Kant's argument is a *non-sequitur* and that there is still a "third alternative": that though our intuitions of space and time are indeed a priori, arising from our own mental activity, they still conform to, or correspond with, things-in-themselves.[82] In other words, a priori representations need not derive from things-in-themselves to correspond with them. For Trendelenburg, an absolute idealist, thinking and being conform to one and the same order and are parts of the same fundamental structure. Hartmann accepted the core of Trendelenburg's argument, which, he said, "hit the nail on the head" (102). Like Trendelenburg, he held that, unless we are to be skeptics, we have to hold that "the basic forms of the existence of things correspond with the basic forms of our intuition and thinking" (114).

Whatever the merits of Hartmann's critique of Kant—it lacked subtlety and sympathy, to say the least—it was still a valiant effort to provide some justification for the transcendental realism behind his own metaphysics. Hartmann admitted that he could not provide a dogmatic demonstration for transcendental realism, which is ultimately based more upon instinct than logic. It was still possible for a skeptic to dispute his transcendental realism, and he could not refute him without assuming the validity of his cognitive faculties and thus begging the question (114). Still, Hartmann was convinced that the consequences of transcendental idealism—"absolute illusionism"— made it necessary to abandon it and to accept transcendental realism instead, which provides the best explanation for the possibility of knowledge. Whether there really is such knowledge, however, was a question he could not answer in the confines of his treatment of Kant.

---

[80] For this controversy, see my *Late German Idealism*, pp. 107–20.

[81] Hartmann wrote an article on the controversy for a popular journal. See his 'Zur Kantischen Philosophie', *Blätter für literarische Unterhaltung*, 10 (2 Mar. 1871), 151–4.

[82] Trendelenburg first made this argument in his *Logische Untersuchungen* (Berlin: Bethge, 1840), I. 123–33. He then restated it in response to Fischer in his 'Ueber eine Lücke in Kants Beweis von der ausschliessende Subjectivität des Raumes und der Zeit', in *Historische Beiträge zur Philosophie* (Berlin: Bethge, 1867), III. 215–76.

7. Eudemonistic Pessimism

Now that we have examined Hartmann's new religion and major aspects of his metaphysics—its concept of the unconscious, its monism and its realism—we are finally in a position to discuss the most controversial side of his philosophy: its pessimism. The chief exposition of that pessimism appears in part C, chapters 11–13, of *Philosophie des Unbewussten*;[83] but Hartmann also wrote several articles in its defence,[84] and another whole monograph on the topic, his *Zur Geschichte und Begründung des Pessimismus*, which first appeared in 1880.[85] Hartmann once said that his pessimism was the one aspect of his philosophy that he had altered least;[86] but it is clear that in later years, in reaction to criticism, the doctrine went through significant reformulations.

One of these reformulations concerns Hartmann's relation to Schopenhauer. Nowhere, it seems, are Hartmann's debts to Schopenhauer more evident than in his pessimism. In chapters CXI–XIII of the second edition of the *Philosophie des Unbewussten* he constantly cites Schopenhauer, and much of his argument there can be seen as a reaffirmation and defence of Schopenhauer's thesis that "life is suffering". In an 1870 article Hartmann said that "the foundations for Schopenhauer's arguments are correct in themselves", and he claimed that all his critics had failed to refute him.[87] It is striking, however, that in later years Hartmann went to great pains to put a distance between himself and Schopenhauer.[88] He felt that his critics had unfairly condemned his philosophy chiefly because of its apparent similarity with Schopenhauer's pessimism. To sidestep these criticisms, Hartmann stressed that neither his conclusions nor his methods were Schopenhauerian. His conclusions were very different from Schopenhauer's, because his theory of value ended not with the denial but the affirmation of the will to life.[89] His methods were also very different, because they were based more on empirical investigation rather than metaphysical arguments. Hartmann criticized Schopenhauer's metaphysical arguments severely, insisting that they rested on two false premises: the blindness of the absolute will and the negativity of pleasure.[90] Where he once endorsed the foundation of Schopenhauer's arguments, he now complained about Schopenhauer's complete lack of rigour in justifying his pessimism,

---

[83] Chapters CXI–XIII, pp. 564–681 (1870). Unless otherwise noted, all references in parentheses are to this edition.

[84] 'Ist der pessimistische Monismus trostlos?', *Philosophische Monatshefte*, 5 (1870), 21–41; 'Ist der Pessimismus wissenschaftliche zu begründen', *Philosophische Monatshefte*, 15 (1879), 589–612; 'Ist der Pessimismus schädlich?', *Gegenwart*, 16 (1879), 211–14, 233–5; 'Zur Pessimismusfrage', *Philosophische Monatshefte*, 19 (1883), 60–80; 'Der Pessimismus und die Sittenlehre', *Blätter für literarischen Unterhaltung*, 1 (1 Jan. 1883), 6–9.

[85] Eduard von Hartmann, *Zur Geschichte und Begründung des Pessimismus* (Berlin: Duncker, 1880). A 2nd enlarged edn appeared in 1891 with Hermann Haacke Verlag, Leipzig.

[86] 'Mein Entwickelungsgang', *Gesammelte Studien und Aufsätze*, p. 39.

[87] 'Ist der pessimistische Monismus trostlos?', in *Gesammelte Studien und Aufsätze*, p. 74.

[88] See 'Mein Entwickelungsgang', in *Gesammelte Studien und Aufsätze*, pp. 38–40; 'Mein Verhältnis mit Schopenhauer', in *Philosophische Fragen der Gegenwart* (Berlin: Duncker, 1885), pp. 25–37.

[89] Cf. 'Mein Entwickelungsgang', p. 39, and *Philosophie des Unbewussten* (1870), p. 675.

[90] 'Mein Entwickelungsgang', p. 34.

which he claimed is based more on his bleak moods and misanthropic temperament than any rigorous reasoning.

Whatever the precise differences between Hartmann and Schopenhauer, it has to be said that Hartmann's efforts to place a distance between himself and Schopenhauer were more tactical than truthful. What is most striking about the first and main exposition of his pessimism—chapters CXI–XIII of the second edition of *Philosophie des Unbewussten*—is its sympathy and affinity with Schopenhauer.[91]

How, exactly, did Hartmann conceive pessimism? Although he provides no precise definition, he understands it in the same general terms as Schopenhauer: as the thesis that nothingness is better than being, that non-existence is preferable to existence. Hartmann wagers, like Schopenhauer, that no sane person would choose to live his or her life over again; he or she would prefer instead annihilation, complete nothingness (567, 586). The reason that nothingness is better than being, Hartmann argues, is because life brings more suffering than happiness.

Hartmann insists that we do *not* define pessimism as the thesis that this is the worst of all possible worlds. That was how Schopenhauer once defined it, by making pessimism the antithesis of Leibniz's thesis that this is the best of all possible worlds.[92] Not only are Schopenhauer's argument for his thesis spurious, Hartmann contends, but the Leibnizian thesis is compatible with pessimism (558). The pessimist can hold that this is the *best* of all possible worlds, because that does not entail that this world is good, still less that it is perfect; it is still possible for it to be the least bad of many bad options. More importantly, it is also possible that, though this existing world is better than all other possible worlds, its non-existence is better than its existence.

Although Hartmann, like Schopenhauer, understands pessimism as the doctrine that nothingness is better than being, he puts an essential qualification upon this thesis, one that does not appear in Schopenhauer: that life is not worth living *only* when measured according to eudemonic standards, i.e. according to the ideal that the good life is happiness, which consists in the greatest possible pleasure and the least possible pain. Hence Hartmann defines his pessimism completely and strictly in eudemonic terms.[93] It is for him simply the thesis that there is more pain than pleasure, more suffering than happiness, in life.[94] But this qualification leaves open the possibility that life is worth living by other than eudemonic standards. This, as we shall soon see, is exactly Hartmann's position.

Like Dühring, Hartmann was troubled by the question whether the value of life could be arbitrated in philosophical terms. Is it not entirely a matter of personal

---

[91] The admiration and sympathy never really disappeared. In *Phänomenologie des sittlichen Bewußtseins*, p. 619, Hartmann paid handsome tribute to Schopenhauer for his rebellion against theism, which he regards as a major contribution to cultural history.

[92] See above Chapter 3, section 3.

[93] 'Ist der Pessimismus wissenschaftlich zu begründen?', in *Zur Geschichte und Begründung des Pessimismus* (1880), pp. 67, 69.

[94] Ibid., p. 67.

decision? There are passages in the *Philosophie des Unbewussten* where Hartmann seems to accept that point. He writes that each person has to judge the value of life from his or her own experience and perspective, and that no one can decide for someone else (569). "Every person is exactly as happy as he feels", as he once put it (569). But Hartmann goes no further in this subjectivist direction, and even seems to backtrack. He corrects himself on the grounds that people are sometimes mistaken about the value of their own lives. People, he insists, are not the most impartial judges about themselves. The mere instinct for self-preservation makes them biased about the worth of their existence (570). As Jean Paul said: they love life not because it is beautiful but they find life beautiful because they love it. The mere fact that people so fervently desire and pursue happiness makes them assume and hope that it is achievable in life. Because people are not the best judges of their own experience, and because they are predisposed to assume that happiness is attainable in life, the philosopher has to intervene; only he can determine, from an objective and impartial standpoint, whether happiness is really obtainable in this life.

True to his eudemonic definition of pessimism, most of Hartmann's argument in chapters XI–XIII of part C of *Philosophie des Unbewussten* is an attempt to prove that life consists more in pain than pleasure, and therefore more in misery than happiness. To prove his case, Hartmann draws our attention to the following facts about human nature, desire and experience.

(1) Human beings are more sensitive to pain than pleasure (576-7). Any human being, when presented with the options of feeling neither pleasure nor pain, or pleasure and pain in equal amounts, would choose the former (581).

(2) The great goods of human life—youth, security, health and freedom—consist not in the presence of pleasure but in the absence of pain. We feel pleasure in having these goods only if we have lost them and then regained them (582-3).

(3) The pleasure in the satisfaction of our desires is much shorter in duration and intensity than the misery of their frustration (578-9).

(4) The chief desires of human life—for food and sex—are the source of more suffering than happiness. Hunger and sexual frustration take us below 0 in the scale of happiness; and when these desires are satisfied, we are only back at 0 (589, 594, 599). The few moments of pleasure in sex hardly compensate for its great disappointments and for the huge investment of time and energy (592). On the whole, Hartmann affirms Schopenhauer's thesis about the metaphysics of sexual love: that we persist in such a painful activity not for our individual happiness but for the survival of the species (595).

(5) The desires for power, fame and money are inexhaustible; the more we get, the more we want; but the greater our wants, the less likely they are to be satisfied (610, 614).

Although Hartmann disagrees with Schopenhauer's theory that pleasure has only a negative value—he points out that some pleasures are not preceded by any pains—he still thinks that most pleasures arise indirectly from the diminution of pain (575). Practically speaking, Hartmann admits, Schopenhauer is correct: all that we can achieve in this life is something negative, i.e. the diminution of pain; but we cannot achieve anything positive, i.e. the predominance of pleasure over pain (578–9). Summarizing all his arguments, Hartmann finally draws the damning general conclusion that life, as measured by the hedonic calculus, is not worth living (586). We can summarize his case in the following syllogism. If (1) the best possible life for a human being consists in the absence of pain; if (2) the absence of pain is equivalent to 0 on the scale of happiness; and if (3) complete absence of pain is unattainable for anyone in life, then (4) the value of life falls *below* 0. But if the value of life falls below 0, then it is not, by eudemonic standards, worth living.

In chapters CXI–XIII of *Philosophie des Unbewussten* Hartmann explains that there are three fundamental illusions about the value of life. The first illusion is that "Happiness is attainable in the present stage of development of the world" (573). This is an illusion, Hartmann argues, because, for all the reasons just given, happiness in a positive sense is unattainable, and because pain and suffering far outweigh pleasure and contentment. The prevalence and persistence of this illusion in human beings, Hartmann maintains, is due to hope, which is grounded in our instinct for self-preservation. Although our hopes are almost always disappointed—nine times in ten, Hartmann estimates—they constantly reassert themselves because of this instinct. If we had no hope for a better future, we would not be able to bear this life and we would commit suicide. The second illusion is that "Happiness is attainable for an individual in a transcendent life after death" (635). This is an illusion too, Hartmann explains, because there is no world beyond ours, a supernatural one that is better than our own; the only world is the natural world, the world as it exists in space and time. The will, which is the source of everything, exists only in and through its embodiments in this world; and if there were no will, there would be nothingness (642). The prevalence of this illusion arises from egoism, which longs for the continuation of our individual existence beyond the grave; those who are denied individual happiness in this world seek compensation in another (642). Although Hartmann is critical of Christianity for fostering this illusion, he still thinks that it marks an important step beyond paganism because it at least sees that this life is a vale of tears and that the highest good is not attainable in it (635, 643). The third illusion is that "Happiness lies in the future through the world-process" (645). Here Hartmann criticizes those philosophers (Lessing and Hegel) who believe in human progress, and who find the meaning and purpose in life in contributing to the ends of world-history. He maintains that, however much humanity progresses, it will never get rid of the greatest sources of human misery: sickness, age, dependence on the will of others, sexual frustration and hunger (650). The state has only a negative ideal—to protect our rights to life and liberty—but it cannot help us to achieve the good life or make us happy (658). The best we can ever accomplish through political activity is security, health and freedom; but that brings us at best only to 0 on the scale of pleasure (659). Hartmann does not dispute the enormous technical progress that has been made through the arts and sciences; but he insists that it at best only makes life easier and that it never brings happiness (659). However far we progress in medicine, agriculture and chemistry, he argues, this will still leave us with the difficult question: "What content should we give our lives?" (660).

The culmination of Hartmann's eudemonic pessimism comes with his fantastic theory of redemption, which he outlines in the penultimate chapter of *Die Philosophie des Unbewussten*.[95] Here Hartmann teaches that we will achieve complete deliverance from suffering—the state of utter painlessness—only when we, the whole of humanity, collectively resolve to deny the will. If one person alone denies the will, this ends suffering for him or her; but the rest of humanity goes on suffering because the will continues to exist in its many other self-conscious embodiments in other people. If, however, we together in unison resolve to deny the will, this destroys the will itself, which exists only in and through its self-conscious embodiments. Having eradicated the will itself, we thus destroy the very source of existence, and so we create nothingness. With nothingness, we reach our ultimate goal: nirvana, complete painlessness. Redemption thus takes place when humanity takes it upon itself to rectify the worst mistake ever made—the primal decision of the will to come into existence.

It was a remarkably nihilistic theory, one that developed Schopenhauer's own nihilistic sentiments at the end of *Die Welt als Wille und Vorstellung*. The theory attracted considerable comment and even ridicule—Nietzsche would famously spoof it in his *Unzeitgemäße Betrachtungen*[96]—though Hartmann himself admitted that it was very speculative (676). It is indeed difficult to place this nihilistic fantasy within the context of Hartmann's philosophy as a whole. For it is scarcely compatible with the more optimistic side of Hartmann's philosophy, which maintains that life is still worth living after all. We must now consider this side of Hartmann's philosophy.[97]

8. Evolutionary Optimism

Despite all his arguments and efforts in behalf of eudemonic pessimism, Hartmann insists that it is still only one half of his general theory about the value of life. He describes his general theory as a synthesis of "eudemonistic pessimism" with "evolutionary optimism".[98] While the eudemonistic pessimist holds that it is impossible to achieve happiness in this world, and that life consists essentially in suffering, the evolutionary optimist maintains that it is possible to make progress in diminishing human

---

[95] Chapter CXIII, 'Das Ziel des Weltprocesses und die Bedeutung des Bewusstseins', pp. 664–81.

[96] See §9 of *Vom Nutzen und Nachtheil der Historie für das Leben, Sämtliche Werke, Studien Ausgabe*, ed. Giorgi Colli and Mazzino Montinari (Berlin: de Gruyter, 1980), I. 311–24.

[97] It is a mistake to neglect this side of Hartmann's philosophy. Some accounts stress the nihilistic theory as the culmination of Hartmann's pessimism, leaving out the optimistic side of his theory. See, for example, Pauen, *Pessimismus*, pp. 127–31; and the otherwise brilliant account in Lütkehaus, *Nichts*, pp. 223–42. Pauen maintains (pp. 127–8), incorrectly, that Hartmann intends to undermine the belief in progress.

[98] *Geschichte und Begründung des Pessimismus* (1880), pp. ix–x, 36.

suffering and in achieving greater morality and perfection. If life is not worth living by eudemonic standards, it is still very much worth living by moral ones. We human beings have a purpose in life and we have good reason to go on living: to diminish suffering, and to promote human culture and perfection.

Hartmann is convinced that the two sides of his theory are not only compatible but complementary.[99] It is only when we are ready to renounce the illusion that we can achieve happiness in this life, he argues, that we are fully ready to devote ourselves to our moral ideals. The search for happiness is based on egoism, which places my self-interest above everyone else; it is therefore contrary to the moral law, which demands that I act for the sake of principle alone. The eudemonic pessimist therefore promotes morality by discouraging egoism, the chief source of the temptation to act contrary to our moral ideals. And so, for Hartmann, pessimism is not the enemy but the friend of morality.

Hartmann saw his syncretic theory—his synthesis of optimism and pessimism—as an attempt to complement Schopenhauer's pessimism with Hegel's optimism. If Schopenhauer was right to be pessimistic about the prospects for human happiness, Hegel was correct to be optimistic about the prospects for greater human freedom and moral perfection. Like a good Hegelian, Hartmann believed in progress in world-history, which he understood in terms of the growth of self-consciousness and reason. History was for him a struggle between the irrational will and reason, between the forces of unconsciousness and those of consciousness, where reason and consciousness would gradually take control over subconscious feelings and impulses (327–8, 670).[100] The more the realm of consciousness and reason grew, the more we would learn to limit our desires and take control over our lives, and the less we would be frustrated by the vain pursuit of pleasure. Hartmann's enduring optimism surfaces in his conviction that the forces of reason and consciousness will ultimately triumph over those of the unconscious will (330, 675).

It is the evolutionary optimism of Hartmann's theory that marks his greatest distance from Schopenhauer. This side of his theory was, from the very beginning, conceived in opposition to Schopenhauer's pessimism. Where Hartmann took issue with Schopenhauer's pessimism—even in the days when he otherwise endorsed it—concerned its "quietism", i.e. the thesis that all attempts to improve the human condition are futile.[101] He insisted that his own pessimism, unlike Schopenhauer's, makes it meaningful and rewarding to strive to improve the world, to try to make it a better place; it includes, he stressed, social and political programmes for the improvement of the human condition (650). Like Dühring, Hartmann affirmed a social and political

---

[99] See Hartmann's article 'Ist der pessimistische Monismus trostlos?', as reprinted in *Gesammelte philosophische Abhandlungen*, pp. 71–89, esp. 77–8; and 'Ist der Pessimismus schädlich?', as reprinted in *Geschichte und Begründung des Pessimismus* (1880), pp. 86–100, esp. 92–100.

[100] All references in the next paragraphs, until otherwise noted, are to the second edition of *Philosophie des Unbewussten*.

[101] See 'Ist der pessimistische Monismus trostlos?', p. 74.

activism, insisting that we have the obligation to strive to change the world, however little we might actually accomplish. He deplored Schopenhauer's quietism because it virtually sanctioned suffering and evil by depriving us of any reason to do something about them. It was ultimately because of his activism that Hartmann believed he was justified in affirming the will to life. He stressed his difference with Schopenhauer on this score by ending chapter XIII of *Philosophie des Unbewussten* with a ringing *"affirmation of the will to life"* (675; his italics).

In the retrospective essays of his later years Hartmann always insisted that his differences with Schopenhauer's pessimism were there from the very beginning, and that he never refashioned his pessimism to avoid the criticisms of Schopenhauer's.[102] Although this is not true—his position did evolve and he did respond to the criticisms of Schopenhauer's pessimism—it is still the case that the evolutionary side of his pessimism was present since at least the second edition of *Die Philosophie des Unbewussten*. While this side of his theory is stressed more in later years, as Hartmann distances himself from Schopenhauer, it was already explicit in his earlier work. It was even implicit in Hartmann's early religious writings. One of the main reasons for Hartmann's advocacy of religion is that it provides the individual with some sense of purpose in life, with some reason to strive to make the world a better place. On these grounds, Hartmann was opposed from the very beginning to Schopenhauer's pessimism, which saw all such striving as pointless.

There is still the deeper question, though, whether the two sides of Hartmann's theory are completely consistent. For Hartmann's eudemonistic pessimism is sometimes so severe that it begins to undermine his evolutionary optimism. It is an essential aspect of his evolutionary optimism that mankind can make progress at least in decreasing pain and suffering even if it cannot increase pleasure and happiness. Yet Hartmann also says that all our striving does not do much to ameliorate misery (650–1). So small is our approximation to the ideal of the best life on earth, he maintains, that one has to raise again the question of the value of life (660). There is also Hartmann's nihilistic theory of redemption, according to which the end of history should be annihilation, nirvana or nothingness (662). But if we aspire toward that lofty goal, what is the point in struggling toward moral and cultural perfection?

Hartmann's evolutionary optimism underwent considerable reformulation and clarification in the 1870s, reaching its culminating exposition in his chief work on ethics, his *Phänomenologie des sittlichen Bewußtseins*, which first appeared in 1878.[103] The tension between his eudemonistic pessimism and evolutionary optimism is now, at least partially, resolved by removing all traces of eudemonism from his concept of historical development. Hartmann now makes it clear that the process of evolution

---

[102] See 'Die Schicksale meiner Philosophie in ihrem ersten Jahrzehnt', in *Philosophische Fragen der Gegenwart*, pp. 8–9.

[103] Eduard Hartmann, *Phänomenologie des sittlichen Bewußtseins* (Berlin: Duncker, 1878). All references in parentheses in the next paragraphs are to the third edition, edited by Alma Hartmann, which appeared in Berlin in 1924 with Wegweiser Verlag.

consists essentially in "cultural development", which has little to do with the mitigation of misery, still less with the promotion of happiness. Rather, it is all about the development of human powers in the arts and sciences, about the promotion of excellence in human culture, about the evolution of the species *homo sapiens*. Hartmann stresses that we pay an enormous price for such evolution: the more we develop these powers, promote this excellence and advance as a species, the more miserable we become (529). We are presented with a clear dilemma: "Either promotion of happiness at the cost of cultural development or promotion of cultural development at the cost of human happiness" (517). But the dilemma is not a choice that we humans have to make: nature and history are moving *inevitably* in the direction of greater and higher culture, for which we have to pay the price in terms of less happiness and even greater misery.

It is a fundamental thesis of Hartmann's evolutionary optimism that history, and the world-process in general, are teleological or purposive, that they are inevitably but unconsciously working toward a goal or end, which is the development of higher human culture. Hartmann saw this teleological conception of history as the main result of "the historical worldview", which he regarded as one of the great achievements of 19th-century thought (518). It seemed a decidedly old-fashioned perspective, given that the reaction against Hegel's historicism had been under way for decades, a reaction first voiced by Ranke and Savigny and later epitomized by Dilthey, who declared all philosophy of history to be dead. Yet Hartmann had a trump card up his sleeve to counter Hegel's critics and to revive the philosophy of history. The teleological conception of history, he claimed, had now received major impetus and endorsement from Darwinism, which had finally closed the gap between human and natural history (520). Darwinism was indeed "the triumph of the Leibnizian-Hegelian principle of development" (521). Hartmann knew all too well that many of Darwin's disciples had interpreted evolution strictly in mechanical terms; but he protested that this was not the true meaning of their master's doctrine. Thanks to Darwin, he argued, it was now possible to show that the higher development of human culture is the goal of human evolution itself. The process of natural selection is now working toward the growth of greater refinement and organization of brain processes, which will eventually manifest themselves in higher levels of culture (521). Darwin's theory of evolution also shows us very clearly, Hartmann maintained, that the goal of evolution does not consist in the happiness of individuals, still less the masses, but in the development of the human species, and more specifically the perfection of its distinctive capacities for art and science (521). To be sure, the process of natural selection, which crushes the sick, weak and unfit, seems to be very brutal and harsh; but that, Hartmann reassures us, is only when it is measured by inappropriate eudemonist standards. The elimination of the weaker and less fit is necessary to promote the evolution of the stronger and more fit, where "stronger" and "fitter" means more advanced in powers for the promotion of human culture.

The task of each individual in the modern world, Hartmann taught, is to promote, as much as he or she can, the goals of history. This means that each individual will have to exert him or herself to promote culture, to create progress in the arts and sciences. In other words, he or she will have to be what Hartmann dubbed "a fighter for culture" (*Kulturkämpfer*). The phrase was an unmistakable allusion to current political events. The *Kulturkampf*, the struggle between the Bismarckian state and the Roman Catholic Church, was only beginning to wind down in 1878, the year Hartmann published the first edition of his *Phänomenologie des sittlichen Bewußtseins*. In this struggle Hartmann stood entirely and passionately behind the Bismarckian state, which for him represented the realm of culture against the forces of darkness. Who were these forces of darkness? They were the Jesuits and the social democrats (528–9).[104] The Jesuits represented the principle of heteronomy in ethics—complete subjugation to the Catholic hierarchy—which threatened to take Germany back to the Middle Ages. The social democrats advocated social and economic equality on the basis of the principle of utility, the greatest happiness of the greatest number (497–8). Their programme, Hartmann argued, not only suffered from the illusion that happiness is attainable in this life, but it also led inevitably to mediocrity in the arts and sciences, to a general levelling where everyone has and does the same, and where no one strives to achieve more than anyone else (499–503). Like Nietzsche,[105] Hartmann believed that cultural achievement could be created only by a small minority, an elite few, those who had the necessary talents, and that the great mass of individuals were incapable of it. If this elite were allowed to pursue excellence, they would eventually improve the lot of everyone, because they would raise the standards for all. Bringing everyone down to the same level, as the social democrats would have it, would ultimately only worsen the state of the working classes (498–9).

How would the elite *Kulturkämpfer* promote culture? What means were necessary to achieve a higher level of it? Hartmann's answer to these questions is shocking for a modern reader. In explaining these means he reveals his harsh and pitiless vision of the world, his own version of social Darwinism. There are several means to achieve higher culture, we learn, and each is brutal. One is war, which forces a people to develop its powers to the fullest (529). Wars are means for natural selection among peoples, where the victors prove their superiority over the vanquished. The development of culture not only permits but requires, Hartmann opines, colonization, where the more advanced nations should rule over more primitive races (530). Another means for cultural evolution is economic competition (532–3), which forces individuals to develop their skills and improve their talents so that they can get ahead of others and improve

---

[104] Remarkably, Hartmann argued that social democracy, if pursued to its logical conclusion, would lead to Jesuitism. Since it would become obvious that the social democrats could not justify their theory that the masses could attain happiness in this life, they would preach the doctrine of happiness in another life, just like the Jesuits. See *Die Phänomenologie des sittliche Bewußtseins*, pp. 510–12.

[105] Despite this affinity with Nietzsche, Hartmann was one of his bitter foes. See Hartmann's 'Nietzsche's «Neue Moral»', *Preussische Jahrbücher*, 67 (1891), 504–21. The article was reprinted in *Ethische Studien* (Leipzig: Hermann Haacke, 1898), 34–60. For further materials on Hartmann's critique of Nietzsche, see *Eduard von Hartmann: Zeitgenosse und Gegenspieler Nietzsches*, ed. Jean-Claude Wolf (Würzburg: Königshausen & Neumann, 2006).

their lot. Still another means is social, political and economic *inequality*, which allows for the development of an elite few to pursue cultural ends (530, 535). War, competition, inequality, exploitation, colonialism—all these lead to the unhappiness of the great majority of people; but that, Hartmann insists, is the price that we have to pay for evolution and the development of culture.

We can now see clearly the conservative political intention and motivation behind Hartmann's theory of the value of life. It was all a defence of the monarchy and aristocracy of the old order, and more specifically of the Prussian establishment, of which Hartmann's family was such a proud member. As an admirer of Kaiser Wilhelm I, Bismarck and the Prussian military, Hartmann firmly believed that the Prussian state was the only bulwark to preserve the realm of culture against the emerging forces of barbarism in the modern world. Both sides of Hartmann's theory—its eudemonic pessimism and evolutionary optimism—were crucial in his defence of the old order. Eudemonic pessimism was meant to discourage the masses, whose demands for social and economic equality were based upon the false premise of eudemonic optimism, the assumption that it is possible to achieve happiness in this life. Evolutionary optimism was meant to encourage the elite, to justify their existence by making social and political inequality both the precondition and product of evolution and historical development.

When we place Hartmann's philosophy in this social and political context, it becomes clear how much it was a product of his age. We can now see why the younger pessimists charged Hartmann with bolstering the status quo. We can see also why Hartmann's philosophy became so popular in the 1870s after the foundation of the Reich, and why its star sank so rapidly after the First World War. After that catastrophe, Hartmann's world and culture would cease to exist. For all his philosophical importance for his age, it is not surprising that we have forgotten him.

8
The Pessimism Controversy, 1870–1890

1. The Eye of the Storm

Because or in spite of all its problems, Hartmann's *Philosophie des Unbewussten* proved to be a very controversial book. Indeed, no book in the late 19th century was more controversial. Hartmann's tome sparked "the pessimism controversy", the greatest intellectual controversy—measured in terms of duration, intensity and number of participants—in the second half of the 19th century in Germany. This controversy cast in the shade the disputes over historicism, materialism and Darwinism, which had also attracted much attention. It lasted from 1870 until the beginning of the First World War, and virtually every major intellectual in Germany took part in it. After all, nothing less was at stake than the very value of life itself.

The most intense phase of the pessimism controversy—if we can divide that controversy into phases at all—took place from 1870 to 1890, roughly the first two decades after the publication of the first edition of Hartmann's *Philosophie des Unbewussten* in 1869. We know from two contemporary bibliographies that in the 1870s alone hundreds of reviews, scores of articles and dozens of books were published on pessimism.[1] For the 1880s, one can safely predict, the volume of literature would at least have doubled.[2] Most of this literature focuses on Hartmann's pessimism, which was thought to be a more sophisticated and systematic form of Schopenhauer's doctrine. No one, however, was under any illusion that the Frankfurt sage stood behind it all. If he were not alive in spirit, there would have been no controversy at all.

Standing in the very centre of the storm, Hartmann himself inevitably played a major role in the pessimism controversy. Though a reluctant polemicist, he was very sensitive to criticism, so he never hesitated to respond to the many objections against

---

[1] O. Plümacher, 'Chronologische Verzeichniss der Hartmann-Literatur von 1868–1880', in *Der Kampf um's Unbewusste* (Berlin: Duncker, 1881), pp. 115–50; and Ferdinand Labau, *Die Schopenhauer-Literatur* (Leipzig: Brockhaus, 1880). Neither of these bibliographies extends beyond 1880. On the first decade of the reception of Hartmann's philosophy, see his own article 'Die Schicksale meiner Philosophie in ihrem ersten Jahrzehnt (1869–1879)', in *Philosophische Fragen der Gegenwart* (Leipzig: Wilhelm Friedrich, 1885), pp. 1–25.

[2] There is no reliable or complete bibliography of the controversy for the 1880s. Both Plümacher and Labau published their work in the early 1880s, too early to record the writings of that decade.

his philosophy. Throughout the 1870s and 1880s he wrote numerous articles, and no less than four books,[3] in reply to his many critics. In the course of responding to their objections he would often clarify, and even reformulate, his pessimism. To understand his pessimism, then, we need to consider these objections and his replies to them.

2. Two Classic Objections

One of the oldest objections against pessimism is that it is immoral because it saps the motivation to fight evil and to alleviate suffering.[4] If we know that we cannot achieve happiness or diminish unhappiness in this life—so the objection goes—then there is little incentive in trying to make the world a better place. For these critics, all pessimism leads to quietism, an acceptance of, and surrender to, the evil and suffering of the world. This is immoral, however, because morality demands that we actively struggle against evil and suffering rather than passively resigning ourselves to it. While this objection was originally made against Schopenhauer, Hartmann's critics did not hesitate to dump it on him too. The immorality of pessimism was such a favourite topic that it eventually became the subject of an essay competition in the early 1880s.[5]

Hartmann had two responses to this objection. The first was to take the moral high road: although pessimism does indeed undermine egoism, the selfish striving for personal happiness, it supports morality, which demands that we act for the sake of moral principle alone.[6] When the pessimist argues that we cannot achieve personal happiness, Hartmann explains, he undermines only the motivation to pursue *selfish* ends, which is the chief motive to *violate* moral principles, which require nothing short of duty for the sake of duty. Hartmann then threw the objection back in the optimist's face: it is the optimist who is guilty of undermining morality. For if the optimist were

---

[3] The books were his *Erläuterungen zur Metaphysik des Unbewussten, mit besonderer Rücksicht auf den Panlogismus* (Berlin: Duncker, 1874), which eventually became part of a much larger work, *Neukantianismus, Schopenhauerismus und Hegelianismus in ihrer Stellung zu den philosophischen Aufgaben der Gegenwart* (Berlin: Duncker, 1877). In the 1880s Hartmann published two further polemical works: his *Zur Geschichte und Begründung des Pessimismus* (Berlin: Duncker, 1880); and *Philosophische Fragen der Gegenwart* (Leipzig: Wilhelm Friedrich, 1885).

[4] This criticism was first made by Johann Friedrich Herbart in his review of *Die Welt als Wille und Vorstellung* in *Hermes*, Stück 3 (1820), 131–49; reprinted in *Sämtliche Werke*, ed. Karl Kehrbach and Otto Flügel (Langensalza: Hermann Beyer & Söhne, 1887–1912), XII. 56–75. After Herbart, the criticism was made constantly and by virtually every critic.

[5] Among the works submitted for the prize were Johannes Rehmke, *Der Pessimismus und die Sittenlehre* (Leipzig: Verlag von Julius Klinkhardt, 1882); Albert Bacmeister, *Der Pessimismus und die Sittenlehre* (Haarlem: De Erven F. Bohn, 1882); Hugo Sommer, *Der Pessimismus und die Sittenlehre* (Haarlem: De Evren F. Bohn, 1882); and Paul Christ, *Der Pessimismus und die Sittenlehre* (Haarlem: De Evren F. Bohn, 1882). The prize was set by a Dutch congregation, 'Godgelaerde Genootenschap te Haarlem', and was shared by Christ and Rehmke.

[6] See Hartmann's articles 'Ist der pessimistische Monismus trostlos?', *Philosophische Monatshefte*, 5 (1870), 21–41, reprinted in *Gesammelte philosophische Abhandlungen*, pp. 71–89, esp. 77–8; and 'Ist der Pessimismus schädlich?', *Gegenwart*, 16 (1879), 211–14, 233–5, reprinted in *Geschichte und Begründung des Pessimismus* (1880), pp. 86–100, esp. 92–3, 96–7, 99. The first two works are here referred to in their later editions.

correct that we *can* achieve happiness in this life, then self-interest in one's own pleasure would be the irresistible motivation for human action, which would make it impossible to do duty for its own sake. Hence pessimism, Hartmann concludes, does not undercut but assists morality, because it is a potent antidote against egoism or selfishness, which is the main enemy of all morality.

Hartmann's second response to this objection was to stress that his pessimism is entirely eudemonistic, and that it is not only compatible with, but the best support for, his evolutionary optimism, which does give us reasons and incentives to fight against evil and suffering. According to that optimism, if we only strive and exert ourselves, we can achieve progress toward creating greater culture, morality and human perfection. Hartmann stressed that his eudemonic pessimism and evolutionary optimism are interdependent: that we are fully motivated to act for moral ends only if we know that we cannot achieve happiness in this life. The moral optimist has to be, therefore, a eudemonistic pessimist. As for the charge of quietism, Hartmann stressed that Schopenhauer was indeed guilty of it,[7] but for just this reason he limited his own pessimism to the eudemonic sphere.

To an extent, Hartmann's responses to this criticism beg the question. Hartmann simply denies what his critics assume: that we human beings, finite and imperfect as we are, need personal happiness as a motivation for moral action. Hartmann's position is a morally severe one, insisting that everyone could and should strive for moral ends for their own sake, regardless of any concern for personal happiness. He saw his own position as a reaffirmation of Kant's rigorism, though even Kant had recognized the need for personal happiness as an incentive for the achievement of the highest good.[8]

But, quite apart from such moral severity, Hartmann's responses to this criticism were more likely to incite than quell the concerns of his critics. For in reply to the question whether his monistic pessimism leads to despair, Hartmann argued that there is nothing to fear in his monism, because it extinguishes individual personality in the oneness of the absolute.[9] If my individual self disappears, then for me there is only nothingness; and if there is nothing to fear, there is no reason to despair. So Hartmann wrote: "I console you about being with the promise of nothingness; it is being for which we need consolation; nothingness needs none at all."[10] But this was an odd argument, because, for many, nothingness is precisely the most horrifying prospect of all. What could be more terrifying than complete annihilation? Against that fear, Hartmann once again took the moral high road, preaching against a selfishness that presumes to extend itself beyond this life. But it is remarkable to see nihilism advocated as the advantage rather than *reductio ad absurdum* of an ethical position. To that extent, Hartmann simply fell into the trap set by his critics, who complained constantly about the short distance from pessimism to nihilism.

---

[7] See Hartmann, 'Ist der pessimistische Monismus trostlos?', 74–5; and *Philosophische Fragen*, pp. 34–5.
[8] Kant, *Kritik der praktischen Vernunft*, V. 25, 110, 127.
[9] Ist der pessimistische Monismus trostlos?', p. 88.   [10] Ibid.

Another closely related objection against pessimism is that it sanctions, even enjoins, suicide.¹¹ If nothingness is preferable to being, if we were better off never having been born, these critics argue, then we have no reason to continue existing at all, and we will be better off putting an end to ourselves right away. We have already seen how suicide was indeed a prudent option on the premises of Schopenhauer's pessimism, which gave the average individual no reason to hope for redemption.¹² Hartmann readily agrees that suicide is indeed the proper result of Schopenhauer's pessimism, but he protests that it is not the right conclusion to draw from his own. Remarkably, he regrets that his early writings might have caused *Weltschmerz* in some and strengthened it in others, and he even admits that this might have been due to his lack of personal maturity and philosophical sophistication.¹³ But he strongly denies that the principles of his philosophy recommend, or even permit, suicide.¹⁴ We have to accept suicide as the proper conclusion of pessimism, he argues, only if (1) we adopt an egoistic, eudemonist ethic, and (2) we accept the argument of eudemonistic pessimism. Then there is indeed no reason to go on living, because there are strong reasons for believing that we could never achieve the highest good in life, which would be personal happiness. But Hartmann repudiates the first premise, the egoistic or eudemonist ethic. All those who claim that his pessimism leads to suicide, Hartmann charges, assume such an ethic. In making such an objection, the eudemonists were throwing stones but living in glass houses because it is their ethic that ultimately sanctions suicide, given that life presents so few opportunities for true happiness, and given that they allow no other motive to live. Hartmann denies that his own version of pessimism leads to suicide because it is combined with his evolutionary optimism, which gives the individual other reasons to live than the illusion of personal happiness. Evolutionary optimism encourages the individual to participate in social and political activity, and to contribute toward social and political progress; in making such demands, it gives him a sense of meaning and purpose in life even if he never attains personal happiness.

3. Hartmann versus the Neo-Kantians and Dühring

Of all Hartmann's critics, the most persistent and pesky were the neo-Kantians, who were the most powerful school of academic philosophers in the late 19th century.¹⁵ In 1880 Hartmann hit upon a remarkable strategy to foil them. He would demonstrate that the true father of his pessimism was not Arthur Schopenhauer, as everyone

---

¹¹ See, for example, Johannes Huber, *Der Pessimismus* (Munich: Theodor Ackermann, 1876), p. 79.
¹² See Chapter 4, section 4.
¹³ In the essay 'Ist Pessimismus schädlich?', in *Geschichte und Begründung des Pessimismus* (1880), p. 89.
¹⁴ See 'Führt der Pessimismus zum Selbstmord?', in *Geschichte und Begründung des Pessimismus* (1890), pp. 204–39, esp. 231–4. This article is only in the 2nd edn of this work.
¹⁵ On the neo-Kantian campaign against pessimism, see my *The Genesis of Neo-Kantianism* (Oxford: OUP, 2014), pp. 398–421.

thought, but Immanuel Kant. If he could show this, he reckoned, his neo-Kantian critics would have to reappraise their hostile attitude toward pessimism. And so Hartmann wrote a long article, 'Kant als Vater des Pessimismus', which appeared as chapter I of his *Zur Geschichte und Begründung des Pessimismus.*[16]

Hartmann's insinuation that Kant was the father of *his own* pessimism is a post-facto invention, the result of polemical need and his attempt to distance himself from Schopenhauer. The whole thesis seems an implausible and desperate strategy. Kant, the believer in progress and defender of practical faith in God and immortality, a pessimist? But we should not prejudge Hartmann. By exhaustively combing through and citing from the Kantian corpus, which Hartmann knew quite well, he manages to make a solid case for his thesis that Kant was indeed a "eudemonistic pessimist", i.e. someone who held that it is not possible to achieve happiness in this life. Hartmann is perfectly correct that Kant had denied that happiness is the purpose of life, and that Kant had doubted the likelihood of achieving happiness in this world. Of course, it is not plausible to claim that Kant is a *moral* pessimist, given that he maintains that we can achieve progress in history by striving toward human perfection and morality. But, then again, that is just Hartmann's point. He insists that Kant is a moral optimist, and that he is one too. Kant's theory of the value of life is very much the precedent for my own, Hartmann claims, because it too combines eudemonistic pessimism with evolutionary optimism. Kant had taught that the goals of history—the growth of culture and the perfection of human faculties—are attainable but only at the expense of happiness.[17]

Whatever the merits of Hartmann's interpretation of Kant, it did not really work as a polemical strategy. Rather than silencing his neo-Kantian critics, Hartmann's article only provoked them; and so instead of avoiding polemics, Hartmann soon found himself mired in them all the more.[18]

In all Hartmann's polemics in behalf of pessimism one hopes to find some encounter with Dühring, his great contemporary antipode. But it was not to be. The two men thought too little of one another to engage in a philosophical exchange. In the second edition of *Philosophie des Unbewussten* Hartmann took issue with Dühring only on one minor point (603–4). Since he had read *Der Werth des Lebens,*[19] it is likely that he believed many of his arguments a sufficient response to it, though exactly how is never made explicit. In 1870 Hartmann wrote a severely negative review of Dühring's *Kritische Geschichte der Philosophie,*[20] which he condemned for its lack of historical sense and for its purely subjective judgements about past philosophers. It was "beyond such a completely prosaic nature", Hartmann intoned, to write an objective history of

---

[16] Hartmann, *Zur Geschichte und Begründung des Pessimismus* (1880), pp. 1–64.

[17] Hartmann was thinking of the 'Vierter Satz' of Kant's 'Idee zu einer allgemeinen Geschichte in weltbürgerlicher Absicht', Kant, *Schriften*, VIII. 20–2.

[18] See his 'Zur Pessimismus-Frage', *Philosophische Fragen der Gegenwart*, pp. 112–20. On p. 113 Hartmann refers to the many articles written against his.

[19] See *Philosophie des Unbewussten* (1870), p. 603, where Hartmann cites Dühring's book.

[20] Eduard von Hartmann, *Blätter für literarische Unterhaltung* (January 1870), pp. 9–12.

philosophy. Just how little Hartmann thought of Dühring is apparent from his remarks on Hans Vaihinger's book *Hartmann, Dühring und Lange*.²¹ Hartmann took offence that Vaihinger even dared to compare his philosophy to Dühring's "*seichter Trivialphilosophie*", in which one "sought in vain for the least glimmering of spirit".²² Such damning comments utterly dashed any hopes for a meaningful encounter between the chief optimist and pessimist of the decade.

Dühring did not hesitate to repay Hartmann's comments in kind. In discussing recent developments in the second edition of his *Der Werth des Lebens*, Dühring dismissed Hartmann as "der in Reclame grösste Philosophast".²³ With that nasty tit-for-tat, Dühring could not expect a sober and serious review of the second edition of his book; and, sure enough, he did not get one. Hartmann deigned to make only one comment about Dühring's work. In the first edition of his *Zur Geschichte und Begründung des Pessimismus*, he dismissed Dühring's worldview as an "*Entrüstungspessimismus*", i.e. as "a pessimism of indignation" that encouraged people to complain about life and to make them unsatisfied with everything in contemporary social and political institutions (86). He later called Dühring's worldview "a contemptible deviation from purely contemplative pessimism".²⁴ The remark shows how little Hartmann understood Dühring, who conceived himself as an optimist, and who formulated his optimism to avoid just the kind of problem Hartmann attributed to him.

4. Two Female Allies

In his memoirs Carl Heymons, Hartmann's publisher, tells us that the Hartmann household in the 1870s resembled a war room.²⁵ It was filled with the latest reviews, articles and books, and the scene of lively discussions about strategy, about how best to respond to Hartmann's many opponents. As Heymons's description implies, Hartmann was not alone in his struggle against his many critics. Such was the volume of criticism against him that he was in desperate need of help. He was fortunate in having two very talented allies, two fellow devotees to the pessimist cause.

One of these allies was a certain A. Taubert, who wrote one of the most important contributions to the pessimism controversy: *Der Pessimismus und seine Gegner*,²⁶ which appeared in spring 1873. Taubert's book was a spirited defence of Hartmann's pessimism against the first wave of critics. Among these critics were some minor theologians, some amateurish literati, but also some major professional philosophers, most

---

²¹ Hans Vaihinger, *Hartmann, Dühring und Lange: Zur Geschichte der deutschen Philosophie im XIX Jahrhundert* (Iserlohn: Baedeker, 1876).

²² See Hartmann *Neukantianismus, Schopenhauerismus und Hegelianismus*, p. 7 n.

²³ Eugen Dühring, *Der Werth des Lebens*, Zweite, völlig umgearbeitete und bedeutend vermehrte Auflage (Leipzig: Fues, 1877), p. 23.

²⁴ See *Philosophische Fragen der Gegenwart*, p. 48.

²⁵ Carl Heymons, *Eduard von Hartmann, Erinnerungen aus den Jahren 1868-1881* (Berlin: Duncker, 1882), pp. 48-9.

²⁶ A. Taubert, *Der Pessimismus und seine Gegner* (Berlin: Duncker, 1873).

of them neo-Kantians: Gustav Knauer, Jürgen Bona Meyer (1828–97), Rudolf Haym (1821–1912) and Johannes Volkelt (1848–1930). Taubert's book became a focal point of controversy itself, the subject of many reviews, articles and books.[27] It treats systematically all the major philosophical issues surrounding pessimism, and so it provides a good survey of the pessimism controversy in its early phase.

It is worth mentioning the exact identity of this 'A. Taubert'. The 'A' stands not for Albert or Anton, not even Andreas or Augustus, as most contemporaries assumed,[28] but Agnes. Agnes Taubert (1844–77) happened to be the wife of Hartmann, 'Frau von Hartmann', and her defence of his pessimism was partly an act of spousal solidarity. She also had, however, a fearsome intellect and will all her own, one not hesitant to criticize her husband's views as well as those of his critics. According to Heymons, Taubert played a major role in the organization and strategy of the dispute, and her tone and style influenced Hartmann himself.[29] But Taubert deserves credit not only for her part in the pessimism controversy: she was also one of the first women in German letters to participate in a major national intellectual controversy. *Der Pessimismus und seine Gegner* was a landmark not only in the pessimism controversy but also in women's place in philosophy in Germany. Sadly, such a promising beginning ended much too soon. Agnes Taubert died in May 1877, in the very middle of the controversy, only thirty-three years old.[30]

Taubert was not alone in her pioneering role. After her came another remarkable Hartmann apologist, 'O. Plümacher', where the 'O' stood for neither Otto nor Oskar but Olga.[31] Olga Plümacher (née Hünerwadel) (1839–95) was a prominent figure in the pessimism controversy, and wrote three major contributions to it: *Der Kampf um's Unbewusste*, *Zwei Individualisten der Schopenhauer'schen Schule*, and *Der Pessimismus in Vergangenheit und Gegenwart*.[32] These works show a complete mastery of the polemical literature, and great intellectual acumen in discussing the issues. Such was

---

[27] See, for example, F. A. von Hartsen, *Die Moral des Pessimismus* (Nordhausen: F. Förstemann's Verlag, 1874), which focuses almost exclusively on Taubert's work. G. P. Weygoldt's *Kritik der philosophischen Pessimismus der neuesten Zeit* (Leiden: Brill, 1875) also gives prominent treatment to Taubert.

[28] Without exception, Taubert's critics, using the masculine pronoun 'er' to refer to her, assumed her to be male.

[29] Heymons, *Erinnerungen*, p. 49.

[30] According to Heymons, *Erinnerungen*, p. 47, she suffered from "heftigen Anfällen eines Gelenkrheumatismus".

[31] On Plümacher, see Rolf Kieser, *Olga Plümacher-Hünerwadel: eine gelehrte Frau des neunzehnten Jahrhunderts* (Lenzburg: Lenzburger Ortsburgerkommision, 1990).

[32] For the first work, see n. 1 above. *Der Pessimismus in Vergangenheit und Gegenwart* (Heidelberg: Georg Weiss Verlag, 1883). A second edition appeared in 1888. *Zwei Individualisten der Schopenhauer'schen Schule* appeared with Duncker Verlag, Berlin, 1882. Plümacher also wrote the article 'Pessimism' for *Mind*, 4 (1879), 68–89, which is a critique of James Sully's *Pessimism: A History and a Criticism* (London: Henry King, 1877). It is an interesting question whether Plümacher met Hartmann. There is no evidence that she did. At the very least she carried on a correspondence with Hartmann, who greatly admired her. See his references to her in his correspondence with Arthur Drews, *Arthur Drews, Eduard von Hartmann, Philosophischer Briefwechsel 1888–1906*, ed. Rudolf Mutter and Eckhart Pilick (Rohrback: Verlag Peter Gul, 1995), pp. 60, 153–5, 258.

her grasp of the literature, and of the general state of the controversy, that she often had the final word—logically if not historically—in many of the disputes. It has been rightly said: had Hartmann's critics read her, they would not have bothered to make their criticisms in the first place.[33] Plümacher's achievement is all the more remarkable considering that she had no formal university education, that she was a mother and housekeeper, and that she spent much of her life in the backwoods of Tennessee![34] It is unfortunate that her library, most of her correspondence and personal documents have disappeared.[35]

Though Taubert and Plümacher were in the social-political vanguard regarding the role of women in intellectual life, we would be mistaken to see them as champions of progressive or liberal political causes. This is especially clear in the case of Taubert, who very much shared the conservative views of her husband. She entered the pessimism controversy first and foremost for political reasons: to defend the realm of culture against social democracy. Taubert believed that pessimism was the only gospel that could curb the dangerous egalitarian ideals of the social democrats, who falsely believed that everyone on earth could be happy if only wealth were shared. Show the leaders of social democracy that it is impossible to attain happiness on this earth—that happiness exists neither in the palace nor in the cottage—and they would learn to curb their ambitions and to accept their place in society. Pessimism should be the philosophy of the ruling classes—the *Bildungsaristokratie*—who should be the guardians of culture against social democracy, which would reduce all culture down to the lowest common denominator. It was to this end that Taubert wrote her book.[36] The task was to defeat the enemies of pessimism, so that it would seem a more reasonable ideology for the intelligentsia and ruling classes.

We shall now examine the episodes of the pessimism controversy surrounding Talbert's and Plümacher's work. It will become abundantly clear from their work that many philosophical issues were involved in the pessimism controversy. No one who studies the controversy will think that pessimism is only a matter of personal attitude or that it raises no serious philosophical problems. At stake were questions about the nature of pleasure, the role of beauty in life, the meaning of love and the significance of work. All these questions had to be settled for the pessimist to make his case that there was, in the final analysis, more suffering than happiness in life. We shall, therefore, devote a section to each of these topics.

---

[33] This was the opinion of Arthur Drews, *Eduard von Hartmanns philosophisches System im Grundriss* (Heidelberg: Winter, 1906), p. 59.

[34] Plümacher's husband, Eugen Plümacher, founded a Swiss colony in Grundy County, Tennessee. Plümacher lived there from 1869 to 1881, after which she returned to Switzerland. On the Swiss colony there, see Francis Helen Jackson, *The Swiss Colony at Gruetli* (Gruetli-Laager: Grundy County Swiss Historical Society, 2010). Plümacher returned to Tennessee in 1886 in the hope of curing her son's tuberculosis; but he died there in December of that year. Plümacher herself died in Tennessee in July 1895.

[35] See Kieser, *Plümacher*, pp. 7, 62–3.

[36] See *Der Pessimismus und seine Gegner*, pp. 116–17.

5. The Whip of Cords

One of the most striking early polemics against Hartmann's philosophy was that of Gustav Knauer, *Das Facit aus E. v. Hartmann's Philosophie des Unbewussten*,[37] which appeared in 1873. Knauer was a Lutheran pastor from Erfurt, but also a trained philosopher who had written a book on logic.[38] His philosophical leanings were decidedly neo-Kantian, and very much hostile to the metaphysics of the idealist tradition, which, in his view, was not a step forward but a step backward from "the clear Königsberg thinker". Given his vocation, training and neo-Kantianism, a clash with Hartmann's philosophy was inevitable. Sure enough, Knauer could only censure Hartmann's metaphysics, which he regarded as a "swindle"; and he could only condemn his plans for a new religion, which he considered "a thoughtless conceit".

It would not have been worth Knauer's while to voice his protest against Hartmann's philosophy had *Philosophie des Unbewussten* received the attention normally accorded hefty philosophical tomes. But Knauer was amazed, appalled and alarmed that Hartmann's book had become so successful and so fashionable in the salons. For sure, these were signs of the shallowness and corruption of the times. To crush the infamy, he would have to shout and scream as loud as he could; only then would people listen and come to their senses. Hence Knauer's *Facit* is a *Schmähschrift,* an abusive, belittling satire on Hartmann's whole way of thinking. It is dramatic and derogatory in its tone, and unscrupulous and abusive in its language. The rhetoric is not a little reminiscent of Hamann, who took on the prophetic mantle of "the voice in the wilderness" to decry the mainstream of enlightenment philosophy.

Despite its splenetic rhetoric, Knauer's tract does manage to make some very serious criticisms of Hartmann's philosophy. One noteworthy criticism concerns the logic of Hartmann's concept of the unconscious (14–23). Knauer finds Hartmann's concept a hypostasis, the reification of an adjective of a psychological state into an entity on its own. The basic fallacy of Hartmann's philosophy is that it confuses an accident with a substance, as if the accident existed independently apart from its substance. The unconscious is an adjective that qualifies psychological states, which in turn are accidents of the psyche of some human being. There is no single thing called the unconscious which somehow exists on its own in nature, and of which all human beings are only accidents. The unconscious is in fact a second-order accident, an accident of an accident (a psychological drive or disposition) which exists only in particular persons; it is indeed a negative adjective, and as such does not designate anything specific, though for just that reason it seems to be a mysterious entity.

Another weighty criticism concerns Hartmann's pessimism (33–5). Remarkably, unlike most critics, Knauer accepts Hartmann's bleak portrait of human life, which, he

---

[37] Gustav Knauer, *Das Facit aus E. v. Hartmann's Philosophie des Unbewussten* (Berlin: L. Heimann, 1873).
[38] Gustav Knauer, *Conträr und Contradictorisch (nebst convergirenden Lehrstüken) festgestellt und Kants Kategorientafel berichtigt: eine philosophische Monographie* (Halle: Pfeffer, 1868).

admits, is in perfect accord with his own Christian views. But he thinks that Hartmann has left out of account the most important phenomenon of all in drawing his negative portrait of life: the fear of death. This fear is so pervasive, Knauer argues, that it affects everything that we think and do. Just imagine a life without death. We would no longer worry about ageing, sickness or injury, knowing that we would always live through them. Of all emotions, the fear of death is the most horrible and unbearable, and we keep it at bay only by distracting ourselves with little pleasures. Reckon it into the eudemonic calculus of life, Knauer was saying, and it will sink far in the negative direction.

Still another interesting criticism concerns Hartmann's latent theism (58–60). Although Hartmann professes to be a pantheist, Knauer says, he still harbours theist tendencies because he sees no problem in ascribing personality to his absolute. Hartmann's absolute possesses two salient characteristics of personality: will and representation. Hartmann also comes even closer to theism in attributing purposes to the cosmos and his God. But now, ironically, it seems we have to choose between the historical God of Christianity and Hartmann's absolute. There should be no mistake, however, which is better: Hartmann's absolute is an abstraction, whereas the God of Christianity is a real presence lying deep in the human heart.

In the introduction to *Der Pessimismus und seine Gegner* Taubert, in a brief description of Hartmann's most vocal opponents, duly took note of Knauer's book.[39] Knauer, she said, wrote from "the heights of the Christian worldview", and he had dismissed Hartmann's book in peremptory terms from the pulpit. In it one could find, she wrote, "the intellectual crudity of clericalism". With such an introduction one could not expect Taubert to discuss Knauer's criticisms; and so she did not. Since Knauer had dealt with Hartmann so contemptuously, she felt he deserved to be treated in kind. The best expression for such contempt, she believed, is total silence.

The whole matter should have been left there. Such were the differences between Taubert and Knauer that there was little point in trying to bridge them. But sometime in October 1873 Taubert's publisher, Carl Heymons, had received a sealed letter from Knauer addressed to Taubert with the request that he deliver it to her.[40] Knauer was offended by Taubert's remarks about "the intellectual crudity of clericalism". Taubert's exact word for "clericalism" was "*Pfaffenthum*", i.e. something more like "priestdom", a stinging rebuke for any Lutheran pastor, who has no high opinion of Catholic clergy. For such insulting language, Knauer demanded an explanation, even an apology.

Knauer got a reply, though no apology. Taubert wrote him a six-page letter,[41] which is very revealing about her lofty attitude and the whole tone of debate between Hartmann and his opponents. From the very beginning Taubert made it clear that she regarded Knauer's letter as inappropriate. He had made a personal matter out of what should have been an impersonal public discussion. Though she was very busy, she was

---

[39] Taubert, *Der Pessimismus und seine Gegner*, p. 36.
[40] Heymons, *Eduard von Hartmann*, p. 35.
[41] Heymons cites the letter in full, ibid., pp. 34–41.

willing to take the time and trouble to reply to it; but she was not going to apologize. Since Knauer himself had used insulting language, he should not be a whiner; he could only expect to receive as he gave. Taubert also made it clear that she regarded it as pointless to have a philosophical debate with Knauer: "With a Kantian of your ilk there cannot be a fruitful discussion" (36). But if she would not apologize or philosophize, she was willing to explain what she meant by "Pfaffenthum" and why Knauer was guilty of it. "Pfaffenthum" means, she explained, the hypocritical use of religion for one's own personal ends. It occurred whenever "under the pretence of seeking God's cause one sought one's own cause, either consciously from hypocritical falsity or unconsciously from a lack of moral judgement and an education of the heart" (39). Knauer's critique was a perfect example of such "Pfaffenthum" because, to condemn Hartmann's philosophy, he invoked all the standard language of religious obloquy, viz., he called Hartmann's philosophy "a swindle", "enthusiasm" and "craziness". She then made perfectly clear where she felt Knauer had been at fault:

Ask yourself whether this has been a proper intellectual tone. Nobody has forced you to use such language. There is no excuse. Surely what drove you was zealotry for the house of God—that is what drives everyone of your profession; but was it proper to use the whip of cords with which your saviour drove the changers from the temple, or the harsh words of the pharisees and sadducees, for the sake of a philosophical discussion? (*wissenschaftlichen Erörterung*)? One should have thought about that. (39)

Yes, indeed, Knauer should have thought about that. But it was a point that would have been well observed by Talbert herself, whose sharp temperament in the controversy was wielded much like "a whip of cords".

6. A Hyperontology?

Of all the questions raised by the pessimism controversy, perhaps the most fundamental concerned the very meaning and possibility of pessimism itself. Some critics held that the central thesis of pessimism—that nothingness is better than being, that non-existence is preferable to existence—is meaningless, or at the very least unverifiable. They argued that such a thesis amounts to metaphysics, a theory about the world as a whole or existence in general, for which there can be neither verification nor falsification. Clearly, though, the optimist could derive no polemical advantage from this argument. If it were correct, it would apply as much against himself as the pessimist. It implied that the entire attempt to determine the value of life—whether in positive or negative terms—cannot succeed because it transcends the limits of knowledge.

One of the first to make this criticism was Rudolf Haym, a prominent neo-Kantian, in an extensive early review of Hartmann's philosophy for the *Preußische Jahrbücher*.[42]

---

[42] Rudolf Haym, 'Die Hartmann'sche Philosophie des Unbewußten', *Preußische Jahrbücher*, 31 (1873), 41–80, 109–39, 257–311. These articles were reprinted in book form as *Die Hartmann'schen Philosophie des Unbewussten* (Berlin: Reimer, 1873). All references here are to the original articles.

Hartmann's central thesis that existence is worse than non-existence, Haym charged, goes beyond the limits of all possible knowledge. One could meaningfully make that statement only if it were possible to compare existence and non-existence against one another; but no human being is in a position to make such a comparison. "Who does not become dizzy", Haym asked, "with the demand to compare the existence of the world with its non-existence?" (258). We can compare one thing with another *within* the world, because both belong to a common genus and we have experience of both. "But the whole world itself!" How do we compare it with another world when we have no experience of another? And how do we compare being, possible or real, with nothingness? To determine which is better, being or nothingness, Haym argued, we need to have a standpoint beyond both, a privileged perspective where we could somehow compare them against one another, as if they were species of some common genus or "superbeing" (*Ueberseiende*) (258). But what is this superbeing? We find it impossible to give it a content, and so we cannot make any meaningful comparison. We are just not in possession of such a "hyperontology", as Haym dubbed it. "The pretension to judge the world from some standpoint beyond it", he concluded, "is immediately nonsensical; it is the caricature of the old, defensible belief of all genuine idealism, that the value of the external sensible world must be judged by the forum of the inner world of the soul and conscience" (260). Abandoning such a pretension, Haym argued, drives us back to the view that "the worth of the world must be measured by its own standards" (260).

Taubert was quick to respond to Haym's critique.[43] She insisted that there is no need to postulate a standpoint beyond the world to compare its existence with its non-existence. All that is necessary to make such a comparison, she argued, is the power to abstract from our life and existence and to compare it with non-existence. Just as a person with hearing and sight can imagine the world of someone deaf and blind, so the philosopher can imagine that the world he knows with all his senses does not exist (23).

Non-existence is not an unknowable strange realm beyond conceptual access; rather, it is immediately and completely knowable because it is simply the negation of the concept of existence in general, which we acquire by abstraction (24). Haym has confused two things: our feelings as existing realities and the concepts the philosopher abstracts from these feelings. The philosopher is not comparing feelings themselves, which are indeed incomparable, but only the concepts of them, which are easily comparable because they are only abstractions (23). It was completely beside the point for Haym to insist that "the value of the world has to be measured by its own standard", Taubert replied, because such a measurement would demonstrate nothing about the value of existence as such (25). Many things are perfect in their kind—parasites and fleas—when they are measured against the standard of their own genus; but that tells us nothing about the value of their kind or species itself.

[43] Taubert, *Der Pessimismus und seine Gegner*, pp. 23–6.

Another Protestant pastor, Georg Peter Weygoldt, in his *Kritik der philosophischen Pessimismus*,[44] responded to Taubert and defended a position similar to Haym's, though he gave his argument a twist of his own. The starting point of Weygoldt's argument is the primacy of the concept of being for all our thinking. Nothingness cannot be thought at all, he insisted, and therefore cannot be the object of comparison with existence or being. Taubert had not really proved but had only claimed that nothingness is thinkable and that it has priority over being (134). On closer inspection "his" claims prove to be false, Weygoldt argued. Existence (*Dasein*) is the form in which being (*Sein*) is given to us; and we have no relation to anything beyond being. The possibility of thinking, and all its content, comes from being. We cannot think of anything as nothingness, which can never be a meaningful object of thought. Whenever we think of something at all, it *ipso facto* is something and ceases to be nothingness. Because nothingness is nothing at all, we cannot compare being with it, and so we cannot say that one is better than the other. This means, Weygoldt then concluded, that it is meaningless to talk about "the pointlessness or irrationality of being" (*Zweckwidrigkeit oder Unvernünftigkeit des Seins*), as the pessimists are wont to do. Since we cannot compare being with anything beyond itself, the purpose or rationality of existence cannot be denied or called into question (135). We cannot say that nothingness is preferable to existence, because both are abstracted from all characteristics in terms of which one could be superior or inferior to the other (135).

Perhaps the simplest—and most effective—argument against the grand claims of pessimism came from the theist critic Johannes Huber.[45] To Huber, it is utterly clear that the pessimist is going beyond the limits of possible experience in making his generalizations about the value of existence. It is not necessary to invoke any technical epistemological argument to show this. Why? Simple. Because the pessimist is first and foremost talking about life on this earth; he knows no other. Granted, this life is "a vale of tears", just as the pessimist tells us; but it is still only one planet in the universe. For all we know, people are very happy on other planets. So the pessimist has no right to make his vast generalizations, his grand claims about the universe in general and existence as such. On purely empirical grounds, which the pessimist insists are his own, there could be no reply to Huber's simple but telling objection. If he were to be a good empiricist, the pessimist would have to limit his claims to life on earth. Remarkably enough, neither Schopenhauer nor Hartmann nor Taubert had made this important qualification.

A more epistemologically sophisticated objection came a year later from Wilhelm Windelband.[46] As a neo-Kantian, Windelband suspected all metaphysics, and for that

---

[44] G. P. Weygoldt, *Kritik der philosophischen Pessimismus der neuesten Zeit* (Leiden: Brill, 1875), pp. 134–6.

[45] Huber, *Der Pessimismus*, p. 96.

[46] Wilhelm Windelband, 'Pessimismus und Wissenschaft', *Der Salon*, 2 (1877), 814–21, 951–7. Reprinted in *Präludien*, ninth edition (Tübingen: Mohr, 1924), II. 218–43. All references in parentheses are to this later edition. A parenthetical note on the first page of this edition assigns this article the date 1876.

reason he banished pessimism from the intellectual market place. In his view, neither pessimism nor optimism are scientific theories, because they do not make verifiable or falsifiable statements about the nature of things; rather, they are simply expressions of "moods", of our "attitudes", about things, which grow out of generalizing feelings about life (e.g. disillusionment, indignation). Such moods do not provide "judgements" (*Urtheile*) which are true or false, but they consist in appraisals or evaluations (*Beurteilungen*) about the goodness or badness of things (227). Optimism and pessimism therefore deserve a place in science only as subjects of individual or cultural-historical psychology (232). Windelband's critique of pessimism and optimism does not, as it first appears, derive from a positivist rejection of the cognitive status of all value judgements. He believes that some value judgements are cognitively justifiable; the problem for him concerns *metaphysical* value judgements about the nature of the world in general or existence as such. Windelband explained that appraisals or evaluations are *teleological* judgements, i.e. appraisals where we assess something according to its purpose or end. Some teleological judgements are justifiable, provided that they presuppose the appropriate purpose or end; it is then only a matter of determining from experience whether the particular action or thing conforms to that purpose or end. For example, if I order a pair of dancing shoes from my shoemaker, and if I complain that I cannot eat them, I have made an absurd appraisal, because shoes are not food; if, however, I complain that I cannot use them as skates, I come closer to an appropriate appraisal, because shoes can be modified to be skates, though in this case it is still inappropriate because I asked for dancing shoes; but if, finally, I complain that I cannot dance with the shoes because they are really too heavy and inflexible for that end, then my complaint is perfectly defensible and correct. Now the problem with value judgements about the world in general, or existence as such, Windelband contended, is that it is not clear whether the world has a purpose, and how we could know that. We cannot jump outside or beyond the world to see the purpose of the world itself. We make value judgements perfectly well within the world; but we cannot take them and apply them to the world in general (230). Hence pessimism, as well as optimism, go beyond the limits of knowledge and the conditions of a meaningful value judgement.

Whatever the merits of Haym's, Weygoldt's and Windelband's arguments against metaphysics, Hartmann and Taubert responded that they are ultimately irrelevant to the central claims of pessimism.[47] Their pessimism, they stressed, is not a metaphysics, and it does not even presuppose one; it is rather a strictly empirical theory about the attainability of happiness and the prevalence of suffering in life. Hartmann and Taubert insisted that their pessimism is essentially a eudemonistic theory, according to which

---

[47] Taubert, *Der Pessimismus und seine Gegner*, pp. 11–12; and Hartmann, 'Ist der Pessimismus wissenschaftlich zu begründen?', *Philosophische Monatshefte*, 15 (1879), 589–612; reprinted in *Zur Geschichte und Begründung des Pessimismus* (1880), pp. 65–85. See also Hartmann, 'Die Stellung des Pessimismus in meinem philosophischen System', in *Zur Geschichte und Begründung des Pessimismus*, Zweite Auflage (Leipzig: Hermann Haacke, 1891), pp. 18–28, p. 25. (This article appears only in the second edition of this work.)

there is more pain and suffering than pleasure and happiness in life. Whether this is so, they argued, does not demand going beyond the realm of human experience, because it is a thesis true or false of human experience itself. To determine whether it is true or false, we only have to see whether there is, for most people most of the time, more pain than pleasure, more suffering than happiness. If that is so, we then have reason to conclude from experience itself whether life is worth living or not. With this response, Hartmann and Taubert believed, they had ducked the charges of metaphysics. Never did they need, and never did they suppose, something like Haym's "Hyperontology".

It is necessary to add, however, that this attempt to escape metaphysics was really a tactical manoeuvre to avoid critical blows. For it was Hartmann's and Taubert's more considered position that ethics and metaphysics are inseparable, that we cannot know the meaning and value of life without knowing our place in the universe as a whole. Sure enough, only a few pages later Taubert reminded Hartmann's critics that his pessimism is the necessary result of his metaphysical principles (26); and Hartmann, despite all his disclaimers, never tired of stressing that ethics without metaphysics "floats in the air".[48]

7. The Nature of Pleasure

Granted that pessimism is not committed to a metaphysics to determine the value of life, Hartmann's critics were still not satisfied. They also questioned his attempt to measure the value of life in empirical terms according to pleasure and pain alone. All kinds of objections were raised against Hartmann's eudemonic standards and measurements. His critics were opposed to his conception of pleasure, to how he measured pleasure and pain, and the consequences he drew from his measurements.

A common objection against Hartmann's eudemonic calculus was that it is pseudo-scientific, presupposing the comparability of incommensurable values. According to this objection, if we consider all the different kinds of value in life, it becomes impossible to compare and summarize them, so that we can never say that misery preponderates over happiness.[49]

Hartmann's response to this objection is mainly to dig in his heels and to stress the purely quantitative aspects of pleasure and pain.[50] He readily admits that sensations have a qualitative dimension which makes them incommensurable with one another;

---

[48] See Chapter 7, section 1.

[49] For this objection, see Johannes Volkelt, *Das Unbewusste und der Pessimismus* (Berlin: F. Henschel, 1873), pp. 286–7; Julius Duboc, 'Eduard von Hartmann's Berechnung des Weltelends', *Deutsche Warte*, 6 (1874), 350–61, esp. 360–1; Adolf Horwicz, 'Die psychologische Begründung des Pessimismus', *Philosophische Monatshefte*, 16 (1880), 264–88; Friedrich Paulsen, 'Gründen und Ursachen des Pessimismus', *Deutsche Rundschau*, 48 (1886), 360–81; and Albert Weckesser, *Der empirische Pessimismus in seinem metaphysischen Zusammenhang in System von Eduard von Hartmann* (Bonn: Universitäts-Buchdruckerei von Carl Georgi, 1885).

[50] See 'Ist der Pessimismus wissenschaftlich zu begründen?', in *Zur Geschichte und Begründung des Pessimismus* (1880), pp. 65–85.

but he still insists that in determining their pleasure or pain alone, we can abstract from their content or qualitative dimension and consider strictly their quantitative one, i.e. their duration and intensity. Just as we can determine whether on a given table top the weight of the pears is greater than that of the apples—however different pears are from apples—so we can determine whether different sensations bring more pleasure over pain. If the sum of pleasure in the world is negative, then we have to accept pessimism, which is entirely an inductive truth from experience.

Hartmann later explained that there are three fundamental presuppositions involved in arriving at such a conclusion.[51]

(1) That one gives each sensation a value strictly corresponding to its actuality in consciousness, independent of memory and moral values.
(2) That pleasure and pain relate to one another as positive and negative quantities, irrespective of their qualitative aspects.
(3) The quantity of pleasure and pain is determined entirely by the product of their intensity and duration.

Regarding the qualitative dimension of sensation, Hartmann now took a somewhat equivocal stand: first, that we can abstract from it entirely, because it is not relevant to the assessment of pleasure and pain; and, second, that we can reduce it down to its quantitative dimension, because higher pleasures are simply greater in intensity and duration than lower ones. Both these reductive theses soon became the subject of considerable controversy.

One of the first and most thoughtful discussions of Hartmann's eudemonic calculus was that by Jürgen Bona Meyer, a neo-Kantian critic, in his *Weltelend und Weltschmerz*.[52] Meyer laid down several rules about measuring the value of life according to eudemonic standards (12). First, the nature of each kind of pleasure must be accurately determined; more specifically, one must not describe the pleasure in too bleak or negative terms, biasing the scales in favour of pessimism. Second, the whole mass of pleasures and pains must be measured against one another, i.e. one must not leave out any kind of pleasure or pain. Third, one must take into account not only the quantitative but also the qualitative dimension of pleasure and pain. If any one of these rules were infracted, Meyer insisted, one would make inaccurate comparisons, and so come to the wrong conclusion about the value of life.

Meyer contended that Hartmann infringes each of these rules, making his pessimism suspect three times over as a general conclusion about the value of life. Against the first rule, for reasons we shall soon see, Hartmann gives a much too negative account of some basic pleasures, viz., work and love. Against the second, for reasons

---

[51] See section 2 of 'Zur Pessimismus-Frage', in *Philosophische Fragen der Gegenwart*, pp. 91–102.

[52] Jürgen Bona Meyer, *Weltelend und Weltschmerz: Eine Rede gegen Schopenhauer's und Hartmann's Pessimismus* (Bonn: Marcus, 1872). Later published in an enlarged version as 'Weltlust und Weltleid', in *Probleme der Weltweisheit*, Zweite Auflage (Berlin: Allgemeiner Verein für Deutsche Literatur, 1887), pp. 253–95. All citations here are to the original edition.

we shall also see, he leaves out of account some very important pleasures, viz., the pleasure we take in nature. Worst of all, though, Hartmann violates the third rule, failing to consider the qualitative dimension of pleasure and pain. Meyer knew that Hartmann expressly intended to ignore this dimension, that he wanted to provide a strictly quantitative comparison between pleasure and pain, because that alone could provide an objective conclusion. Meyer could not understand, however, how we could leave out the qualitative dimension of pleasure and pain if we wanted to have a complete and accurate account of the value of life.[53] Not all pleasures and pains are on the same footing, and some pleasures are better or higher than others just as some pains are worse and lower than others. We could not, then, simply compare units of pleasure and pain against one another in terms of intensity and duration, as if that settled the question. It is just a fact, Meyer pointed out, that people endure great pains for the sake of higher pleasures, or that they prefer brief moments of pleasure over longer moments of pain. Although people quickly tire of pleasures, they also get used to, and bear with equanimity, longer periods of pain. The reason for this, Meyer hypothesized, is that "the human soul is more intensively gripped by joy than by pain" (21–2). Such was the human hankering for happiness that people would remember vividly the few moments of joy in their lives and forget the long periods of suffering.

Haym too felt that Hartmann had made a mistake in ignoring the qualitative dimension of pleasure and pain.[54] The price of ignoring that dimension, he argued, is a completely abstract and artificial comparison which has nothing to do with the real values of life, which lie in the realm of quality and particularity (263). Haym identified two questionable presuppositions behind Hartmann's eudemonic calculus. First, a completely sensual and physical conception of pleasure, because that alone could be measured quantitatively (263). Second, the reduction of the realm of feeling down to the satisfaction or dissatisfaction of the will (68, 262). Because of his reductive analysis of feeling, Haym complained, Hartmann fails to evaluate feelings on their own terms, regarding them as illusory in the same way as secondary qualities. But even if we take Hartmann's quantitative analysis of feeling on its own terms, Haym argued, he is too hasty in drawing negative conclusions from it. It is not true that the relaxation of nerves after a pleasant sensation is painful; it is also not true that there is more indirect and relative pleasure (i.e. pleasure from the removal of pain) than indirect and relative pain (i.e. pain from the removal of pleasure); and still less is it true that pleasure must be greater than pain to be noticed in consciousness (264–5).

Taubert did her best to defend Hartmann's eudemonic calculus against these objections. Part of her defence is purely methodological. It was Hartmann's aim to reach some general conclusions about the balance between pleasure and pain in the world; and to do that he had to abstract entirely from the qualitative dimension of pleasure.

---

[53] See also Meyer's argument in *Arthur Schopenhauer als Mensch und Denker* (Berlin: Carl Haber, 1872), pp. 44–5.

[54] 'Die Hartmann'sche Philosophie des Unbewussten', pp. 261–5.

What all pleasures have in common simply as feelings is their quantitative dimension, their intensity and duration; they differ from one another in terms of their qualities or contents alone. We have to take quality into account, then, only when we consider the specific kinds of pleasures and attempt to make comparisons between instances of them (20). Though perfectly correct to make this point, Taubert failed to address the wider issue: how accurate is our account of the value of life if we consider solely its quantitative dimension?

Taubert was indignant about Haym's claim that Hartmann has a physical or sensual concept of pleasure (21). This was an old "priest's trick" (*Pfaffenkniff*), which tries to discredit eudemonism by claiming that it reduces all pleasure to sensuality. She pointed out that Hartmann recognized the positive pleasures of science, art and religion, which he was far from reducing down to carnal pleasures (21). Haym's point, however, is that Hartmann has to treat pleasure as sensual or physical if it is to be measured purely quantitatively and taken into account by his calculus. To the extent that the pleasures of art, science and religion are not so measurable, they fall out of the calculus, and thus give an inaccurate estimate of the pleasures of life.

Another issue in weighing the pleasures and pains in life arose concerning Hartmann's assessment of "the four great values": health, freedom, youth and security. Hartmann had claimed that these values have a strictly negative or relative worth, because we appreciate them only when we are deprived of them; otherwise, we take them for granted, so that they give us only a '0' when measured by the utilitarian calculus. Although Meyer, Haym and Julius Duboc admitted that these values are indeed negative or relative, they also insisted that people are not as inclined to take them for granted as Hartmann supposed.[55] Everyone in life has experienced illness, oppression and insecurity, and so they have all felt great pleasure in repossessing them. Meyer claimed that, even if we are not self-conscious of these values, they should still be weighed heavily in any accounting of the value of life. "Happiness remains happiness, even when I do not repeat hourly that it is happiness; it still remains happiness as a lasting source of pleasure" (19). In making this point, Meyer raised a general question that would loom larger in the course of the controversy: namely, to what extent must I be conscious of having a pleasure for it to be one?

Undaunted by these arguments, Taubert defended Hartmann's analysis of the four great values. She admitted that we do not live, as Haym put it, in "an Epicurean middle world" where no one experiences illness, oppression and insecurity. It is indeed often the case that we learn to treasure health, freedom, youth and security. Nevertheless, it is still true that these are only relative or negative goods, that we value them only because we fear their opposite (31). Taubert also questioned Meyer's assumption that we could derive great pleasure from these values even if we are not conscious of them. It is "a bold assumption", she said, to think that there can be pleasures of which we are

---

[55] Meyer, *Weltelend und Weltschmerz*, pp. 18–19; Haym, 'Die Hartmann'sche Philosophie des Unbewussten', pp. 266–7; and Duboc, 'Hartmann's Berechnung', pp. 356–8.

not conscious. If that were so, it would not help the optimist's case, because the pessimist might just as well refer to unconscious pain (32).

The whole question of unconscious pleasure raised by Meyer and Taubert was taken up in an interesting way by Weygoldt, who made clear its importance for assessing the general value of life.[56] It was a mistake of Schopenhauer and Hartmann, he urged, to think of our normal experience strictly in terms of pleasure and pain, as if we were always in one state or the other. Pleasure and pain are far from exhausting our normal life of sensation, and they are the exception rather than the rule (94). The normal state of experience is neither pleasant nor painful but is a state in between them, a state of equanimity or balance which we could call "an indifference point". This normal state does not exist before or beyond sensation, but it is rather the sum of all those countless, unconscious sensations, the stirrings and strivings of organic life, just beneath the surface of consciousness (94). We can be sitting hours long in this normal state, perfectly content, without feeling either pleasure or pain. It would seem that Schopenhauer and Hartmann could accept this "normal state", given that they are generous in giving importance to the realm of the unconscious. But Weygandt pointed out that there is still an outstanding issue between him and the pessimists. The pessimists want to assign the normal state a '0' in the calculus of pleasure and pain. While Weygoldt did not contest its null value in the eudemonic calculus, he still insisted that we should give it some value in the general assessment of life. The normal state does not consist in conscious pleasure, to be sure, but it does consist in a subconscious feeling of contentment or satisfaction, a feeling which needs to be given a positive valence in assessing the general value of life. The equanimity and tranquillity of the normal state of consciousness cannot be neglected in accounting for the value of existence, even if we cannot measure it in terms of conscious pleasure and pain. So, ironically, Weygoldt agreed with Taubert in not accepting subconscious pleasures; but he refused to draw the conclusion that we should measure value in terms of pleasure or pain alone. There was the entire subconscious realm of inner contentment and equanimity of our normal consciousness which had to be assigned a positive value. Hartmann should have been willing to acknowledge this realm, Weygoldt remarked (97), given that he stressed so much the influence of the subconscious on our mental life. That he did not acknowledge it was the result of the undue influence of Schopenhauer's pessimism upon him.

One of the more interesting critiques of the pessimist's concept of pleasure came from Johannes Rehmke, a doctoral student in Zurich, who wrote a short tract titled *Die Philosophie des Weltschmerzes*,[57] which appeared in 1875, shortly after Taubert's work and partly in response to it. Rehmke thought that there is a fatal weakness in the pessimist concept of pleasure: it makes all pleasure subjective and individual, as if it

---

[56] Weygoldt, *Kritik des philosophischen Pessimismus*, pp. 93–7. Cf. Volkelt, *Das Unbewusste und der Pessimismus*, pp. 280–1, who espouses similar views.

[57] Johannes Rehmke, *Die Philosophie des Weltschmerzes* (St. Gallen: Zollikofer, 1876).

involves some reference to the selfish desires of the individual (40). The premise behind this concept of pleasure comes from Hartmann's analysis of feeling, which regards all feelings, especially pleasure and pain, as the result of satisfaction or dissatisfaction of the will. According to Schopenhauer and Hartmann, the will, as it appears in the individual, always involves some egoistic gratification or frustration of individual and subjective desire. Against this analysis of pleasure, Rehmke made a telling objection: that though all satisfaction of the will involves pleasure, not all pleasure involves satisfaction of the will (44–5). This opens the possibility for another source of pleasure besides the egoistic satisfaction of desire. This source becomes apparent, Rehmke argued, when we consider the specific content of the will, its particular kinds of goals. While some of these goals are indeed subjective and individual, just as the pessimist insisted, others are objective and universal (46–7). These latter goals are moral or social, and involve doing our duty or contributing to the common good. We could take pleasure in the achievement of these goals just as much as in the subjective and individual, Rehmke insisted, so that there is another source of positive pleasure independent of the egoistic strivings of the will. Rehmke went on to argue that there are some pleasures that are completely independent of the will, whether its goals are subjective or objective, individual or universal. These are aesthetic pleasures or agreeable states of mind, which normally do not involve any antecedent desire. These pleasures could come from outside us, in the pleasures in nature, or they could come from inside us, in the pleasures of memory or hope (52–3).

Rehmke's and Haym's protests against Hartmann's reductive psychology were developed more systematically and thoroughly by Hugo Sommer, a disciple of Lotze, in his *Der Pessimismus und die Sittenlehre*.[58] Flatly contrary to Hartmann, Sommer stressed the primary role of feeling in mental life, which was for him the basis for, and not the product of, the will. All willing has its origin in feeling, he argued (31, 83). To will something we must first take an interest in it; and to take an interest in it, we must have a feeling for its value (31, 83). Without a feeling for some particular thing, willing is only an abstraction, because it lacks a particular object. It was a mistake of Hartmann, therefore, to reduce feeling down to the will, to contentment or discontentment, to the satisfaction or dissatisfaction of desire. There are as many kinds of feelings as there are objects in which we take an interest, and in which we find some value, Sommer maintained, and it is absurd to think that they are all alike simply because they amount to either satisfaction or dissatisfaction of desire (41). When we determine the value of life, we have to take into account all these different kinds of feelings, which resist reduction down to any common denominator.

Having stressed the irreducibility of feeling, Sommer then explains, more clearly than Haym or Rehmke, how Hartmann's psychology leads inevitably to his pessimism. Because Hartmann thinks of pleasure and pain as either satisfaction or dissatisfaction of desire alone, he has no difficulty in treating them as if they were all homogeneous

---

[58] Hugo Sommer, *Der Pessimismus und die Sittenlehre* (Haarlem: De Erven F. Bohn, 1882).

and comparable, although what he is comparing are mere abstractions, separable from their particular objects (40–1). Because Hartmann assumes the will is the primary power of the soul, and because pleasure is only the satisfaction of the will, he thinks that he is justified in calculating the general value of life in terms of pleasure alone (77–8). Furthermore, because he thinks of pleasure in terms of satisfaction of desire, he also thinks of it in sensual terms, as a kind of physical pleasure (79). All these premises, Sommer argues, are decisive for Hartmann's pessimism. Measured in terms of sensual or physical pleasure, he is correct to conclude that life does not have much value, given that life rarely consists in intense and enduring sensual pleasures. But the conclusion follows, Sommer argues, only because of Hartmann's psychological and metaphysical premises, which reduce the life of feeling down to abstract units of satisfaction or dissatisfaction (89). If, however, we look at the concrete content of life, what is revealed to us through feeling, we can see that life consists in all kinds of different values, each of which has to be taken on its own terms. The values revealed to us by feeling do not all consist in pleasure; and if they do consist in pleasure, it is not necessarily sensual or physical. Hence the most important values in life, Sommer concluded, resist Hartmann's eudemonic calculus.

8. A Pessimist Counterattack

After Taubert's *Der Pessimismus und seine Gegner* appeared in 1873, there was no lull in hostilities between the pessimists and their enemies. Taubert's book was more a stimulus than a stop to Hartmann's critics, whose attacks only grew in number, depth and intensity. Taubert's early death in May 1877 had left Hartmann surrounded by his foes and bereft of his most loyal ally. He was in desperate need of aid to carry on the struggle for the pessimist cause. That aid came in the early 1880s with Olga Plümacher's books, her *Der Kampf um's Unbewusste*, which appeared in 1881, and her *Der Pessimismus in Vergangenheit und Gegenwart*,[59] which was first published in early 1884. It is the latter book, whose content is more directly relevant to pessimism, which especially concerns us now. This book is not only a history but also a defence of pessimism. Its second part is a systematic and thorough examination of all the latest criticisms of pessimism, especially those which had appeared since Taubert's book. Because it is so solid and lucid, Plümacher's counterattack is worthy of careful examination. One of its avid readers was Nietzsche, whose copy was filled with annotations.[60]

Plümacher first raised the question whether individual differences regarding pleasure are so great that they invalidate any generalization about pleasure and pain among human beings (181–4). She admitted that, within certain limits, sensations between

---

[59] O. Plümacher, *Der Pessimismus in Vergangenheit und Gegenwart* (Heidelberg: Georg Weiss, 1884). All references in parentheses above are to the second edition, which appeared with the same publisher in 1888.

[60] See Thomas Brobjer, *Nietzsche's Philosophical Context* (Urbana, IL: University of Illinois Press, 2008), p. 99.

people are indeed very different. What gave one person pleasure gave another displeasure. Such differences in feeling depend on a host of factors, viz., on age, physical constitution, state of health, custom, education and social class. Nevertheless, Plümacher insisted that the differences are not limitless, that they are not so great that they are absolute (182). There is a certain point at which all people, regardless of differences in physical constitution, feel pain. No one, for example, can bear putting their hands in water heated to boiling point. This is sufficient, Plümacher maintained, to justify the kind of generalizations that the pessimist needs to make about life. All that matters in the first instance is simple pleasure or pain and their temporal relations to one another (viz., how long one lasts compared to the other); and only in the second instance does one have to examine variations in the stages of psychic and physical organization (183). To take these variations into account, one has to specify the circumstances and conditions under which feelings of pleasure or pain take place; and the more specific these are, the more reliable the generalizations will be, holding for all people regardless of nationality, race and social class (183–4).

Next, Plümacher examined the objection that reliable generalizations are impossible because the value of different pleasures are incommensurable (184–90). Even if all people feel the same upon the same stimulus and occasion, there is still the problem that feelings arising from different stimuli and occasions will be too heterogeneous to make comparisons and reliable generalizations about them. In response to this objection, Plümacher dug in her heels and fell back on the old line of Maupertuis.[61] It was already clear to him in the 18th century, she pointed out, that all pleasures and pains are alike as simple feelings, regardless of their causes and content; they differ from one another in their duration and intensity alone (184). The pessimist does not deny that there are great qualitative differences between feelings, and that as such they are incommensurable with one another (184–5). But his chief aim is to determine simply whether there is more pleasure than pain in the world, and to that end he does not have to consider the qualitative dimension of pleasure and pain at all (185). The great axiological question of the value of life depends on *how much* pleasure or pain is present, regardless of its origins and content (186). This point is decisive, Plümacher insists, against all the latest criticisms by Hugo Sommer and Adolf Horwicz.[62] Their objections against pessimism, she opined, have not progressed beyond the days of Maupertuis (185). Hartmann's critics wrongly think that he has to make qualitative comparisons between different pleasures; but it is precisely this qualitative dimension from which the pessimist abstracts in order to make comparisons about amounts of pleasure (187).

---

[61] Though she did not explicitly cite it, Plümacher probably meant Pierre Louis Moreau de Maupertuis, *Essai de philosophie morale* (Berlin: Akademie der Wissenschaften, 1749), which argued that pleasures and pains could be compared purely quantitatively in terms of intensity and duration, and that, because pains outnumbered pleasures, non-being was preferable to being. Maupertuis was thus a pessimist *avant la lettre*. Hartmann was well aware of Maupertuis's work and discusses it in *Zur Geschichte und Begründung des Pessimismus* (Berlin: Duncker, 1880), p. 21.

[62] Sommer, *Pessimismus und die Sittenlehre*, 40–3; and Horwicz, 'Begründung', pp. 264–88.

While Plümacher helped to clarify the kinds of generalizations the pessimist wants to make, she had also inadvertently revealed a weakness in his argument. Granted that there is much more pain than pleasure in life, this still does not warrant general conclusions about its value. For that reckoning, her critics insisted, still leaves out the qualitative dimension, which cannot be so easily ignored. What if the few pleasures of life, though greatly outnumbered by pain, are of much greater quality or value than the pain? Such pleasures might make life worth living after all. Take the case of a man who is ill with cancer and who constantly suffers great pain; nevertheless, he chooses to go on living because of his love for his children, which is a joy of such value to him that all his suffering pales in comparison.

In the course of her argument against Hartmann's critics, Plümacher made some major concessions about the measurement of pleasure and pain. She conceded that there is no "feeling meter" or "sensation scale" even for the intensity of pleasure and pain. Many feelings, even those like one another, remain incommensurable. One could not say, for example, that the feelings of a mother for the loss of her child are more intense than those for the death of her husband, or that the feelings for the loss of a fiancé are more intense than those for the death of a sibling. All that one can say in these cases is that these experiences are intensely painful, even if one cannot make precise comparisons. She also accepted, however, Horwicz's point that pleasure and pain cannot be added and subtracted like quantities in mathematics.[63] If I have a pleasure that I assign the value +10, and then I have a pain that I assign the value -5, it does not follow that I am left with a pleasure of +5 and that the pain disappears (187). Pleasures and pains do not relate to one another in such precise increments, Plümacher realized, and so she states that they are "overleaping" (*überspringende*), i.e. their values increase not by continuous increments but by whole quantities, so that a pleasure can completely vanquish a pain or conversely. Hence the pessimist cannot make exact mathematical calculations after all (188).

Plümacher did not fail to respond to Haym's and Rehmke's objection that pessimism rests upon a false theory of feeling (195–9). Haym and Rehmke had contended, it will be recalled, that Hartmann incorrectly claims that all pleasure derives from the will, and that he neglects other sources of pleasure that do not come from it. Among these pleasures are aesthetic ones, so it seems as if Hartmann has failed to consider the entire aesthetic dimension of life, one of the most important sources of pleasure, and one that sometimes makes life worth living. Plümacher's first line of defence against this objection is that feeling remains the same—it has the same qualitative and quantitative properties—whether or not it is an accident of the will (195). The psychological theory about the origin of pleasure makes no difference to the pessimist, then, who in his calculations counts all pleasures and pains, whatever their source (196). This dismissal of the relevance of theories of pleasure did not prevent Plümacher, however, from defending Hartmann's theory. Rehmke's theory that there are some pleasures that are

---

[63] Horwicz, 'Begründung', pp. 267–70.

independent of the will derives all its plausibility, she argued, from limiting the will down to its conscious dimension alone, though the causes of pleasure are largely subconscious (197). Plümacher admitted, however, that it is difficult to demonstrate Hartmann's theory because, in some cases, it is difficult to determine whether the will is always really present as a source of pleasure (198).

The most interesting phase of Plümacher's counterattack is her response to those critics who maintain that pessimism is a pathological response to the tragedy of life (199–210). According to these critics,[64] pessimism is the product of a morbid sensitivity or choleric temperament which fully exaggerates the negative side of life. A more normal sensitivity and temperament would also grasp the positive side of life, which it would not allow to be overshadowed by its negative side. Plümacher is willing to concede such an abnormal sensitivity and choleric temperament in the case of Schopenhauer and Bahnsen; but nothing of the kind is to be found in Hartmann, she maintained, whose temper, judging from his writings and autobiography, is sanguine and equable. Plümacher then turns this objection against the optimists: Are they not the blind and obtuse ones who fool themselves (and others) because they cannot really appreciate the tragedy of life? Is it not the case, she asked, that it takes a good dosage of obtuseness and superficiality (*Stumpfsinn und Leichtsinn*) to keep melancholy and worry within bounds? Whoever has suffered real tragedy in this life knows that all that quietens and softens their justified grief and sorrow is "a mild forgetting", "a sweet melancholy", which derives from the instinct for self-preservation (201). If we did not forget, if we did not grow numb, the sorrows of life would destroy us.

Among those who charged pessimism with morbid pathology was Dühring, whom Plümacher duly subjects to scrutiny (201–2). Dühring saw pessimism as an ideology of the idle, decadent and vain who no longer care about life.[65] Theirs is a "*Katzenjammerphilosophie*", which arises from overindulgence in liquor and narcotics. The only defensible form of pessimism for Dühring is "a pessimism of indignation" (*Entrüstungspessimismus*) because it recognizes the social and political causes of human misery and motivates people to do something against them. Unfortunately, Plümacher, like Hartmann, does not engage in a detailed discussion of the merits of Dühring's optimism and she limits herself only to a few general comments. She maintains that Dühring stays only on the surface of the problems of suffering and evil; his pessimism of indignation goes only so far in recognizing the tragedy of life, which does not have only social and political causes. In its naïve belief in the human causes of evil and the power of human beings to remedy them, Plümacher riposted, Dühring's philosophy reveals itself to be an obsolete standpoint, a relic of the French Enlightenment (202).

---

[64] Plümacher discusses the views of Dühring (see n. 65) and Julius Duboc, *Der Optimismus als Weltanschauung* (Bonn: Emil Strauβ, 1881), pp. 92–108.
[65] See his diagnosis of pessimism in the second edition of *Der Werth des Lebens* (1877), pp. 1–37.

9. The Value of Work

Whatever the problems with his general concept of pleasure, Hartmann held that the case for pessimism has to be based on induction, in the consideration of particular cases. The pessimist could draw his dreary conclusions about the value of existence only after an examination of each particular aspect of human life. Withholding all general principles, he had to consider each aspect for its own sake. Hence the pessimist controversy covered a wide array of special topics, such as work, art and love.

One topic that became an intense battleground between the pessimists and their critics was work (*Arbeit*). Clearly, work is a crucial theme in the pessimist's portrait of life. Our days are filled with work, nine to five most days of the week for many of us, so if work proves to have a negative value in the general accounting of life, the scales will be tipped heavily in the pessimist's favour. Mainly for this reason, Hartmann's analysis of work in the *Philosophie des Unbewussten* is very bleak, even cynical.[66] There can be no doubt, Hartmann declares, that work is an evil for whoever must engage in it. Nobody works if they do not have to, and we do it only to avoid a greater evil, whether that be poverty or boredom. So work is not an end in itself, only a means to other ends. Usually, work is the price someone must pay to have a secure existence; but that is not a positive but a negative good, i.e. one to avoid greater evils; and, furthermore, it is a good (unlike health and youth) that we must purchase through much pain. We also must not underestimate, Hartmann adds, the misery that work often imposes upon us. He then cites Schopenhauer's lines about the factory work of 5 year olds, who sit twelve to fourteen hours a day doing repetitive tasks, and who thus "buy very dearly the mere pleasure of drawing breath".[67] The best we can do with work, Hartmann thinks, is to get used to it, to make it habitual, so that we become just like the cart horse who learns to bear his load.

For Hartmann's critics, this was an unduly grim, wildly inaccurate, conception of work. Haym thought that Hartmann's conception was suitable only for the galley slave, and that he completely neglected the satisfaction work gave us in exercising our powers and in realizing our will.[68] Work, Meyer argued in a similar vein,[69] is not simply a means to other ends but it is a pleasure in itself, because it activates our powers, directs our energies, and satisfies our human need for "the good, beautiful and true". Of course, there is toil and trouble connected with work; but these negative factors do not outweigh the positive ones, and eventually they become part of the pleasure. By exaggerating the negative aspects of work, Hartmann falsifies one of the chief sources of human happiness: pleasure in acting (*Freude am Thun*).

---

[66] *Philosophie des Unbewussten* (1870), CXII, pp. 584–5.
[67] See Schopenhauer, 'Von der Nichtigkeit und dem Leiden des Lebens', *WWV* II. 740 (P 578).
[68] 'Die Hartmann'sche Philosophie des Unbewussten', p. 267.
[69] *Weltelend und Weltschmerz*, p. 17.

None of these objections impressed Taubert.[70] She was skeptical whether the pleasure in work came strictly from work itself. There are so many other sources of that pleasure, she argued, that is not likely that it comes simply from working. One must consider the greater evils that work avoids, viz., the absence of boredom and idleness; the means it provides for obtaining many other things, viz., the happiness of one's family; and the anticipation of the rewards of work (33–4). When we consider all these factors, the pleasure in work itself seems to evaporate, so that we have to acknowledge, Taubert insisted, that "the activity of work in and for itself is onerous and unpleasant" (35). In responding to Haym and Meyer, Taubert went on to mention another important factor that diminished the value of work in modern life: the division of labour. In the past a craftsman could derive great pleasure from creating something for which he contributed all the parts and labour; in producing it, his talents and skills would be exercised. But such work had been superseded by modern mass forms of production, which made each worker engage in a single monotonous task. It is impossible for a worker in the modern factory to take pleasure in his work when he does one small task over and over again, and when he has little role in its design and mode of production. If Haym only considered the consequences of labour in modern forms of production, Taubert tartly retorted, he would not have made his tasteless comment about galley labour.

An important voice in these exchanges about the meaning of work was Johannes Volkelt, a young neo-Kantian and social democrat, whose *Das Unbewusste und der Pessimismus* appeared shortly after Taubert's *Der Pessimimus und seine Gegner*.[71] Volkelt, like Haym and Meyer, felt that Hartmann had given a much too negative conception of work and its value in life. Work is the means by which we exercise and become self-conscious of our powers; and in exercising and becoming self-conscious of them, we gain a sense of our self-worth, which is a great source of inner pleasure. Of course, work involves challenges, obstacles and difficulties; but it is precisely in overcoming them that we develop our powers and grow in self-confidence and self-consciousness. Volkelt did not underestimate, however, the problems posed for work by modern methods of production. All the problems raised by Taubert he fully recognized. Work had become dull, routine, mindless and even degrading in the modern division of labour. But, Volkelt explained, these problems are not intrinsic to work itself but only its present form. Many of them will disappear in the socialist state of the future. Although there will still be forms of mass production and a division of labour, working hours will be shorter and working conditions much better; more importantly, everyone will receive a liberal education where they learn to develop all their faculties and not only those needed on the factory floor. There would be not only bread for everyone, but, as Heine put it, "roses and myrtle, beauty and pleasure".

---

[70] *Der Pessimismus und seine Gegner*, III, 'Die private Güter und die Arbeit', pp. 33–6.
[71] Johannes Volkelt, *Das Unbewusste und der Pessimismus*, pp. 287–92.

For Taubert, however, the socialist state is no solution to the problems of modern work and production.[72] She shared Hartmann's conviction that a socialist state, which promised happiness for everyone, is an illusion. There will always be social and economic inequality, because resources are always scarce, and because people are born with very unequal capacities to attain them. A socialist state, which would control all aspects of the economy, and which would impose social and economic equality, would be a threat to property, liberty and talent. Remarkably, Taubert and Volkelt had a very similar diagnosis of the social problem: the modern economy has increased the standard of living for everyone, especially the working classes; but it has also increased their needs and expectations beyond the means of the government and economy to satisfy them.[73] This has created a crisis, because the people now demand more than they can possibly have. Nevertheless, despite their common diagnosis, Volkert and Taubert had very different solutions to the crisis. For Volkelt, the solution is socialism; but for Taubert, it is pessimism, because only it exposes the illusions of socialism, the pointless striving for happiness in life.

An interesting take on Taubert's solution to the social problem was given by Georg Peter Weygoldt in his *Kritik des philosophischen Pessimismus*.[74] Weygoldt shared Taubert's conservative views, and he too was a critic of socialism. He believed that the demand for higher wages and better working conditions had become excessive, the result of socialist agitators among the workers. Because of the increased expectations and demands of the working class, and because of the limited means of satisfying them, discontent was growing and revolution was on the horizon. But, for Weygoldt, pessimism was not the solution to that looming danger but part of its cause, chiefly because the pessimists had painted such a bleak portrait of labour. Work has an intrinsic value, and people should work because it is a pleasure. But because the pessimists have portrayed work as an evil to be avoided, they have encouraged the workers to demand higher reward for their sacrifices. Nowhere are the dangers of pessimism more evident, Weygoldt contended, than in its conception of work. By describing work in such negative terms, the pessimists have encouraged the very evil they so deeply fear: revolution.

In 1884, a decade after Taubert's death, and well after the initial dust had settled, Olga Plümacher provided a new analysis of the concept of work from a pessimist perspective.[75] She took a broad and mature view of the topic, one which attempted to take into account all that the critics had written, but also one which could reveal the strengths of the pessimist's case. Plümacher began with a general definition of work. In

---

[72] See *Der Pessimismus und seine Gegner*, 'X: Die Glückseligkeit als historische Zukunftsperspektive', pp. 101–22, esp. 114–16.

[73] See Johannes Volkelt, 'Die Entwicklung des modernen Pessimismus', *Im neuen Reich*, II (1872), 952–68. Taubert cites p. 967 of this article, which outlines Volkelt's very similar take on the social problem, but she takes exception to the conclusions that Volkelt draws from it.

[74] Weygoldt, *Kritik des philosophischen Pessimismus*, pp. 101–4.

[75] *Der Pessimismus in Vergangenheit und Gegenwart*, pp. 210–16.

its initial natural form, work is a species of movement, one where the goal lies not within but beyond the movement itself (210–11). Insofar as movement expresses a physiological need, and insofar as it provides for a person's needs, it can be an important source of pleasure. To that extent, Plümacher conceded, Hartmann is "perhaps" wrong to underestimate the degree of pleasure that can be involved in work (211). However, it is wrong to assume, as the optimists did, that the sheer activity of work is intrinsically pleasant. Work is often unpleasant for many reasons: it involves more movement than necessary for a person's needs; it requires too much of one kind of movement; or it inhibits other forms of movement (211). All too often work develops only one side of our nature, leaving the other sides frustrated or atrophied. Although Plümacher conceded that Hartmann might have exaggerated the negative aspects of work, she stressed that he never meant to demean its value. He had always emphasized its importance as a means for realizing higher social ends; and in that respect he had given work a much greater value than his critics, who measured its worth solely in terms of the pleasure it gave to the individual (212). Critics like Weygoldt were completely unfair, then, when they charged Hartmann and Taubert with demeaning the value of work.

Recognizing the value of work does not mean, Plümacher was eager to explain, regarding it as an intrinsically pleasant activity (212, 214). The moral, social and cultural value of work is one thing, its eudemonic value for the individual is quite another. To be sure, people often take pleasure in knowing their work to be of moral, social and cultural value; but that is often small compensation for their trouble and toil; and in many cases all the effort and struggle in trying to do good comes to nothing because circumstances make it impossible to realize one's plans (212). For the philosopher, who takes a broad historical perspective, work plays an important role in advancing social ends and world progress. But for the individual, who sees only particular ends in concrete circumstances, work is often just a gruelling and unpleasant task (214).

Plümacher admitted that work sometimes could be very rewarding and pleasant. But to be so three conditions have to be fulfilled: (1) the activity of one's vocation is in balance with the individual's desire for action; (2) the activity also promotes the individual's personal ends; and (3) the activity has a higher meaning as something socially useful (212). But these conditions are rarely fulfilled; in most cases, where a worker has to earn the means of subsistence, the demands of work exceed the natural need for movement and require a great expenditure of physical and psychic energy. The sad truth of the matter is that, for the great majority of people, work means sacrificing one part of one's life to gain another. Of the work of the great majority, that old dictum is sadly true: "If you do not put your life into it [i.e. work], you will never receive it"[76] (213). It was for this reason that the goal of the great majority is not work but leisure, i.e. they work only so that they do not have to work anymore (215).

---

[76] Plümacher implies this is an old saying, which is in the original German: "*Und setzt ihr das Leben nicht selber ein, nicht wird euch das Leben gewonnen sein.*"

Plümacher regarded this situation as "a tragic contradiction of cultural life", and not as the temporary result of a historical form of political or economic organization. She had sympathy with the condition of the workers, whose wages could barely cover their needs, and whose work was often exhausting and meaningless to them (213). But she could see no social or political solution to it, and seemed to disapprove of social democracy as a remedy (213). In one remarkable passage she seems to admit that the social problem is the result of defective social, economic and political organization. She writes that "in our cultural situation" the poor work too much for their reward. It then turns out, however, that their labours are the result of climate and geography. With her experience in Tennessee in mind, she writes that in many parts of the southern US people can earn a living from the soil without much trouble or labour.

Work, Plümacher explained, is not something accidental or arbitrary in the human predicament, but something necessary and natural. It lies in the plan of the world as much as breathing in the plan of an organism. This plan is not something imposed upon us but lies deep within our inner nature (214). In this respect the optimists are right to speak about "the blessings of work"; hence Hartmann, Plümacher implied, was one-sided in seeing work only in negative terms as something we want to avoid (214). Nevertheless, though work in one respect fulfils our inner selves and our natural needs, in another respect it demands self-denial and even self-destruction (214). The fact that work is a blessing does not speak against but for pessimism, Plümacher insisted, because that blessing demands nothing less than "the forgetting of one's self and one's existence", "self-alienation through the mechanical expenditure of energy" (215).

10. Aesthetic Redemption

In the course of their polemics against Hartmann's pessimism, Jürgen Bona Meyer and Rudolf Haym had both made a point of mentioning the many pleasures in life that Hartmann had left out of his equations. Almost *en passant* both of them cited the pleasure we derive from nature (*Naturgenuss*) and stressed its importance for human well-being.[77] It seemed a serious omission that Hartmann had never considered this pleasure, especially given the importance that had been bestowed upon it since the romantic era. For Schiller, Goethe, Herder and the romantics, contact with nature regenerates and inspires human beings. One escapes the drudgery and despair of life, which is the product of culture, by turning to nature. While culture divides us, nature makes us whole again. But if this is so—if nature really restores us, makes us whole and happy—then the pessimist's case against life needs significant qualification.

---

[77] Meyer, 'Weltelend und Weltschmerz', p. 20; and Haym, 'Die Hartmann'sche Philosophie des Unbewussten', p. 275. The same point was made in much greater detail by Johannes Volkelt in his *Das Unbewusste und der Pessimismus*, pp. 294–8. Though published in the same year as Taubert's work, Taubert does not mention it.

Even though made *en passant,* this objection did not go unnoticed. It was fully appreciated by Taubert, who devoted a full chapter to it in *Der Pessimismus und seine Gegner*.[78] It was true, Taubert admitted, that Hartmann, in calculating the pleasures of life, had failed to consider those we derive from nature. But then, she added, he also did not mention the suffering often caused by nature, viz., volcanoes, earthquakes, hurricanes and floods. And that suffering is often very great indeed. In Japan millions have lost their lives from earthquakes; in Bengal 10,000 people a year die from Tiger attacks; and in sailing across the Atlantic, thousands of ships have been lost. So, as these facts attest, nature does not only heal us; she also destroys us. If any objection is to be made against Hartmann, then, it is that he failed to consider such a weighty argument *in favour of* his pessimism (56).

If we find nature beautiful, Taubert went on, that is only because we read our feelings and purposes into it (58, 61). The peace, tranquillity and harmony of nature is really only an illusion that we create to calm and charm ourselves. The "laughing meadows" conceal as much suffering as "the torment of the cities"; and "the peace of the night" is the occasion for predators to stalk their prey. A view of a forest from the distance might be beautiful and uplifting; but it is an illusion to think that its denizens are happier than people in cities. One creature is the prey of another, and thousands of innocents lose their lives from hunger and cold. There is terror, need, struggle in the forest just as in the city.

Taubert regarded pleasure in nature as a fiction because it is, in her view, more a cultural construction than a natural feeling (56–7). Pleasure in nature is a very modern phenomenon, she pointed out, the product of the romantic age and Rousseau's rebellion against modern culture. We derive pleasure from nature only when we want to return to it; and we want to return to it only after we have become alienated from it in the first place. That alienation has been the product of modern urban life, which has enclosed man in a shell of art, technology, customs and laws. The ancient Greeks felt no longing for nature, because they were really part of it; and the medievals did not want to become one with nature, because they saw their resting place in heaven. It was only after the infliction of the wounds of modern urban life that people began to long for nature. This only goes to show, Taubert believed, that pleasure in nature is really negative in value: we appreciate nature only if we do not have access to it (57). Nature cannot be regarded, therefore, as a constant source of pleasure, especially for those who live close to it.

But even if we admit that nature is the source of pleasure in the modern age, Taubert continued, it still should not be given much weight in calculating the general value of life. Why? The problem is that this pleasure is becoming more and more rare and inaccessible for most people in contemporary life. Nature has been so polluted by modern industry and technology, it has been so trammelled and spoiled by human habitation, that there are few places left on earth that offer people tranquillity and beauty (59).

---

[78] VI: 'Der Naturgenuss', pp. 55–62.

If we want to find unspoiled nature, we have to travel far to see it; and the further we have to travel, the more stress we have to endure before we get to it. We have to ask ourselves whether travelling to exotic locations to enjoy nature is worth all the trouble; in most cases, it would be more relaxing simply to stay at home (60). What is the pleasure of the Alps if, to enjoy its occasional vistas, one has to endure poor food, rough roads and dirty hotels? As the reader can see, all the arguments for stay-at-home vacations were already well in place in the 19th century.

So far the thrust of Taubert's case against Haym and Meyer is to show that pleasure in nature should not be given much weight on the scales of the value of life. That we take pleasure in nature is a fact that we should not dispute. But that pleasure is not natural or universal; it is not positive and constant; and it is not accessible or common. But, beside these points, Taubert had another kind of argument up her sleeve to show that pleasure in nature should not count as evidence against pessimism. The pessimist is in a better position than the optimist, she contended, to explain why we take pleasure in nature in the first place. That pleasure has its source in our longing to become one with the universe, in our striving to lose our individuality and to rest in peace "in the harbour of nothingness" (57). If life were truly beautiful and desirable, as the optimist assures us, we would never feel this longing; we would not strive to lose our individuality; we would not feel separated from nature; and we would not want to return to her (58). The longing and striving to return to nature stands as evidence for the sorrow and suffering of our normal existence, where we are caught in the toils and troubles of our own individuality. So the pleasure we take in nature, properly examined and explained, turns out to be one of the strongest proofs for pessimism.

The dispute about pleasure in nature was only a foreshadowing, however, of a much bigger issue dividing Taubert and her critics. Haym's complaint about Hartmann's neglect of pleasure in nature had its source in a much broader and deeper criticism: that Hartmann had ignored the aesthetic dimension of life. Hartmann, he insisted, had "stubbornly closed his eyes to the aesthetic element" (273),[79] and he had done his utmost "to reduce the aesthetic to a minimum" (275). For Haym, this was a major weakness of Hartmann's pessimism, because the aesthetic dimension of life is proof that it is not a scene of sorrow and suffering. Beauty is a source and sign of pleasure, and the omnipresence of beauty is therefore proof of the happiness of life. "The existence of beauty in the world, and the sense for it, is the guarantee of all pleasure that exists, and it is an indisputable original phenomenon of pleasure... The enjoyment of art is in truth striking testimony of happiness, which flows in streams through the veins of the earth" (274). A strikingly romantic sentiment from one of the greatest critics of romanticism![80]

---

[79] References in parentheses are to 'Die Hartmann'sche Philosophie des Unbewussten'.

[80] It is worth noting that Haym was the author of *Die romantische Schule* (Berlin: Gaertner, 1870), the first comprehensive scholarly account of the early romantic movement. Though Haym's treatment is sympathetic, it is often highly critical.

Never one to shirk a challenge, Taubert engaged Haym's criticism in the very next chapter of *Der Pessimismus und seine Gegner*.[81] Haym, she charged, had simply confused aesthetic pleasure with happiness. It is one thing to enjoy beauty; it is quite another to equate such enjoyment with happiness, with contentment in life. Even if one sees beauty everywhere, it does not follow that the world is a happy place. After all, beauty lies more in the mind of the perceiver than in things themselves. The conflation of beauty with the happiness of the world becomes especially apparent, Taubert claimed, from the highest form of art, from tragedy, which depicts not the happiness but the suffering of humanity (64). The purpose of art is to take us beyond the realm of ordinary life, where there is so much sorrow and suffering, and into a higher realm, where we can enjoy forms for their own sake (65). It is art that gives human beings some consolation about the misery of life and that reconciles them to life through the magic of aesthetic illusion (66–7).

Such views about the power of art sound strikingly Nietzschean, though it was probably only a coincidence that Nietzsche's *Geburt der Tragödie* had appeared just a year earlier.[82] Unlike Nietzsche, though, Taubert did not think that art could provide a path of redemption, a remedy for all the sorrows and suffering of life. She doubted the possibility of "an aesthetic redemption of the world, i.e., an overcoming of suffering through beauty" (77). The problem with such a programme, in her view, is that the aesthetic dimension of life is too rarified, accessible only to an elite few, the artist and the highly educated. The great masses of people are too poor and ignorant to appreciate beauty, and so this antidote for their toils and troubles lies out of reach. Haym, for his part, was not so skeptical about the powers of art. Though he admitted that beauty is fully appreciable by only a few, he still insisted that beauty is omnipresent in life and that everyone can take pleasure in it, at least to some degree (274).[83] But Taubert believed that Haym was too naïve and idealistic, that he had little conception of the poverty and weaknesses of the masses. He had underestimated how poor most people are, and how little time, energy and money they have for the pleasures of art (77). He was like Queen Antoinette recommending that the people should eat cake when they could not afford bread (76).

The exchange between Taubert and Haym raised the question: why not aesthetic education? Why not educate the people so that they can appreciate art? In that case the pessimist's reckoning about the value of life would have to be reformulated, throwing much more pleasure into his equations. Aesthetic education was indeed the idea behind Haym's thesis: "Happiness is in truth an ethical-artistic task" (276). Haym's point is that beauty is not something given in human life, but that it is something we create by making our lives works of art. Through such an aesthetic education we give our lives a much greater value than they would otherwise have. Hartmann had treated

---

[81] 'VII: Die Glückseligkeit als ästhetische Weltanschauung', pp. 63–84.
[82] Friedrich Nietzsche, *Die Geburt der Tragödie aus dem Geiste der Musik* (Leipzig: Ernst Wilhelm Fritzsch, 1872). Taubert never mentions Nietzsche in her book.
[83] Haym, 'Die Hartmann'sche Philosophie des Unbewussten'.

beauty and happiness as a given, as if they had to be handed down to us by fate, and he had failed to appreciate the simple point behind the old adage that everyone is the forger of his own happiness.[84]

Aesthetic education, though, was not an ideal for which Taubert had much patience. She wilfully misread Haym's remarks about it, interpreting them as a proposal for a eudemonistic ethic.[85] Haym had no such intention, and all her criticisms of his attempt to attach rewards to virtue were beside the point. We should not be misled by Taubert's apparent sympathy with the masses, as if she deplored their poverty and lack of education. The truth of the matter is that Taubert did not sympathize with the people but feared them. She stated that they are not really interested in art and the realm of the ideal, and that they are content with eating, drinking and material well-being (77). Worst of all, their ambitions were to steal the property of the elite and privileged. Goaded by socialist agitators, their goal was complete social and political equality, a world where there would be no place for art at all (77).

Nearly a decade after Taubert's exchanges with Haym, Olga Plümacher revisited the aesthetic question in her *Der Pessimismus in Vergangenheit und Gegenwart*.[86] The charges against Hartmann for ignoring the aesthetic dimension of life had not abated, and the optimists continued to maintain that taking it into account would tip the eudemonic scales in their favour. Art and pleasure in nature—so the argument went—made life more pleasant than painful, and therefore worth living after all. Plümacher, however, remained skeptical of this argument. She insisted that pessimism does not exclude aesthetic contemplation, and that it can take account of the pleasure derived from it (227). But the question remains whether aesthetic pleasure really counts that much in weighing the general amount of pleasure versus pain in the world. The aesthetic realm, Plümacher conceded, is indeed very wide, extending to all kinds of objects and experiences. But the problem is that the pleasure of beauty is, for most people, very weak, fragile and uncommon (231). To appreciate the fragility and weakness of beauty, one only had to go to a concert with a toothache, visit an art gallery with a stomach-ache or watch a sunset while seasick (231–2). So, even if the aesthetic realm is wide, the conditions for enjoying it are narrow (231). Such pleasure requires disinterested contemplation, which is a rare state of mind, one hard to attain and sustain in life (232). The aesthetic attitude demands tranquillity and peace of mind, which are easily upset by those passions that are inevitably involved in the usual business of life, viz., longing, fear, dread and anxiety. Whoever insists upon having an entirely aesthetic existence would have to abandon the normal feelings of life, and renounce "two thirds of the richness of the life of the soul" (232). So, unlike Nietzsche, but like Taubert, Plümacher did not think that life could be made worth

---

[84] Haym (p. 276) refers to the old German adage: "*Jeder ist seines Glückes Schmied.*"
[85] See ch. 8: 'Die Glückseligkeit als Tugend', pp. 79–84.
[86] *Der Pessimismus in Vergangenheit und Gegenwart*, Zweite Ausgabe, VI, Cap. 8, pp. 233–7.

living as an aesthetic phenomenon.[87] Art was at best a faint and fleeting escape from the suffering of life, providing no hope for enduring redemption.

11. Love

It was an old truth dear to Christianity and Romanticism that what makes life worth living is love. No matter how much evil and suffering there is in this world, love conquers all and redeems all. Novalis, epitomizing this core belief of Christianity and Romanticism, wrote in a revealing passage from his notebooks: "The heart is the key to the world and life. One lives in this helpless condition to love, and to be committed to others... So Christ, seen from this standpoint, is the key to the world."[88]

So if the pessimist were to make his case against the value of life, he had no choice but to tackle the theme of love. Whether love is really so valuable and redeeming clearly depends on one's conception of it. What, after all, is love?

Schopenhauer had taken his stand on this question in his famous essay on the metaphysics of sexual love in the second volume of *Die Welt als Wille und Vorstellung*.[89] There he had argued that love is rooted in sexual desire, and that its chief purpose is procreation, the propagation of the species. Because it is based on instinct, a drive of nature over which we have no control, love has no moral value. Love, Schopenhauer insisted, is filled with illusions. While the lover believes to be pursuing his self-interest, he is really in thrall to the sexual instinct acting through him. The lover is enchanted by the beauty of the beloved, though beauty is really only the bait to capture him. We think that love is a matter of reciprocity, of giving and receiving; but the lover really does not care about the interests of the beloved and cares only about satisfying his desires. While the lover thinks that he will be forever happy in the arms of the beloved, his passions quickly fade after sexual satisfaction. Soon disillusionment grows and prevails. All these illusions arise from the fact that we are not self-conscious, that we are not aware of the will of nature which acts through us and which uses us as instruments to preserve the species. Because he was so bent on exposing these illusions, Schopenhauer called his own attitude toward love "a crude realism"; but its crudity was also its honesty, which he believed so much better than all the idealist and moral afflatus surrounding love. When we see love from this broad metaphysical perspective, Schopenhauer concluded, we can see that it does not redeem life but simply perpetuates it, keeping in motion the cycle of desire and suffering. Love brings a short moment of ecstasy in sexual orgasm; but that hardly compensates for all its despair and

---

[87] Plümacher does not respond to Nietzsche in *Der Pessimismus in Vergangenheit und Gegenwart*, though she does briefly refer to him, p. 176. She had certainly read him. In an early article, a survey of Hartmann's foes, she took into account Nietzsche's critique of Hartmann in *Unzeitgemässe Betrachtungen*. See 'Die Philosophie des Unbewussten und ihre Gegner', *Unsere Zeit*, 15 (1879), 321–45, esp. 329.
[88] 'Teplitzer Fragmente', no. 62, in *Novalis: Werke, Tagebücher und Briefe Friedrich von Hardenbergs*, ed. Hans-Joachim Mähl and Richard Samuel (Munich: Hanser Verlag, 1978), II. 396.
[89] 'Metaphysik der Geschlechtsliebe', *WWV* II. 678–727.

disillusionment. A wise man, seeing the cause of love and all the sorrows it brings, would strive for self-renunciation and extirpation of sexual desire.

In *Philosophie des Unbewussten* Hartmann explicitly and emphatically endorsed Schopenhauer's metaphysics of sexual love.[90] That metaphysics was as important to his pessimism as it had been to Schopenhauer's. Hartmann differs from Schopenhauer only in the bluntness and clarity of his exposition, and in introducing a Darwinian element into his theory. Love, on the face of it, Hartmann wrote, appears completely absurd. What is it that people are after? Why are they going to all this trouble? Why are they so gripped by their desires? The more one thinks about it, the more one feels like a sober man in a party of drunks. All the mystery of love disappears, however, when we admit the hard and honest truth about it: that its goal is sexual satisfaction, not just with any individual but with just this particular individual (190). Whenever sexual desire abates, so does love itself (189). Love is the instinct to mate with another particular individual to produce the best possible offspring for the species. Though we think we are making a conscious choice, the selection of another partner is really natural selection working through us, striving to find the most suitable mate to create the best offspring (192, 193). The reason that love seems so mysterious to us is simply because we are unconscious of its goals. We think that we are pursuing our own self-interest, because we desire nothing more than to be with the beloved; but we also know that it cannot be solely our self-interest when we have to sacrifice so much of ourselves for the beloved, and when we are so often disappointed and disillusioned after the satisfaction of our desires. When, however, we become wise to nature's purpose with us, the mystery of love disappears; yet, despite our better knowledge, we still find ourselves pushed again by recurring desires, though with decreasing enthusiasm (595–6).

The importance of this theory of love for Hartmann's pessimism should be clear. If love is only sexual desire, and if the satisfaction of this desire is momentary, the intense but brief pleasure of orgasm, then love does not weigh much in the hedonic calculus of life (598). Against its momentary pleasures, we have to weigh its many troubles and disadvantages. There is all the stress and frustration we endure *before* we satisfy our desires; and there is all the disillusionment and disappointment *after* we satisfy them. The sadness of disillusionment lasts much longer than all the happiness of our illusions (592). The intense pains of childbirth far outweigh the passing pleasures of sex (590). Although love affairs sometimes lead to marriage, few marriages are happy, and those that are happy are so not because of love but because of friendship between the partners (593).[91] On all these grounds, reason advises us to abstain entirely from love; but

---

[90] See *Philosophie des Unbewussten* (1870), Kap. BII: 'Das Unbewusste in der geschlechtlichen Liebe', pp. 181–98; and 'Hunger und Liebe', in Kap. CXII.: 'Die Unvernunft des Wollens und das Elend des Daseins', pp. 586–99.

[91] It is noteworthy that Hartmann distinguishes love from friendship, which he says are "*himmelweit verschiedene Dinge*", *Philosophie des Unbewussten*, 187. Plümacher claims that Hartmann made "*Liebesfreundschaft*" an important element of marriage. But Hartmann, at least in the second edition of *Philosophie des Unbewussten*, would have regarded this concept as a contradiction in terms.

then the torment of repressed desires makes abstemiousness an even greater evil than indulgence (599). Ultimately, then, reason must advise an even more drastic remedy: extermination of the drive, i.e. castration. That is the only possible result from the eudemonological standpoint, Hartmann admits (599). If there is anything to be said against it, that must be from some moral standpoint beyond the self-interest of the individual.

It should not be surprising that the reaction against this theory of love was swift, strong and severe. No other aspect of pessimism created such indignation and hostility among its critics. For the theists, Schopenhauer's and Hartmann's theory of love clashed with their deepest convictions and ultimate values. Some of Hartmann's first theist critics were so shocked, their moral senses so offended, that they accused Hartmann of advocating promiscuity, free love and prostitution. By reducing love down to sexual desire, Hartmann seemed to be advocating the pursuit of sexual desire for its own sake, regardless of moral restraints. Thus Knauer said that Hartmann's views about love were surrounded by "the pestilential air of prostitution", and that they were "laden with the egoism of old bachelorhood".[92] Another early theist critic, Ludwig Weis, wrote that Hartmann's treatment of love was "spiced with a tickling of the palate and the arousal of the senses", and that for this reason his philosophy should have all the success of Offenbach's pieces for the theatre.[93] Both Knauer and Weis insinuated that Hartmann's work sold so well only because it aroused pornographic interests, especially among young women.

Taubert swiftly condemned these early critics.[94] They were moralizing like the principal of a girl's school, and they had little appreciation for the fact that Hartmann was trying to get to the truth about love without the blinkers of moral scruples. First and foremost philosophers had an obligation to tell the truth, even if it were difficult for people to admit on moral grounds (37–8). Taubert did not dispute that there might be people who were attracted to Hartmann's writings for salacious motives; but that hardly discredited the writings themselves, still less the author (39). That Hartmann was not condoning, let alone recommending, free love and prostitution was clear, Taubert pointed out, from some passages in the third edition of *Philosophie des Unbewussten* where he explained that following instinct leads to marriage, and that free love and prostitution are a corruption of instinct (40–1).[95] All the moral indignation about Hartmann's theory of love is entirely beside the point, Taubert argued,

---

[92] *Das Facit*, pp. 48–9.
[93] Ludwig Weis, *Anti-Materialismus oder Kritik aller Philosophie des Unbewußten* (Berlin: F. Henschel, 1873), p. 129. This work is volume III of his *Anti-Materialismus* (Berlin: F. Henschel, 1871-2). Regarding Offenbach, Weis was probably referring to the scandal created by his *Galop infernal* of Act II, Scene 2, of *Orphée aux enfers*, which contains the infamous cancan dance.
[94] *Der Pessimismus und seine Gegner*, Kap. IV: 'Die Liebe', pp. 37–50. See also her long review of Weis's *Anti-Materialismus*, which appears as an appendix to her book, pp. 147–64.
[95] Taubert cites *Philosophie des Unbewussten*, dritte beträchtlich vermehrte Auflage (Berlin: Duncker, 1871), pp. 192, 209. These passages were probably added by Hartmann to respond to critics like Weis and Knauer.

because it was never his intention to treat the *ethical* meaning of love (42). Hartmann's aim was to determine only the *eudemonic* value of love, i.e. he wanted to see whether and how its miseries outweigh its joys. If people thought that Hartmann was denying or underestimating the ethical value of love, that was only because they confused his theory with Schopenhauer's, which was indeed guilty of destroying its ethical dimension by reducing it to sexual gratification (42). Having thus defended Hartmann, Taubert went on to give her own views on love, which are more positive than Hartmann's. While she did not dispute Hartmann's main finding that love creates more suffering than happiness, she weighed it more heavily on the eudemonic scales than he by stressing its importance in overcoming loneliness (46). Besides science and art, love alone could at least give us "a dream of happiness", which was sometimes enough to get us through "the night of life" (46).

Though Taubert's defence was widely read, it hardly staunched the flow of criticism against Hartmann. While later critics did not stoop to the level of Knauer and Weis, they were still indignant about Hartmann's reduction of love to sexuality. The conservative theist Weygoldt thought that Hartmann's theory was faulty on eudemonic grounds alone, because the miseries Hartmann found in love do not arise from love itself but only from contemporary social mores.[96] Hartmann had judged the metal from its dross, Urania from *Venus vulgivaga*, Weygoldt claimed. That young men nowadays suffer from repressed sexual drives has much to do with contemporary mores, which prevent early marriage. That young woman too feel sexual frustration has more to do with lax morals than their natural desires. And that there are so many unhappy marriages has nothing to do with love itself but with the low morals of the age, which allow flirtation and *mariages de raison*.

Paul Christ, another conservative theist critic, said that he could not read Hartmann's theory without a deep inner indignation.[97] Like Weygoldt, he thought that much of the unhappiness of love came from a lack of morality and reason, and that it had nothing to do with love itself. Of course, there are many illusions in love; but it is the responsibility of everyone to learn to control them and to keep them within realistic limits. Every happy marriage—and there are more of them than Hartmann wanted to admit—stood as a refutation of Hartmann's theory. Experience shows us that in happy marriages there is no disillusionment but only fulfilment. Hartmann's theory is dangerous for morals, Christ believed, because it encourages people to seek sexual satisfaction alone in their personal relationships. And the Darwinist strands of Hartmann's theory, which stressed the importance of racial improvement, raised serious moral questions: could it not lead to abortion and mistreatment of those who were not born so perfect?

Remarkably, the social democrat critic, Johannes Volkelt, agreed with his conservative colleagues, Weygoldt and Christ, that contemporary social conditions are

---

[96] *Kritik des philosophischen Pessimismus*, pp. 105–7.
[97] Christ, *Der Pessimismus und die Sittenlehre*, pp. 164–6.

responsible for much of the misery of love.[98] But his solution to this problem was very different from theirs: a new socialist order rather than a return to old customs and beliefs. In a socialist republic, Volkelt was convinced, there would be much less sexual misery: there would be fewer unhappy marriages, because divorce would be easy; there would be much less sexual frustration because men and women could marry young and whoever they really loved; and there would be little prostitution because there would be public careers for women as a well as men, and because there would be no standing armies (soldiers being the main customers of prostitutes).

Whatever the merits of these later criticisms, it is important to see that they could at best affect only one half or side of Hartmann's thinking about love. For, besides his theory about love as sexual instinct, Hartmann harboured another very different theory about love. This other theory is latent in his monism, and it was only a matter of developing its implications. It is an important implication of that doctrine, Hartmann thought, that each individual is essentially one with all other individuals, and that each fully realizes itself only when it forfeits those aspects of its individuality that separate it from others and only when it recognizes its identity with all others. There is a single universal will in all of us, which makes up our inner identity; and it is our task as moral agents to make this identity, which is normally subconscious, fully self-conscious, so that we understand the moral consequences of our actions. When I become self-conscious of this will, I know that whatever I do to others I also do to myself, and that whatever others do to me they do to themselves. Schopenhauer had given great importance to this theme in Book IV of *Die Welt als Wille und Vorstellung*.[99] The same theme was no less important for Hartmann, who developed its implications into another theory of love. While the theme is not explicit in the first two editions of *Philosophie des Unbewussten*, it appears in a later article, 'Ist der Pessimismus trostlos?'[100] Here Hartmann writes about "the mystical roots of love" which come from the longing for identity with all other beings. This longing, we learn, is really a form of love: "All love is in its deepest root longing; and all longing is the longing for unification [with others]" (86). In this unity people do not retain their individuality but surrender it, Hartmann stresses. "Whoever has not felt the longing for self-annihilation in the loved person does not know what love is" (87). Taubert developed this theme in *Der Pessimismus und seine Gegner*, stressing how love is "homesickness", the longing of the lover to surrender his or her individuality and to become one with the absolute (47).

In fundamental respects this mystical theory of love differs from the instinct theory. While the mystical theory sees the goal of love as unity with the absolute, the instinct theory finds it in procreation. Whereas the mystical theory demands the surrender of individuality, the instinct theory affirms it, because the goal of love is self-replication in

---

[98] Volkelt, *Das Unbewusste und der Pessimismus*, p. 309.
[99] Schopenhauer, *Die Welt als Wille und Vorstellung*, §§63, 66; *Werke*, I. 484, 508–9.
[100] Eduard von Hartmann, 'Ist der Pessimismus trostlos?', *Philosophische Monatshefte*, 5 (1870), 21–41. Reprinted in *Gesammelte philosophische Abhandlungen zur Philosophie des Unbewussten* (Berlin: Duncker, 1872), pp. 147–65. All references above are to this later edition.

one's progeny. In the mystical theory the individual penetrates through the veil of Maya and finally discovers the truth about the world; but in the instinct theory the individual is subject to all kinds of illusion, the abolition of which leads to self-renunciation but not identification with the universe as a whole. Whatever its merits, the very different logic of the mystical theory deflects some of the criticisms of the instinct theory. No one could charge the mystical theory with egoism or immorality, the most common complaints against the instinct theory.

Some of Hartmann's critics, however, were not blind to the mystical theory, which they found as faulty as the instinct theory. Johannes Volkelt questioned that the two theories, having such different logic, could ever be reconciled.[101] Meyer saw in the mystical theory not a negation of egoism but a superegoism because the individual sees him/herself as the universe as a whole.[102] The reason he or she seeks identity with others is still egoistic because he or she wants *self*-redemption. Hugo Sommer thought that the mystical theory rests on a simple logical mistake.[103] Even if all individuals are ultimately one that has little or nothing to do with love, for love arises despite this oneness and not because of it. Love occurs only in the interaction between individuals, because it requires recognition of, and respect for, another's individuality. It demands that we take pleasure in the well-being of another not because he or she is the same as us, but because he or she is different from us.

Obviously, much more could be said about the topic of love—and much more was said during the pessimism controversy. What we have said about it here is a mere sample of a much broader and richer discussion. At the very least it is another case in point of how pessimism, in questioning the general value of life, had raised the profoundest philosophical questions.

---

[101] Volkelt, *Das Unbewusste und der Pessimismus*, pp. 305–8.
[102] See Jürgen Bona Meyer, 'Weltlust und Weltleid', *Probleme der Weltweisheit*, pp. 291–2. Meyer makes this criticism only in this revised version of his original article 'Weltelend und Weltschmerz'. It is noteworthy that he made it after corresponding with Hartmann.
[103] Sommer, *Pessimismus und die Sittenlehre*, pp. 125–6.

9

Mainländer's Philosophy of Redemption

1. The Heroic Pessimist

On the night of 1 April 1876, the young Philipp Batz, only 34 years old, standing on stacked copies of his just published philosophical work, hanged himself. Some thought Batz was insane; others said he had been depressed. But his suicide, which had been long planned,[1] was also an act of conviction; it was indeed the final will and testament of his philosophy. In a pessimistic age, Batz was perhaps the most radical pessimist of them all. Like all pessimists, he taught that life is suffering, and that it is not worth living. Unlike the others, however, Batz not only taught pessimism; he lived it and breathed it, making its ascetic principles the basis of his conduct. He alone was willing to take pessimism to its ultimate conclusion: suicide.

The book that provided the platform for Batz's suicide on that sad night was his life's work, *Die Philosophie der Erlösung*,[2] whose first volume appeared in 1876, just days before his death. In the months before his suicide, Batz had written a second supplementary volume, which would be published only in 1886.[3] Apart from his philosophical work, Batz wrote dramas, a long historical play, *Die letzten Hohenstaufen*,[4] and a comedy, *Die Macht der Motive*.[5] His knack for poetry made him a good prose writer.

Die Philosophie der Erlösung is an idiosyncratic masterpiece. It is the exposition of a complete worldview, containing an epistemology, metaphysics, aesthetics, physics, ethics and politics. All these elements of the book support its underlying gospel: that salvation from the misery of life lies only in death, which is nothingness. Batz was

---

[1] On Batz's final reflections before his suicide, see Walther Rauschenberger, 'Aus der letzten Lebenszeit Philipp Mainländers: Nach ungedruckten Briefen und Aufzeichnungen des Philosophen', in *Süddeutsche Monatshefte*, IX (1911/12), 117–31. It is noteworthy that Batz's older brother and older sister also committed suicide.

[2] The first edition appeared as *Die Philosophie der Erlösung* (Berlin: Grieben, 1876). We will cite Mainländer's works according to *Schriften*, ed. Winfried H. Müller-Seyfarth (Hildesheim: Olms Verlag, 1996). 4 vols. An abridged version, selected and edited by Ulrich Horstmann, appeared with Suhrkamp Verlag in 1989. For a complete catalogue of Mainländer's works, see *Schriften*, IV. 474.

[3] *Die Philosophie der Erlösung*, Zweiter Band. *Zwölf philosophische Essays*. Frankfurt: C. Koenitzer, 1886. Second edition 1894.

[4] *Die Letzten Hohenstaufen: Ein dramatisches Gedicht in drei Theilen* (Leipzig: Heinrich Schmidt & Carl Günther, 1876). Reprint 1997 as volume III of *Schriften*,.

[5] *Die Macht der Motive* was first published in 1998 in *Schriften*, IV. 79–187.

confident that his system was the culmination of all philosophy. He claimed that it combined into a single vision, into a perfect organic whole, all the essential truths of idealism and realism, monism and pluralism, Christianity and Buddhism.[6]

The primary purpose of Batz's work was to explain the cardinal doctrines of Christianity—"the greatest of all world religions"—on a secular or rational basis. His soteriology can be equally described as Christianized paganism or paganized Christianity. We learn that the esoteric meaning of all the essential truths of Christianity—the incarnation, trinity, the resurrection—is that the suffering of life is redeemed only in death, which is the peace of utter nothingness. That death is nothingness is, of course, what the pagan Epicurus taught; but it is also, Batz tells us, what Christ really meant. In the course of explaining Christian doctrine, Batz introduces a very modern and redolent theme: the death of God. He popularized the theme before Nietzsche, though he gives it a much more metaphysical meaning.

Besides the death of God, Batz's philosophy contains another signature doctrine, one no less powerful, puzzling and original. This is his idea of the death wish, i.e. that the inner striving of all beings, the final goal of all their activity, is death.[7] At the core of everyone, Batz teaches us, lies their deep longing for utter nothingness. Schopenhauer's aimless and blind will turns out to have a goal after all: death. Batz admits that there is an instinct for self-preservation in all of us; but he insists that, upon reflection, this desire for life is really only the means for death. We will life only for the sake of death. Batz finds this longing for death not only in each individual, but in the general process of history, whose sole and ultimate goal is death. In some following sections I shall examine the metaphysical and ethical basis for this paradoxical doctrine.[8]

In a letter to his publisher Batz expressed the wish for his work to be published under the pseudonym *Philipp Mainländer*, a name that honoured his home town, Offenbach am Main.[9] Batz told his publisher he wanted to be called this until his death and for all time. Ever since, Batz's request has been honoured, and he has been known almost exclusively by his pseudonym. Henceforth I will honour that custom.

Mainländer gives the lie to the common generalization that pessimism goes hand-in-hand with a conservative or reactionary politics. He was a social democrat or communist, preaching the value of free love and the equal distribution of wealth. He had the deepest sympathy for the suffering of the common man and much of his thinking was preoccupied with "the social question", i.e. the poverty of the mass of people and the workers. One of the chief aims of his *Philosophie der Erlösung* was to provide a message of redemption for the common man. While Schopenhauer limited deliverance to the elite few—the saint or artistic genius—Mainländer extended it to the whole

---

[6] See Batz's summary of his philosophy, 'Die Philosophie der Erlösung', in *Die Philosophie der Erlösung*, II. 233–42.

[7] According to Ludger Lütkehaus, Mainländer was the proper discoverer of the death wish, and Freud only rehabilitated the idea. See his *Nichts* (Frankfurt: Zweitausendeins, 2003), p. 251.

[8] See sections 2 and 4 below.   [9] See 'Aus meinem Leben', *Schriften*, IV. 366–7.

of humanity.¹⁰ It is not the least token of Mainländer's humanity that he was sympathetic to the Jews, whose charity and sagacity he much admired.¹¹

Mainländer's radical politics raises, however, a problem of consistency. If we take his pessimism seriously, as we must, it becomes difficult to reconcile with his left-wing convictions. For while his pessimism preaches resignation and quietism, his radical politics teaches the value of resistance and activism. This tension lies at the very heart of Mainländer's philosophy, and poses its deepest challenge. I will consider in the final section Mainländer's attempt to address this apparent inconsistency.

The task of the following chapter is to provide an introduction to the basic ideas of Mainländer's philosophy, the study of which has lately undergone a renaissance.¹² It is a mistake to underestimate Mainländer as a philosopher, as Nietzsche once had.¹³ Mainländer not only makes penetrating criticisms of Kant and Schopenhauer, but he also creates a coherent and original worldview. His interpretations of traditional Christian doctrines, while not historically accurate, are interesting in their own right as attempts to rehabilitate them from a modern perspective. Few philosophers thought with as much passion as Mainländer, and few attempted to live so completely and honestly according to their philosophy. We must pay him high tribute: Mainländer was the heroic pessimist, the only one willing to live—and die—by his convictions.

2. Life and Philosophical Education

Mainländer's death brought to an end a remarkable career, one filled with a passionate devotion to the life of the spirit. He was born 5 October 1841, the youngest son of a wealthy bourgeois family. From 1848 to 1856 Mainländer attended the Realschule in Offenbach, and then went to a business school in Dresden. Mainländer never went to a university, and he was self-taught in literature and philosophy. Such an education gave his thinking not only its simplicity but also its originality. After finishing business school in 1858, he went to work in various trades in Italy, where he lived for five years. The Italian years were the happiest of his life. Mainländer learned Italian, wrote poetry

---

[10] See Mainländer's critique of Schopenhauer in his 'Aehrenlese', Essay 11 of the second volume II of *Die Philosophie der Erlösung*, *Schriften*, IV. 481–505.

[11] See his comments in the 'Anhang' to *Philosophie der Erlösung*, I. 597–8.

[12] Recently, in addition to the new editions of Mainländer's works stated in n. 2, several collections of articles on Mainländer have appeared. See *"Die modernen Pessimisten als décadents": Von Nietzsche zu Horstmann. Texte zur Rezeptionsgeschichte von Philipp Mainländers Philosophie der Erlösung*, ed. Winfried Müller-Seyfarth (Würzburg: Königshausen & Neumann, 1993); *Was Philipp Mainländer ausmacht: Offenbacher Mainländer Symposium 2001*, ed. Winfried Müller-Seyfarth (Würzburg: Königshausen & Neumann, 2002); *Anleitung zum glücklichen Nichtssein: Offenbacher Mainländer-Essaywettbewerb*, ed. Winfried Müller-Seyfarth (Würzburg: Königshausen & Neumann, 2006). Also see the monograph by Winfried Müller-Seyfarth, *Metaphysik der Entropie: Philipp Mainländers transzendentale Analyse und ihre ethisch-metaphysische Relevanz* (Berlin: Van Bremen, 2000).

[13] See Nietzsche, *Die fröhliche Wissenschaft* §357, in *Sämtliche Werke*, III. 601–2. Nietzsche asks himself whether the *"süsslichen Virginitäts-Apostel Mainländer"* can be counted among the genuine Germans, and concludes *"Zuletzt wird es ein Jude gewesen sein (—alle Juden werden süsslich, wenn sie moralisieren)."* I leave Nietzsche scholars to ponder the meaning and value of his opinion.

and read Italian literature. In 1863 he was called home to Germany to take over his father's factory. But the work did not suit him, and he longed to escape. He dreamed of a romantic life as a Prussian soldier. But, because of his age, his efforts to enlist failed, so he went to work with a banking firm in Berlin. This work too stifled him; he strived to earn a fortune through speculation, so that he could devote the rest of his life to philosophy and literature; but the crash of the stock market in 1873 ruined him. Mainländer's attempt to become a soldier finally succeeded in October 1874 when he was allowed to join the Halberstädter Kürassieren, a cavalry regiment. His autobiography provides a fascinating portrait of a cavalryman in the last days of that dying profession. The one year Mainländer spent as a cavalryman proved exciting but exhausting. He had enlisted to stay for three years; but for family and health reasons, he lasted only one and left in November 1875. The five months after leaving the army and before his death were some of his most productive. Mainländer left behind, unpublished, a novel, drafts for two dramas, and the second volume of *Die Philosophie der Erlösung*.

Mainländer's philosophical education began early, in 1858, while he was apprenticed to a banking firm in Naples. The first philosophical work he read was Spinoza's *Tractatus theologico-politicus*. This book, he later wrote, "created a revolution in me" (97).[14] "It was as if a thousand veils fell before my eyes, as if an impenetrable morning fog had sunk and as if I saw for the first time the sun rising. I was only seventeen, and I must praise the director of fate that the first philosophical writing put into my hands was this treatise of the great man." It was probably Spinoza who made him skeptical of traditional theism, and who taught him that the truth of the Christian mysteries lay in their ethical message alone. Mainländer also said that Spinoza's views about the state and natural law became "my flesh and blood" (97). He read the *Ethica* too; though he perused it slowly and brooded over some sentences for hours, he confessed he found it too difficult to understand. Significantly, he felt an inner resistance to Spinoza's pantheism—an anticipation of his later rejection of monism.

Two years later, in February 1860, while on a return trip to Germany, Mainländer made another momentous discovery, encountering another philosopher who would have an even greater influence upon him. That philosopher was, of course, Arthur Schopenhauer. He reckoned "the most important day of his life" the one when he ran across Schopenhauer's *Die Welt als Wille und Vorstellung* in a bookstore. This is how Mainländer himself tells the tale:

I went into a bookstore and leafed through the latest books from Leipzig. There I found Schopenhauer's *Welt als Wille und Vorstellung*. Schopenhauer? Who was Schopenhauer? I never heard the name. I paged through the work, and I read of the denial of the will to life;...the text had now entranced me. I forgot my surroundings and sank into myself. Finally I asked: 'What does it cost?' '6 dukats'. 'Here is the money'. I grabbed my treasure and stormed

[14] See Fritz Sommerlad, 'Aus dem Leben Philipp Mainländers. Mitteilungen aus der handschriftlichen Selbstbiographie des Philosophen', *Zeitschrift für Philosophie und philosophische Kritik*, 112 (1898), 74–101. Reprinted in Müller-Seyfarth, *"Die modernen Pessimisten als décadents"*, pp. 93–113. All references in parentheses here are to the later edition.

like a crazy man from the bookshop and went home, where I read the first volume from beginning to end. It was broad daylight when I finished; I had read it the whole night through. When I finally stood up, I felt myself newborn." (98)

After that fateful February day, Mainländer would continue to read Schopenhauer, studying all his writings until they became part of himself. "I read Schopenhauer's work as a pious soul reads the Bible: to strengthen oneself" (101). Yet, despite his veneration for the Frankfurt sage, Mainländer insists that, from the very beginning, he was still critical of him and that he disagreed with him on many points (98). After reading Spinoza, he found Schopenhauer's political views to be naïve. Furthermore, he already had doubts about Schopenhauer's "half-monism". These early doubts would eventually surface in his later philosophy. Mainländer was slow, however, in articulating them. It was only in 1865, after the trauma of his mother's death, that he began to commit them to paper. From his critique of Schopenhauer, he later wrote, he could see, though only through a glass darkly, the outlines of his chief work (102).

Given that Mainländer's philosophy grew out of his *critique* of Schopenhauer, we should beware of reducing him down to a mere disciple or apostle.[15] Mainländer accepts two of Schopenhauer's cardinal doctrines: that the will is the thing-in-itself; and that life consists in suffering, so that nothingness is better than being. But he departs from central doctrines of Schopenhauer's metaphysics and ethics: his transcendental idealism, i.e. the theory that the external world consists only in our representations; his monism, i.e. the postulate of a cosmic will that exists in all individual wills; and the thesis that the criterion of morality consists in selfless actions.

The beginning of the Franco-Prussian war in 1870 had a powerful effect on Mainländer. Not only did it arouse his patriotism: it also inspired his philosophy. "The feelings that the war aroused in my breast", he later wrote, "were the birth pangs of my philosophy of redemption" (102). But the path from conception to execution is often a long one, and so it was in Mainländer's case. Starting in June 1872, he wrote in three months the first draft of his system; and, after rereading Kant and Schopenhauer, he wrote in the next four months the second draft (104). It was only in the summer of 1874, before beginning his year of military service, that he finished the final draft, which had now grown enormously in size, many times its original length (107). After finishing the work he was filled with elation and foreboding. This is how he described his feelings:

I felt serene that I had forged a good sword, but at the same time I felt a cold dread in me for starting on a course more dangerous than any other philosopher before me. I attacked giants and dragons, everything existing, holy and honourable in state and science: God, the monster

---

[15] Otto Siebert classified Mainländer among Schopenhauer's "*Anhänger*". See his *Geschichte der neueren deutschen Philosophie seit Hegel* (Göttingen: Vandenhoeck & Ruprecht, 1898), pp. 239–40. Olga Plümacher placed Mainländer in the "*Schopenhauer'schen Schule*", though she stressed that she used the term "*Schule*" in the widest sense to designate only a general tendency of thought. See her '*Einleitung*' to *Zwei Individualisten der Schopenhauer'sche Schule* (Vienna: Rosner, 1881), pp. 1–6.

of 'the infinite', the species, the powers of nature, and the modern state; and in my stark naked atheism I validated only the individual and egoism. Nevertheless, above them both lay the splendour of the preworldly unity, of God... the holy spirit, the greatest and most significant of the three divine beings. Yes, it lay 'brooding with wings of the dove' over the only real things in the world, the individual and its egoism, until it was extinguished in eternal peace, in absolute nothingness. (108)

Having finally finished his masterpiece, and having said all that he wanted to say, Mainländer felt empty and exhausted. His mission was accomplished, his life at a close. What better time to end it all?

3. The Gospel of Redemption

The heart and soul of Mainländer's philosophy lies in its gospel of redemption. That gospel is very simple, and it can be summarized in two propositions: (1) that redemption or deliverance comes only with death; and (2) that death consists in nothingness, complete annihilation. All of Mainländer's philosophy is devoted to the explanation and defence of this gospel.

Fundamental to Mainländer's gospel is Schopenhauer's pessimism. With few reservations, Mainländer endorses Schopenhauer's bleak doctrine.[16] He accepts its central thesis: that nothingness is better than being, that existence is worse than non-existence. And he approves the justification for it: that life is suffering. If we calculate all the pleasures and pains of this life, we find that, on balance, the pains vastly outweigh the pleasures.[17]

This fundamental fact about human existence—the primacy of suffering, the preponderance of pain over pleasure—means that we stand in need of redemption, of some form of deliverance. Release from suffering, Mainländer insists, comes with death alone. Since death extinguishes all desire, it destroys all suffering, which has its source in the frustration of desire.

Although Mainländer insists that redemption comes only with the fact of death, he also thinks that contemplating this fact—facing the reality of death and accepting its forthcoming annihilation—gives us the appropriate attitude to withstand the sorrow and suffering of life.[18] If we firmly keep in mind that death is nothingness, if we fully realize that our existence ends in annihilation, we will come close to the tranquillity

---

[16] See 'Ethik', §12, *Die Philosophie der Erlösung, Schriften*, I. 183–4; and 'Anhang', I. 575. Mainländer does not accept Schopenhauer's thesis that pleasure has only a negative quality. See 'Aehrenlese', *Die Philosophie der Erlösung, Schriften*, II. 467. In his 'Kritik der Hartmann'sche Philosophie', *Die Philosophie der Erlösung*, II. 529–653, Mainländer, though otherwise severely critical of Hartmann, praises his pessimism and accepts its main conclusions (p. 629).

[17] See 'Aehrenlese', *Die Philosophie der Erlösung, Schriften*, II. 467.

[18] Mainländer describes this attitude in most detail in 'Das wahre Vertrauen', in *Die Philosophie der Erlösung*, II. 243–70.

and serenity preached by the Stoic sage and the Christian mystic (217).[19] We will realize that nothing in the world really matters anymore, so that we will accept all that happens to us with equanimity. The final lines of the main text of *Philosophie der Erlösung* express this teaching with utter clarity: "The wise man looks in the eye, firmly and joyfully, absolute nothingness" (358).

In a revealing passage from his autobiography,[20] Mainländer tells us about the personal origins of his gospel. After quitting a hated job at a Berlin banking firm, he was desperate and destitute. He had no idea of what the future would bring. For several days he wandered through the streets as if lost in a trance. "Then suddenly an electrifying flash drove through my heart, and I was filled with an insurmountable longing for death. And then there began a new life within me ... a period of my life, where I sacrificed myself to fate with love and out of conviction. What happened to me is what the Christians called the effect of grace." It was an experience straight out of the playbook of the *Theologica germanica*, a text which Mainländer revered and made his guide in life.[21] The central concept of that inspiring work—acceptance, resignation or *Gelassenheit*—would become the heart of Mainländer's ethics.

While Mainländer's gospel of redemption has great debts to Schopenhauer, we understand its motivation and purpose only if we recognize that it is a reaction against him.[22] Mainländer praises Schopenhauer for his doctrine of the denial of the will to life, which he thinks should be the basis for ethics (559). But Schopenhauer, he argues, compromises this important principle by clinging to a doctrine of immortality and an afterlife. He held that there is in everyone a cosmic will; and though the individual is destroyed by death, this cosmic will remains and is eternal.[23] It is as if we never escape the cosmic will and never find true annihilation. We are in its clutches even in death because our individuality dissolves into it. Schopenhauer regarded this eternal core in every individual as a source of metaphysical comfort, a proof of eternal existence against the fact of death. For Mainländer, however, this belief in immortality is only a self-deception, a betrayal of the doctrine of self-renunciation, which requires a complete denial of the will in all its forms. The only will that exists, Mainländer insists, is the *individual* will, so that when that will dies nothing remains. If we are to achieve complete tranquillity and composure in the face of death, then we have to realize that nothingness triumphs totally, leaving no trace of the will. Only when the will dies, utterly, entirely and completely, is there deliverance and liberation.

---

[19] All references in parentheses are to the main text of *Die Philosophie der Erlösung*, *Schriften*, I. 1–358, or to its appendix, *Schriften*, I. 359–623.
[20] *Aus meinem Leben*, *Schriften*, IV. 338.
[21] On its importance for Mainländer, see *Aus meinem Leben*, *Schriften*, IV. 374, 403.
[22] In a later essay, 'Der Idealismus', attached to the second volume of *Die Philosophie der Erlösung*, Mainländer makes clear the importance of this point for his own philosophy. He states that if it were not for Schopenhauer's postulate of a cosmic will in addition to the individual will he would have had little to correct in his philosophy. See II. 65–6. See also 'Aehrenlese', *Philosophie der Erlösung*, *Schriften*, II. 485.
[23] See Schopenhauer, 'Über den Tod', *Die Welt als Wille und Vorstellung*, *Werke*, II. 590–651.

Mainländer saw his philosophy of redemption as timely, as the solution to the most urgent problem of modern humanity. This problem came from a terrible tension in the modern soul: on the one hand, a deep need for religion; on the other hand, a loss of religious faith. Since suffering is the eternal fate of mankind, there is still the great need for deliverance from it; but the traditional sources of religious belief are no longer credible to the general educated public.[24] No one believed anymore in the existence of a heaven beyond the earth where a paternal God rewarded the virtuous and punished the wicked. Hence Mainländer saw the purpose of his philosophy as the formulation of a modern doctrine of redemption, a doctrine that should be completely consistent with the naturalistic worldview of modern science. His philosophy, he was proud to say, would be "the first attempt to ground the essential truths of salvation on the basis of nature alone" (223). The only doctrine of redemption consistent with a modern scientific view of the world, Mainländer maintained, is that which preaches utter nothingness, the complete annihilation of death.

There was, of course, nothing new to such a theory of death. The thesis that death is complete nothingness, the annihilation of the individual, was a central pillar of the Epicurean tradition. The wise Epicurus knew that there is nothing to fear in death, because death means the dissolution of the body, which is the source of all pleasure and pain. Since good and evil are measured in terms of pleasure and pain, death is neither good nor evil; it is just a simple fact that we have to accept at the end of our natural lives. We can accept it easily if we only firmly keep in mind the maxim: "When I am there, it [death] is not; when it is there, I am not." Mainländer accepts the essence of this theory of death; yet he gives it a completely different twist from the Epicurean. For Mainländer, death means deliverance, because life is essentially suffering and there is a need to escape from it. For Epicurus, however, death is not deliverance but simply the natural end of life. Since Epicurus held that we can achieve the highest good on this earth and in this life, he could see no reason for redemption. It is here, in preaching the need for redemption, that we see the deep Christian roots of Mainländer's philosophy.

Mainländer's gospel of redemption was not, however, entirely Christian. It was a paradoxical fusion of the classical pagan and Christian traditions. Mainländer accepted one central principle common to these traditions: that the highest good is happiness, which consists in tranquillity, equanimity, peace of mind. This ideal of the highest good appears in the Epicurean, Stoic and Christian traditions. Its greatest Christian exponent was Augustine, who had turned it against the Epicureans and Stoics by arguing that the highest good cannot be achieved in this life.[25] This life was too filled with suffering and sorrow, Augustine argued, for someone to achieve tranquillity within it. Since Mainländer shares Augustine's pessimism about this life, he endorses his argument against the pagans. He disagrees with Augustine, however, by

---

[24] On this crisis, see 'Das wahre Vertrauen', *Die Philosophie der Erlösung*, II. 249–50.
[25] See Augustine, *The City of God*, translated by R. W. Dyson (Cambridge: CUP, 1998), Book XIX, pp. 909–64.

denying the existence of a heavenly realm where all suffering will be redeemed. It is only when we realize that death brings complete annihilation, Mainländer holds, that we achieve the tranquillity of the highest good. So Mainländer joins Christian pessimism to the pagan view about the end of life.

Mainländer's attitude toward the traditional Christian conception of the highest good emerges from his statements about Christian mysticism. The happiest person on earth, Mainländer teaches, is the Christian mystic (197). Because he understands that life is suffering, the Christian mystic attempts to stand above it and to steel himself against its misfortunes. He gets to this point, though, because he believes that there is a heaven beyond this world where he will find his true happiness; but this belief, Mainländer insists, is only the first stepping stone toward true redemption (198–9). Only when the mystic grasps the true meaning of Christ's gospel—that serenity resides in pure nothingness alone—does he develop the equanimity and tranquillity of real happiness. The true mystic learns that salvation comes not with belief in a supernatural realm that satisfies our desires but in the complete renunciation and eventual extinction of desire; only then do the troubles and torments of life cease to matter to him.

It is in this context that we should understand Mainländer's paradoxical doctrine of the death wish. The inner striving of the will is for death because it is only in death that we find true happiness, which is the highest good for every human being. Such happiness resides in complete tranquillity and peace, which comes only with death, the utter nothingness of annihilation. If Mainländer describes life as a means toward death that is because death promises what life really wants: tranquillity and peace.

4. Mainländer and the Young Hegelian Tradition

Much of the motivation behind Mainländer's philosophy of redemption is revealed in the 'Vorwort' to the *Philosophie der Erlösung*. Mainländer writes there that the mission of his philosophy is self-emancipation, the liberation of humanity from its own self-imposed bondage. The history of the world is the story of this self-emancipation, Mainländer tells us. In its path towards self-liberation, humanity goes through the stages of polytheism, monotheism and atheism; in this process humanity learns to be more self-critical and self-conscious of its own powers; it sees how it has enslaved itself to entities of its own making; and so it grows in autonomy, its power to lead life according to its own self-conscious goals and ideals. Humanity is at present at the end of the stage of pantheism, the last stage of monotheism, which appears either in a dynamic (Hegel) or a static (Schopenhauer) form. Now, as humanity nears the final stage, the individual demands the restoration of his rights, the repossession of the powers that he once squandered on heaven.

Mainländer's statement about the mission of his philosophy, and his narrative about the self-emancipation of humanity, show his great debt to Feuerbach and the neo-Hegelian tradition. In his emphasis upon the rights of the individual, Mainländer resembles no one more than Max Stirner, the most radical of the neo-Hegelians, who would free the individual of every form of self-bondage, whether it came from morality, the state or religion. Like Stirner, Mainländer wants the modern individual to make his own will the centre of his universe, so that all value stems from it alone.

Despite these similarities, there is still the greatest difference between Mainländer and Stirner, and indeed all his neo-Hegelian contemporaries and predecessors. Namely, Mainländer wants self-liberation not so that we *reclaim* the earth but so that we *renounce* it. The neo-Hegelians believed that life can be redeemed if only human beings regain their powers and create the world in their own image; but Mainländer holds just the opposite: that life is irredeemable suffering and that redemption lies only in leaving it. For all their criticisms of state and church, the neo-Hegelians were fundamentally optimistic about life, believing that life is worth living if we only have the power to create it according to our own ideals; the source of suffering for them lay not in existence itself but in corrupt and exploitative moral and political institutions. Mainländer's pessimism divides him utterly from the neo-Hegelians. He finds their optimism naïve. For him the chief sources of suffering lie in existence itself; even in the best state, and even with the greatest progress of the sciences, the main forms of suffering will remain. There will always be the traumas and troubles of birth, sickness, age and death (206–7).

Besides their opposing views about the value of life, there is another important difference between Mainländer and the neo-Hegelian tradition. This concerns their opposing attitudes toward the Christian heritage. Both saw traditional theism as a source of self-imposed bondage, as the hypostasis of human values and powers. Hence both believed it necessary to break with traditional Christian dogma, especially its belief in the supernatural and the kingdom of heaven beyond this earth. For the neo-Hegelians, however, the reckoning with the Christian tradition concerns not only its dogmas but also its values (viz., faith, hope, chastity, humility, self-renunciation). These values will have no place in the brave new earthly kingdom created by man alone. But, for Mainländer, the break with Christian dogma should *not* also be a break with Christian values. We can reinterpret those values so that they are in accord with modern secular life. The old ethics of chastity, humility and self-renunciation still have their importance in a world where evil and suffering prevail, and where people remain caught in the snares of natural desire. If we realize that the only escape from suffering, the only cure for natural desire, lies in the denial of the will to life, we are on the way to a reinterpretation of Christian ethics.

Despite his proclamation of egoism and atheism, it is astonishing how much Mainländer continues to see his own life in religious terms. In his autobiography he finds the workings of providence in all the major events of his career, and he sees his mission in life as an apostle to spread the gospel of redemption.[26] His aspiration to be a common soldier in the cavalry was inspired by the Christian doctrine of self-humiliation.

---

[26] See 'Aus meinem Leben', *Schriften*, IV. 318, 363, 405.

The core of his ethical doctrine—"surrender to the universal", i.e. submission to the higher ethical order of the state—was his substitute for the Christian cross.[27]

Mainländer retains and reinterprets at least three core Christian values, which he strived to realize in his own life. First, the virtues of chastity and self-denial. Second, the mystical ideal of *Gelassenheit*, i.e. complete indifference to the world, resignation to all the slings and arrows of outrageous fortune. Third, the importance of faith and trust in providence, the belief that the universe is governed for the good and that each individual gains by it.

5. Philosophical Foundations

Although the heart of the philosophy of redemption lies in its ethics, and more specifically in its gospel of redemption, Mainländer knew that his ethics requires an epistemological and metaphysical foundation. Without such a foundation, its gospel could be misunderstood, misinterpreted or corrupted. Even worse, there would be no reason to accept his gospel over its rivals, the many competing accounts of redemption. Confident that redemption could be found through his philosophy alone, Mainländer set about providing it with an epistemological and metaphysical foundation. Accordingly, most of the first volume of *Die Philosophie der Erlösung* is devoted to a discussion of the epistemological and metaphysical issues behind his ethics.

A central pillar of Mainländer's philosophy of redemption is its principle of *immanence*, i.e. the demand that philosophy stay within the limits of human experience and that it not postulate causes that transcend or cannot be confirmed by it (3, 199). This means for Mainländer that the content of our concepts has to be taken from human sensation or intuition, which alone gives us knowledge of existence. An immanent philosophy is also for Mainländer a *naturalistic* philosophy, i.e. one that explains everything on the basis of efficient or mechanical laws, and that refuses to grant constitutive status to final or supernatural causes.[28] Since it is immanent and naturalistic, Mainländer believed that his philosophy of redemption is based upon strictly the modern scientific view of the world.

The principle of immanence has the profoundest moral implications for Mainländer. It lays down the basis for a purely humanist ethics, one that banishes any ethics based on alleged supernatural authority, whether that is a holy book or a mystical experience. It also means that redemption cannot be found in any belief in a supernatural world in the hereafter. Although Mainländer thinks that the meaning of life is found in death,

---

[27] Ibid., p. 368.
[28] On Mainländer's critical stance toward teleology, see *Philosophie der Erlösung*, I. 20, 480, 484. See also his important statement in *Philosophie der Erlösung*, II. 570–1. Here Mainländer states that the purposiveness of the world is not to be denied, and that he has appealed to teleology only once in his work, namely, regarding the original creation of the world, although even there he understands the purpose of the creation in a strictly regulative sense.

which is not within our experience, death is nothingness to him precisely because it is the end of human experience, which determines the limits of intelligibility for us.

Another central pillar of Mainländer's philosophy of redemption is its *nominalism*, i.e. its belief that only particular or determinate things exist. The pillars of immanence and nominalism support one another. Everything in our experience, everything that we sense, feel or intuit, is particular; references to abstract entities—species, ideas, universals or archetypes—are transcendent because we cannot have any experience of them. Although Mainländer gives no systematic defence or exposition of his nominalism, it is perfectly explicit all the same: "There are only individuals in the world" (482; cf. 144).[29] Following this principle, Mainländer often states that the world consists only in a *collection* of individuals; it is only the sum of its individual members; there is no unity above and beyond them (144, 199).

It is on the basis of his nominalism that Mainländer justifies one of his foundational doctrines: "There is only *one* principle in the world: the *individual* will for life; it has nothing else alongside it" (50). Whenever he refers to the will, Mainländer constantly italicizes the adjective "*individual*". The point of such emphasis is entirely polemical: he is prohibiting Schopenhauer's postulate of a single cosmic will within all individuals. This postulate, as we have seen, undermines the gospel of death, because *ex hypothesi* the cosmic will remains after the death of the individual will. In stressing that only the individual will exists, Mainländer is disputing the existence of this cosmic will and the hope for immortality based upon it. Having banished the cosmic will, Mainländer is then in a position to maintain that death will really bring redemption. With the destruction of the individual will, there will be only nothingness.

For Mainländer, the philosophy of redemption is also, crucially and necessarily, "idealism" (3). Idealism is indeed the basis for the immanence of the philosophy of redemption. Since idealism holds that we cannot jump beyond the powers of the knowing subject, it warns us not to transcend our experience and not to aspire to knowledge of another realm behind or beyond it (3). Idealism is for Mainländer closely connected with criticism, the examination of the powers and limits of our knowledge. As such, it advises us to know these powers and limits before we attempt to solve "the puzzle of the world".

Mainländer described his idealism as a "critical" or "transcendental" idealism, though he understood these terms in a specific sense, one that differs markedly from their meaning in Kant and Schopenhauer (40). A *critical* idealism is for Mainländer one that recognizes the subjective sources of our representations of space and time, and that refuses to ascribe *mathematical* space and time to things-in-themselves. A *transcendental* idealism is one that includes an *empirical realism*, though an empirical realism in a full-bodied sense, i.e. it assumes that experience gives us some knowledge of things that exist independent of our representations of them, namely, knowledge of

---

[29] Cf. *Die Philosophie der Erlösung*, II. 578. Here Mainländer criticizes Schopenhauer's belief in the real existence of species and declares: "*Es giebt nur Individuen in der Welt...*"

their extension and movement (41). Such idealism is "transcendental" in the sense that it gives us knowledge of the *objective* properties of a thing, i.e. properties that transcend our own consciousness of the thing, that exist in the thing itself, apart from and prior to awareness of it (12, 21).[30] Mainländer was critical of Kant's and Schopenhauer's version of empirical realism, because it did not ascribe sufficient independent existence to the objects of experience.[31] According to their empirical realism, experience consists in nothing more than representations, where these representations have objective validity only in the sense that they are governed according to universal and necessary rules; the representations, however, represent nothing beyond themselves, showing us nothing about things as they exist independent of us (454). Mainländer complains that Kant's and Schopenhauer's transcendental idealism comes too close to the idealism of Berkeley, which would ascribe reality only to representations (446–7). Kant's transcendental idealism, Mainländer objects, makes the thing-in-itself something completely unknowable, an indeterminable X, which he might as well have eliminated entirely (369).

As we have described it so far, there seems to be a contradiction in the heart of Mainländer's idealism. On the one hand, it intends to be completely immanent, refusing to make transcendent claims about any reality independent of our experience; on the other hand, however, it insists upon a full-blooded empirical realism that assumes we have knowledge of how things exist independent of our experience of them. The question then arises: how does the empirical realist know that the objects of experience give us knowledge of things-in-themselves, i.e. of things that exist independent of our consciousness of them? Mainländer himself explicitly raised this issue in the long appendix attached to the first volume of the *Philosophie der Erlösung*. The fundamental problem of epistemology, he explains, is this: how do we know that the object of experience is an appearance of the thing-in-itself? How do we know that it is more than a mere representation within consciousness? (437). Mainländer's response to this problem is that we are perfectly justified, on the basis of our experience, in assuming that the cause of a change in our perceptual states lies not in us but outside us, and in assuming that this something indeed exists independent of our consciousness of it (439). The cause cannot lie inside us, because the contents of our consciousness appear independent of our will and imagination; they change and vary when the activity of consciousness remains the same (439). So when we apply the principle of causality to the cause of our sensations, we are not really going beyond experience itself, because it is just *a fact of our experience* that its contents do not depend on us but on some factor independent of it.

---

[30] On these grounds Plümacher held that Mainländer's idealism is really a form of transcendental realism. See her *Zwei Individualisten*, p. 7. Yet Mainländer warned against conflating properties as we experience them with properties of things-in-themselves. See *Philosophie der Erlösung*, I. 3, 8.

[31] Mainländer did not recognize, therefore, the objective side of Schopenhauer's philosophy. See below chapter 3.5, and 5.5.

Mainländer maintains that Kant and Schopenhauer failed to recognize the objective or realistic dimension of experience because of their theory of space, according to which space is only an a priori intuition. This made them think that *all* spatial properties of an object are only the product of the mind, depending upon nothing more than the innate powers of our sensibility. Mainländer thinks that it was a great achievement of Kant's Transcendental Aesthetic to have demonstrated that *mathematical* space and time are not properties of things-in-themselves, and that they are constructions of the mind. Yet he insists that all Kant's arguments are valid only for *mathematical* space and time, i.e. space and time understood as homogeneous, uniform and continuous media. We construct such a space through the activity of synthesis, by extending a point in three directions (6). We construct such a time by drawing a line through all past and future moments of the present (15). However, particular spaces and times—the particular distances and intervals between things—are real and cannot be the creation of our consciousness alone. Particular spaces are marked by the limits of the efficacy of an object, i.e. its power to resist other bodies occupying its location (6–7, 446); and particular times are marked by movements, by how far something moves or changes place (15).

It is chiefly because the mind does not have the power to create *particular* spaces and times, still less the *particular* qualities of sensation, that Mainländer thinks we must introduce a realistic dimension to our experience. The a priori functions and forms of our mind consist in the activity of synthesis, which is essential to the constitution of our experience, just as Kant always argued. This activity is crucial for objects appearing as wholes and unities to us, and for us to understand the systematic interconnections between them. However, synthesis by itself is a merely formal activity, and it does not have the power to create everything in our experience, viz., the particular qualities of sensations, still less when, where and how they appear to us. The particular *manner* of synthesis—how, when and where we synthesize just these sensations and no others—depends on the cues given to us by things acting upon us, things that exist entirely independent of our consciousness (12, 21). Our activity of synthesis is therefore circumscribed by the individuality of things; only in following that individuality do we know what, when, where and how to synthesize (446).

In a retrospective essay on idealism in the second volume of *Die Philosophie der Erlösung*,[32] Mainländer summarized in an illuminating way both the strengths and weaknesses of Kant's and Schopenhauer's idealism. Kant and Schopenhauer were entirely correct to stress the a priori aspects of the cognitive faculty, and the contribution they make to knowledge of experience, he acknowledged. Without these a priori aspects, knowledge would be indeed impossible for us. But Kant and Schopenhauer went too far and were guilty of an elementary confusion. For it is one thing to say that the forms and functions of the mind are necessary for *knowledge* of the external world; and it is quite another to say that they are necessary for the *creation* of that world (69).

---

[32] 'Der Idealismus', *Philosophie der Erlösung*, II. 37–70.

Kant and Schopenhauer, Mainländer implies, have confused the *ratio cognoscendi* with the *ratio essendi*. Nowhere is this confusion more apparent than in Schopenhauer, who argues that because the principle of sufficient reason is a priori, having its origins in our mental activity, the cause of sensation lies within consciousness; in saying this, he confuses, Mainländer maintains, the *actual* efficacy of a thing acting on our sense organs with the conditions of our *perceiving* or *thinking* that this thing acts on them (440). But the principle of sufficient reason alone has no power to create our experience; it is only the condition under which we have knowledge of it. Once we separate *ratio cognoscendi* and *ratio essendi*, Mainländer holds, it is possible to incorporate a strong dose of empirical realism within idealism, for idealism then ceases to be a theory about the *existence* of things, and strictly one about the *knowledge* of things. Was that not for Kant himself, Mainländer could ask, the decisive difference between a critical and metaphysical idealism?

Why was Mainländer so bent on introducing a realistic dimension to his idealism? It is fundamental to pessimism, he insisted. If we hold that experience consists in nothing more than representations, as Kant and Schopenhauer say, then we cannot grant the reality of the suffering of others. Their apparent suffering will be nothing more than representations floating in our minds, and we will have no reason to grant them a reality equal to and independent of ourselves. Hence, Mainländer argued, Schopenhauer's idealism undermines his own pessimism.[33]

6. The Death of God

We have already seen how Mainländer, following his nominalism and his demand for a strictly immanent philosophy, made his basic principle the existence of the *individual* will. He stresses that this principle is the basis of his *entire* philosophy, of his epistemology, ethics, physics, metaphysics and politics (45). His immanent philosophy is distinguished from Schopenhauer's by its refusal to grant the reality of a cosmic universal will above and beyond the individual will. The individual will alone is the ultimate reality, which we cannot transcend, and which conditions all that we think or do.

But no sooner does Mainländer announce his first principle than he admits it suffers from a serious difficulty (102). His first principle means that each individual will is self-sufficient and independent; but natural science shows that all things in the world stand in systematic interconnection, so that every thing depends on every other thing according to necessary laws. How can there be such interconnection if everything is self-sufficient and independent? Or, conversely, how can there be such independence if everything is interconnected? Mainländer declares that this problem is "extraordinarily important", and indeed "the most important of all philosophy" (103). At stake for him is nothing less than the freedom of the individual. For the systematic interconnection of all things will be inevitably grounded in their unity, in a single universal

---

[33] See 'Aehrenlese', in *Die Philosophie der Erlösung*, II. 483.

substance; and such unity will leave no place for the freedom of the individual, who will become only "a puppet". When the individual acts, his action will be not his own but only the single universal substance acting through him.

Mainländer has another formulation for his difficulty: how can we conceive the unity of the one and the many? We cannot conceive the single universal substance existing in a plurality of individuals. For if it exists as much in Hansel as in Gretel, then it has been divided, and it ceases to be one. So it seems we cannot have both unity and plurality. Nevertheless, both are necessary: science postulates a single universe because of the interconnection of all things according to laws; and ordinary experience teaches us that things are independent of one another, that the destruction or removal of one does not change everything else.

What is the solution of this difficulty? Mainländer proposes a compromise between the conflicting sides of the antinomy. It is necessary to recognize the truth of each side, because there is *both* systematic interconnection and individual independence, *both* unity and plurality. The conflict between them can be resolved, however, by introducing the dimension of time, by making each side true for different stages of development of the universe (104–5). In the beginning, there was indeed a primal unity, a single universal substance, which was an undifferentiated, indivisible oneness. However, that unity no longer exists; its existence lies entirely in the past. The original unity of the world, the single universal substance, gradually split into a multiplicity of individual things; there is enough of its unity left for their interconnection, but not so much that they cannot be independent. The process of the world is therefore from unity to difference, from one to many, where that original oneness gradually and continually differentiates itself, splitting into many fragments, which are more independent units (94, 107). The individual is then *partly* free or independent, according to how much the original unity has dissolved, and *partly* interconnected and dependent, according to how much unity still remains. Freedom and necessity are partial truths, because the individual acts upon the world and changes it, just as the world acts upon the individual and changes it.

It is in this context that Mainländer introduces his dramatic concept of the death of God (108). This primal unity, this single universal substance, has all the attributes of God: it is transcendent, infinite and omnipotent. But since it no longer exists, this God is dead. Yet its death was not in vain. From it came the existence of the world. And so Mainländer declares in prophetic vein: "God is dead and his death was the life of the world" (108). This is Mainländer's atheistic interpretation of the Christian trinity, to which he devotes much attention in the second volume of *Die Philosophie der Erlösung*.[34] "The father gives birth to the son"—Article 20 of the Nicene Creed—means that God (the father) sacrifices himself in creating the world (the son). God exists entirely in and through Christ, so that the death of Christ on the cross is really the

---

[34] See his later essay 'Das Dogma der Dreieinigkeit', in *Die Philosophie der Erlösung*, II. 189–232, esp. 195–8.

death of God himself. With that divine death, Mainländer proclaims, the mystery of the universe, the riddle of the Sphinx, is finally resolved, because the transcendent God, the source of all mystery, also disappears.

The main subject matter of Mainländer's metaphysics, which makes up the culminating section of the *Philosophie der Erlösung*, is the death of God. Although Mainländer stresses, following his immanent guidelines, that this original unity is unknowable, he also maintains that we know three things about it: (1) that it has fragmented itself in making the world; (2) that because of this primal unity, the individual things in the world still stand in interconnection; and (3) this primal unity once existed but it does so no more (320). To these three points, Mainländer adds a fourth, as if it were an afterthought: that the transition of the primal unity into multiplicity, of the transcendent into the immanent, is the death of God and the birth of the world (320). Having said this much, Mainländer then insists that we cannot know anything more about this God. We can determine his essence and existence only negatively (320), and it is meaningless to ask why he created the world (325).[35] Since the transcendent is *toto genere* distinct from the immanent, we should not venture speculations about the transcendent by analogy with our world (322). So *why* the primal unity fractured itself, *why* the one became many, remains a mystery for us.

Nevertheless, despite such words of caution, Mainländer cannot resist the temptation to speak about the unspeakable. He excuses himself on the grounds that we can say a little something about God's creation after all—provided, of course, that we give it a strictly *regulative* validity. We have to think and write *as if* God were like human beings. If we allow this assumption strictly as a working hypothesis, then we can understand the creation on analogy with our own human actions, namely, as the product of will and intelligence (321–2). Adopting this assumption as his starting point, Mainländer then proceeds to construct a remarkable mythology of the creation.

Before the creation, Mainländer tells us, God had the freedom of the *liberum arbitrium indifferentiae* (323). His absolute power and will meant that there were no causes determining him into action, and that he could have done otherwise with no contradiction to his nature. God had the power to do whatever he willed; but there was one point over which he had no power at all: his sheer existence. Although absolutely free in *how* he existed, he was limited in the mere fact *that* he existed (324). God, for all his omnipotence, could not immediately negate his own existence. After all, if he did not exist, he could not exert his power whatsoever. But once God saw that he existed, he was not amused. Sheer existence horrified him, because he recognized that nothingness is better than being. So God longed for nothingness. Since, however, he could not immediately negate his existence, he decided on a suicide by proxy. God would destroy himself through other things, by creating the world and fragmenting his existence into a multitude of individual things (325). To achieve his goal of complete non-existence,

---

[35] On these grounds it is unfair to criticize Mainländer, as Lütkehaus does (*Nichts*, pp. 258, 260), for not explaining the reason for the existence of the world.

the total serenity of nothingness, God had to create the world as the necessary means toward his self-destruction.

On the basis of this myth, Mainländer then proceeds to sketch, in the final chapter of *Die Philosophie der Erlösung,* his "metaphysics", which is his general theory of nature and history. Metaphysics, he tells us, gives us a view of the world as a whole, so that all the partial perspectives of the earlier chapters of his book now appear as a single vision. That vision is, to put it mildly, macabre. We now enter the darkest recesses of Mainländer's imagination, which fabricate for us a grim cosmology of death. What the metaphysician sees from his exalted standpoint of the whole of things, Mainländer attests, is that everything in nature and history strives for one thing: death (330, 335). There is in all things in nature, and in all actions in history, "the deepest longing for absolute annihilation" (335). In his earlier chapters of his book, in the discussion of physics, ethics and politics, Mainländer wrote about the individual will to life as the very essence of everything, not only of every human being, but also of every thing that exists, whether inorganic or organic. Now in metaphysics, however, we see that this was only a limited perspective, because the striving for existence or life is really only a means for a deeper goal: death (331, 333, 334). We live only so that we die, because the deepest longing within all of us is for peace and tranquillity, which is granted to us only in death. In this longing of all things for death, we are only participating, unbeknownst to ourselves, in the deeper and broader cosmic process of the divine death (355). We long to die, and we are indeed dying, because God wanted to die and he is still dying within us.

Mainländer sees this process of cosmic death taking place all throughout nature, in both the organic and inorganic realms, and he goes into great detail about how it takes place everywhere in the universe. The gases, liquids and solids of the inorganic realm all reveal an urge toward death. A gas has the drive to dissipate itself in all directions, i.e. to annihilate itself (327). Liquids have the striving for an ideal point outside themselves, where, should they ever reach it, they destroy themselves (327–8). Solids, or fixed bodies, have a longing toward the centre of the earth, where they too, if they ever reach it, will eliminate themselves (328). The plants and animals of the organic realm also show a drive toward nothingness; they have a will to life, to be sure, but it coexists with a will to death, which gradually and inevitably triumphs over the will to life (331–3). Although Mainländer has in general little sympathy for the teleological conception of nature, it is remarkable that he still attributes a strange kind of purposiveness to everything in nature: namely, the striving toward self-destruction and death.

The drama of cosmic death and decay in nature Mainländer also finds in history. Kant, Fichte, Schelling and Hegel misunderstood history, he argues, when they saw it as a progression toward the creation of a moral world order. If we examine the development of human civilization from ancient Asia, Greece and Rome, we have to admit that it is a long history of steady decline and decay (260). All these civilizations participated in the general process of dissolution involved in the dying of God, and so they gradually but inevitably became worse (261). Mainländer's vision of history appropriates the old Christian conception of history, whereby mankind progresses inevitably toward its final day of judgement. But in Mainländer's version we are all saved in the end, goats and sheep alike, simply because we all die. All of humanity is saved in this generous eschatology, not despite death but because of it.

It is hard to know what to make of Mainländer's cosmology of death. If we take his regulative guidelines seriously, then we cannot deem it a conjecture or hypothesis; rather, we have to regard it as a fiction, treating it only *as if* it were true.[36] We do best, then, to take it simply as mythology, as a story meant to replace the religious myths of the past. The justification of such a myth is purely pragmatic: it gives us the power to face death because we imagine ourselves moving inevitably towards it.

7. Ethics

Ethics is for Mainländer essentially "eudemonics" or the doctrine of happiness (169). The task of ethics is to determine happiness in all its forms, and in its most perfect form, i.e. the highest good, which he describes as "complete peace of heart". It also finds the means by which a human being achieves happiness. This definition of ethics is simply axiomatic for Mainländer. He does not consider alternatives to it, still less the challenge to all forms of eudemonism posed by Kant.

Central to Mainländer's ethics is the basic principle of his metaphysics: the individual will (169). According to this principle, there is no will above or beyond the individual will, no cosmic or universal will that exists within everyone alike. This principle is the foundation of moral freedom for Mainländer: it means that the individual will alone is the source of its actions, because when it decides or acts there is no cosmic will deciding or acting through it. Hence the individual will is the basis and source of human responsibility and autonomy.

It is a crucial fact about Mainländer's individual will that it is egoistic, i.e. it strives only for its *own* happiness (57, 169, 180). All human actions are motivated by self-interest, and even those done from charity or sympathy derive from some interest on the part of the agent (180). Mainländer insists on distinguishing the drive for self-preservation from self-interest.[37] A person who sacrifices his life for the community in time of war is still acting from self-interest (e.g. the love of glory). Self-interest therefore has to be understood as the striving for one's own happiness, even if that means ending one's life.

Mainländer's egoism is significant not least because it leads him to question the basic principle of Schopenhauer's ethics, which finds the source of morality in selfless actions. If moral actions have to be selfless, Mainländer argues, then there are no moral actions, because all actions, even the most holy or saintly, derive from self-interest

---

[36] Mainländer stresses the regulative status of his theory of history in 'Aehrenlese', *Die Philosophie der Erlösung*, II. 506.
[37] See 'Eine naturwissenschaftliche Satire', *Die Philosophie der Erlösung*, II. 527.

(193, 570). There are in fact moral actions, Mainländer insists, but Schopenhauer did not understand them. For an action to be moral, it is *not* necessary that it be selfless, as Schopenhauer thought; it is only necessary that (1) it be legal, i.e. according to the law, and that (2) it be done gladly or with pleasure (189). For an agent to perform an action gladly, it is not necessary that he deny his nature for the sake of duty but only that he realize that the action is in his long-term or enlightened self-interest (193).

Because of his egoism, Mainländer also doubts Schopenhauer's doctrine of pity or sympathy as the basis of morals (202, 569). Schopenhauer believed that pity or sympathy is selfless because the individual gets outside himself and places himself in the position of another. But Mainländer contends that we never leave ourselves in sympathizing with others; it is *myself* that I put in the place of the other. When we sympathize with another, we feel miserable within ourselves; and in helping the other person we are simply attempting to remove this inner misery. Of course, there is such a thing as love; but the very essence of love consists in the *expansion* of the self so that it includes the other (61). Hence love is little more than extended egoism.

Though a potent weapon against Schopenhauer's ethics, Mainländer's egoism also gets him into trouble. For he stresses, no less than Schopenhauer, that the denial of the will is the fundamental virtue (559). If life is not worth living because the selfish pursuit of desire leads to suffering, then the only path to happiness resides in the denial of desire, in self-renunciation. But Mainländer then faces the same problem as Schopenhauer: How is it possible to deny the will if the will is the force behind all human actions? Schopenhauer could get around this difficulty because, unlike Mainländer, he did not maintain egoism; he held that an individual, through rare acts of mystical insight, could get outside himself and sympathize with others. But, by insisting that even these rare acts of insight are ultimately self-interested, Mainländer seems to close off even this escape route. The problem is even more pressing for Mainländer because egoism also seems to undermine his gospel of redemption. If we are to find redemption, he argued, then we must cease to will life and we must instead learn to will death. But if the very core of our being is the will to life, as Mainländer insists (45), then how is it possible for us to will death?

Mainländer's way around this difficulty is to stress the central role of knowledge in human decision-making and action. No less than Schopenhauer, Mainländer is a determinist about human action, and he too denies the existence of the *liberum arbitrium indifferentiae* (176). Each action and decision is the product of an individual's character and motive, where his character is innate and the product of birth. Given a person's character, and given their motive, the action follows of necessity (176). Nevertheless, Mainländer maintains that human beings still have within themselves the power to act contrary to their original character, and to change their character, in the light of knowledge they acquire (563, 565). This power consists in nothing less than reason (178). Reason shows us all the different options and their consequences, so that we can make wise decisions about what is best for us. On this basis we can resist temptation or restrain our inclinations toward certain actions, and so learn to act differently from what we originally would have done. This power to act according to our better knowledge means, Mainländer maintains, that we have the power to renounce or deny our will, for we see that acting on our original inclinations, pursuing our natural desires, is self-destructive, having worse consequences for us than self-restraint and abstinence.

Mainländer still insists, however, that the role of reason in shaping human decisions and actions does not mean violating egoism. This is because reason teaches us what is in our *long-term* or *enlightened* self-interest rather than our *short-term* or *benighted* self-interest (193). The power of acting according to our better knowledge is really the power to act according to our informed self-interest. For when we see that the struggle to satisfy our desires leads to suffering, we learn that it is more in our enlightened self-interest to deny our desires (215–17). Our enlightened self-interest then consists in acting contrary to the desires of our original nature or character, the pursuit of which is a form of benighted self-interest. So the ascetic or saint, for all the appearances of selflessness, is still egoistic, acting according to his enlightened self-interest.

In his ethics of self-denial and renunciation of the will to life, Mainländer laid great importance on the virtue of chastity. Perfect chastity was for him the inner core of Christianity, and the crucial step toward redemption (578). To some extent, Mainländer's emphasis on chastity is perfectly understandable. The will to live is most apparent in the sex drive; and in acting on that drive, we perpetuate suffering by creating another human being. Only through chastity, then, do we break the cycle of desire and end the suffering of mankind. But Mainländer's emphasis on chastity is sometimes extreme; he went beyond the demand for chastity and called for nothing less than virginity, which was for him the only certain sign of self-denial (219). There is, of course, a great difference between chastity and virginity: a chaste person has learned to control his or her sex drives, though he or she has *perhaps* indulged in them; a virgin, however, has *never* acted on his or her sex drives. Mainländer insists on nothing less than virginity because—in a world of uncertain birth control—this alone ensures that life does not perpetuate itself. The demand for virginity caught the notice of Nietzsche, who dismissed Mainländer as the "sentimental apostle of virginity".[38]

We can begin to understand Mainländer's ethic of virginity—at least from a psychoanalytic perspective—if we trace its personal roots. Mainländer's mother died on 5 October 1863, on his 24th birthday. Her loss was deeply painful, and he never overcame it. In his essay on free love in the second volume of *Die Philosophie der Erlösung* he reveals that he had the best conceivable relationship with his mother; but he would now, because her loss has been so painful, gladly lose his memory of her.[39] But forget her he could not. In his autobiography Mainländer informs us that on 26 September 1874, he visited her grave and swore to her "virginity until death".[40] Virginity was thus

---

[38] See Nietzsche, *Die fröhliche Wissenschaft*, §357, in *Sämtliche Werke*, III. 601–2.
[39] 'Die freie Liebe', *Die Philosophie der Erlösung*, II. 322.
[40] 'Aus meinem Leben', IV. 372. Mainländer's italics.

Mainländer's vow of love and loyalty to his mother. In Freudian terms, it was an extreme case of an unresolved Oedipal complex.

The most vexing question of Mainländer's ethics is that of suicide. Suicide, it seems, is the straightforward conclusion of Mainländer's pessimism no less than Schopenhauer's. If life is worse than death, then why go on living? Why not get life over with sooner rather than later if all that it promises is more suffering? Mainländer was much troubled by this question, which he addressed on several occasions.[41]

Mainländer strived to remove prejudices against suicide, and he insisted that there should be no moral law against it. Nothing filled him with more indignation, he confessed, than those clergy who condemn suicide and who even preach withholding pity for those who take such a drastic step (II. 218). To counteract this prejudice, he argued that the two great world religions, Christianity and Buddhism, had nothing against suicide, and that they even approved it. Christ said nothing about suicide; and so there is no reason to think that he would have denied a suicide a resting place in heaven. Indeed, his whole ethics, in the high value it gives to chastity and self-denial, is little more than a prescription for "a long suicide". Buddha not only allowed but recommended suicide, forbidding it only for his priests, who had the solemn duty of teaching redemption (II. 109, 218). He regretted only that the prescription against suicide for his priests would be a burden upon them.

As we might expect, Mainländer rejects Schopenhauer's argument against suicide. Schopenhauer held that suicide is in vain because it cannot destroy the cosmic will behind our actions. Since Mainländer disputes the very existence of such a will, Schopenhauer's argument holds no weight for him. When we destroy our individual will, Mainländer contends, we destroy the will itself, the thing-in-itself behind appearances. The suicide does not intend to destroy the will as such, a cosmic will, Mainländer further implies, but simply his own individual will, in which effort he can be entirely successful.

There are passages in *Die Philosophie der Erlösung* where Mainländer is perfectly explicit in his advocacy of suicide. Whoever cannot bear the burden of life, he says unequivocally, should "throw it off" (349). Whoever cannot endure "the carnival hall of the world", he adds more poetically, should leave through "the always open door" into "that silent night". If we are in an unbearably stuffy room, and a mild hand opens the door for us to escape, we should take the opportunity (545–6). More directly and explicitly, he advises: "Go without trembling, my brothers, out of this life if it lies heavily upon you; you will find neither heaven nor hell in your grave." (II. 218).

There are other passages, however, where Mainländer seems to hesitate before prescribing suicide for everyone. In one place he states that, though the philosophy of redemption does not condemn suicide, it also does not demand it (350). It will even attempt to encourage a would-be suicide to stay in this miserable world. Why? Because, Mainländer answers, each individual should work with others to help all to achieve

---

[41] See the passages in *Die Philosophie der Erlösung*, I. 349, 545–6, 579, 600; and II. 109, 218.

redemption (349–50). There is, however, something almost evasive, even duplicitous, in Mainländer's explanation. For the work of redemption the disciple should help to promote is really the value of death and non-existence. It would seem, then, that it is best for him to encourage rather than discourage suicide.

Although Mainländer sometimes hesitates before the abyss, on one occasion he even declares his readiness to leap into it. He wants to destroy, he writes, all the convoluted motives that people give to stop themselves from "seeking the still night of death", and he confesses that he would happily "shake off existence" if it would serve as an example for others (II. 218). Given his own suicide, we can hardly charge him with weakness of will or hypocrisy.

8. Theory of the State

Schopenhauer, Mainländer opined, "lacked all understanding for political questions" (596). This was unfair, because Schopenhauer understood well enough the political and social currents of his age; it was just that he disapproved of them. There is, however, a solid core of truth in Mainländer's remark: Schopenhauer had little interest in politics. Because of that lack of interest, his political thought is undeveloped. Not that Schopenhauer completely neglected politics. There is the significant chapter on the state in *Die Welt als Wille und Vorstellung*, which, as we shall soon see, heavily influenced Mainländer.[42]

As we might expect, Mainländer's politics reflects his very different attitude toward the issues of his day. He stood on the opposite end of the political spectrum from Schopenhauer. Schopenhauer was on the extreme right, whereas Mainländer was on the extreme left. While Schopenhauer despised the nationalist and democratic movements of 1848, Mainländer fully supported them. He was not only an ardent nationalist, but also a staunch advocate of democracy. Unlike Schopenhauer, he was deeply troubled by "the social question", and he was fully sympathetic to the workers' movement founded by Ferdinand Lasalle.[43] Although Mainländer did not advocate violent revolution, he was a defender of social democracy and what he called "communism", i.e. equal distribution of property, free love and the abolition of the family.

The fundamental problem with Schopenhauer's political attitude, in Mainländer's view, is that he lacked the very virtue he praised the most: pity, sympathy for the suffering of others. If Schopenhauer had that virtue, Mainländer maintains, he would never have been so indifferent about the social question. Schopenhauer provides little consolation, little hope of redemption, for the common man (600). He is like Mephistopheles, Mainländer declares, because he tells the people that their reason will never help them to solve the problem of existence. According to Schopenhauer's system, only the rare

[42] See §62 of Buch IV, *Werke*, I. 457–78.
[43] See Mainländer's brilliant portrait of Lasalle, 'Das Charakterbild Ferdinand Lassalle's', in *Die Philosophie der Erlösung*, II. 343–71.

genius, someone who has the power of intuition to pierce the veil of Maya, can save himself. As for the common man, Schopenhauer condemns him "to languish eternally in the hell of existence". It was one of the more important advantages of his philosophy over Schopenhauer's, Mainländer believed, that it offered hope and redemption for everyone alike.

Given his harsh verdict on Schopenhauer's neglect of politics, we have every reason to expect Mainländer to devote more attention to it. Sure enough, he wrote two sections on politics for the first volume of *Die Philosophie der Erlösung*;[44] and the second part of the second volume, nearly 200 pages, is devoted to a discussion of socialism.[45]

For all his criticism of Schopenhauer, Mainländer's theory of the state, as he first expounds it in *Die Philosophie der Erlösung*,[46] still bears a remarkable resemblance to Schopenhauer's own theory. Like Schopenhauer, Mainländer builds the state on a social contract, on the mutual commitment among individuals not to harm or steal from one another. The major premise behind this theory also comes straight from Schopenhauer: that human beings are egoistic, seeking of necessity their self-interest. A state formed by a contract proves to be the most effective means to satisfy the demands of self-interested agents. The true state, Mainländer declares, gives its citizens more than it takes, i.e. it ensures them some advantage that they would not have otherwise had without it (180–1). People enter into the contract out of self-interest, he explains, because it is the best way to protect their lives and property (181–2). The fact that the strong and smart can be defeated even by the weak and dumb means that the mutual limitation of power is in the interests of everyone, even the stronger and smarter (180). Hence self-interested agents enter into a contract, i.e. they mutually agree not to harm and to respect the property of one another. According to this contract, everyone has certain rights and duties: the rights to have life and property protected; and the duties to respect the similar rights of others (182). The result of this contract is the establishment of a common power or authority which protects the rights of everyone through force.

Following his egoistic theory of human nature, Mainländer stresses how every human being is a reluctant and resentful citizen in the state. Each individual harbours a discontent and mistrust of its powers. Although every man enjoys his rights under the social contract, he complains about his duties, which he performs only begrudgingly (184). Towards the state he feels like man in nature feels toward his enemy (165). He hates having to pay taxes, and he attempts to avoid conscription in times of war. Mainländer leaves us with the impression that if his citizens only had Gyges ring, they would murder and steal to their heart's content.

---

[44] In the main text of *Philosophie der Erlösung*, see the section entitled 'Politik', I. 225–316; and in the Anhang the section with the same title, I. 583–600. The two sections entitled 'Ethik', I. 167–224 and I. 527–81, are of no less importance for Mainländer's political views.

[45] See section II, 'Der Socialismus', II. 275–460, which includes three of the essays of volume II.

[46] See especially §11 of 'Ethik', I. 180–5, and §25, I. 210–14.

Also in tune with that theory, Mainländer paints a virtual Rousseauian picture of the state of nature, where each individual leads a solitary life in complete independence from others. Man is by nature a-social, he maintains, and it was only extreme need or boredom that drove him to seek out the company of others (230). Men formed families for the sake of procreation and for protection of the young; families then joined together into wider groups for the purposes of self-defence and hunting (231–2). The heads of these families then entered a social contract not to harm one another, because only by that means could they live together in peace (232).

Given these egoistic and individualistic premises, it is not surprising that Mainländer's social contract ends in "a watchguard state", i.e. one whose chief function is to ensure that people do not violate their rights to one another. The task of the state, he writes, is to ensure that we do not steal or murder; but it cannot do anything more (185). Above all, we cannot expect the state to make people happy. Even if it effectively protects the rights of everyone, it is still possible for them to be miserable. There are four fundamental evils of human life that are constant and that cannot be eradicated by political means: birth, sickness, age and death (206). Mainländer's pessimism was immune to political change or reform, because no state, even a socialist one that cares for all human needs, could make life worth living.

9. Communism, Patriotism and Free Love

So far, so good. Mainländer has expounded a theory of the state that is perfectly in accord with his egoistic and individualist anthropology. It is a theory that seems to differ little from Schopenhauer's. We are left wondering, then, why Mainländer is so critical of Schopenhauer and where his differences with him really lie. But Mainländer's political theory is much more complicated; the side we have explained so far accounts for only one half of it. There is not only the *liberal* Mainländer who expounds a watchguard state; there is also the *communist* Mainländer who champions state ownership of the means of production and the equal distribution of wealth. There is not only the *individualist* Mainländer who stresses the citizen's mistrust of the state; there is also the *patriotic* Mainländer who advocates complete devotion to the state, the readiness to serve the state in all its goals even to the point of death. And there is not only the *ascetic* Mainländer, who preaches the value of chastity and even virginity; there is also the *indulgent* Mainländer, who teaches the value of free love and the abolition of marriage.

Mainländer's more radical political views emerge most forcefully in the essay on communism he wrote for the second volume of *Die Philosophie der Erlösung*.[47] The purpose of this essay was to remove the fears of communism among the bourgeoisie and aristocracy, though Mainländer's views are so extreme that they were more likely to have alarmed than calmed them. He attempts to reassure his readers: communism is

[47] 'Der Communismus', *Die Philosophie der Erlösung*, II. 280–305.

not the devil, having neither hooves nor horns. It does not mean the abolition of private property, so that the state will own everything; but it does mean public distribution of wealth, and profit sharing between workers and capitalists. Even after the establishment of communism, people will still own their own things, and no one, not even the government, will have a right to appropriate them; it is just that everyone will own an equal amount of things, so that no one suffers from need. Communism also does not mean the abolition of marriage, as if people could no longer form lifelong partnerships; but it does mean allowing divorce and the right to polygamy. All this sounds reassuring enough, perhaps, but there were other aspects of Mainländer's political ideal that would have only horrified his bourgeois or aristocratic readers. He tries to reassure the wealthy that they will continue to enjoy their lifestyle in a communist state; but he insists that is so only because everyone will enjoy such a lifestyle; he optimistically assumes that there is enough wealth for everyone to lead such a life. Even more alarmingly, Mainländer advocates giving children over to the state. Free love is possible, it seems, only when the burden of caring for children is taken over by the state. All the care and concern that parents have for their children, and all the joys of free love, make surrender of children to the state the most advantageous policy.

The only side of Mainländer's communism that would have diminished the fears of the public was his insistence on the value of gradual and peaceful political change. The mechanisms for such change, Mainländer believed, were popular agitation and representation of workers in parliaments. Mainländer was a great admirer of Lasalle's approach to the social question, which stressed the importance of peaceful protest and political representation rather than revolution. With Marx's and Engel's belief in the value and inevitability of revolution Mainländer had no sympathy whatsoever.

These clashing sides of Mainländer's political theory—his watchguard state and communism—are *not* the product of his intellectual development, as if one side evolved after the other to correct and complement it. Both appear explicitly in the first volume of the *Philosophie der Erlösung*. It is as if Mainländer were so troubled by the moral consequences of the watchguard state that he retreated from it and voiced his reservations about it. Such a state, he notes, demands nothing more than respecting the lives and property of others; it requires only that we obey the law in our actions, but not that we act for the sake of the law in our motives or intentions (185). It is perfectly compatible with this state, therefore, that we do not help others in need, and that we even allow them to starve. Mainländer's misgivings are most clear and vocal when it comes to discussing Schopenhauer's theory of the state. He finds it incredible that Schopenhauer had confined the state to a watchguard role—the very state Mainländer himself endorsed in an earlier passage (592). The state should give more than security of life and property, he says. It provides education; it protects religion; and it helps its citizens develop their moral qualities. Although Schopenhauer himself has enjoyed all the benefits of life in the state, he still refuses to acknowledge them.

Repelled by the moral vacuum of the watchguard state, Mainländer puts forward an antithetical conception in *Die Philosophie der Erlösung*. He envisages an ideal state that will provide for the basic needs of humanity (210). It is not in accord with the fate of humanity, Mainländer says, for each person to be left on his own, or for one person not to help others (212). Each individual should devote himself to an ideal state where human need disappears, and so that misery can be diminished even if it cannot be fully eradicated (212, 214). It is only in the second volume of *Die Philosophie der Erlösung*, however, that Mainländer fully specifies how human need will disappear in the communist state (viz., through distribution of wealth).

How do we reconcile these clashing sides of Mainländer's politics? It is not clear that we can. They stem from two deep strands of Mainländer's thinking whose ultimate consequences push him in opposing directions. These strands are his pessimism and his ethics of compassion. The pessimistic strand, because of its egoistic theory of human action, moves him toward the watchguard state and the political realism that the state cannot make people happy. His ethic of compassion, however, pushes him toward communism and political idealism, the demand that we do all we can to relieve the sources of human suffering. While the pessimistic strand leads to resignation and quietism, the ethical strand leads to indignation and activism, the attempt to relieve suffering through political action.

There is also the even more troubling question whether Mainländer's radical politics is compatible with his pessimism. If we were complete pessimists, utterly convinced that death is preferable to life, then we should have no motivation at all to strive for the ideal state. For we have it in our power to commit suicide right here and now and we need not trouble ourselves further. Of course, we should have pity for the suffering of our fellow human beings; but we need not act on that feeling, because they too have the option of suicide, which they can enact whenever they want. There is also the question whether the communist state, when it is finally and fully realized, will eradicate pessimism. Mainländer attempts to smooth over the inconsistency by stating that the communist state will not make people happy; it will only remove their suffering.[48] But he also is clear that the communist state will not only satisfy people's basic needs; it will also help them realize their desires for the good life; it will indeed allow workers to work less and enjoy the same lifestyle that the bourgeoisie and aristocracy now have.[49] But if this is so, will people not be happy under communism? If offered the choice between being or non-being, would they not choose being in the communist state? The precondition of opting for non-being is suffering, which the communist state will eradicate.

Toward the close of his discussion of communism in the second volume of *Die Philosophie der Erlösung*,[50] Mainländer attempts to address these difficulties. He writes that communism and free love are not his highest ideals, and that he has something better than them: namely, poverty and virginity (333). His highest ideals, he assures us,

---

[48] Ibid., II. 305.
[49] Ibid., II. 290, 291, 302–3. See also 'Höhere Ansichten', where Mainländer says that ideal state will satisfy the "*Genusssucht Aller*".
[50] 'Höhere Ansichten', II. 333–8.

are those of Christ and Buddha, who preach resignation. Better than life in the ideal state is complete tranquillity and deliverance, which comes only with death. Why, though, bother with creating the ideal state if we can have death now? Mainländer answers: though he personally can find redemption in all political conditions, so that he does not need to bother with the ideal state, the same is not true for the masses, who need to live in the ideal state before they find redemption. Why, though, must they first live in such a state? To that question Mainländer responds somewhat cryptically: before we turn against life, we must learn to enjoy all that it has to offer (337). Only he who attempts to enjoy all the rotten fruits of this earth will see through its emptiness and discover for himself the true value of death.[51]

Perhaps, in the end, it is impossible to square Mainländer's pessimism with his communism, in which case his political philosophy lies shipwrecked on the shoals of inconsistency. Still, there is something admirable about that philosophy. Mainländer's communism was at least an attempt to address the social question, and it did so in a realistic manner by advocating peaceful agitation and parliamentary representation rather than violent revolution. Even if some aspects of his ideals—complete equality of wealth and free love—are naïve, his ideals still stem from a very deep humanity, from a real sympathy for the plight of the working man in modern society. His political philosophy avoids the deepest pitfalls of his contemporaries: the elitism of Schopenhauer, Nietzsche, Hartmann and Taubert on the right, and the anti-Semitism of Dühring on the left.[52] Despite his obsession with death, the core of Mainländer's thought, and of his very being, was his hope to redeem humanity, *all* of humanity. For that noble cause, his suicide was an act of martyrdom.

---

[51] See 'Das wahre Vertrauen', *Die Philosophie der Erlösung*, II. 252, 255.
[52] Mainländer was critical of Schopenhauer's anti-Semitism. See *Philosophie der Erlösung*, I. 597–8.

10

The Pessimistic Worldview of Julius Bahnsen

1. An Original and Powerful Worldview

One of the most ardent, original and profound pessimists of the age of *Weltschmerz* was Julius Bahnsen (1830–81). Though the discovery and publication of his autobiography in 1905 saved him from oblivion,[1] and though there was a brief revival of interest in his psychology in the 1930s,[2] Bahnsen has been largely forgotten.[3] If he is remembered at all, it is usually because of Nietzsche, who once regarded him as a fellow pessimist.[4] Yet to make Nietzsche the sole reason for interest in Bahnsen betrays a skewed historical perspective. Bahnsen deserves to be treated as an end in himself, as an object of investigation in his own right, just as much as Nietzsche.

The main reason for unearthing Bahnsen lies in his original and powerful worldview. His perspective on the world derives from a single vision: that the essence of reality lies in the inner conflict of the will. Since Bahnsen held this conflict to be incessant, interminable, irresolvable and the source of all suffering, his worldview is utterly tragic. For the warring sides of the will, there is no higher synthesis, no reassuring compromise, no soothing mediation. The most intense suffering, even insanity, arises because the self is divided within itself, "willing what it does not will and not willing what it wills". Such constant and irredeemable suffering is for Bahnsen the inescapable

---

[1] This was the work of Rudolf Louis. See his edition of Bahnsen's autobiography, *Wie ich Wurde Was ich Ward* (Munich: Georg Müller, 1905).

[2] For the centenary of his birth, several of Bahnsen's writings were republished in 1931 by the Ambrosius Verlag, Leipzig. Among these writings were *Mosaiken und Silhouetten*, edited by Alfred Görland; *Beiträge zur Charakterologie*, edited by Johannes Rudert; *Das Tragische als Weltgesetz und der Humor*, edited by Anselm Ruest-Bernau; and a second edition of Louis's autobiography, also edited by Anselm Ruest-Bernau. For the centenary, Harry Slochower wrote an excellent summary of Bahnsen's philosophy. See his 'Julius Bahnsen, Philosopher of Heroic Despair, 1830–1881', *The Philosophical Review*, 41 (1932), 368–84.

[3] Largely but not entirely. The main work on Bahnsen since the centenary has been Heinz-Joachim Heydorn, *Julius Bahnsen: Eine Untersuchung zur Vorgeschichte der modernen Existenz* (Göttingen: Verlag Öffentliches Leben, 1952). In his 'Vorwort', p. 1, Heydorn notes that the centenary was unsuccessful in rehabilitating Bahnsen. For a discussion of Bahnsen's reception, see Winfried H. Müller-Seyfarth, 'Julius Bahnsen. Realdialektik und Willenshenadologie im Blick auf die "postmoderne" Moderne', in *Schopenhauer und die Schopenhauer-Schule*, ed. Fabio Ciracì, Domenico Fazio and Matthias Koßler (Würzburg: Königshausen & Neumann, 2009), pp. 231–46.

[4] On Nietzsche's relationship to Bahnsen, see Thomas Brobjer, *Nietzsche's Philosophical Context* (Urbana, IL: University of Illinois Press, 2008), pp. 39, 48, 55, 99, 136 n. 28, 139 n. 21, 140 n. 23.

fate of humanity. No wonder, then, that he, like a true pessimist, thinks that it would be better if we were not born.

One reason for Bahnsen's lapse into virtual oblivion—despite his original and powerful worldview—lies with his challenging prose. It has the exasperating power of exhausting even the most sympathetic reader. Its syntax is twisted and trying, its vocabulary vast and eccentric, its meaning elusive and vague. Never, it seems, does Bahnsen rewrite his sentences; it is as if it never occurred to him to strive for the simplest and most elegant formulation. He copies aspects of Schopenhauer's style—the colourful metaphors and the classical allusions—but never does he achieve his master's clarity and directness. Bahnsen himself admitted these shortcomings, and he recognized that they were a major reason for his lack of literary success; but he excused himself on the grounds that he did not have the time or opportunity to polish his prose.[5] But the difficulty of his writing was also partly a matter of choice. For Bahnsen deliberately does not discipline himself: he spurns conceptual elaboration and tight reasoning for the sake of the insight and inspiration of the moment.[6] While this makes his prose vivid and emphatic, it also makes it confusing and erratic.

The major reason for the neglect of Bahnsen, however, comes from the classification of him as a member of "the Schopenhauerian school".[7] Taken too strictly, these historiographical terms are reductive. They suggest that there is little need to consider a thinker in his own right because, it seems, if one knows the head of the school one knows all that is necessary about its members. In the case of Bahnsen this is especially misleading. For a short while, he was indeed a close disciple of Schopenhauer, and he always acknowledged his great debts to his "master". But he soon broke with him over so many fundamental points that it becomes impossible to consider him a Schopenhauerian in any strict or narrow sense. Bahnsen's worldview contradicts Schopenhauer's on three fundamental points. First, Bahnsen denies, like Mainländer, Schopenhauer's monism and he maintains instead that there is a plurality of individual wills; second, he disputes Schopenhauer's transcendental idealism and defends a transcendental realism; and, third, he makes Schopenhauer's will dialectical, so that it contradicts itself. Even Bahnsen's voluntarism—the point where he is closest to Schopenhauer—is a more radical and consistent version of his master's doctrine, for Bahnsen denies that the intellect can ever escape, let alone govern, the will. The apparent inconsistency in Schopenhauer's voluntarism—that the will dominates yet is controlled by the intellect—is resolved entirely in favour of the will.

Rather than just a variation of Schopenhauer's philosophy, Bahnsen's worldview is more a synthesis of Schopenhauer with Hegel. Hartmann's philosophy, as we have

---

[5] *Wie ich Wurde was ich Ward*, p. 112. [6] Ibid., p. 105.

[7] Otto Siebert, *Geschichte der neueren Philosophie seit Hegel* (Göttingen: Vandenhoeck & Ruprecht, 1898), pp. 233–5. For a more accurate assessment of Bahnsen's problematic place in "the Schopenhauer Schule", see Domenico Fazio, 'Die "Schopenhauer-Schule": Zur Geschichte eines Begriffs', in *Schopenhauer und die Schopenhauer-Schule*, pp. 15–41, esp. 25.

seen,⁸ should be described in similar terms. But there is something unique about Bahnsen's synthesis, something that sets it apart from Hartmann's. While Hartmann's synthesis attempts to tame and moderate Schopenhauer's pessimism with Hegel's optimistic belief in historical progress, Bahnsen's synthesis is completely tragic: it excludes evolution or development because history is cyclical and contradiction is constant. What Bahnsen takes from Hegel is not his historicism but his dialectic, and specifically and solely the *negative* moment of his dialectic—its emphasis on contradiction, the very aspect of Hegel's dialectic that Hartmann had rejected in his early days.⁹ We shall see later how these opposing syntheses became self-conscious for Bahnsen and Hartmann in the 1870s, and how they were the chief source of their philosophical differences.¹⁰

Bahnsen's pessimism has been described as the most extreme and radical in the age of *Weltschmerz*.¹¹ A strong case can be made for this view. Bahnsen is indeed more radical than Schopenhauer and Hartmann, because he denies the possibility of redemption. He is skeptical that art, asceticism or culture can remove us from the world of suffering, or that they provide escape from the self-torment of the will. Bahnsen's irrationalism is also greater than Schopenhauer's and Hartmann's, because he maintains that the striving of the will is not only incessant but also self-contradictory. But whether Bahnsen is more radical and extreme than Mainländer is contestable. If Bahnsen denies the possibility of redemption, Mainländer maintains that there is redemption only in death. While Bahnsen disapproves of suicide, Mainländer beckons us toward this ultimate step. Who, then, is more pessimistic? Bahnsen or Mainländer? I leave it to the reader to decide.

The main theme of Bahnsen's philosophy is his "real dialectic" (*Realdialektik*), which represents his central thesis that reality is irrational because the will is self-contradictory. Since Bahnsen saw the inner conflicts of the will as self-contradictory in a strict logical sense, he was committed to the bold and controversial claim that reality itself is self-contradictory. That flies in the face of the standard logical doctrine that contradiction applies to propositions rather than things. The point of Bahnsen's real dialectic, however, is to deny just that standard doctrine; it is a *real* and not an *artificial* dialectic precisely because it holds that contradiction applies to reality itself. Only in his later years did Bahnsen begin to explain and defend his controversial thesis in what became his magnum opus, his two-volume *Der Widerspruch im Wissen und Wesen der Welt*.¹² We will have occasion to examine Bahnsen's thesis below.

The task of the following chapter is to trace the genesis of Bahnsen's worldview, his early encounter with Schopenhauer and the steps by which he gradually emancipated

---

⁸ See Chapter 7, section 4. ⁹ See Chapter 7, section 5. ¹⁰ See section 8 below.
¹¹ Thus Louis in the 'Einleitung' to his edition of *Wie ich Wurde Was ich Ward*, p. xxiii; and Slochower, 'Bahnsen', p. 369.
¹² Julius Bahnsen, *Der Widerspruch im Wissen und Wesen der Welt* (Berlin: Theobald Grieben, 1880); vol. II was published in Leipzig by the same publisher in 1882. It was published posthumously, though Bahnsen had completed the work except for minor editorial matters.

himself from his master's legacy to develop his own unique worldview. We will see how Bahnsen moved away from Schopenhauer's monism and idealism toward a pluralism and realism, and how he removed the inconsistencies in Schopenhauer's voluntarism to formulate a radical pessimism all his own.

By no means is this chapter the first study of Bahnsen's intellectual development. The most important effort in that direction was undertaken more than seventy years ago by Heinz-Joachim Heydorn. His *Julius Bahnsen*,[13] which is based largely on a study of Bahnsen's unpublished manuscripts, is still an indispensable source for Bahnsen scholarship. My own account has relied heavily on Heydorn's research and bibliography. I differ, however, from Heydorn in one important respect: he thinks that Bahnsen's intellectual development is essentially complete by the middle 1860s, and that his later philosophy simply carries out a metaphysics he had fully envisioned in that decade. We shall soon see, however, that Bahnsen was still working out his philosophy well into the 1870s, and that it came into something like its final form only after his dispute with Hartmann. Even Bahnsen's pessimism, I argue, found its ultimate and characteristic formulation only in the final years of his life.

A significant chapter in Bahnsen's philosophical development came with his friendship with Hartmann. For some four years, from 1871 to 1875, the two philosophers met and corresponded. Each learned from the other and developed his views accordingly. For Bahnsen, the discussions with Hartmann were decisive in forming his own worldview, which was not least a reaction against Hartmann's. In its intensity and importance Bahnsen's relationship with Hartmann is not a little reminiscent of another relationship between two pessimists: that between Nietzsche and Wagner. Since so little is known about the former relationship; since it was so crucial for Bahnsen's intellectual development; since it was no less important in the history of pessimism; and since it is of the greatest philosophical interest, this chapter will devote several sections to a discussion of it.

2. The Making of a Pessimist

It should come as no surprise that Bahnsen's tragic worldview arose from a tragic life. His philosophy was very much the product of a broken heart and thwarted ambition. What life gave birth to such a sad philosophy?

Julius Friedrich August Bahnsen was born on 30 March 1830, in Tondern, Schleswig, the son of Christian August Bahnsen, the director of a training college for school teachers. His mother died when he was young, which was the source of persistent grief. Her loss, he later wrote, made it hard for him to participate in the pleasures of childhood (4n.).[14] He dated the beginning of the misery in his life to December 1842, the

---

[13] See n. 3 above. Heydorn informs us in his 'Vorwort' that he resolved to study Bahnsen in 1938.

[14] All references in parentheses are to Louis's 1905 edition of *Wie ich Wurde Was ich Ward*. All references in Roman numerals are to Louis's introduction.

day his father brought the *Noverca* home "as a Christmas present" (7). Bahnsen regretted deeply the provincial circumstances of his early childhood, and complained bitterly about their monotony and *"Kleingeisterei"*. There was no cultural stimulus, and there were few children with whom he could share his interests. He felt utterly isolated on the desolate moors of Schleswig, which he called his "intellectual Siberia". Nothing more seemed to demonstrate the conspiracy of the fates against him than the fact that he had to spend most of his life in the provinces. After a university education in Kiel and Tübingen, and after one short journey to London, he would work for the rest of his life as a school teacher in the Prussian hinterland. Bahnsen wanted nothing more than to be a university professor; but that was not to be.

If Bahnsen's professional life was a failure, his personal life was a disaster. In 1862 he married Minnita Möller, whom he loved dearly; but she died the next year giving birth to their only child. In 1868 Bahnsen married again, now to Phillipine Clara Hertzog, who bore him three children. But the marriage was a very unhappy one and ended in divorce in 1874. The experience of deep loss, followed by a bitter divorce, made Bahnsen a broken man. Hartmann, who saw Bahnsen often during the 1870s, described him as a psychopath, "a male hysteric".[15] Though this is the self-serving diagnosis of an exasperated and disillusioned ex-friend, it probably does reflect something of Bahnsen's desperate state of mind during these years.

Given his unpropitious beginnings, it was only fitting that Bahnsen's pessimism began early. In his autobiography he tells us that, when he was only 17, he had already formed "the nihilistic core idea" behind his worldview. That idea was not the result of reading philosophy or poetry, but the product of experience and temperament. On March 10, 1847—Bahnsen is very precise with his dates—he was sitting in his "gloomy little room" next to the stove when he was overcome with a profound sadness, "a melancholy contemptuous of the world and men" (20). He felt "finished with the world", and even contemplated suicide, happy that he could quickly end it all by throwing himself off a nearby bridge. Ever since that day, he wrote, he felt the rest of his life was only a *"Galgenfrist"*, i.e. a short delay before the gallows.

From December 1849 to July 1850, while a student at Kiel University, Bahnsen began to write down his moody musings in a notebook.[16] He called his worldview "nihilism", because it revelled in the theme of nothingness, the heady idea that there are no goals or values in life. He summarized this worldview in the striking lines: "History is the becoming of nothingness, going from nothingness and to nothingness" (xxxviii). Or, as he later put it: "Man is only a self-conscious nothingness" (161). The nihilistic theme is resonant of no one more than Max Stirner, whose chief work, *Der Einzige und sein Eigenthum*, Bahnsen had consumed at an early age.

---

[15] See Louis, 'Einleitung', p. xlv. Even Louis, who is skeptical of Hartmann's comment, describes Hartmann in those years as "im buchstäblichen Sinne des Wortes ein gehetzes Wild", p. xlvi.

[16] The notebook seems to have been lost. Louis provides substantial excerpts from his introduction, 'Einleitung', pp. xxxvii–xxxix. Heydorn, *Bahnsen*, p. 262, calls this manuscript 'Jugendmanuskript ohne Titel' and maintains that it was written from 17 Dec. 1849 to 2 July 1850.

Already in these early sketches we can see the germ of Bahnsen's later real dialectic.[17] Bahnsen had been reading Hegel and the left Hegelians, Feuerbach, Stirner and Ruge, who were all the rage in the 1840s. It is in their idiom that he casts his first philosophical reflections. He takes up the idea of the Hegelian dialectic, but conceives it coming to no positive result so that it ends only in "the idea of nothingness". "The unspoken sense of the Hegelian dialectic", he writes, is "the idea that opposites exist next to one another, so that the one is only as powerful, absolute, and justified as the other" (xxx–viii). But the result of their opposition, Bahnsen adds against Hegel, is not their synthesis in a higher unity but their utter destruction, which yields "nothingness". He is perfectly explicit in taking issue with Hegel on this point:

Hegel and his opponents rescue their "positive result" by speaking of a dialectical *movement*, while there is only a dialectical *being*, i.e. something purely null, in which there can be no middle and no mediation but only a nullification. If one were without prejudice and presupposition and true to the "method", one would have seen that the new dialectically discovered "absolute", or whatever you want to call the end point, must have another opposite than absolute perfection, and that it must show itself to be something logically impossible. (xxxviii–xxxix)

It is striking that the young Bahnsen takes issue with not only Hegel but also his left-wing critics. His dialectic will not end with Feuerbach's new humanism, not even with Stirner's radical ego; it will have no culmination or positive result at all but will end in utter nothingness. Although the neo-Hegelians have been dreaming of redemption, Bahnsen thinks that they need to be brought to their senses; he envisages a programme for destroying even their illusions:

The "individual freedom of the ego" in Lafaurie, "the ego and its own" in Stirner, the "humanism" of Ruge, and whatever other idols of the imagination pretend to be the truth, will be reduced down to their nothingness. (xxxix)

We can see from these early fragments, then, that Bahnsen has already conceived two central themes of his later real dialectic: (1) the idea that reality is dialectical, i.e. that it consists in the struggle of opposites; and (2) the thesis that this dialectic has no positive result. There is still something missing, however, another crucial ingredient: the will. Bahnsen has still not arrived at his signature doctrine that all conflict derives from the will. That theme would appear only later, after Bahnsen's discovery of Schopenhauer.

In the spring of 1850 Bahnsen moved from Kiel to Tübingen to continue his studies. He was a student there for two years, from the Spring Semester of 1850 until the Winter Semester of 1852/53, when he heard lectures on philosophy, psychology, theology, history and philology.[18] His most important teachers there were Jakob Friedrich Rauff

---

[17] This is the thesis of Louis, 'Einleitung', p. xxxvii, which is fully corroborated by the excerpts cited by him.

[18] For a list of the lectures Bahnsen attended, see Louis, 'Einleitung', p. xxxi.

(1810–79), who taught him psychology, and Friedrich Vischer (1807–87), who taught him aesthetics. He received his doctorate under Vischer with a thesis on aesthetics.[19]

Bahnsen's notes on Vischer's lectures reveal much about his own thinking during these years.[20] Under the influence of Feuerbach and the left Hegelians, Bahnsen sketched the outlines for a materialist metaphysics. The central concept of this metaphysics is the concept of force, which is used to explain all psychic phenomena (viz., the will, consciousness). Matter is conceived as "the unity of force and stuff", a formula that anticipates Büchner's own more famous version.[21] The doctoral dissertation was an attempt to apply this materialism to aesthetics. The central concepts of aesthetics—the tragic, comic and beautiful—are explained in terms of the concept of force. The aim was to eradicate the last nimbus of transcendence surrounding these aesthetic concepts.

Why Bahnsen abandoned this early materialism is unclear. According to Heydorn, the materialist phase of Bahnsen's thought ends in a crisis sometime in 1855, before his meeting with Schopenhauer.[22] He maintains that the manuscripts Bahnsen wrote from 1854 to 1855 show him struggling—but failing—to resolve the contradictions of his real dialectic. It is as if Bahnsen, for a short while, lost faith in his nihilistic vision and was striving to get beyond it. But exactly why this crisis arose, and why it should lead to the abandonment of materialism, remains uncertain.[23]

3. The Disciple of Schopenhauer

Bahnsen informs us that he first heard about Schopenhauer in the Winter Semester 1851/52 while still a student at Tübingen (45–6).[24] He learned about the Frankfurt sage from Rauff, who told him about "the paradoxes" of his philosophy. His curiosity aroused, Bahnsen duly read *Die Welt als Wille und Vorstellung*, which came to him like a revelation. He found especially appealing the fourth and final part, that which contains Schopenhauer's pessimism. Having earned a little money from teaching, Bahnsen immediately went out and bought a copy of the second edition, the first book he had ever owned. After the death of his brother, Bahnsen said that he derived much comfort from Schopenhauer, whose philosophy became for him a substitute for religious ritual and dogma (46). Thus for Bahnsen, as indeed for Frauenstädt and Mainländer, Schopernhauer's philosophy offered the core values of religion without the questionable baggage of theism.

---

[19] Heydorn, *Bahnsen*, no. XLVI: 'Versuch, die Lehre von den drei ästhetischen Grundformen genetisch zu gliedern nach den Voraussetzungen der naturwissenschaftlichen Psychologie' (1852).
[20] Heydorn, *Bahnsen*, no. XLIII: 'Bahnsens Kollegbuch über die bei Prof. Reiff in Tübingen gehörten Kollegs mit persönlichen Anmerkungen'. For an analysis of these notes, see Heydorn, *Bahnsen*, pp. 68–76.
[21] Louis Büchner, *Kraft und Stoff* (Frankfurt: Meidinger, 1855).   [22] Heydorn, *Bahnsen*, pp. 77–8.
[23] According to Heydorn, *Bahnsen*, p. 80, crucial manuscripts from these years have been lost.
[24] References in parentheses are to *Wie ich Wurde Was ich Ward* (1905).

In the summer of 1856 Bahnsen finally summoned the courage to request an audience with the great sage. To his delight and surprise, his wish was granted. He duly made the pilgrimage to Frankfurt, where 17 Schöne Aussicht seemed like "the antechamber of a world potentate". Despite his reputation as a recluse and misanthrope, Schopenhauer greeted Bahnsen kindly. From their meeting Bahnsen went away with a feeling of awe and devotion, as if he had just received "the blessings of a first communion" (47). "Everything of the mystic that had been slumbering in me was now, in one stroke, awakened and unleashed" (47). A remarkable *volte face* for an erstwhile materialist!

After his first meeting with Schopenhauer, Bahnsen resolved to master his philosophy completely, so that he would be a disciple second to none. Although he had to work as a private tutor some thirty hours a week, he devoted every spare minute to the study of Schopenhauer's philosophy. Such was his knowledge of his teacher's works that at their next meeting, some fourteen months later, Schopenhauer rewarded him with a remarkable tribute: his mastery of the texts put him on par with Frauenstädt! Since Schopenhauer regarded Frauenstädt as his chief apostle, this was high praise indeed. It was during these years of discipleship that Bahnsen published his first writing, an exposition of Schopenhauer's theory of mathematics.[25]

The young Bahnsen embraced Schopenhauer's philosophy not only as his worldview but also as his guide to life. Since Schopenhauer had preached that redemption could be achieved only through self-denial, Bahnsen started to practise asceticism. He aspired to be the next Saint Francis of Assisi. Despite much fasting and abstention, he began to despair that he would ever attain Schopenhauer's ideal. He worried constantly about relapses into the ways of the flesh; and never did he warm to the idea of castration (48). Remarkably, Bahnsen seemed little worried about Schopenhauer's own Epicurean lifestyle, which was hardly an example for a young ascetic.

Bahnsen's discipleship did not last long, at most four years.[26] He later wrote that he was especially troubled by two points in Schopenhauer's philosophy, and that in thinking through them he began to abandon it (48-9). The first point was "the famous merely" (*das famose "bloss"*) in Kant's Transcendental Aesthetic. Though Bahnsen does not explain what this means, it is an obvious reference to Trendelenburg's famous criticism of Kant's argument in the Transcendental Aesthetic, according to which Kant has not demonstrated that space and time are "merely" subjective. Kant's argument, Trendelenburg noted, had left open a possibility for realism: namely, that though the forms of space and time are subjective in their origins, arising from the a priori forms of sensibility, they still correspond to things-in-themselves. Bahnsen will later explore

---

[25] 'Der Bildungswerth der Mathematik', *Schulzeitung für die Herzogtümer Schleswig-Holstein und Lauenberg*, 21 Feb. and 21 and 28 Mar. 1857, nos. 21, 25, 26.

[26] Louis claims (p. xl) that Bahnsen was "Schopenhauerian strengster Observanz" for only "ein Paar Jahre", but this seems an underestimate because the discipleship seemed to last from May 1853, when he first resolved to meet Schopenhauer, until 1857, just before he published his essay on Schopenhauer's theory of mathematics.

this gap in Kant's argument, making it the basis for his own realism.[27] The second point was "the possibility of successful asceticism", which seemed to conflict with other cardinal theses of Schopenhauer's philosophy. Though Bahnsen again did not go into any details, he surely had in mind the impossibility of denying the will when it is the dominating force in human life and action.[28]

Quite apart from his later reservations about Schopenhauer, we have to ask whether Bahnsen was ever a completely faithful and unbiased interpreter of his philosophy. Like Frauenstädt and Mainländer, Bahnsen read his own ideas into Schopenhauer's writings. In a letter to Schopenhauer written February 21, 1858, Bahnsen describes the core of his master's philosophy as "the world law of negativity".[29] That phrase signifies nothing less than his own real dialectic, the thesis that not only opposition but self-contradiction lies at the heart of reality. But this was to read more into Schopenhauer's work than the texts would bear, given that Schopenhauer never conceived his will in dialectical terms, as if it somehow developed through opposition to itself. Schopenhauer's will is an irrational force, to be sure, but its irrationalism consists more in its blind and incessant striving rather than its inner conflicts. In seeing the will as not only blind but also self-contradictory, Bahnsen was casting it in Hegelian terms, which could only have been utter heresy for Schopenhauer.

According to Heydorn, in the period from 1858 to 1864, which are roughly the years after his discipleship under Schopenhauer and before his first major book, Bahnsen sketched in three manuscripts the elements of his own system of philosophy.[30] In them Bahnsen not only states the central thesis of his later real dialectic—that the heart of reality lies in the self-contradiction of the will—but he also expressly breaks with Schopenhauer in at least two fundamental respects. First, he rejects Kant's theory of space and time, specifically the Kantian thesis, which is accepted by Schopenhauer, that space and time are only a priori forms of intuition.[31] Bahnsen argues that Kant's theory cannot explain the given element of sensation, the manifold of particular sense qualities, and that, insofar as it cannot do so, we have reason to assume a degree of realism, i.e. that space and time are, at least in part, properties of things-in-themselves. Second, like Mainländer, Bahnsen also criticizes Schopenhauer's monism, his thesis that there is a single cosmic will behind all the phenomena of nature and within every individual ego.[32] Bahnsen maintains instead that there is a multiplicity of

[27] See section 7 below.
[28] In *Der Widerspruch im Wissen und Wesen der Welt*, II. 192, Bahnsen informs us that he was skeptical about the moral worth of asceticism when he first read Schopenhauer's "chief work" in 1857. In his marginal notes he argued that asceticism by itself has no moral value, i.e. that a person can be ascetic for strictly self-serving reasons.
[29] See *Schopenhauer Briefe*, ed. Ludwig Schemann (Leipzig: Brockhaus, 1893), p. 357.
[30] These manuscripts are as follows: no. LI, 'Wille und Motiv als Weltgesetz der Negativität', written between February 1858 and July 1866; no. LIII, 'Beträge zur Philosophie der Sprache', written between July 1859 and April 1863; and no. LV, 'Die Negativität in Leiden und Taten der Menschen', written between September 1863 and March 1864.
[31] See the excerpts cited by Heydorn, *Bahnsen*, pp. 84–8.
[32] See again the excerpts cited by Heydorn, *Bahnsen*, p. 92.

things-in-themselves, that there is one will per individual ego. These conclusions are indeed crucial for the formation of Bahnsen's later system, which will differ from Schopenhauer's philosophy in both its realism and pluralism.

Although these excerpts indeed show that Bahnsen was moving away from Schopenhauer in these years, Heydorn is going too far when he maintains that his system was already essentially complete and that it was only a matter of filling in details.[33] As Bahnsen himself insisted, he was still too unsure of himself in the 1860s, and he will attain full clarity, confidence and certainty only in the 1870s in the course of his controversy with Hartmann.[34] Bahnsen was especially tentative about his pluralism, which he would state boldly at times only to lapse into reaffirmations of Schopenhauer's monism.[35]

4. Literary Debut

Bahnsen's literary debut came with his *Beiträge zur Charakterologie*, which appeared in 1867,[36] though it had been finished as early as autumn 1865.[37] The subject of his book, which Bahnsen calls "character", is what psychologists nowadays describe as "personality", i.e. the individual identity of a human being. Characterology was thus for Bahnsen the study of character or personality, i.e. what makes for the individual differences between people. The fundamental task of his book was how to define and describe these individual differences. He believed that such an enterprise is of great importance for moralists, jurists and educators, whose professions require them to appreciate the differences between people.

Bahnsen's *Beiträge* is a sprawling two-volume work, covering all kinds of topics in ethics, psychology, law and pedagogy. Volume I sketches a theory of temperament and examines the topic of responsibility. Volume II is essentially an essay on moral psychology, on the various kinds of emotion and their moral implications. Throughout, Bahnsen's cardinal vice—his lack of thoroughness and rigour in pursuing a question—is especially in evidence. Important issues are raised, only to be dropped and lost sight of in constant digressions. On any given topic the reader is forced to pull together Bahnsen's arguments and observations from scattered sections of the text. Bahnsen himself admits that he had no definite plan in writing the book, that it has more the form of a diary than a treatise, and that he originally had no intention of publishing it.[38]

---

[33] Heydorn, *Bahnsen*, pp. 68, 80, 99.   [34] *Wie ich Wurde Was ich Ward*, p. 49.
[35] See below, section 4.
[36] Julius Bahnsen, *Beiträge zur Charakterologie: Mit besonderer Berücksichtigungen pädagogischer Fragen* (Leipzig: Brockhaus, 1867), 2 vols. All references in parentheses are to this edition. Although the *Beiträge* was not Bahnsen's first published writing, it was his first major work. Bahnsen himself referred to it as his literary debut in *Wie ich Wurde Was ich Ward*, pp. 67–72.
[37] As Bahnsen informs us in his 'Vorrede', p. ix.
[38] See *Wie ich Wurde was ich Ward*, pp. 69–70.

Yet, for all its faults, the *Beiträge* met with some success. It has been generally regarded as a pioneering work in the study of personality. One of its admirers was Nietzsche.[39] Another was Hartmann, who gave it a favourable review in the *Philosophische Monatshefte*.[40] Ludwig Klages (1872–1956), the psychologist, saw Bahnsen's work as the ancestor of his own theory of personality.[41]

The *Beiträge* is an important document in Bahnsen's *philosophical* development. It is a mistake to shove it aside as if it were only a work on psychology.[42] The basic concept that Bahnsen develops in this work—the idea of individual personality—became the central theme of his entire philosophy. Bahnsen's later metaphysics attempts to justify this concept as basic and irreducible, fundamental for the understanding of existence and each human being. It defends this concept against monists, who would reduce the individual down to a mere mode of the absolute, and against materialists, who would reduce it down to a mere complex of material parts.[43]

There is another reason the *Beiträge* is important for Bahnsen's philosophical development: it demonstrates his growing independence from Schopenhauer. The erstwhile disciple now spreads his wings. Though complete autonomy is not achieved, big steps are taken toward it. What had been stated privately in the notebooks of the late 1850s and early 1860s is now stated publicly, even if somewhat tentatively and hesitantly.

Despite his fledgling steps away from Schopenhauer, Bahnsen was still very much under his spell in the *Beiträge*. He compares his own work to the attempt of an architect to make revisions in the design of a beautiful palace (i.e. Schopenhauer's system), whose structure is firm and solid, but which needs here and there a few new windows and doors (I. 124).[44] Bahnsen not only states that the philosophical foundation of characterology lies in Schopenhauer's philosophy (I. 1), but he also defines his discipline in Schopenhauerian terms. The whole discipline revolves around Schopenhauer's central concept: the will. Characterology, Bahnsen writes, is "a phenomenology of the will" whose task is to describe how the will appears in different individuals (1). The debt to Schopenhauer is especially apparent when Bahnsen makes the will and its various motives the basis for his classification of personality. The classical four temperaments—melancholic, choleric, sanguine and lethargic—are defined in terms of the formal relationship between will and motive (I. 32). And the extreme states of the soul,

---

[39] See Nietzsche to Paul Deussen, *Briefwechsel, Kritische Gesamtausgabe*, ed. Giorgo Colli, Renate Müller-Buck, Annemaire Pieper et al. (Berlin: de Gruyter, 1975), I/2. 258.
[40] Eduard von Hartmann, *Philosophische Monatshefte*, 4 (1870), 378–408.
[41] On Klages's relationship to Bahnsen, see Müller-Seyfarth, 'Bahnsen', pp. 233–4.
[42] I cannot accept, therefore, Heydorn's procedure (*Bahnsen*, p. 3) of ignoring the *Beiträge* on the grounds that it is not a philosophical work. This is not only an anachronistic assumption but also contrary to Bahnsen's own view of psychology, which stresses its philosophical foundations. Because he does not consider the *Beiträge*, Heydorn oversimplifies Bahnsen's philosophical development, for reasons which will be clear below.
[43] See especially *Der Widerspruch im Wissen und Wesen der Welt*, chapters 3 and 4, II. 65–106.
[44] Given the importance that Bahnsen still gives to Schopenhauer's system, it is difficult to accept Heydorn's thesis, *Bahnsen*, pp. 97, 99, that Bahnsen had broken with Schopenhauer and had completely worked out the foundations of his system before the *Beiträge*.

Dyskolos and *Eukolos*, i.e. depression and euphoria, are understood as an individual's specific capacity for pleasure or pain, which are also treated as a function of the will (I. 20, 49).[45]

Since determining personal differences is an empirical matter, Bahnsen deems characterology "a descriptive science", and he calls it "a phenomenology" whose task is to describe the phenomena of the will. As an empirical science one would therefore expect characterology to be far removed from Bahnsen's philosophical interests. Yet Bahnsen, like a good student of Schopenhauer, drew no sharp distinction between philosophy and empirical science. He insists that characterology, like any discipline, has metaphysical foundations, and that it is necessary to examine them (I. 1). Sure enough, in the two chief chapters of the first volume of his work,[46] Bahnsen focuses on two fundamental metaphysical questions, both of them from Schopenhauer's philosophy. First, what is the relationship between the will as such and its manifestations in individuals? Second, what is the relationship between the will and representation? It was in thinking through both these questions that Bahnsen began to depart, markedly and in principle, from Schopenhauer.

These disagreements with Schopenhauer come as something of a surprise. Given Bahnsen's declaration of his debts to "his master", and given that he applies his philosophy on so many points of doctrine, it would seem that the *Beiträge* should be essentially a Schopenhauerian work, indeed an exercise in Schopenhauerian psychology. Yet the great mystery of the work, as Hartmann pointed out,[47] is that Bahnsen so dutifully expresses his debt to Schopenhauer only to depart from him on point after point. There is an astonishing tension, or at least disproportion, between Bahnsen's declaration of allegiance and his actual thinking.

Writing about the first question, that concerning the relationship between the cosmic and individual will, Bahnsen notes that Schopenhauer himself regarded it as one of the greatest difficulties for his own philosophy (I. 51 n., 202–3).[48] Is the will one and the same in all its individual phenomena? Or does it divide itself into each of them, so that there is not one single will but many different wills, and as many as there are individual persons? (50–1). Characterology cannot avoid this thorny issue, Bahnsen stressed, because as the study of the individual differences between people it has to determine the basis for the *principium individuationis* (I. 118). After posing this problem, Bahnsen immediately takes issue with Schopenhauer's own account of individual differences. Schopenhauer had limited the *principium individuationis* to the phenomenal

---

[45] Although Bahnsen accepts Schopenhauer's definition of these terms in *Die Welt als Will und Vorstellung* §57, I. 433, he questions his classification of them under the four temperaments.

[46] The chapters, which are unnumbered, are entitled 'Die Imputabilitätsfrage und das Modificabilitätsproblem', I. 118–324, and 'Die Communalprovinz', I. 325–96.

[47] Eduard von Hartmann, *Neukantianismus, Schopenhauerianismus und Hegelianismus in ihrer Stellung zu den philosophischen Aufgaben der Gegenwart* (Berlin: Duncker, 1877), pp. 178–9.

[48] Bahnsen cites (I. 202–3) the lines from ch. 50 of vol. II of *Die Welt als Wille und Vorstellung* where Schopenhauer asks: "wie tief, im Wesen an sich der Welt, die Wurzeln der Individualität gehn?" See WWV II. 822 (P 641).

or empirical world, so that the differences between people are entirely a phenomenal or empirical matter. Since he assigns individual differences to the realm of phenomena, and since he thinks that every action and event in that realm is determined according to natural laws, Schopenhauer cannot explain why we hold *individual* agents responsible for their actions (I. 119). Although his will is free, because it stands above and beyond the realm of phenomena, it has a purely universal or cosmic status, so that it is the same in everyone and everything alike; for just this reason, though, it cannot be the basis for *individual* responsibility. Because it is omnipresent in everything, not only in all human beings but also in all inanimate and animate things, Schopenhauer's cosmic will is useless in determining any responsibility whatsoever (I. 253).

With this critique of Schopenhauer, Bahnsen had stated one of the defining doctrines of his mature philosophy: namely, his individualism. That doctrine, as Bahnsen later expounds it, holds that there is a multiplicity of individual substances in the world, i.e. that there is not just one will but many wills, and indeed one for each person. Bahnsen had already stated this doctrine in an earlier manuscript,[49] but he now gives it a new foundation in the *Beiträge*, one that stresses the importance of individuality for the concept of responsibility. This foundation consists in two premises. First, that the subject of moral imputation is the individual. We hold an individual responsible, he argues, because of his or her individual character, because he or she is just this person and no other (I. 255). It is completely irrelevant whether there is a single cosmic will present in each one of us, because that will is the source of all actions in everyone, regardless of their actions or moral merits (I. 253). Second, that this individual, if it is to be held responsible, must have the power of autonomy, i.e. it should be the source or cause of its own actions (I. 247). But this autonomy it cannot have in the *phenomenal* or *natural* world, where all events are determined according to the principle of sufficient reason. Hence Bahnsen, to save individual responsibility, is led to postulate a plurality of individual substances, essences or natures, in the *noumenal* or *supernatural* world. Schopenhauer's limitation of the *principium individuationis* to the realm of appearances is therefore decisively rejected.

Although Bahnsen was moving toward the individualism and pluralism of his later philosophy, he was still not there yet. The break with Schopenhauer's monism was still not complete, clean or clear.[50] For that to happen, Bahnsen would have to deny the existence of Schopenhauer's single cosmic will; but in the *Beiträge* Bahnsen has still not

---

[49] See no. LI: 'Wille und Motiv als Weltgesetz der Negativität', pp. 6, 24 (as cited in Heydorn, *Bahnsen*, pp. 92–3). According to Heydorn, the basis for this pluralism is the concept of polarity.

[50] In this respect I now have to take issue with Hartmann, who thinks that Bahnsen was already a complete individualist and pluralist in the *Beiträge*. See *Neukantianismus, Schopenhauerismus und Hegelianismus*, p. 179. To prove his case Hartmann cites a passage from Bahnsen's later 1870 work *Zum Verhältniß zwischen Wille und Motiv* (Lauenberg: H. Eschenhagen, 1870), p. 17 n. However, this work was written much later, after 1869 at the earliest. For similar reasons, I cannot accept the conclusion of Christo Thodoroff, *Julius Bahnsen und die Hauptprobleme seiner Charakterologie* (Erlangen: Junge & Sohn, 1910), pp. 33–8, who also thinks that the break with Schopenhauer's monism is complete in the *Beiträge*.

taken that drastic and dramatic step. He has shown that the cosmic will is useless in defining questions of responsibility; but he has not stated, let alone demonstrated, that it does not exist. On the contrary, in the final section in the chapter on imputability, Bahnsen commits himself to the existence of the single cosmic will. He states that the absolute independence of the individual is impossible, and that the individual is always only one part of the cosmic one or whole (I. 319).[51]

Concerning the second question, i.e. the relationship between will and representation, Bahnsen again departs from his master. Schopenhauer, he complained, goes too far in distinguishing will from representation, and he is indeed on the verge of sanctioning a dualism between them (I. 13). Schopenhauer's unacceptable dualism is especially apparent, Bahnsen contends, in his account of aesthetic experience. Schopenhauer describes aesthetic experience as "will-less" or "disinterested contemplation", as if the will were not present at all, and as if that experience consists in nothing more than pure representation or consciousness; furthermore, he refers to the subject of aesthetic experience as a "pure subject", as if its actions were entirely contemplative, completely unperturbed by the will. Bahnsen protests, however, that even aesthetic interest has its basis in the will, and that it is an exaggeration to write of its "disinterestedness" (I. 327). Although aesthetic experience abstains from lower ends or interests like self-preservation and procreation, that does not mean that the will is absent; on the contrary, it appears in feelings of "self-promotion, self-confirmation, self-satisfaction" (I. 328). The pleasure we take in art, and in intellectual activity in general, Bahnsen claims, is a species of "self-affirmation" (328–9). The experience of beauty consists not in the elimination but the expansion of our willing self (351 n.). If we were to cut the umbilical cord connecting knowledge with the will, we would be utterly bored by what we see, even if it were the forms of Plato (329). And if we were pure subjects in aesthetic contemplation, having no interests or feelings deriving from the will, we could not explain why we are touched and moved by aesthetic objects (I. 351 n.). Complete absence of the will from aesthetic experience would remove every tincture of happiness from the pleasure of beauty.

Despite contesting Schopenhauer's distinction between will and representation, Bahnsen insists that he does not want to question his criterion for the highest objectification of the will: namely, the final separation of intellect and will (I. 330). But he immediately qualifies this apparent concession by stressing that he wants to push the separation to the point where intellect and will *join* one another again. Just as the will should know, so the intellect should will. This unity of will and intellect is apparent, Bahnsen claims, not only in the desire for knowledge, but also in acts of sympathy or pity (330–1).

In tune with his critique of Schopenhauer's dualism, Bahnsen stresses throughout the *Beiträge* the close connection between will and representation. Volition and cognition should never be separated, in his view, because the will is always the force and

---

[51] See also the traces of monism in volume II. 31, 113, 177–8.

power behind cognition. He summarizes his investigation into this topic with the proposition: "intellectual functions are only a special case of functions of will" (I. 356). Despite his criticisms of Schopenhauer, Bahnsen still insists that he is loyal to the spirit of his thinking, which stresses the *inseparability* of will and intellect. Schopenhauer's great insight, he declares, is that will and representation, subject and object, are identical in the self-knowledge of the will (I. 13).

Apart from these metaphysical issues, there is another respect in which Bahnsen begins to depart from Schopenhauer in his *Beiträge*. This concerns the meaning of pessimism itself. Bahnsen insists that it is a misunderstanding of pessimism to think that it rests upon a eudemonic calculation about the preponderance of suffering in life. What makes someone a pessimist is not simply the recognition that life is miserable and that we are not going to be happy—if that were the criterion, Bahnsen argues, even animals would be pessimists—but the realization that it is often difficult, if not impossible, to achieve our ideals in this life (II. 156, 213). The pessimist knows all too well that most of his hopes and ideals will be frustrated by the world, and that he can realize a few of them only through enormous struggle and then by paying a price. He sees that realizing one ideal often requires sacrificing another, or that realizing a goal only partially often requires compromising with those who hold opposing ones (II. 214). Never, though, does the pessimist surrender his ideals entirely and become a cynic. Rather, he stands and fights for them even when he knows that it requires sacrifice and sorrow. Gradually, beginning in the *Beiträge*, Bahnsen was moving away from Schopenhauer's ethic of quietism and toward one of heroic struggle. Yet the transition is still incomplete, because Bahnsen continued to affirm an ethic of resignation (II. 196, 214).

Bahnsen remains the disciple of Schopenhauer in another important respect: he still believes in the possibility of redemption. Despite emphasizing the inseparability of will and representation, he still believed that the intellect, the power of representation, is just autonomous enough, and indeed just powerful enough, to transform the will and to turn it against itself. Knowledge of the worthlessness of life, he claimed in true Schopenhauerian fashion, can lead to the denial of the will (I. 339–40). Through the effective use of the cognitive apparatus at its disposal, the will can learn about the consequences of its actions; and after recognizing that its striving leads to misery, it becomes dissatisfied with itself, where such self-dissatisfaction consists in not willing what one wills, i.e. in self-denial. It was in this manner that Bahnsen explained to himself the possibility of freedom from the urgings of the will. It is almost as if, in spelling it out so carefully, he was trying to convince himself that the idea of self-denial still had merit.

Yet even here doubts persisted. Bahnsen's loyalty to this idea was already wavering. In a striking passage he said that self-denial, because it involves a conflict of will, never really leads to peace or satisfaction (I. 229). That was his negative dialectic asserting itself, striking against the limits imposed by Schopenhauer's doctrine. Already in the *Beiträge*, then, Bahnsen was doubting, if only hesitantly, the possibility of redemption, and he was on the verge of taking the final decisive step toward his more radical pessimism.

5. Foundations of Pessimism

One of the decisive moments in Bahnsen's intellectual development came in 1869 with the publication of the first edition of Hartmann's *Philosophie des Unbewussten*. After reading a review of the book in the *Blätter für literarische Unterhaltung*,[52] Bahnsen immediately bought a copy and studied it with care. Here, he thought, was a kindred spirit, a fellow pessimist, a potential colleague, who had the same philosophical interests. More importantly, Hartmann had investigated in great depth some of the same metaphysical issues he had already discussed in his *Beiträge*. Bahnsen was troubled, however, that Hartmann had come to opposing conclusions. If Hartmann's metaphysics were correct, it would undermine the guiding idea behind his characterology: the principle of individuality. So, to respond to this threat, Bahnsen wrote a short tract clarifying his differences with Hartmann, his 1870 *Zum Verhältniß zwischen Wille und Motiv*.[53]

Bahnsen saw the greatest danger to his principle of individuality in Hartmann's monism. Like Schopenhauer, Hartmann held that there is a single cosmic will working its way throughout all of nature and objectifying itself in every individual thing. He too placed the realm of individuality, i.e. the plurality of particular things, in the phenomenal world, so that each individual thing is only a phenomenal manifestation or objectification of the universal will. The will in itself is uniform, homogeneous and undifferentiated; it assumes different forms according to its different objects in the realm of appearance. But if we accept this view of the will and its various manifestations, Bahnsen argues, we give no room for character or individuality. The principle of individuality demands that each person has his or her own will, that there be one will per person (38). But Hartmann, like Schopenhauer, thinks that there is only one and the same will in all persons. If that is so, Bahnsen fears, the whole science of characterology, which is based on the principle of individuality, will collapse.

Against Hartmann's monism, Bahnsen makes a firm stand in favour of an ontological pluralism. Hartmann, he claims, does not appreciate one basic ontological principle: "that each power is a power to be in general" (6). This means that each power is a striving to realize a specific nature; it is, in the old Latin nomenclature, a "*vis essendi eademque existendi*". This implies that it has not only an individual nature or essence but also an individual existence, i.e. it does not derive its essence or its existence from something else outside itself but has them in itself. Having thus declared his pluralism,

---

[52] The review, which was by Rudolf Gottschalk, appeared in the *Blätter für literarische Unterhaltung*, Nr. 8, 18. February 1869, pp. 113–18. No one who read this review would want to ignore Hartmann's book. Though very critical of Hartmann, Gottschalk declares Hartmann's work "the product of an original thinker" and "one of the most preeminent publications of recent philosophical literature".

[53] Julius Bahnsen, *Zum Verhältniß zwischen Wille und Motiv: Eine metaphyische Voruntersuchung zur Charakterologie* (Stolp and Lauenberg: H. Eschenhagen, 1870). All references in parentheses are to this edition. Heydorn, *Bahnsen*, p. 85 n, points out that this work was based on an earlier manuscript, no. LI, 'Wille und Motiv als Weltgesetz der Negativität', which was composed between Feb. 1858 and July 1866. In his opinion, the earlier work is clearer than the later one, which is marred by polemics against Hartmann.

Bahnsen then proceeds to reject monism, at least tentatively and implicitly. We can talk about the unity of each individual thing, and we can claim that this unity exists, he writes in a footnote, but if we do so we cannot talk about any unity above and beyond these individual things, i.e. a unity *of* all these individual things; instead, all that we can speak about is "a *tendency* toward unification" (17 n.). We must not confuse, however, this *tendency* toward unity with an *actual* unity, as if it already exists, Bahnsen continues, firmly rejecting the hypothesis of "some transcendent interference" pushing all particular things together. Reading behind the lines, as Bahnsen bids us, he is saying that there really is no single cosmic will; to assume that it exists would be to hypostasize a mere "tendency".

There was another issue that troubled Bahnsen about Hartmann's metaphysics, one closely connected to the principle of individuality though still distinct from it. This was Hartmann's strict distinction between will and representation.[54] In distinguishing between will and representation, Hartmann had given autonomy to the realm of representation, which is governed by the self-conscious intellect; such autonomy then allows the intellect to take control of the will and to demand that it conform to rational ends. Bahnsen, however, wants to stay true to Schopenhauer's original irrationalism. He insists that the content of the will comes from the will itself; in other words, its striving and longing is inseparable from its specific objects (12–13). The crucial question for the will, he writes, is not *that* it is satisfied but *in what* and *how* it is so (14).

In giving such great power to the realm of representation, Hartmann is guilty of a simple mistake, Bahnsen argues. He conflates the content of the will with its representation, so that it appears as if what the will wants, its objects or ends, are due to representation alone, which is the work of the self-conscious and rational self. Hartmann's reasoning, which Bahnsen formulates in the following syllogism, seems plausible enough: (1) the content of the will comes from its motive; (2) each motive is a representation; and therefore (3) only representations form the content of the will (27). His mistake comes in premise (2), Bahnsen contends. Representation does not create the content of the will but it is only the self-consciousness of that content; it does nothing more than give a name to the object of the will, which is really produced by the will itself (28).

For all its brevity, density and obscurity, Bahnsen's *Zum Verhältniß zwischen Wille und Motiv* marks an important stage in his philosophical development. Bahnsen had now stated, firmly and self-consciously, two of the signal doctrines of his mature philosophy: individualism and voluntarism. To be sure, both doctrines were already present in the *Beiträge* and the manuscripts from the early 1860s; but they lay side-by-side, uncomfortably, with incompatible doctrines, viz., Schopenhauer's monism and his belief in the power of the intellect over the will. In the *Beiträge* Bahnsen had still

[54] See Chapter 7, section 4.

affirmed the existence of Schopenhauer's cosmic will;[55] and he had continued to assume that representation has some form of power over the will, so that it can make the will turn against itself.[56] Now, however, these incompatible doctrines, these remnants of Schopenhauer, disappear in favour of individualism and voluntarism alone. There is no cosmic will but only a multitude of individual wills; and the will has complete power over representation, which never has the power to redirect it.

Although in discussing these metaphysical niceties we seem to have strayed far from Bahnsen's original pessimism, the truth of the matter is that we are now moving toward its deepest and darkest core. With the denial of Schopenhauer's monism, and with the rejection of any dualism between will and representation, Bahnsen leapt into the very depths of despair: for now there could be no possibility of redemption. The denial of monism means there can be no redeeming insight that we human beings, despite all the competition and dissension between us, are at bottom one. Now that Schopenhauer's cosmic will had been downgraded to regulative status, there was nothing left but a plurality of individual wills, each striving for itself and against all others. Individualism had always meant for Schopenhauer egoism, the competitive free-for-all where each individual asserts his own self-interest at the expense of everyone else. But it is just such individualism that Bahnsen now affirms; he is committed to the view that this egoism is indeed the only reality. There is no single cosmic will in which we can see ourselves and all beings. The rejection of the will–representation dualism has no less troubling consequences. It means that the will is indeed omnipotent, and that the realm of representation will never have the power to tame it. Whatever the will wants comes from itself, and it will not have to comply with the ends laid down by the intellect. Bahnsen later wrote that it was his dispute with Hartmann that first made him fully aware of "the energy of my pessimism".[57] We can now see what he meant.

6. Hartmann's Review of Bahnsen

No one was more vigilant about the reception and criticism of his philosophical productions than Eduard von Hartmann. No review, article or monograph about his *Philosophie des Unbewussten* would appear without it getting an immediate point-for-point riposte. It comes as no surprise, then, that Hartmann quickly responded to Bahnsen's *Zum Verhältniß zwischen Wille und Motiv*, which he reviewed, along with the *Beiträge zur Charakterologie*, in the *Philosophische Monatshefte*.[58] Hartmann could

---

[55] Bahnsen, *Beiträge*, I. 319; II. 31, 113, 177–8.   [56] Ibid. I. 216–19, 335, 340.
[57] *Wie ich Wurde was ich Ward*, p. 76.
[58] Eduard von Hartmann, Review of 'Beiträge zur Charakterologie' und 'Zum Verhältniß zwischen Wille und Motiv', *Philosophische Monatshefte*, IV (1870), 378–404. This review reappeared in Hartmann's *Neukantianismus, Schopenhauerismus und Hegelianismus*, pp. 175–211. All references in parentheses are to this later edition.

see that there was much at stake in an encounter with Bahnsen. If Bahnsen had felt threatened by his monism, he felt challenged by Bahnsen's individualism.

Hartmann's review of Bahnsen's *Charakterologie* is sympathetic to Bahnsen's general project. There is a need for a more rigorous study of character, Hartmann says, and, though Bahnsen's work lacks systematic structure, it is a great improvement on what has been done before, viz., the theory of temperaments and phrenology. Hartmann praises Bahnsen's work for being "uncommonly stimulating". But he finds one aspect of the work very puzzling: Bahnsen claims that the foundation for his characterology lies in Schopenhauer's philosophy; yet he departs from that philosophy on point after point. Hartmann then lists the fundamental respects in which Bahnsen breaks with Schopenhauer (178–80), all of them completely accurate. First, Bahnsen disagrees with Schopenhauer's subjective idealism because he accepts Trendelenburg's criticism of Kant. Second, Bahnsen advances an individualism that is incompatible with Schopenhauer's monism. Third, Bahnsen disputes the metaphysical status of Schopenhauer's ideas and the possibility of disinterested contemplation of them. Fourth and finally, though he continues to affirm Schopenhauer's doctrine of the unchangeability of character, Bahnsen puts forward a theory according to which character can be improved and perfected through education. So if Bahnsen contradicts Schopenhauer on all these points, Hartmann asks, why does he still call him "master"? Bahnsen duly took note of this criticism, which encouraged him in developing his own independent standpoint.

Hartmann quickly focuses on the main issue dividing him from Bahnsen: monism versus pluralism. The motivation behind Bahnsen's individualism, Hartmann rightly sees, lies in his concern with moral responsibility. To explain moral imputation, Bahnsen, like Kant and Schopenhauer, postulates the existence of a noumenal character, which is distinct from phenomenal character, and which transcends the causal necessity of the phenomenal world. Hartmann finds this postulate entirely pointless. A person deserves moral praise and blame, he argues, because he or she acts with self-consciousness, and because he or she acts in the phenomenal world, i.e. in this particular place at this particular time. To save moral responsibility, we do not need the additional assumption that there is a noumenal self acting through the phenomenal self's actions in the natural world. The phenomenal character alone suffices for the attribution of praise and blame; the noumenal character is a useless spooky presence behind the empirical one (185). Furthermore, if we are to be responsible for our actions, we must be self-aware of them; but *ex hypothesi*, on Schopenhauer's theory, we are not self-conscious of that act of the will by which we choose our characters. How, then, Hartmann asks, can we be held responsible for it? (183). Bahnsen had written about a *pre-existential* merit and a *pre-existential* guilt involved in the choosing of our characters; but that, strictly speaking, Hartmann retorts, is utter nonsense (183). We are responsible only *after* we exist.

It was crucial to Bahnsen's incipient individualism that he attribute an independent essence and existence to moral character. This is what Bahnsen, following

Schopenhauer, had called "aseity", i.e. existence for and in itself, *ens a se* rather than existence from another, *ens ab alio*.[59] Hartmann, however, finds it impossible to attribute such sublime metaphysical status to the individual, which is always dependent and determined by other things. We can attribute such status, he insists, only to one thing: the single universal substance (185). There is no sense, however, in which we can attribute aseity to the individual. We might try to do so in a negative or positive sense (183). In a negative sense, it means the complete absence of determination by external causes. This, however, is hardly applicable to anything individual in the world, which is always determined or conditioned by something else, either in its essence or existence. In a positive sense, it means that the individual has the power to posit or create its own essence and existence. It must do that positing either before or after it exists; but either alternative is absurd: before it exists, it is nothing and so cannot do anything; after it exists, it would have to have *per impossibile* a completely essenceless existence (183).

Hartmann not only attacks Bahnsen's individualism but he also defends his own monism. The most important question facing his monism concerns the relationship between the cosmic universal will and individual wills. How does the single universal will appear in different individuals? How does it remain the same will despite all the different objects of will in different individuals? That was the fundamental question that Schopenhauer and Bahnsen had once posed, and for which Hartmann now thinks he has an answer. All motives for the actions of different individuals, he claims, are ultimately nothing more than different *directions* of activity of the single universal will (206). These motives do not belong to *different* wills in different individuals, but they belong to one and the same cosmic will as it appears or objectifies itself in these individuals. The cosmic will alone has an independent essence and existence, and the actions of individual things are dependent upon it. To make this relationship more intelligible, Hartmann then hit upon a bizarre metaphor. The cosmic will stands to the universe like a spider sits in its web; the motives of this will are like the flies that fall into its web (206–7). They determine the *direction* of its activity, but they do not change its *goal*, which is always the same: catching flies. Hartmann admits that this is not the best of analogies: the spider catches one fly at a time, whereas the cosmic will is involved in an infinite number of individuals. And where, we might well ask, do the flies come from, given that the cosmic will is supposed to be all reality? But we will not push this metaphor further than it deserves.

Hartmann's review takes up another fundamental issue dividing him from Bahnsen: the power of the will *vis-à-vis* the intellect. Hartmann had affirmed and Bahnsen denied the separability of the will from the intellect. Much is at stake in this dispute: the power and authority of reason itself. Does reason have some power to control the will, as Hartmann maintains? Or does the will have complete power over reason, which is

---

[59] See Schopenhauer, *Die Welt als Wille und Vorstellung*, Werke II. 414.

only its servant, as Bahnsen claims? On this important issue, Hartmann's review is a disappointment because it clarifies little and complicates much. Hartmann thought that Bahnsen had simply conflated the content of the will with its motive when these are actually very different. On his own terminology, the motive is the stimulus for the will, what *causes* it to desire something, whereas its content is its goal or end, what is desired (197–8). By identifying content with motive Bahnsen had conflated the beginning and end of the whole process of motivation, Hartmann charges (199). Yet little rests on this point, which is primarily terminological. Hartmann attempts to sidestep Bahnsen's criticisms about his separation of will and representation by insisting that he meant the distinction to hold only for *conscious* representation; regarding *unconscious* representation, he insisted upon their complete inseparability. They are completely inseparable in reality, even if they can be separated in thought (201).[60] But here Hartmann missed Bahnsen's deeper point, which is directed against the *conceptual* distinction.

However much Hartmann distinguishes will and representation, he insists that we identify the content of the will with representation. That the content of the will is representation, he wrote, is "the most simple of all philosophical basic truths" (203). The will can have no content that is in principle inexpressible or unrepresentable (202). This means for Hartmann that the will is, at least potentially, rational, because the realm of representation is that of the intellect or reason. Against Bahnsen's irrational will he emphatically maintained: "all content of the will is absolutely rational" (204). What indeed, Hartmann asked, can the content of the will be other than some representation? There was indeed another possibility, which Hartmann himself acknowledged, and which was indeed Bahnsen's position all along: that the content of the will is *feeling* (*Gefühl*). Prior to its articulation into representation, the content of the will is for Bahnsen feeling, which he defines as "the intuitive innerness of our essential content", or "the will in the innerness of itself before it has posited itself outward in representation".[61] Hartmann, however, would not allow this. In the *Philosophie des Unbewussten* he had already eliminated feeling as the independent middle term between will and representation by analysing it into unconscious representations.[62] For Bahnsen, though, unconscious representation is an oxymoron. That claim, Hartmann protests, is simply a dogmatic fiat. Are there really unconscious representations? Regarding this crucial question, the dispute between Hartmann and Bahnsen ran aground, stuck fast on an aporia of conflicting intuitions.

---

[60] Here Hartmann seemed to be forgetting his own argument that will and representation are indeed inseparable *conceptually*. This was a major point in his critique of Schopenhauer. See *Philosophie des Unbewussten* (1870), pp. 20–1, 90–2. In the final chapter of his book, however, Hartmann had distinguished conceptually what he had once intertwined. He distinguishes between the form and content of the will, where the form is its striving or longing and its content its specific goal. See pp. 690–6. This later distinction was the main target of Bahnsen's criticism.

[61] *Beiträge zur Charakterologie*, II. 63, 135. Cf. II. 43.

[62] *Philosophie des Unbewussten* (1870), Cap. BIII: 'Das Unbewusste im Gefühl', pp. 199–212.

7. In Defence of Realism

We have already seen how Bahnsen, in the manuscripts of the late 1850s and early 1860s, had questioned Schopenhauer's transcendental idealism. Bahnsen had argued that Kant's reasoning in the Transcendental Aesthetic, which Schopenhauer had accepted, leaves a gap: that even though the forms of space and time are a priori, having their origin in the mind, it is still possible for them to correspond to things-in-themselves. Bahnsen had not, however, made his doubts public and explicit. He finally did so, however, in an article he published in 1871 in the *Philosophische Monatshefte*, 'Zur Kritik des Kriticismus'.[63] At the close of this article Bahnsen calls his new position "realistic individualism", a phrase which captures well two of the defining traits of his gradually emerging worldview. While his 1870 *Zum Verhältniß zwischen Wille und Motiv* vindicates individualism, his 1871 article advocates realism.

Bahnsen's article begins with a protest against the dogmatism of the neo-Kantians, who treat any objection against Kant as a *crimen laesae majestatis*. They regard the Transcendental Aesthetic as a paragon of philosophical argument and proclaim Kant's transcendental idealism as the last word of wisdom. But, Bahnsen objects, in clinging to their master's doctrine the neo-Kantians commit the same old mistake as the ancient skeptics: though they claim that we do not know anything, they still make all kinds of claims to knowledge (351). They hold, for example, that we cannot know things-in-themselves, though that is really a claim to knowledge itself. To know that we cannot know, they must already know a lot: they must know the criterion of knowledge, and they must know whether our representations conform to things-in-themselves (352). If the neo-Kantians were to remain true to their own limits of knowledge, Bahnsen maintains, they would have to recognize at least the *possibility* that the a priori forms of intuition of space and time are still true of things-in-themselves (352). When Kant argued in the Transcendental Aesthetic that these a priori forms are true *only* for appearances, for representations of things, he made a dogmatic claim for which he had no further warrant (352). All his arguments for the a priori status, and therefore the subjective source, of the forms of space and time are still logically compatible with these forms applying to things-in-themselves, to the world not only as it appears to us but as it exists independent of us. In other words, it is still logically possible, even if we accept his arguments, that things-in-themselves are in space and time.

In making this point Bahnsen was simply reaffirming Trendelenburg's famous thesis in his *Logische Untersuchungen* that Kant's arguments in the Transcendental Aesthetic for the a priori status of space and time had left open the possibility that these forms still apply to things-in-themselves.[64] Not once does Bahnsen refer to

---

[63] Julius Bahnsen, 'Zur Kritik des Kriticismus', *Philosophische Monatshefte*, 6 (1871), 349–66.
[64] Adolf Trendelenburg, *Logische Untersuchungen*, Zweite ergänzte Auflage (Leipzig: Hirzel, 1862), I. 155–70.

Trendelenburg,⁶⁵ but by 1871 such a reference was entirely unnecessary: the dispute between Trendelenburg and Kuno Fischer about this possibility had become a public spectacle.⁶⁶ Bahnsen's argument for realism begins with and exploits Trendelenburg's possibility. When we eliminate the "only" in Kant's argument, he writes, then "the single reliable gate to the [Kantian] fortress is not merely opened or bashed in; it is lifted off its hinges" (357).

Bahnsen realizes that Trendelenburg's point, as it stands, provides no argument against idealism and no basis for realism. It supplies only a bare logical possibility: these forms might, but also might not, apply to things-in-themselves. Why take one possibility over another? Bahnsen replies that although we have no a priori grounds for realism over idealism, we still have good *empirical* ones, i.e. evidence from experience (361). There is solid empirical evidence, he contends, that the a priori forms of space and time actually correspond with things themselves; in other words, it is highly probable that the world consists in things that actually exist in different places in space and in different moments in time. This is because so much of the content of experience—where some particular thing is in space and when it appears in time—is just given to us and not created by us; it comes and goes independent of our will and imagination. Our experience reveals to us an enormous variety of things whose effects upon our sense organs cannot be due entirely to these organs themselves; these effects must also be produced, at least in part, by causes independent of them (363–4). To be sure, our cognitive faculty and our senses also condition what it is that we know; but this content is also not *completely* conditioned or produced by them. The differences in appearances must be at least partially referable to differences in the objects themselves (364–5).

In making his case for realism Bahnsen had connected that cause with his pluralism. The great difficulty of idealism, he maintains, is that it cannot explain the origins of the empirical manifold, i.e. the sheer variety of things or qualities that are present to our senses. The representations of these things or qualities appear independent of our conscious activity. Schopenhauer argues in book I of *Die Welt als Wille und Vorstellung* that the world is only *my* representation. But that leaves him caught inside his own solipsistic shell from which he can escape only by the weakest analogical inferences (351, 359). He assumes that there are other selves beside myself only because they have bodies similar to my own. But all the bodies of these apparent self-conscious beings are, following his own idealism, only my representations too (358–9). Schopenhauer's idealism gives us no reason to believe that there is a plurality of things in themselves, because he assigns the *principium individuationis* entirely to the phenomenal world. But if we are to avoid solipsism, Bahnsen argues, we have to assume that these other selves are more than my representations, that they are more than appearances existing only in my consciousness; instead, we have to suppose that each one of them is a thing-in-itself just as much

---

⁶⁵ Bahnsen knew Trendelenburg's work very well, citing it constantly in his *Der Widerspruch im Wissen und Wesen der Welt*. See all the references to Trendelenburg in the 'Register' to vol. II.

⁶⁶ On that dispute, see my *Late German Idealism: Trendelenburg and Lotze* (Oxford: OUP, 2013), pp. 107–20.

as myself (358). I know that my representations are mine simply because I also assume that they are not yours or that they are not his or hers; in other words, I assume there are other self-conscious beings like myself whose representations are no less theirs than my own are mine. Bahnsen then summarizes his new pluralistic and realistic worldview in a single sentence: "Self-consciousness and consciousness of the world reciprocally presuppose one another" (359).

With his realism and pluralism now more firmly in place, Bahnsen is much more explicit and firm in his individualism than he had been in *Zum Verhältniß zwischen Wille und Motiv*. He sees no reason at all for Schopenhauer's and Hartmann's assumption for a single cosmic will in the universe as a whole. The will is essentially a will to know, he insists, and as such we cannot separate it from its self-awareness, as if the *ratio essendi* were somehow distinct from the *ratio cognoscendi* (353). But if the will is connected with the subject or knower, Bahnsen implies, it is also an inseparable part of the *individual* who is that subject or knower. Just as I the subject know my representations as mine, so I the subject know my will as mine, so that it is essentially my *individual* will; there is no evidence for a further cosmic will within my own will (355). It is just a fact of my experience that this will in me does not have complete power and control over its world or even its own body; and it is for just this reason that it is fallible and finite, that it makes mistakes (354). This is an experience for which Hartmann and Schopenhauer, whose cosmic will is neither finite nor fallible, have no explanation.

For all his criticisms of Schopenhauer in 'Zur Kritik der Kriticismus', Bahnsen does not disown his old master entirely. "We are not the only ones", he writes probably alluding to Frauenstädt, "who have made the discovery about Schopenhauer that his works, the later ones most clearly, move along realistic paths" (362). In his *Naturphilosophie* Schopenhauer assumed that nature is the manifestation of the will, where the will exists independent of my self-consciousness (361). Like Frauenstädt, then, Bahnsen recognizes that Schopenhauer's system has both idealist and realist sides, While its idealism makes everything my representation, his realism makes everything an appearance of the will.

Yet old habits of loyalty died hard with Bahnsen, who should have let go even more completely. Although he suggests that he is still sympathetic to Schopenhauer's realism, the truth of the matter is that he had rejected the foundation behind it: monism. While Schopenhauer's realism is monistic, Bahnsen's is pluralistic. By 1871, only two links remained between Bahnsen and Schopenhauer: voluntarism and pessimism. We shall soon see how Bahnsen reconceived even these.

8. Philosophy of History

After their first philosophical exchange, Bahnsen vowed to met Hartmann personally, which he finally did in Easter 1871.[67] Bahnsen tells us that he was filled with hope and

[67] See Bahnsen's own account of their first encounter in *Wie ich Wurde Was ich Ward*, pp. 72–5.

anticipation when he finally arrived on Hartmann's doorstep in Berlin. But he was almost immediately disappointed. Hartmann, he felt, was surprisingly reserved, and even rude, because he did not get out of bed! He played the role of the sophisticated Berliner while Bahnsen was supposed to be the naïve country bumpkin. Still, the conversation was "pleasant enough", even though it had none of the intimacy of their previous correspondence.

Despite this shaky beginning, a friendship grew between Hartmann and Bahnsen. They would meet again on several occasions, sometimes vacation together, and Bahnsen even asked Hartmann to be the godfather of his son, whom he named Arthur Eduard Hartmann Bahnsen. It was a somewhat implausible friendship, however, partly because their temperaments were very different, and partly because their social standing was very unequal. Regarding their temperaments, Bahnsen later described himself as "open and lively", whereas Hartmann was "closed and calm". Regarding their social standing, Hartmann was aristocratic, established and successful, while Bahnsen was bourgeois, outcast and struggling.

Still, however improbable, the friendship proved philosophically beneficial. Both learned much from their interchanges. Bahnsen later acknowledged that he came to full clarity about his own position only thanks to Hartmann.[68] Though Hartmann made no such acknowledgement, he could well have done so, for, through his criticism of Bahnsen's individualism, he became much clearer about his own monism. Ultimately, though, it was Bahnsen who got most out of the friendship. While Hartmann was already famous when they met, Bahnsen was still a nobody from the provinces. In writing appreciative and substantive reviews of his early work, and in calling him "the single talent of the Schopenhauerian school", Hartmann gave Bahnsen much more recognition than he would have otherwise received. Thanks to Hartmann, the *Luftmensch* from the backwoods of Pomerania became one of the most controversial pessimists of his age.

In the midst of their friendship, and partly as an act of friendship, Bahnsen wrote one of his most important philosophical works, his 1872 *Zur Philosophie der Geschichte*,[69] which is a revealing account of the basis of his growing pessimism and his fundamental differences with Hartmann. The subtitle of the book is notable: *Eine kritische Besprechung des Hegel-Hartmann'schen Evolutionismus aus Schopenhauer'schen Principien*. Hegel's and Hartmann's "evolutionism" means their optimistic doctrine of historical progress, which is Bahnsen's chief target. Bahnsen professes to examine this doctrine according to Schopenhauerian principles, as if he were the true Schopenhauerian, and as if Hartmann betrayed that sacred legacy. Whether Bahnsen himself deserves that title we shall soon see.

---

[68] Ibid., p. 76.
[69] Julius Bahnsen, *Zur Philosophie der Geschichte: Eine kritische Besprechung des Hegel-Hartmann'schen Evolutionismus aus Schopenhauer'schen Principien* (Berlin: Duncker, 1872). All references in parentheses are to this work.

At the very beginning of *Zur Philosophie der Geschichte* Bahnsen gives a revealing statement of his fundamental differences with Hartmann (2). These differences revolve around their opposing approaches toward Hegel. Put crudely and simply, the opposition in their approaches amounts to this: while Hartmann accepts Hegel's rationalism and rejects his dialectic, Bahnsen accepts Hegel's dialectic and rejects his rationalism. More specifically, Bahnsen thinks that the dialectic is a real or objective process, whereas the logical or rational holds only for our thinking about the world; Hartmann, however, holds just the opposite: that the dialectic is just a method of thinking and the logical or rational is objective or real. Despite such fundamental differences, Bahnsen still praises Hartmann as a fellow pessimist, someone who also heartily wishes for the end of the world. If Hartmann only got rid of his lingering attachment to the realm of ideas, Bahnsen writes, they could walk down the path of nihilism together, fully recognizing that the goal of world-history is its self-destruction and nothingness (2).

Although his initial statement of their differences is very abstract and schematic, Bahnsen devotes most of his tract to explaining its precise meaning. Essentially, what Bahnsen rejects in Hartmann is his attempt to revive Hegel's rationalism, his effort to moderate Schopenhauer's voluntarism through Hegel's rationalism, and more specifically through Hegel's thesis that nature and history are governed by ideas.[70] *Zur Philosophie der Geschichte* is thus Bahnsen's critique of Hartmann's lingering rationalism. He saw that rationalism as problematic first and foremost because it involves a betrayal of Schopenhauer's pessimism and implies a return to optimism. As much as Bahnsen praised Hartmann as a fellow pessimist, he still held, like Nietzsche after him, that Hartmann had compromised that pessimism by combining it with Hegel's rationalism (7). Because Hartmann had so diluted his pessimism, Bahnsen does not know how to classify his philosophy: an optimistic pessimism or a pessimistic optimism (3)?

What, then, is wrong with Hartmann's rationalism? What philosophical grounds could there be against it? Bahnsen fires a whole battery of objections. One salvo revolves around Hartmann's dualism between will and idea. This dualism is so drastic, Bahnsen contends, that it is impossible to understand how the idea has any power over the will, or how it can be the will's driving force and goal (12). According to that dualism, it will be recalled,[71] the will is by itself only a blind striving, an unconscious urge, which does not have any specific goals or ends; the content of the will comes entirely from the realm of ideas, which have a validity independent of the will, and which lay down the ends of its actions. Such a dualism, Bahnsen notes, goes along with a fatal underlying premise: namely, Hartmann assumes that the ideas on their own have no potency and that they cannot act. But if that is the case, Bahnsen asks, how can they have any power over the will? The realm of ideas, as a mere realm of possibilities and abstractions, will be thus an historical irrelevance, standing aloof and apart from the realm of actuality.

---

[70] See Hartmann, *Philosophie des Unbewussten* (1870), pp. 686–7.
[71] See Chapter 7, section 4.

Bahnsen finds this dualism objectionable not least because Hartmann had used it to soften or moderate pessimism. The will itself, in its blind striving and deep urges, Hartmann held, is utterly indeterminate and limitless; it is also the source of all evil in giving rise to existence itself. The ideas, however, limit and restrain that will, giving it form and shape through definite goals and purposes. Bahnsen complains that this distinction is meaningless. He cannot accept Hartmann's view that the "that" of the world, its sheer existence through the will, is the source of evil, whereas its "what", as formulated in the world of ideas, is somehow innocent. "No, the source of our misery is not that we *are*, but that we are *who* we are—and that *who* rests upon the idea" (23). The source of evil in the world, Bahnsen contends, lies not in the mere fact *that* we will, but in the *conflict* of the will, in the tragic fact that the will has contradictory goals. This self-contradiction is the real source of suffering because the will never pursues its goal without also striving after an opposing goal, so that the result is eternal frustration and desperation (14, 53).

Hartmann's rationalism is most evident for Bahnsen in his retention of Hegel's panlogicism, i.e. Hegel's thesis that everything in nature and history is a manifestation of the idea. But that panlogicism, Bahnsen argues, suffers from the same fundamental problem as Hegel's: namely, it cannot explain the particularity and contingency of nature from the realm of ideas (19–21). The ideals form the realm of universal and necessary laws; but these laws, just because they are very general, are compatible with all kinds of particular instantiations, each of which is contingent for them, i.e. the ideas could realize themselves in other possible particulars. Because this aspect of nature falls outside the realm of ideas, Hartmann is then left with a dualism between the realms of the real and ideal, existence and essence. For that reason, Bahnsen concludes, we cannot claim that the realm of nature is governed by ideas; there remains an irrational residue or remainder sticking stubbornly to things.

The upshot of Hartmann's inability to account for the particularity and contingency of nature, Bahnsen contends, is his inadequate treatment of individuality (49). Although he makes it a prerequisite of an adequate idealism, Hartmann cannot explain the individuality of things any more than Hegel; in other words, he cannot account for how the primal absolute one becomes many or how cosmic unity splinters itself into a multitude of individual things. Rather than attributing any substantial reality to the individual, Hartmann ends out making it into a mere accident or mode of the single universal substance, just as Spinoza once did (50, 64–5). He then gives the Spinozist depreciation of the individual a cruel Hegelian twist by making the individual into nothing more than the means or instrument for realizing the ends of the universal idea. Never does Hartmann value the individual as such or for its own sake. He refuses to give it any substantial status, an independent essence and existence, because that would involve fracturing his "one and all", the cosmic unity of his absolute (70–1). Instead, he conceives the individual only as an organization of molecules, denying that there is an essence or nature behind that organization (71).

Because we cannot explain the multiplicity, plurality and individuality of the empirical world from the postulate of a primal unity, Bahnsen questions whether we should assume the existence of such a unity in the first place (50–1). If we do so, then the existence of multiplicity, plurality and individuality becomes an utter mystery (51). All that really exists, Bahnsen insists, is the existence of a plurality of individual wills. The one and all is really nothing more than "the sum of individual factors of life" (50, 64). Each of these individual wills has a substantial reality in itself; together they form only an abstract unity, which does not exist by itself. Bahnsen now makes an important distinction—one characteristic of his mature ontology—between the *essence* and *existence* of the individual will. Although in its *existence* it indeed depends on other individual things, it still has an independent *essence* or *nature* of its own. The realm of aeseity is now understood to hold only for the essences or natures of things. With this strategic distinction, Bahnsen believes he can preserve the independence of individual things and explain their *de facto* dependence on one another.

Another set of Bahnsen's objections against Hartmann's rationalism revolves around Hartmann's faith in historical "evolution", i.e. his belief in progress in history, or that mankind can achieve greater culture and enlightenment even though it cannot make itself happy. That faith involves a kind of rationalism because it presupposes that there is a single universal or absolute standard, deriving from reason, to measure progress in history. Bahnsen questions just this assumption, however, by invoking a standard historicist trope. How, he asks, can there be a single objective standard to measure progress in the face of all the flux of history (8–9)? All the changes in ethos in history make the assumption of universal standards suspect; they appear to be nothing more than the standards of our own time and place universalized for all mankind (10).[72]

Bahnsen swears that he does not intend to deny the existence of all progress in history (38). His only contention is that the movement forward in history should not be understood as a growth of reason itself, as if it were the greater manifestation and realization of the idea. Development is not "the self-exposition of a pure logically formed idea", as Hegel once thought and as Hartmann continues to think (38). There can be progress in this or that respect, in this time and place; but we should not think that this progress is unilinear, constant and accumulative (40, 82). One step forward in one respect often is a step backward in another respect. The wounds civilization cures it also inflicts. For example, the railroads are a cure for isolation in bringing people together; but they are also a source of isolation in putting distance between them. The real motor of historical "evolution", Bahnsen says, is the striving for greater comfort and prosperity in life (41). People are not satisfied with their lot, with what their parents had in the past, and they want to make things better for

---

[72] Despite this objection, Bahnsen himself had his doubts about historicism. In his own political philosophy he affirmed the existence of universal moral standards against the relativism of historicism. See *Der Widerspruch im Wissen und Wesen der Welt*, II. 224. He admitted, however, that the changes of history make it impossible to generalize a single definition of right, II. 237.

themselves. But this very striving creates new needs, so that we are no longer satisfied with the simple life of the past; and with the growth of needs there comes more sources of dissatisfaction (41). There is indeed an interplay, a direct proportion, between development and the receptivity and sensitivity to pain, so that the more we "progress" the more we suffer.

Bahnsen's ultimate objection against Hartmann's attempt to revive Hegel's rationalism derives from his skepticism about teleology. Bahnsen declares that regarding the status of purposes or ends he is a Kantian, i.e. he doubts that we have any right or reason to postulate the existence of ends or purposes in nature or history (17–18). All that we have the right to do is to proceed in our enquiries *as if* there were such ends or purposes. In more Kantian terms, the idea of a purpose, whether applied to history or nature, has a strictly *regulative* and not a *constitutive* status. By invoking this Kantian doctrine Bahnsen undercut Hartmann's and Hegel's theodicy entirely. There is no justification for talking about the *existence* of purposes or ends of history or nature. Bahnsen insists that we have the right to talk about the ends or purposes only of *individual* agents, and that we must not postulate the existence of a single universal subconscious will acting through them.

Such was, in sum and substance, Bahnsen's critique of Hartmann's rationalism in his *Philosophie der Geschichte*. Whatever the power of Bahnsen's arguments, they are interesting in revealing his abiding loyalty to Schopenhauer's pessimism, his resistance to any attempt to dilute or moderate that pessimism by mixing it with Hegel's rationalism. To be sure, Bahnsen would keep part of Hegel too, namely his dialectic; but then only its negative moment: that of contradiction, constantly renewed and never resolved in the eternal conflict of the will with itself.

But was Bahnsen's *Philosophie der Geschichte* the promised *Schopenhauerian* critique of Hartmann? Not entirely, for Bahnsen finally and rightly admits that in one crucial respect he is less Schopenhauerian than Hartmann: namely, Hartmann retained Schopenhauer's monism (72). Ultimately, then, Bahnsen's Schopenhauerian critique of Hartmann proves to be not so Schopenhauerian after all.

9. Hartmann's Offensive against Bahnsen

After the appearance of Bahnsen's *Zur Philosophie der Geschichte* in 1872, the relationship between Bahnsen and Hartmann began to sour. It was not anything Bahnsen said about Hartmann's philosophy that gave rise to their growing alienation. That book had only made explicit philosophical differences that were apparent from the beginning, and these were in any case no occasion for personal animosity. The problem lay rather in the inequality of the relationship, which began to chafe Bahnsen. Older, more successful and established than Bahnsen, Hartmann inevitably became the dominant partner in the relationship. He did much to help Bahnsen, referring him to doctors, supporting his application for a university position and giving him the opportunity to write book reviews. But the more he did for Bahnsen, the more the inequality grew and the more unbearable it became for Bahnsen.[73] Already in debt to Hartmann, Bahnsen felt obliged to support his literary cause, and so he wrote a laudatory review of the second edition of *Die Philosophie des Unbewussten* for the *National-Zeitung*.[74] But he soon regretted having done so, believing that he had violated his intellectual integrity and independence.[75] Worse yet, Bahnsen felt used by a literary clique, of which he was really not a member. When Hartmann wrote an anonymous self-critique,[76] Bahnsen too was duped, believing, like most people, that the work was really by a critic of Hartmann rather than Hartmann himself. When he later discovered Hartmann's authorship, he was offended that he had been left out of the secret. And so, almost as an act of rebellion, Bahnsen began to turn against Hartmann. The final break came in 1875 when Bahnsen—in an anonymous publication—charged Hartmann with "sophistry" for hiding his own views from the public.[77] After that, everything went downhill, rapidly. In 1878 Bahnsen wrote a review, which is really more a diatribe than a critique, of two of Hartmann's books for the *Jenaer Literaturzeitung*.[78] The contrast in tone and attitude between this review and the earlier one could not be starker.

Hartmann, of course, was not going to take this sitting down. He would not humiliate himself by engaging in Bahnsen's style of personal diatribes, still less would he compromise his *noblesse oblige* toward his social inferior. But he was determined to defend himself philosophically. First and foremost this meant responding to Bahnsen's polemic against him in *Zur Philosophie der Geschichte*. Through the screen of a philosophical self-vindication he would also let the world know what he thought of this Pomeranian school teacher and upstart.

Hartmann's main settling of accounts with Bahnsen came in his 1877 *Neukantianismus, Schopenhauerianismus und Hegelianismus*,[79] a polemical work written against the main philosophical currents of the day. Several chapters are devoted to Bahnsen, who looms large in Hartmann's discussion.[80] Hartmann made Bahnsen, along with Julius Frauenstädt, into one of the chief figures of "Schopenhauerism". Hartmann's counter-offensive is of great historical and philosophical interest: here we see clearly Hartmann's reasons for rejecting Bahnsen's individualism and extreme irrationalism

---

[73] In *Der Widerspruch im Wissen und Wesen der Welt*, II. 191, Bahnsen later wrote about how generosity is often motivated by cruelty because its recipient is made to feel powerless and indebted.

[74] *National-Zeitung*, No. 359, August 4, 1871, and No. 361, ug. 5, 1871. Unpaginated.

[75] See *Wie ich Wurde Was ich Ward*, p. 74.

[76] Anonymous, *Das Unbewusste vom Standpunkt der Physiologie und Descendenztheorie: Eine kritische Beleuchtung aus naturwissenschaftlichen Gesichtspunkte* (Berlin: Duncker, 1872).

[77] *Landläufige Philosophie und Landflüchtige Wahrheit: Unprivilegirte Forderungen eines Nicht-Subventionirten* (Leipzig: Krüger & Roskoschny, 1876), pp. 60–82. The tract appeared anonymously to avoid reprisals (p. 62).

[78] Julius Bahnsen, *Jenaer Literaturzeitung*, 23 (1878), 346–8. This is a review of two of Hartmann's books, *Neukantianismus, Schopenhauerismus und Hegelianismus* and *Das Unbewusste vom Standpunkt der Physiologie und Descendenztheorie*

[79] Eduard von Hartmann, *Neukantianismus, Schopenhauerismus und Hegelianismus* (Berlin: Duncker, 1877). Zweite erweiterte Auflage der *Erläuterung zur Metaphysik des Unbewussten*.

[80] Ibid., pp. 11–14, 31–8, 175–257.

and for holding his own monism and qualified rationalism. In this neglected work we can see why the paths of these great pessimists divided so sharply.

Before discussing his writings in detail, Hartmann begins with a general assessment of Bahnsen's talents and achievements. No one knew Bahnsen so well, and no one was more telling in exposing his strengths and weaknesses. Despite his falling out with his younger colleague, Hartmann strives for objectivity; after all, he could afford to be generous. Bahnsen, in his opinion, is "the single talent of the Schopenhauerian school", and it was only "with deep regret" that one could observe his fate "to waste away in the hintermost part of the hinterland of Pomerania" (13). But Bahnsen is to some extent to blame for his lack of recognition, Hartmann claims, because of the extreme obscurity of his writings. They are filled with colourful metaphors and striking ideas, of course, but they lack order and direction, so that no line of thought comes to a clear and definite conclusion (12). What Bahnsen lacks above all is "sobriety", the moderation and focus to make his thinking move in a straight line toward a single goal; instead, "he saunters like a drunk, swerving right and left and never going more than half way" (11). Hence Hartmann complains about the "zigzag movement" of Bahnsen's writing, which make it easy for the reader to lose the point, and which make it necessary to read behind the lines. In a single sentence Hartmann captures Bahnsen's strengths and weaknesses: "He is a completely original philosopher, but the originality is so sharply expressed that it borders on the bizarre" (11).[81]

If the form of Bahnsen's thinking is problematic, so is its content. Though a self-professed pessimist himself, Hartmann finds Bahnsen's extreme pessimism disturbing. Bahnsen wants to give free rein to the self-torment of the will, and to such an extent that that self-torment becomes an end in itself, indeed the very essence of the world (14). "The misery of existence is hopeless; neither the individual, nor the one-and-all, can find an exit from the hell of its self-dismemberment" (13). Bahnsen took too seriously Schopenhauer's thesis that this is the worst of all possible worlds; as a result, his own pessimism is so extreme that, rather than becoming tragic, it "sinks to the level of the most depressing desperation" (13). The net result of his pessimism is a kind of hypochondriac whining, which finds problems, evils and faults everywhere (14). Because it is so dark and depressing, Bahnsen's pessimism has indeed "a pathological character", so that one is led to question all his reasoning and general worldview. Hartmann even doubts the value of humour in Bahnsen's desperate world: his humour is filled with so much gall that it loses its liberating effect (14).

Hartmann characterizes Bahnsen's philosophy as a "system of individualism". Individualism is its most salient and singular characteristic, and the main point of conflict between their systems. The pluralism implicit in this individualism makes Bahnsen a distinctive figure in modern philosophy, Hartmann notes, since it pits him

---

[81] See also Hartmann's later, more generous assessment of Bahnsen in his Dec. 2, 1892, letter to Arthur Drews, in *Arthur Drews, Eduard von Hartmann, Philosophischer Briefwechsel, 1888–1906*, ed. Rudolf Mutter and Eckhart Pilick (Rohrbach: Verlag Peter Guhl, 1995), p. 48.

against the prevalent monism of his day, whether that is his own system, Schopenhauer's or Hegel's (38). In the eternal dilemma between monism and pluralism, the priority of the one or the many, Bahnsen had chosen the latter option, preferring to sacrifice the one-and-all for the sake of the reality of the individual (35). There is a good point to such pluralism or individualism, Hartmann concedes, because monism has a tendency to underrate or ignore the reality of the individual (36). But that does not mean, he quickly adds, that individualism or pluralism is a plausible position, because, on its own, it is only another extreme. The dilemma between the one and many is really a false one, Hartmann argues, because any proper monism can, must and should affirm the reality of the individual. The true monist does not regard selfhood, i.e. the reality of the individual subject, as an illusion but as a reality to be explained (215). When the monist says that the one-and-all is the single self in all individuals that is really only an inexact figure of speech (214). The one-and-all by itself, the single universal substance, is not a self or subject on its own, and it acquires subjectivity or selfhood only in and through the individuals in which it manifests or objectifies itself. The one-and-all is really only "the substantial root" or "the subsisting kernel" of selfhood, not selfhood itself (214). Hence selfhood attaches not to the absolute itself but only to its partial manifestations, to its finite or limited modes. It is the product of the absolute working within the phenomenal sphere and within an individual. The factors that produce the individual are perfectly real: they are (1) the real actions of the will in all the atoms of the organism and (2) the sum of all actions within the one and all which focuses its energy on this particular organism (215 n.).

We can take with good will Hartmann's insistence that the monist has to explain the apparent plurality of things in the phenomenal world. But Hartmann does not address the main difficulty facing his monism, the very difficulty stressed by Bahnsen: namely, how does the one become many? How does the one-and-all differentiate itself, turning into the multiplicity of different phenomena? To say that the individual is the result of the working of the absolute within the phenomenal world only begs the question how that world arises in the first place. In the end, Hartmann ducks the question, excusing himself that this is not the time and place to answer it (230).

But if Hartmann fails to defend his monism, he does go on the offensive against Bahnsen's individualism, and in the most telling and provocative manner. All individualism must collapse, he maintains, in the face of the relativity of the concept of the individual (277). What is an individual is an essentially arbitrary matter, because nature provides no firm and clear guidelines about how any of its productions can be regarded as a unity. Rather than facing this objection, Bahnsen simply sticks his head in the sand hoping that it will go away.[82] In making this point against Bahnsen,

---

[82] Probably provoked by these lines, Bahnsen did reply to this objection in *Der Widerspruch im Wissen und Wesen der Welt*, II. 90. Here he maintains that individuality is supplied by unity of consciousness, which does not depend on biological phenomena.

Hartmann appealed to the latest scientific work, more specifically Haeckel's morphology, which had argued for the relative meaning of the concept of individuality.[83]

Bahnsen's individualism makes it difficult to explain the interaction between things, Hartmann further argues, because each of his individuals has an independent essence and existence (229). On the premises of individualism it is impossible to explain not only interaction between substances but also the unity of each substance, because its unity has to be formed by the coming together of parts, each of which has an independent essence. Interaction is perfectly explicable according to monism, however, because all these apparently distinct individuals are only modes of a single substance (231). Hartmann says that Bahnsen once told him in conversation that there is nothing really that mysterious about the aseity of his individual substances; he admitted that it is difficult to explain how they arose out of anything if they have an independent essence; but he insisted that postulating an infinity of such substances is no worse than monism, which postulates one big mystery with its single substance instead of many little mysteries with individual substances (229–30). Hartmann "decisively" rejects this argument on the amusing grounds that the "craziness" of the world grows in direct proportion to the number of mysteries we postulate within it.

Hartmann's critique of Bahnsen focuses as much on his irrationalism as his individualism. Here again Hartmann felt thrown back on the defensive after Bahnsen's many criticisms of his rationalism in *Zur Philosophie der Geschichte*. He points out that Bahnsen's irrationalism is the result of two fundamental theses: that (1) the will is the ultimate source of reality, and that (2) the will is in constant conflict with itself. Hartmann finds this irrationalism just as extreme as Hegel's rationalism, and wants instead to walk the middle path of moderation between them. There is a problem, he argues, with both extreme positions. The irrationalist cannot explain the rational phenomena of the world, i.e. the fact that there is order and harmony, that things conform to laws and are necessary in their operation. The rationalist, however, cannot account for irrational phenomena, i.e. the fact that the existence of the world is utterly contingent, that it could be as well as not be. To explain these contrary phenomena, the rational form as well as irrational existence of the world, Hartmann argues that we must see the will and idea as two equal but independent attributes of the absolute. The problem with Bahnsen on the one hand, and Hegel on the other hand, is that they take one side or attribute of the absolute at the expense of the other (35). Bahnsen exaggerates the attribute of will, so that he cannot explain the order and harmony of the world; and Hegel overstates the attribute of the idea, so that he cannot account for the contingency of the world. Giving equal weight to both attributes, will and idea, Hartmann contends, allows us to explain both the rationality and irrationality of the world. While the will, as a blind force having no purpose or end, accounts for the contingent existence of the world, the idea accounts for its order and harmony, the subjection

---

[83] Hartmann supplies no specific reference. He probably had in mind Ernst Haeckel's *Generelle Morphologie der Organismen* (Berlin: Reimer, 1866), I. 243–68, esp. 244, 246, 262, 268.

of things to necessary laws. It is in these terms that Hartmann finally explains his rationale for giving equal weight to the realms of will and idea. Bahnsen's irrationalism, because of its one-sided voluntarism, can never explain the rational phenomena of this world, Hartmann charges. Bahnsen warns against hypostasizing ideas, treating them as if they could exist on their own and serve as a check on the power of the will; but he falls into the opposite error of hypostasizing the will, as if it could exist on its own without ideas (251–2).

Although Hartmann agrees with Bahnsen that there is an irrational dimension to the world, he interprets that irrationality in a different sense than Bahnsen. Bahnsen thinks that irrationality arises from the conflict of the will with itself. Hartmann, however, maintains that the irrationality of the world comes from its sheer existence, which is contingent. Such contingency is irrational in the sense that it marks a limit to the domain of law, where everything happens of necessity. It is sufficient to explain this irrationality, Hartmann contends, simply to point to the blind urging and striving of the will, which is a coming into being for no end or purpose (252). Such an urging and striving, because it is eternal and forever unsatisfied, is the source of suffering all on its own, so that we therefore do not have to assume that the will is in conflict with itself. Bahnsen had laughed at the apparent suffering of Hartmann's eternally longing will: since it has nothing opposing itself, it is like a crocodile that has nothing to eat; at least his crocodile, he implied, had something to eat, namely, its other half. Hartmann's reply takes the metaphor one ridiculous step further: if Bahnsen's crocodile always finds something to eat, it should be happier than his, which is forever hungry (254–5).

As the final parting shot of his polemic, Hartmann focuses on Bahnsen's real dialectic, which is crucial to his irrationalism. The central thesis of the real dialectic is that the will is in contradiction with itself. It is not enough for Bahnsen that the will is in *conflict* with itself, Hartmann notes, because he goes further and insists that this conflict is *contradiction*. Bahnsen thinks that, if the will is in contradiction with itself, then the basic law of logic, the principle of non-contradiction, does not have a grip on the world, so that the world is all the more irrational. Hartmann is quick to point out the chief weakness of Bahnsen's thesis: conflict and contradiction are different; conflict is no instance of, or basis for, contradiction (236–7). Conflict means that *two* subjects at the same time strive toward opposed states; contradiction means that *one* subject at the same time, in the same place and in the same respect, has two opposing states or properties. Now while it is true that there is conflict in reality, it is false that there is contradiction; so even if we accept Bahnsen's thesis that everything is in conflict, it does not follow that it is in contradiction; and so it is not the case that the world is irrational or illogical in Bahnsen's strong sense. The real dialectic prides itself on being illogical or irrational; but if we are to take Bahnsen at his word here, Hartmann warns, then he buys the absurdity of the world at a very dear price: the denial of all explanation, justification, reasoning and calculation (258). Hartmann concedes that there is some merit in Bahnsen's real dialectic: it stresses the inner conflicts in our mental life, and so it has made an important contribution to psychology (242). But pointing out these phenomena does not provide evidence for an irrational worldview, Hartmann insists. The real dialectic, as a statement of irrationalism, is worthless, "a knife without blade, heft or handle" (242).

When Hartmann made this critique of the real dialectic in 1878, Bahnsen's major work defending and explaining it—*Der Widerspruch im Wissen und Wesen der Welt*— had still not appeared. Hartmann tells us that he had been waiting for years for Bahnsen to publish his thoughts on the real dialectic (235–6, 240 n.). We will soon see what Bahnsen made of Hartmann's powerful objection.[84]

10. A Tragic Worldview

In 1877, after the demise of his friendship with Hartmann, Bahnsen published a short book on tragedy, *Das Tragische als Weltgesetz*.[85] It was meant to be a popular work, and it is indeed his clearest and most accessible. This is fortunate because this little tract is also one of the most important for understanding his entire philosophy. *Das Tragische als Weltgesetz* reveals the very heart of Bahnsen's philosophy, which is at bottom a tragic worldview. The purpose of Bahnsen's real dialectic is to provide a metaphysical foundation for his tragic vision of the world. Although Bahnsen's theory of tragedy is supposed to be only one application or aspect of his real dialectic,[86] it is really much more: the moral core and content of his worldview.

The characteristic feature of Bahnsen's pessimism, in distinction from that Schopenhauer and Mainländer, is the central place it gives to tragedy. Of course, Schopenhauer's and Mainländer's pessimism could be said to imply a tragic conception of the world; but then again neither Schopenhauer nor Mainländer make much use of the concept of tragedy in formulating their pessimism. For Bahnsen, however, tragedy plays a pivotal role in the formulation of pessimism. The heart of his pessimism lies in his real dialectic, the inner conflict of the will, which he sees as the source of tragedy.

In introducing the concept of tragedy into the pessimistic tradition, Bahnsen enriched and strengthened it. He was not, however, the first to take this step. Nietzsche had already connected pessimism with the theory of tragedy in his *Geburt der Tragödie*, which had appeared in 1872.[87] It is interesting to note, therefore, what Bahnsen has to say about Nietzsche. Although he does not mention him by name, Bahnsen does take silent issue with him in his introduction. "The friends of art", he writes, referring to Schopenhauer and probably also to Nietzsche, tell us that beauty is "a pleasant illusion",

---

[84] See section 12 below.
[85] Julius Bahnsen, *Das Tragische als Weltgesetz und der Humor als ästhetische Gestalt des Metaphysischen* (Lauenburg: Verlag von F. Ferley, 1877). All citations in parentheses are to this edition.
[86] Thus Bahnsen writes in the 'Vorwort' that the book is only "einen Ausschnitt" from his *Realdialektik* (p. vii). The *Realdialektik* was meant to have a much more general meaning, so that the aesthetic dimension is only one of its aspects.
[87] Friedrich Nietzsche, *Die Geburt der Tragödie aus dem Geiste der Musik* (Leipzig: Fritzsch, 1872).

"a resting place in the struggle for existence", "an invocation of the dream of heaven on earth" (5). But, Bahnsen protests, the real purpose of tragedy is just the opposite: it does not shield us from the horrors of existence through pleasant illusions, but it shatters all such illusions and forces us to confront the grim reality of the world, the harsh and brutal fact of self-division (6). Tragedy, then, does not attempt to give us an antidote, escape or reprieve from pessimism; rather, it strives to illustrate the deep truth lying behind it. It is only when we get beyond every illusion of optimism, when we tear away all the threads of the veil of Maya, Bahnsen contends, that we can begin to take pleasure in tragedy (7).

The very heart of tragedy, for Bahnsen, consists in two fundamental facts: first, that the individual has to choose between conflicting duties or incommensurable values; and second, that he or she will be punished, or have to suffer, because he or she obeys one duty or honours one value at the expense of another (87, 88). The tragic hero or heroine always does his or her duty or strives to act on his or her ideals; he or she is always brave and takes a moral stand and acts on principle; but he or she still has to pay the price for their courage and integrity, because there are conflicting duties, principles and values which deserve to be honoured no less. Because duties and values conflict, and because the tragic hero or heroine must act on some duty or value in a particular situation, he or she has no choice but to sin; they must violate another duty or disregard another basic value; and for that infraction or transgression they must be punished (50–1). The essence of a tragedy, then, is that we must do the right or act for the good, but that we will also be punished for it because we cannot help violating other duties and goods. Even with the best intentions and the most scrupulous conscience, we end up doing something bad and wrong, for which we must pay.

Bahnsen's theory of tragedy begins, therefore, with what is often seen as a fundamental fact about the modern world: the conflict between values, between incommensurable visions of the good life. Like Max Weber and Georg Simmel, Bahnsen does not believe that there is a rational solution to these conflicts or these visions. The fate of the modern individual is that he or she must choose between these values and worldviews, where the choice cannot be exclusively or entirely moral, correct or rational. That this fate is tragic is the central contention of Bahnsen's theory.

Bahnsen's tragic worldview was meant to be the antithesis of the optimistic worldview of Christian theism (103). According to theism, there is a divinely instituted harmony between moral virtue and personal happiness. If we do what we ought to do on this earth, then we will be rewarded for it in heaven; and, conversely, if we do what we ought not to do, we will be punished in hell. The tragic worldview not only questions this harmony, but it also denies a central premise behind it: that what we ought to do in life, our moral obligations and conceptions of the highest good, are perfectly clear and consistent. The tragic worldview begins, Bahnsen argues, with the recognition of moral conflict and unclarity. That conflict consists in not only clashing duties but also competing values and opposing conceptions of the good life. For the complicated situations in life, it will not be clear what we ought to do, either because we are subject to conflicting duties, or because of competing values, all of which are incommensurable, and none of which has more authority than another. Whatever we do in these situations will involve violating a conflicting duty or cheating other basic values in life. Every single action in life, Bahnsen remarks, takes place in the face of weighty and worthy counter-motives, and it has consequences so bad that, in some respects, not doing it would have been the better option (84). Hence, for Bahnsen, tragedy begins from a very important fact about our moral life, one not recognized by the traditional theistic worldview: namely, the relativity of morals, the lack of moral absolutes. This relativity is apparent not only from conflicting duties, but also from competing conceptions of the good life, where there is no right or wrong, good or bad, in choosing one course of action over the other.

Bahnsen's theory of tragedy was conceived not only in opposition to the optimistic worldview of theism, but also against competing theories of tragedy. First and foremost among these was Hegel's theory, which had been recently reaffirmed by Friedrich Vischer in his *Aesthetik*.[88] Bahnsen had attended Vischer's lectures on aesthetics in the Winter Semester 1851/52 when he was a student at Tübingen;[89] and he had worked out his own views by playing them against his teacher. According to Hegel,[90] tragedy is about the inevitable moral conflict between individuals, or between the individual and the social whole where the individual separates himself from the whole and takes a stand against it. While the individual is correct from his partial and one-sided standpoint, he is incorrect from the broader standpoint of the social whole, which has to harmonize the interests and standpoints of all individuals. The individual must suffer a tragic fate because his standpoint is one-sided and partial, or because he dares to separate himself from the whole. Tragedy pleases us, Hegel thinks, because it has a moment of reconciliation: we take pleasure in the downfall of the tragic hero because it satisfies our deeper feelings and intuitions about the greater moral authority of the social whole. For Bahnsen, however, there is no such moment of reconciliation. Tragedy is tragedy precisely because moral conflicts are irresolvable, precisely because there are incompatible conceptions of the good. There is no moment of reconciliation because there is no social whole that can resolve these conflicts or harmonize these conceptions of the good.

Bahnsen's theory of tragedy also marks a major departure from Schiller's theory which had played a major role for decades in German thinking about the tragic. Bahnsen was a great admirer of Schiller, praising him in a centennial address for his

---

[88] Friedrich Theodor Vischer, *Aesthetik oder Wissenschaft des Schönen* (Leipzig: Carl Mäcken's Verlag, 1846), §§117–139, pp. 277–321.

[89] As Louis informs us, 'Einleitung', p. xxxi. It is also noteworthy, as Louis explains, pp. xxxiv–xxxvi, that Bahnsen did his doctoral dissertation under Vischer on the subject of aesthetics. His dissertation was, *Versuch, die Lehre von den drei ästhetischen Grundformen genetisch zu gliedern nach den Voraussetzungen der naturwissenschaftlichen Psychologie* (Tübingen: Universität Tübingen, 1853). The work appears to have been lost.

[90] G. W. F. Hegel, *Vorlesungen über die Ästhetik, Werke in zwanzig Bänden*, ed. K. Michel and E. Moldenhauer (Frankfurt: Suhrkamp, 1970), XV. 520–6.

anticipation of Schopenhauer's pessimism.[91] Yet, if we read between the lines of *Das Tragische als Weltgesetz*, it becomes clear that he did not accept Schiller's theory of tragedy. According to Schiller, our pleasure in tragic events derives from the recognition of the moral qualities of the hero, who has the power to act on his duty despite the personal suffering that it causes him.[92] The spectacle of his actions is pleasant because it shows us the power of our moral autonomy and freedom, despite the pressure of circumstances, and despite our opposing personal inclinations. For Bahnsen, however, the autonomy of the tragic actor appears not simply in his resolve to act on his duties but in his willingness to choose one duty over another even though he knows he will suffer for it (86). Schiller, the follower of Kant's moral philosophy, believed that moral duties never conflict, and so he failed to appreciate the dilemmas facing the tragic character. Schiller assumes that the essence of the tragic hero resides in his acting contrary to inclination and self-interest and in following his duty; but, for Bahnsen, there is nothing tragic about having to choose duty over inclination, which is a commonplace of moral life (55, 64). Tragedy arises not simply because we choose to act on our duty against inclination but because in doing our duty we inevitably violate other duties (51). Schiller also wrongly assumes that tragedy somehow lies in acting according to one's conscience and one's better convictions; but here he assumes, wrongly, that our convictions and our conscience are perfectly clear and consistent. As Bahnsen puts it, convictions do not just drop into our heads like rain falls on a flower pot (32–3). Often we do not know what we really believe; and often we have to work this out for ourselves in pressing circumstances without ever really knowing, or having the opportunity to think about, our ultimate convictions and commitments.

In his analysis of tragedy Bahnsen very much emphasizes the inevitability of tragic action, the role of necessity or fate in the hero's downfall. He makes tragic necessity a basic criterion of tragedy. There are two basic criteria of tragedy, he explains. The first is that tragedy reveals some moral conflict (62); and the second is that this conflict, and the consequences that flow from it, be inescapable (67). This is not to say that the tragic hero is "pushed", that his own decision plays no role in his downfall (49). If his own will did not play a role, he would incur no guilt and he would not deserve punishment (67). Nevertheless, Bahnsen still insists that the tragic hero cannot be the complete master of his fate. He must also find himself in a situation over which he has no control; and once he has made his decision, the consequences must unfold inevitably, and in such a manner that he becomes the victim of that decision.

The fact that tragedy is inescapable and inevitable, Bahnsen argues, has an important consequence for pessimism: it shows that there really cannot be, *pace* Schopenhauer, Hartmann and Mainländer, redemption (53, 124). Their ethics of redemption is based

---

[91] Julius Bahnsen, *Schiller: Eine Gedächtnisrede gehalten den 10ten November 1859 im Gymnasium zu Anclam* (Anclam: Schillerstiftung, 1859).

[92] See Friedrich Schiller, 'Ueber den Grund des Vergnügens an tragischen Gegenständen', *Neue Thalia*, 1 (1792), 92–125. Bahnsen does not refer explicitly to Schiller's writing or even mention his name. But Schiller's theory was well-known, so well-known Bahnsen would have assumed his reader knew of it.

on the false assumption that we can somehow escape the world, whether it be through aesthetic contemplation, asceticism or suicide. But tragedy shows us that we are inevitably and inextricably caught in the drama of the world. When we must often prove our integrity by struggling against trying and demeaning circumstances, and when we have obligations and commitments to others and to the community as a whole, we cannot escape into another world or even annihilate ourselves. No, we are trapped here in this world; we must take a stand, fight and suffer the consequences (32).

There is, then, no redemption, no reconciliation, in Bahnsen's deeply tragic view of the world. This is not to say, however, that his worldview is grim or sad. For Bahnsen still offers some relief from all the suffering and tragedy of life. That relief comes from humour, in learning how to laugh at ourselves and our predicament. Humour makes us recognize our predicament and powerlessness but it also allows us to stand above it (107). By laughing at our situation we abstract and detach ourselves from it, and so escape, if only momentarily, from the fate and weight pressing down upon us. Although Bahnsen bids us to appreciate the role of humour in bearing the tragedy of life, he is at pains to insist that it still brings no redemption (123). It offers no enduring remedies, no fail safe recipes to escape from the suffering and moral dilemmas of life; its only power is to lighten the load and to prepare us for even more to come.

11. Prayers of a Pessimist

Always hoping and striving for literary success, Bahnsen wrote a book in the late 1870s that he hoped would capture the pessimistic spirit of his age. This was his *Pessimisten-Brevier*, which first appeared anonymously in 1879.[93] Although the book went on to a second edition, it had none of the success for which Bahnsen had hoped. He believed that he had misjudged the public mood, which was not really so pessimistic after all; and he complained that other events conspired against it: the assassination attempt on the life of the Kaiser made people suspicious of anything "nihilistic".[94] The book has been indeed long forgotten.[95] Yet, as a historical document, Bahnsen's *Brevier* should be judged a success. No other work represents so well the pessimistic spirit of late 19th-century philosophy.

The *Brevier* contains Bahnsen's most personal reflections on all aspects of the experience of life. None of these reflections, of which there are thousands extending over more than 400 pages, is more than a paragraph in length. Because they are so scattered, fragmentary and occasional, they resist easy summary and defy strict systematization. They attempt to capture a passing mood, to formulate an observation or to make a

---

[93] *Pessimisten-Brevier*. The book bears the subtitle *Von einem Geweihten* (Berlin: Theobald Grieben, 1879). The second edition appeared in 1881. All references above are to the second edition.

[94] See Bahnsen's account of the misfortunes of the book in *Wie ich Wurde was ich Ward*, p. 115.

[95] The book is rare. It has not been digitalized and stands in desperate need of preservation because of its brittle paper.

single point about the trials and tribulations of life. Bahnsen organized them according to general headings, though the order they impose is loose and artificial.

The *Brevier* is first and foremost a *modern* book of lamentation. Its modernity comes from the fact that it was written in a new secular age. Bahnsen is trying to come to terms with a world without God and immortality. What is it like to live in a world without providence, one with no divine order ensuring that the virtuous will be saved and the vicious punished? What is it like to live in a world without redemption, one where one's sorrows and losses will not be made good in another world? And what is it like to live in a world without personal immortality, where death promises nothing more than annihilation? Bahnsen's book describes the feelings, moods and thoughts of the modern individual who lives in just such a world.

The literary form of Bahnsen's *Brevier* seems to belie this secularism. He calls it a breviary, a prayer book, and he tells us that the pessimist too has his initiation rites, that he too needs consecration like any prophet (v–vi). It soon becomes clear, however, that the religious meaning is all pose and irony. Bahnsen is appropriating old religious language for new irreligious ends. There is no god to whom this pessimist prays. There is no higher power to hear his lamentations. Rather than an imprimatur from a religious authority, this brevier boasts a certificate of legitimacy signed by the greatest authority of them all: death (v).

Just as we would expect from Bahnsen, the *Brevier* paints a very bleak portrait of life. Many of his reflections reaffirm Schopenhauerian and Hartmannian themes, stressing the predominance of sorrow over joy, pain over pleasure, in life. We are told right away that there is nothing real but pain, which is the axis around which the world turns (6). Although there are indeed a few joys in life, they prove to be based on illusions (224), and they are always bought at a great price (43, 362). While there is no such thing as *pure* joy or pleasure, which is always mixed with sorrow and pain, there is such a thing as *pure* sorrow and pain; and if there are only a few kinds of pleasure, there are innumerable kinds of pain (217). Schopenhauer's old theme of the negative value of pleasure reappears when Bahnsen argues that the satisfaction of a need is never a plus, because it only returns us to normal, whereas the frustration of a need is always a minus, because it takes us below normal (230; cf. 369–70, 400).

The greatest pain of all, Bahnsen maintains, comes from the death of a loved one (6–7). When we lose someone we cherish, someone in whom we have invested all our heart, we are shattered into a thousand pieces; our inner world is filled with "the infinity of nothingness" (7). The most desolate emptiness of them all is "the dark feeling of loneliness" that comes with the loss of our nearest and dearest. In a world without providence, redemption or immortality, this loss is complete, eternal and irredeemable. There cannot be any comfort, there cannot be any compensation, for the loss. Of course, time heals all wounds; but we fear the dead becoming dead for us, because we know that, should we forget them, we too will be dead in our own best part (20). Hence the greatest consolation is not to be consoled at all and to nurture our feelings of loss (17). Those who would mislead us with religious ideas—with the thought of reunion in another world—are only tormenting us and desecrating the memory of the beloved (17). It is fortunate only that life is short and the days go by quickly (11). In saying all this Bahnsen was writing from personal experience. After his first wife, Minnita, whom he dearly loved, died in 1863, and after the second marriage ended in disaster, the memory of Minnitta became even more precious to him. He realized that he had duped himself in trying to replace her and that there was really no escape from her loss.

Although Bahnsen agrees with Schopenhauer and Hartmann that, when measured in eudemonistic terms, life is not worth living, it is noteworthy that he does not stress eudemonistic themes in formulating his own pessimism. The moral idealism that we saw emerge in the *Beiträge* now reappears in the *Brevier*. What makes someone a pessimist, Bahnsen maintains, is not the lack of pleasure, or even the presence of pain, but the frustration of goals, the violation of standards, the disappointment in not achieving ideals (61, 105, 246, 317–18). The great danger to having a worthy existence for Bahnsen comes not from unhappiness but from misfortune, which makes it impossible for us to realize our most important ideals or goals (102, 105). Misfortune can be so demoralizing that it becomes impossible to escape its effects by retreating into "the inner citadel", the favourite strategy of the ancient Stoics; it attacks not only the outer body or physical needs, but even our inner soul, our self-respect and integrity (80, 88, 102). Throughout the *Brevier* Bahnsen is obsessed with the role of fate and fortune in ruining our lives. It is an obsession perfectly fitting for his tragic view of the world; and it is in contrast to Schopenhauer and Hartmann, who stress more the mechanics of desire in making our lives miserable than the role of fickle fate.[96]

Slowly and tentatively, Bahnsen was working toward his own version of pessimism in the *Brevier*. The weak and tentative steps already made in the *Beiträge* now become stronger and firmer. They appear in Bahnsen's occasional critical comments on Schopenhauer's and Hartmann's pessimism. These comments are never explicit—the *Brevier* was not academic polemic—but, to any student of Schopenhauer and Hartmann, the allusions are unmistakable. On several occasions Bahnsen criticizes Schopenhauer's ethic of resignation and withdrawal. Fate can be so cruel to us that it destroys the inner world into which Schopenhauer and the Stoics advise us to withdraw. That inner world is no refuge because it is not immune from tragic conflict. We are often torn between opposing duties, so that the most conscientious and noble person becomes vulnerable and even his sanity threatened (292, 296, 298). It was all well and good for Schopenhauer to preach withdrawal and resignation; he was a hermit who had few responsibilities toward others; but most of us are caught in the web of life and have obligations that make it impossible for us to do anything but act (281, 293, 296). Before we decide to end the game of life, Bahnsen advises, we should make sure

---

[96] The appendix of the second volume of *Der Widerspruch im Wissen und Wesen der Welt* is devoted to 'Moirologie', the doctrine of fate (II. 459–97). Bahnsen sees fate active in the apparently accidental frustration of our most carefully laid plans (p. 464). The more we are concerned to achieve our plans, the more likely they are to fail. Those who most often fail are "the children of anxious care" (p. 459).

that all our obligations are voided; but that rarely happens, so that we are doomed to stay on this gloomy earth (281, 366).

Bahnsen is also critical of Hartmann's pessimism, especially his belief in historical evolution. Though a pessimist about happiness, Hartmann was still an optimist about history. Even if the individual could not be happy, he could find meaning in life by participating in the general struggle of humanity to improve culture. Bahnsen, however, finds the belief in progress illusory (201, 221, 222). History is not moving forward toward greater culture and morality, because it reveals fundamental contradictions that are never resolved in higher syntheses but lead only to nothingness (179). Bahnsen shares none of Hartmann's admiration for Bismarck and his confidence in the modern state. Bismarck's *Realpolitik* shows that the modern state is based upon little more than the lust for power, and that it has no moral scruples about getting it (176). The centralization, bureaucraticization and militarism of the modern state is levelling all differences between people and regions (180). Least of all does Bahnsen approve of the militarism of the modern state, which engages in secret diplomacy and treaties (179). It has no scruples about declaring war, though the result of war is seldom anything of value to the people (180). In criticizing Hartmann for his uncritical faith in the modern state, Bahnsen found an ally in another young pessimist (whose name he misspells): "Nitschke".[97]

For all its bleakness, Bahnsen's *Brevier* is not entirely negative. It has a positive purpose and content, even if it is heavily overshadowed by its gloom and doom. The *Brevier* was meant to be not only a book of lamentation but also a *vademecum*, a guide for the pessimist about how to cope with life in a tragic world. It is as if Bahnsen were aware of Hartmann's criticisms of his pessimism as a doctrine of despair, and as if he were eager to reply to them. For Bahnsen insists that his pessimist is not the "hypochondriacal whiner" that Hartmann made him out to be (212). Although his ideals and goals are often frustrated, the pessimist does not give up all hope (247). All-powerful fate is still impotent to take away the rays of hope for a better future (292). While the pessimist realizes it is unlikely that he will fulfil his highest ideals, he also learns to content himself with the little that he can achieve, and he does not allow the perfect to be the enemy of the good (266–7). Even if circumstances thwart him, he learns to appreciate what he has and how "to make the best of it" (252). The pessimist always struggles to maintain his autonomy, to be the master of himself, even if fate should often overcome him (387, 415). On no account does Bahnsen advise or even approve of suicide. To throw a life away, he admonishes, has no merit and it removes no guilt (294). Like Dühring, Bahnsen also recognizes and stresses that the positive experiences of life have their meaning and value only in contrast to the negative ones. Life has value only because of death (294), and the pains of love are necessary for its joys (295, 392).

---

[97] *Landläufige Philosophie und Landläufige Wahrheit*, p. 6. Bahnsen was referring to Nietzsche's critique of Hartmann in *Unzeitgemäße Betrachtungen*.

In stressing the positive aspects of pessimism, and in criticizing Schopenhauer and Hartmann, Bahnsen was stumbling and fumbling toward his own distinctive version of pessimism in the *Brevier*. He was still not there yet, however. He will formulate his own version of pessimism only in the final year of his life in one of his last writings. We will come to that article in due course.

12. Real Dialectic

From his earliest manuscripts Bahnsen had referred to his "real dialectic" (*Realdialektik*) as his personal philosophy and as the core of his worldview. He had failed, however, to provide a detailed justification or systematic exposition of it. He owed the world, and indeed himself, a fuller explanation. No one was more painfully conscious of this obligation than Bahnsen himself. In the early 1870s he had already set to work on his metaphysics and he had even prepared a cycle of lectures on real dialectic.[98] Still, nothing appeared, as Hartmann complained.[99] Such were Bahnsen's duties as a father, school teacher and administrator that he could not find the time or leisure to complete it. Finally, in 1880, he published the first volume of his systematic philosophy, *Der Widerspruch im Wissen und Wesen der Welt*.[100] The second volume appeared posthumously in 1882, though it was ready for publication before his death.

It is to the introduction of *Der Widerspruch*, which comprises the first half of the first volume,[101] that we must turn for a basic and systematic account of what Bahnsen means by "real dialectic". As Bahnsen explains it there, the real dialectic makes three central claims: (1) that contradiction exists in the very heart of reality itself and that it is not merely an attribute of our thought about reality (2, 5–6, 59, 62, 103); (2) that contradiction cannot be resolved and its result is entirely negative (5, 6, 23); and (3) that the source of contradiction lies in the will, which is the basis of all reality (2, 46, 49).

Bahnsen maintains that these claims are characteristic of his dialectic in distinction from the dialectics of Kant and Hegel. The first claim contradicts Kant's dialectic, which refuses to give objective status to contradiction; although it rightly sees that contradictions are necessary and natural to reason, the Kantian dialectic attributes them to our thinking about the world rather than the world itself (3). The second claim contradicts Hegel's dialectic, which holds that contradiction leads to a positive result, a higher synthesis of opposites (1). Bahnsen also maintains that Hegel, in attributing

---

[98] Bahnsen, *Zur Philosophie der Geschichte*, pp. 18, 57. On p. 18 Bahnsen speaks of a projected work, whereas on p. 57 he says that he has actually written something. Hartmann had seen some manuscripts that seem to have been drafts for his book. See his *Neukantianismus, Schopenhauerismus, Hegelianismus*, p. 240 n.

[99] Hartmann, *Neukantianismus, Schopenhauerismus, Hegelianismus*, p. 235.

[100] Julius Bahnsen, *Der Widerspruch im Wissen und Wesen der Welt: Princip und Einzelbewährung der Realdialektik* (Berlin: Theobald Grieben, 1880). The second volume appeared in Leipzig in 1882 with the same publisher. All references in this section are to the first volume.

[101] 'Das antilogische Princip. Einleitung in die Realdialektik', I. 1–210.

contradiction to becoming rather than being, does not give sufficient objective status to contradiction (1). Real dialectic makes contradiction an attribute of being itself, not simply of becoming or appearance.

These three claims are the basis of Bahnsen's "irrationalism", a doctrine that he expressly and emphatically maintains. They mean, Bahnsen insists, that the world is essentially and ultimately "irrational" or "anti-logical". By pointing out necessary but irresolvable contradictions in the world itself, real dialectic demonstrates the limits of logical or rational thought. While the laws of logic are indeed valid for our *thinking* about reality, they are not so for reality itself, which defies understanding because it is fundamentally contradictory. We must recognize, Bahnsen teaches, "the absolutely enigmatic nature of the world", the fact that we cannot resolve its puzzles because its contradictions are irresolvable (8). Real dialectic takes its starting point, therefore, in the "deep humiliation of thought" (9). "The germs of the real dialectic", Bahnsen writes, "grow from the mold of despair about the logical knowability of the world" (9). Thanks to real dialectic, "primal contradiction" (*Ur-Widerspruch*) finally rises from its Cinderella status and assumes the stature of a princess (11).

The irrationality of the world means, Bahnsen further explains, that what is impossible for logic—contradiction—exists in reality itself (94). The real dialectic affirms the reality of the logically impossible or the non-reality of the logically necessary (94). What logical thinking regards as impossible it therefore regards as factually necessary. But if this is so, if reality in itself is self-contradictory, then we have to abandon the old maxim *Ab esse valet consequentia ad posse* (105). This is because reality, as the self-contradictory, is *impossible* for the logician. Although the real dialectician maintains that the world is impossible logically speaking, he also holds, paradoxically, that it is (factually but not logically) necessary. This is because the self-contradictions of the world are necessary and cannot be otherwise. Necessity in itself is purely objective, attached to being and facticity and not secondary to the subjective necessity of knowing (112). Although the real dialectician acknowledges that there is contingency in the world, he insists that it is entirely with reference to its existence and not its essence (112).

The foundation for the central claims of the real dialectic Bahnsen finds in a "metaphysics of will" (2, 46, 49). The reason that reality is contradictory, and that its contradictions are irresolvable, is because it consists in the will, which contradicts itself (5–6, 46). Hence Bahnsen says that "the object" of real dialectic is the self-division of the will, which is the fact that the will contradicts itself (98). Bahnsen seems to hold that the will contradicts itself in two senses: first, it wills contradictory ends; and, second, it turns against itself, so that it denies itself or wills to not will anything (47, 52–3, 98, 174, 187, 207). Just why this is so Bahnsen does not fully explain. He leaves us, however, with many hints. We learn that the will desires death as well as life, that it loves and hates itself, that it is selfish yet self-sacrificing, that it wants solitude as well as company, that it is active and passive, sadistic yet masochistic, and so on.

In basing his real dialectic on such a "metaphysics of will" Bahnsen seems to relapse into his old Schopenhauerian ways, to cling still to the Schopenhauerian postulate of a single cosmic will which he had rejected in the early 1870s. But his argument need not presuppose that postulate: all his talk about "the will" could be seen as an abstract figure of speech, shorthand for talking about the multiplicity of wills in individuals. At least some such paraphrase of Bahnsen's language is necessary because he is explicit in *Der Widerspruch* in reaffirming his individualist metaphysics (21, 172, 200). Yet Bahnsen, as his critics pointed out, still vacillates. He also insists that, despite the importance it places on the self-division of the will, real dialectic has "a decisive anti-dualistic tendency" which appears in its assumption that there is a *single* substance divided into itself (44). It is only the indivisible unity of this will, he adds, that prevents the will from dividing the universe into distinct halves (46). No system is more jealous of the predicate "monistic", Bahnsen reveals in his penultimate chapter, than the real dialectic (430). Real dialectic, we learn, upholds the continuum of nature, which gives us "a true uplifting feeling for universal identity"; and it does not renounce "the consciousness of knowing itself to be one with the necessity of universal being" (431). It is fair to say, then, that Bahnsen never completely erased Schopenhauer's monism, traces of which persist even in his mature system.

The method used by the real dialectic, Bahnsen explains, is chiefly that of intuition (*Erschauen*) (30). Since his aim is to show the *existence* of contradiction, the real dialectician has to focus attention upon what is given within the realm of experience. His task lies more in showing facts (*Erweisen*) than in providing reasons (*Beweisen*) (28). Hence the real dialectician makes little use of the deductive method, viz., syllogisms, definitions, axioms and arguments (28). His method is more analytic or inductive than synthetic or deductive, i.e. he begins from observations and particular facts and from them ascends to more general propositions (28). But in observing the world and in drawing conclusions from his observations, the real dialectician, just like any other philosopher, still proceeds in a logical manner following the rules of ordinary logic (30). In revealing and explaining the contradictions inherent in the will, the real dialectician clarifies "the illogical through logical means". His task is "to make the antilogical thinkable", which he can do "only in logical ways" (35).

Following Schopenhauer's suggestion that the proper method of the philosopher is interpretation, Bahnsen states that the task of real dialectic is not to conceive or explain the world but "to understand" it, where understanding consists in interpretation (13, 14). Bahnsen was clearly writing after the development of hermeneutics by Boeckh, Schleiermacher and Droysen, and he is happy to claim this method for his own philosophy. But he immediately points out that hermeneutics, as it has been preached and practised so far, suffers from a false presupposition: the prejudice that the author is rational and consistent. His own hermeneutics will strive for just the opposite goal: to find contradiction.

The real dialectic is not speculation for its own sake, Bahnsen says, because it has an underlying ethical motive (13). His book will be "a work of redemption" (*Erlösungswerk*), because it will show, like Paul before the Jews, that it is impossible to find redemption through the law alone. Here, of course, "the law" is not moral commands but the laws of logic. Since the real dialectic shows that it is impossible to resolve the contradictions of the world, it shows that redemption cannot come from logic. But if we ask where redemption lies if not through the law, Bahnsen leaves us with no answer. Since the real dialectic shows that contradiction is irresolvable and the source of all suffering, it provides the basis for a complete pessimism (50). Redemption, it seems, lies in nothing more than abandoning all hope in redemption.

The most controversial aspect of Bahnsen's real dialectic concerns its claim about the objective status of contradiction. In saying this it appears as if Bahnsen violates the law of non-contradiction, i.e. that he maintains in one and the same time, place and respect, both P and not-P are true. Since denying that law is very problematic—it is to say the least self-defeating—the most charitable reading of Bahnsen would seem to be that he confuses *contradiction* with *conflict*: while contradiction is an attribute of speech or thought, only conflict can be an attribute of reality itself. While it makes perfect sense to say that things in reality are in conflict with one another—so this objection goes—it is absurd to say that they contradict one another. We have already seen how Hartmann made just this objection against Bahnsen.[102] Yet Bahnsen is utterly unrepentant: he wants to hold that there is not only conflict but contradiction in reality. He states emphatically and repeatedly that the *existence* of contradiction—in the full-blooded logical sense—is the central and characteristic claim of his real dialectic (2, 5–6, 59, 62, 103, 242, 418).[103]

There is, however, a simple and straightforward reply to this objection, one that removes the charge of committing a fallacy, and one that preserves something of Bahnsen's original intention in attributing not only conflict but contradiction to reality. On this reading, Bahnsen is not committed to denying the law of contradiction, i.e. to saying that propositions of the form 'P and ~P' or 'S is F and ~F' are true or valid in the same time, place and respect. All that he is saying is that *it is a fact that* the will contradicts itself, that it holds in the same time, place and respect contradictory goals or propositions of the form that 'S is good' and 'S is not good'. Just as it is a fact that people contradict themselves or hold contradictory beliefs, so it is a fact that the will contradicts itself and believes in contradictory values or pursues contradictory goals. So Bahnsen is not committed to saying 'S is good' and 'S is not good' are both true or valid, but only that the will *believes* and *acts* as though both were true or valid. Though the laws of logic are valid, they cannot prevent people from violating them.

[102] See section 8 above.
[103] This inevitably raises the question: had Bahnsen not read Kant's famous 1763 *Versuch den Begriff der negativen Größen in die Weltweisheit einzuführen*? In that work Kant had distinguished sharply between logical contradiction and real opposition, claiming that rationalists had confused the former with the latter, and that only the latter is found in nature (as a conflict of forces). Bahnsen had not only read Kant's work but refers to it frequently; see *Der Widerspruch*, I. 93–4, 195, 216, 241, 255, and II. 453. Bahnsen praises Kant's distinction between real and logical contradiction, making it seem as if all he wants is real contradiction (i.e. an opposition between forces). But he continues to write as if it does not prohibit talking about *contradiction* in reality (I. 241, 255). In II. 453, however, he appears to realize that Kant's limitation of real opposition to forces is not sufficient to represent the real dialectic. It is fair to say that Bahnsen deliberately misread Kant's text to serve his own purposes.

According to this reading, this is just what Bahnsen means when he stresses that it is simply *a fact* that the will contradicts itself (59). The laws of logic still have a normative validity because they tell us how we *ought* to think; but they do not banish the *existence* of contradictions themselves because it is a simple fact that people do contradict themselves (indeed, if they did not, there would be little purpose to the norms). Bahnsen's point is that we must not let the normative validity of the laws of logic blind us to the nature of reality itself. He indeed insists that we must not hypostasize these laws, as if they were true of reality itself, when they are valid only for our thinking about reality (154-5). The nature of reality consists in the will—a metaphysical or psychological thesis about which logic is entirely neutral—and it is a fact that the will contradicts itself, and that it does so in a perfectly straightforward logical sense, because, as Bahnsen explains, it "wills what it does not will and does not will what it wills" (53; cf. 98, 174, 187, 207). Here we must keep in mind, of course, that Bahnsen, as a pluralist, is talking only about *individual* wills and not about a cosmic will. For the thesis of the reality of contradiction to be true, all that Bahnsen needs is the fact that particular people have contradictory desires.

As evidence for this reading there stands Bahnsen's insistence that he does not intend to dispute or deny the laws of ordinary logic. Against those who charge him with advocating or allowing nonsense,[104] he protests he is no rebel against the laws of logic, which he regards as perfectly true for our thinking about things (56–7, 61, 63–5, 207). The real dialectic, he expressly says, does not permit or seek contradiction in the field of logic (63), and it leaves "the logical relationship between concepts entirely intact" (64, 82, 88). It concedes that reason should hold sway over "the faculty of abstraction" (i.e. concepts, judgements and reasoning) (82, 88), and it thus "leaves to Caesar what is due to Caesar" (65; cf. 82, 88). All that the real dialectic maintains, however, is that reality itself is not logical, and that it is not logical because its source is the will which contradicts itself.

Even for this charitable reading, however, there are still serious problems with Bahnsen's real dialectic. Although Bahnsen is perhaps not guilty of violating the law of contradiction, he still fails to provide sufficient evidence for his central thesis that reality itself is contradictory. All the evidence Bahnsen mounts for his real dialectic show only that there is conflict, not contradiction, in reality. His evidence comes from two different areas: psychology, which points out the inner conflicts of the soul; and physics, which points out the interplay of opposing forces in magnetism, electricity and gravity. The second volume of the *Beiträge* goes to great lengths in talking about the "antinomies" of the soul;[105] and the second part of volume I of *Der Widerspruch* goes

---

[104] In addition to Hartmann, *Neukantianismus, Schopenhauerismus, Hegelianismus*, pp. 242, 258, this charge was made by Johannes Volkelt in his review of *Zur Philosophie der Geschichte* in *Philosophische Monatshefte*, VIII (1872), 282–96, esp. 295, and by Johannes Rehmke in *Unsere Zeit*, November 1876, p. 776.

[105] See *Beiträge zur Charakterologie*, 'Problematische Naturen', II. 1–35, and 'Die Antinomien des Gemüths', II. 125–224.

into great detail about the workings of the real dialectic in natural phenomena.[106] The more closely we examine this evidence, however, the more plain it is that it demonstrates conflict but not contradiction. Never does Bahnsen succeed in showing, or even in explaining, that in one and the same respect, and in one and the same time and place, the mind or nature is both F and ~F. It is indeed the case, for example, that the soul both loves and hates, is self-preservative and self-destructive, abhors loneliness and desires solitude, that it is intensely selfish yet self-sacrificing. All this is true, but not at the same time and in the same respect, as if we could both affirm and deny any given proposition about the soul. Similarly, though it is also the case that gravity consists in attractive and repulsive forces—that its force of attraction will shrink it to a single point and that its force of repulsion will expand it to infinity—this does not demonstrate for one and the same force that it is both attractive and repulsive. Even if we can view the same force as positive and negative, it is still not the case that it is positive and negative in the same respect and at the same time. The problem with the real dialectic, then, does not so much reside in its "absurdity", in its attributing reality to contradictions, but in the lack of empirical evidence for these alleged contradictions.

Limiting the real dialectic to the existence of conflict rather than contradiction makes it a much more plausible worldview, and still an interesting and informative one. But such a limitation also comes at a price: for Bahnsen then has to abandon his irrationalism, which is committed to the thesis that reality violates the law of contradiction. It is still open for Bahnsen to argue for the limits of reason, as he indeed goes on to do in the second half of volume I, where he contends that reason or the discursive intellect cannot grasp central aspects of reality, viz., the realms of individuality, continuity and quality. None of this would show, however, that the world is *irrational*, i.e. that it *violates* logical laws, but only that it is *non-rational*, i.e. that it does not fall under their jurisdiction.

13. Ethics and Politics

Bahnsen's magnum opus—*Der Widerspruch im Wissen und Wesen der Welt*—intends to be nothing less than a general system of philosophy, the systematic expression and justification of an entire worldview. While volume I sketches Bahnsen's epistemology, logic and natural philosophy, volume II outlines his ethics, politics, philosophy of history and theory of religion. The meaning of Bahnsen's worldview becomes clear and concrete only when we examine its application to the ethical and political sphere.

The central theme of Bahnsen's ethics and politics is his *individualism*, i.e. his belief in the irreducible reality and ultimate value of the individual in society and state. This

---

[106] See *Der Widerspruch im Wissen und Wesen der Welt*, '17. Die Polarität in ihrer allgemeinen Gesetzmässigkeit als Verhältniss des Physischen zum Logischen', I. 341–59; '18. Das homöopathische Princip', I. 359–74; '20. Die Gravitation nach physikalischer und metaphysischer Auffassung', I. 380–410; '22. Der Chemismus', I. 424–36.

is exactly what we expect from the author of the *Beiträge zur Charakterologie*, who had not only explained but advocated individual difference. But it is also just what we expect from the author of *Die Philosophie der Geschichte*, who had defended a metaphysical pluralism against Hartmann's monism. Hence the foundation for Bahnsen's ethical and political doctrines lies with his psychology and metaphysics. If psychology shows the uniqueness of the personality, and if metaphysics demonstrates the irreducible reality of individual things, then society and the state must recognize, and indeed revolve around, personality and individuality.

The individualistic theme of Bahnsen's ethical and political doctrines is immediately apparent in his theory of the basis of right or law. The source of right or law, Bahnsen maintains, derives from the individual self (238, 250).[107] This is not the *egoistic* self with its present desires and needs, Bahnsen hastens to add, but the *autonomous* self who has the power to impose laws upon itself and to restrain its desires and needs according to them. In the tradition of Rousseau and Kant, Bahnsen maintains that the will of the autonomous self is the source of all law, i.e. no law has legitimacy unless it has the consent of the individual (250–1).

The close connection of Bahnsen's ethics and politics with his metaphysics becomes clear as soon as we consider the antithesis of his individualism: metaphysical holism, according to which the reality of the individual exists only in the cosmic whole or absolute. When applied to ethics and politics, this holism maintains that the rights of the individual derive from the community or the state. Just as Bahnsen rejects Hegel's and Hartmann's metaphysical holism, so he repudiates their ethical and political holism. He maintains the precise opposite of such holism: that the rights of individuals are not based on the community or state, but that the legitimacy of the community or state is based on the rights of individuals. The state is not an end in itself but only a necessary evil, the indispensable check against evil impulses where one individual encroaches on the rights of others (338).

Against the holists, Bahnsen makes two arguments. First, to justify the lawful relations between individuals, to establish their duties and rights, it is not necessary to postulate the existence of an absolute substance or whole. It is sufficient, he maintains, if we just assume the existence of *interrelations* between individuals (209, 229, 251). The community arises from need, the need of individuals for one another, and the resulting mutual dependence between them (291). Second, to assume the existence of an absolute whole or substance is not only unnecessary; such an assumption also undermines the rights of the individual because it treats them as mere modes or parts of the whole, a mere means for the ends of the state (287–8).

Given his rejection of holism, it not surprising to find Bahnsen warning against the growing powers of the state in the modern world. He abjures its increasing centralization, bureaucratization and militarization, which he regards as threats to individual

---

[107] All references in parentheses are to volume II of *Der Widerspruch im Wissen und Wesen der Welt* (Leipzig: Theobald Grieben, 1882).

freedom and diversity. The modern state is taking over many functions that once belonged to the family, the church or the individual, so that virtually all aspects of life are becoming regulated and directed from above (299, 378–9). But if the weight of the collective whole is too great, Bahnsen cautions, then it smothers individual initiative, autonomous groups and personal freedoms (221–2). Bahnsen's warnings about the growing power of the state apply to the right as well as the left. He hated the conservative Bismarckian state as much as the radical social-democratic one. Though they had opposing ends, both kinds of state were still alike in their means, in giving greater powers to the state over the individual. It was no accident, in Bahnsen's view, that Ferdinand Lassalle, the leader of the social democrats, began as an Hegelian: he divinized the state as much as Hegel, only he did so for his egalitarian ends (370). As a bulwark against the centralization and bureaucratization of the modern state, Bahnsen advocates a social and political pluralism, i.e. a society which consists in many autonomous groups and local forms of authority.

Because of his individualism, one might surmise that Bahnsen is a liberal of the classical 19th-century variety, i.e. someone who advocates free trade, the restriction of the powers of the state and the right to pursue self-interest. But Bahnsen decidedly rejects what he calls "Manchesterism", i.e. the doctrines of Smith, Ricardo and Mill as they were developed and applied by the Manchester school in early 19th-century England.

Bahnsen regards Manchesterism as a form of "pseudo-individualism", because it does not appreciate the real diversity among people but reduces all individuals down to a standardized mould (304, 375). The individual is nothing more than a unit of labour or consumption, where each such unit is like every other in qualitative terms, and where it is unlike others only in quantitative ones, i.e. *in how* much it produces or consumes (304, 375). Bahnsen regards Manchesterism as little more than a generalized egoism, which allows the individual the maximal freedom to pursue its natural appetites and self-interest. But the individual that is the basis of the state, he insists, is not the egoistic but the autonomous individual. While the egoistic individual chases after its own natural desires, the autonomous individual submits to law of its own free will, limiting its natural desires according to the mandates of the law.

It is in the name of his true individualism that Bahnsen rejects the egalitarianism of the social democrats and communists. Like Hartmann, Nietzsche and Taubert, Bahnsen regards this egalitarianism as a dangerous levelling force which threatens to make everyone alike by ensuring that everyone has the same education and income. The homogeneity implicit in the modern principle of equality is for him "one of the most despotic of political maxims" because it will suffocate natural differences and spontaneity (303, 382–3). According to his principle of individuality, the best society and state is not one where everyone receives and contributes the same, but one where everyone receives and contributes differently according to their unique talents and abilities (356–7). In thus repudiating egalitarianism Bahnsen insists that he does not mean to promote or protect the old rights of the aristocracy. Although he wants people to contribute, earn and receive differently according to their naturally different talents and abilities, he does not believe in the value of inherited wealth and privilege (303). What he wants is an aristocracy of merit rather than an aristocracy of money or privilege, i.e. what he calls an *Aristokratie des Geistes* instead of an *Aristokratie des Geldes*.

Bahnsen's individualism is the central theme not only of his politics but also of his ethics. It plays the leading role in his long treatment of love, sex and marriage, which comprises five chapters of volume II.[108] Like any romantic, Bahnsen celebrates the power of love in overcoming our natural egoism; love involves the natural desire to surrender ourselves, to give ourselves over to the needs and desires of the other (193–6). But he also insists that love cannot and should not be mere selflessness, as if the lover should completely deny or abandon himself for the sake of the beloved (138, 163). If the loving self humiliates itself—if it demeans itself, thinks nothing of itself and allows the beloved to dominate itself—then it makes itself less worthy of love (139). Love should be not only self-surrender but also appropriation of the other, so that the self gains as much as it loses (172). Because whom we love is not just any instantiation of an ideal but this or that *particular* person, love presupposes the value of individual differences (169). For just this reason, then, each lover should maintain his or her individuality in their love.

The same individualistic theme emerges in Bahnsen's critique of the ethics of sympathy and asceticism. Schopenhauer had praised the triumph of the ascetic and mystic over the individual ego, his or her power to extinguish their individuality in the cosmic whole. But Bahnsen maintains that the value of self-denial has to be balanced by self-affirmation (180). We should never be so sympathetic to others or so self-sacrificing that we deny the value of our own selves. Absolute devotion to others still demands that we have a self to give to them (181). A person who goes beyond the limits of self-respect to serve others makes himself contemptible (183). He deserves no more respect than someone who sells himself into slavery (181). In Bahnsen's critique of selfless devotion it is possible to detect his reservations about Mainländer's ethics, one of the few instances in his writings where he explicitly refers to his fellow pessimist.[109]

Nothing more aroused Bahnsen's moral indignation than *Realpolitik*, which had been practised so shamelessly by Bismarck. The *Realpolitiker* assumes that the end justifies the means, and that the end is first and foremost power. Like Rousseau and Kant, Bahnsen insists that politics must be founded on the principles of morality, and that the statesman has no right to exempt himself from them. The only difference between power and rightful power, he tells us, is that rightful power has a moral foundation. But what are the principles of morality? And what foundation do we give them? If the basis for law is the will of the autonomous individual, what ensures that its will is moral? It

---

[108] Chs 5–9, II. 106–205.
[109] Bahnsen explicitly mentions Mainländer by name, II. 192. He denies that there is any necessary moral value in desiring to destroy all existence, given that desire might have an egoistic motivation alone. But beyond this particular point, it is plausible to see the general critique of asceticism as directed against Mainländer as well as Schopenhauer.

cannot be that whatever it wills is right just because it wills it, which would be the worst form of *Realpolitik*.

The question remains how Bahnsen attempts to provide a moral foundation for his individualism. But on this all important question Bahnsen does not develop a clear and consistent position. He states his commitment to the existence of universal and necessary norms which have an unconditional validity (224), and he disputes the historicist claim that the change of norms in history provides evidence for a complete relativism (224, 237). But what grounds superhistorical norms—what gives them their universal and necessary validity—is a question that Bahnsen does not systematically answer. He flatly rejects Kant's attempt to base moral principles upon pure reason. He dismisses the categorical imperative as "the discovery of old wives' wisdom" (216), and he stresses its emptiness, claiming that "nothing is so bad that it cannot be justified by subsumption under a universal concept, and nothing is so good that it in the same way can be made to appear damnable" (276). Of utilitarian doctrine he has an even worse estimate, because he regards questions of pleasure and pain as irrelevant for a consideration of the rightness or wrongness of an action (88, 216–17).

Despite his dismissal of utilitarianism, Bahnsen still suggests in some passages something like a eudemonistic foundation for ethics. As a good pessimist he states that the basis of moral obligation arises from the experience of human suffering, from our awareness that things are not as they should be because we suffer (211–12). The fundamental norms or obligations of morality are for him, as for Schopenhauer, negative, commanding us to avoid suffering and evil (213). They find their basic expression in the *Neminen laede* of classical natural law theory. If we were to put the basic duties of morality in a more positive form, Bahnsen proposes, they would prescribe that everyone should share the burden of existence, so that no one takes on too much or does too little (214). In determining how these general laws apply to any specific situation, Bahnsen advises the use of "tact" and "instinct" (235). We know from intuition and feeling, rather than from any abstract reasoning, how we should act in particular circumstances; general principles are at best only rules of thumb. How we ground these principles, though, Bahnsen still leaves up in the air. His eudemonistic foundation is never developed in any detailed manner. Never does he explain, for example, how the principle of sharing burdens equally follows from the basic principle of avoiding harm.

One might argue that in asking for a foundation of morals from Bahnsen we are pursuing the wrong question, given that, in an important sense, he disputes whether there can be any such thing as a foundation for morality. The central contention of his real dialectic is that moral obligations conflict and that, for any given situation, there is no right or wrong answer about what we should do. Sure enough, Bahnsen never ceases to remind us of his real dialectic—the panacea for all conceptual ills—in his chapters on ethics and politics. Real dialectic reveals itself in the philosophy of right, he explains, when it shows the impossibility of deriving absolute right from one side or perspective alone (273). Still, it is not so clear that we are asking the wrong question. Arguably, Bahnsen's real dialectic comes into play not with regard to the *basis* of moral principles but with regard to their *application*. We find contradictions in moral principles, in other words, only when we attempt to apply them in the complicated situations of moral and political life. It is these situations, not the abstract principles themselves, that give rise to the contradiction. In any case, Bahnsen's own firm espousal of universal and necessary moral principles makes it necessary to limit his real dialectic to the application of morals rather than the principles themselves. But then we are still left high and dry regarding the foundation of these principles. As so often in Bahnsen's philosophy, the demand for answers ends with a question mark.

14. The Pessimist as Tragic Hero

Although for decades Bahnsen had described his worldview as "pessimism", he had devoted surprisingly little attention to the meaning of this concept. He had done much to explain the real dialectic, which was meant to be the foundation for his pessimism; but he had done little toward explaining the attitude itself. How, precisely, does pessimism differ from optimism? How does it differ from cynicism? Is it a form of quietism? Is it guilty of immoralism? All these basic questions lacked answers. While Bahnsen had addressed some of them in the *Brevier*, he had not done so in a sustained and systematic fashion; his reflections were sporadic and scattered over hundreds of pages.

The need to fill this gap became painfully clear to Bahnsen in the late 1870s. By then "pessimism" had become a *Modebegriff* and it was on everyone's lips. Popular use had so stretched the word that it virtually emptied it of meaning. Even worse, pessimism had become the target for all kinds of censure and criticism, which all too often were based on misunderstandings. So Bahnsen had not only to define the term but also to parry these criticisms. Yet that was not all. The need to provide a fuller explanation of "pessimism" became all the more pressing when Bahnsen finally realized that the meaning he gave to this concept differed in important respects from Schopenhauer and Hartmann. By the late 1870s Bahnsen had developed a pessimism all his own, and it was high time that he distinguish it from that of his former teacher and from that of his ex-friend and now rival.

Bahnsen turned to this pressing task in one of his last writings, an article he wrote from 24 April to 5 May 1881,[110] 'Zur Verständigung über den heutigen Pessimismus'. The article was not published in his lifetime and appeared first as a chapter of his posthumous autobiography.[111] Although nearly forgotten, Bahnsen's essay is an important document in making clear the final meaning he gave his pessimism.

"Pessimism" nowadays, Bahnsen complains, is used to justify every negative mood and fit of hypochondria (165). It appears as if it describes only a personal or individual attitude toward the world, as if one person could be an optimist and another a pessimist. But Bahnsen decidedly rejects any attempt to reduce pessimism down to a matter

---

[110] The dating is that of Louis in his introduction to *Wie ich Wurde was ich Ward*, p. xxiii.
[111] *Wie ich Wurde was ich Ward*, pp. 163–83.

of personal attitude or individual temperament. Pessimism would be utterly "lame", he insists, if it were not a worldview (168). For it to be a worldview means that it must make a claim to universality, that it should put itself forward as the proper attitude toward life for everyone alike. This is not to say, however, that pessimism should be only a theory, an academic doctrine. Ultimately, it has to be based upon the life of its protagonist, who knows from personal experience what it means to suffer (173–4). All philosophy, Bahnsen insists like a good Kantian, has to be based upon experience, and the pessimist's worldview is no exception to that rule. It is just that the pessimist should not leave his experience on the level of the strictly personal; he should draw general conclusions from it, so that it claims to represent the experience of human beings in the world.

It is one of the greatest misunderstandings of pessimism, Bahnsen believes, to think that it should involve withdrawal from the world, a complete indifference and resignation to what happens within it. Pessimism, he insists, is opposed to everything "mollusc-like" (177), and it offers no narcotics for someone to retreat into "a spineless and fibreless quietism" (172). Rather than letting the world run over him, the pessimist should take a stand and fight against it; he adopts a "defensive posture" and engages in battle with the world. The pessimist's motto is *Vivere est militare*, and his attitude is "Never cease to fight" (*Zu-kämpfen-nicht-aufhören-können*) (175). In rejecting quietism as the proper attitude of the pessimist, Bahnsen had taken issue, though only silently, with Schopenhauer's pessimism. His departure from his former master is unmistakable, even if still not explicit, when he abjures asceticism as an "impotent velleity" (173).

The pessimist, Bahnsen makes it clear, is at heart an idealist (168). What makes someone a pessimist is not suffering, the failure to achieve personal happiness, but all too frequent disappointment, all too common frustration of their ideals. But disappointment and frustration does not mean, Bahnsen insists, that the pessimist abandons his ideals; rather, he continues to fight for them, even in the face of probable defeat (175). Even if the pessimist has little hope, he still has much courage (180). Someone who loves nothing, who is not convinced of the value of anything, Bahnsen writes, is a mere "Murrkopf", i.e. a moaner and whiner, who has no right to judge the world (174). Because he is still an idealist, the pessimist would like to be an optimist (175); but he realizes, as the optimist does not, that life is never easy and that he will have to fight to advance only a little way toward his goals (175).

Pessimism, as Bahnsen describes it, is therefore utterly opposed to cynicism, the Mephistophelian spirit that ridicules all ideals. That cynical spirit was a commonplace in his day, appearing in the *Realpolitik* of Bismarck and the German conservatives. For Bahnsen, however, *Realpolitik* is contemptible, abandoning the very ideals which the pessimist wants to defend (179).

The true pessimist, Bahnsen explains, is neither cynic nor dreamer; he strives for the middle ground between these extremes because he has "an idealist heart" and "a realist head" (171). He has an idealist heart insofar as he is devoted to his ideals and never abandons them, because he feels for the suffering of others and wants to improve their lot. He has a realist head insofar as he realizes that nothing important is achieved in this world without struggle, and that all too often struggle ends in defeat or at best incremental gains. Though he has to battle against trying circumstances, he still resolves "to make the best of it", Bahnsen writes, using the English phrase.

What is it, though, that keeps the pessimist fighting for his ideals in the face of so much defeat? What motivates him to persist? Bahnsen has an interesting answer to this question. The enduring source of the pessimist's idealism, he explains, lies in his sympathy for the suffering of others (170, 182). The "heart" of his idealism lies exactly here: in his power of feeling, in placing himself in the position of others and doing all he can to help them. Because he is motivated by his sympathy, the pessimist will do all he can to alleviate the suffering of his fellow human beings, even if it means sacrificing himself. Those cynics who dismiss all moral devotion as an illusion, Bahnsen claims, cannot feel the deepest pain of the human heart (182).

Throughout his essay Bahnsen swipes at Hartmann's pessimism, which he now carefully and vigorously distinguishes from his own. He rejects entirely Hartmann's attempt to base pessimism on a hedonic calculus, as if someone should become a pessimist simply because of the preponderance of pain over pleasure in life. The pretension of objectivity behind this calculus is completely bogus, Bahnsen claims, because the scale has to be set differently for every individual (166). More importantly, though, Hartmann's calculus cannot provide a foundation for pessimism, because it assumes, wrongly, that pessimism is based on the lack of personal happiness; it fails to take into account the moral basis of pessimism: sympathy for the suffering of others (182). What makes someone a pessimist is the recognition that they cannot achieve anything in life without struggle and sacrifice; but that is entirely independent of how much pleasure or pain they acquire (168). Furthermore, it is a complete misconception on Hartmann's and Taubert's part, Bahnsen argues, to talk about "the uses" of pessimism, as if the pessimist mentality were only an effective instrument to promote evolution and world progress (170). This degrades the pessimist's ideals into a mere means toward collective ends. The true pessimist does not believe in progress in history; but, in any case, the ends of history are a complete irrelevance to him. He will fight for his ideals even when he knows that history is not moving in his direction, and even when he knows that it is against him.

Although Bahnsen is never so explicit, the underlying theme and thesis of his article is that the pessimist is a tragic hero. Like the tragic hero, Bahnsen's pessimist fights for a higher ideal even though he knows that he will have to suffer for it, and even though he realizes that he will probably never succeed. This theme is just what we should expect given Bahnsen's account of tragedy. Here again we see how the core of his pessimism lies in his tragic conception of the world, according to which there are no higher powers that guarantee justice and happiness in the world, or that ensure redemption for all our pain and suffering. The only source of justice and happiness has to come from the struggle and striving of the individual, who is more likely to endure defeat than victory.

This conception of the pessimist as a tragic hero is confirmed when we compare Bahnsen's later essay with an earlier piece of writing he completed in the 1870s when working out his tragic view of the world. Namely, the chapter on 'Heldenthum' or heroism in his *Mosaiken und Silhouetten*.[112] Here Bahnsen provides a vivid portrait of the tragic hero which perfectly corresponds to his later account of the pessimist. He identifies three characteristics of the tragic hero. First, he is an idealist who fights for his ideals and sacrifices himself for them. There is a greatness to his character because he is selfless and utterly devoted to the good of others. Second, he has equanimity because he maintains his composure in the face of the slings and arrows of outrageous fortune, and even in the face of inevitable defeat. Third, he is autonomous, adopting goals and ideals he personally believes in; he does not simply accept orders, like a soldier, or follow the mandates of a religious order, like a knight.

In the final pages of his article Bahnsen makes a passing swipe at another erstwhile pessimist: Friedrich Nietzsche (179–80). Though Bahnsen does not mention him by name, there can be no mistake that he is referring to the author of *Menschliches, All Zu Menschliches*. Referring to Nietzsche's new "historical philosophy", Bahnsen claims that such a programme of exposing the base origins of morality will undermine the moral heroism on which pessimism is based. If we deprive even the tragic hero of his illusions, what then? Bahnsen does not answer that question, contenting himself with rebuking Nietzsche for having betrayed Schopenhauer's legacy. Given his own radical departures from Schopenhauer, this was, to say the least, a remarkable criticism.

It was a great merit of Bahnsen's essay that it had set forth a new and original version of pessimism, one distinct from Schopenhauer's quietism and asceticism on the one hand and Hartmann's evolutionism and eudemonism on the other hand. It was another of its great virtues that it steered pessimism clear of the charges of immoralism, cynicism and quietism. It did so by making the heart of pessimism lie in moral sympathy and heroism. If sympathy for others can truly motivate the tragic hero, then Hartmann's objection that Bahnsen's pessimism leads to despair loses its value.

A new conception of pessimism—one that never lapsed into cynicism or despair and one that was based on the greatest moral sympathy—was only one of Bahnsen's contributions to the philosophy of his age. We have already seen some of his other contributions: an interesting theory of tragedy; an original and powerful worldview that places conflict at the very heart of reality; a plausible defence of realism, individualism and pluralism against the idealism and monism of Schopenhauer and Hartmann. On the whole, Bahnsen's contributions to the philosophy of his age are in inverse proportion to the scanty recognition he has received. His obscurity might seem a fitting fate for someone who so deeply believed in the tragedy of life. But it is the obligation of the scholar to correct the fickleness of fate according to higher standards of intellectual merit. By those standards Bahnsen deserves much greater attention than we have given him.

---

[112] Julius Bahnsen, *Mosaiken und Silhouetten* (Leipzig: Wigand, 1877), pp. 1–41.

Bibliography

Primary Sources

Augustine, *The City of God*, tr. R. W. Dyson. Cambridge: Cambridge University Press, 1998.
Avenarius, Richard, ed., *Vierteljahrschrift für wissenschaftliche Philosophie*. Leipzig: Fues, 1877–1901. 24 vols.
Bachmann, C. F., 'Idealismus', in Johann Samuel Ersch and Johann Gottfried Gruber, eds, *Allgemeine Encyclopädie der Wissenschaften und Künste*, XV. 113–18. Leipzig: Brockhaus, 1838.
Bacmeister, Albert, *Der Pessimismus und die Sittenlehre*. Haarlem: De Erven F. Bohn, 1882.
Bahnsen, Julius, *Versuch, die Lehre von den drei ästhetischen Grundformen genetisch zu gliedern nach den Voraussetzungen der naturwissenschaftlichen Psychologie*. Tübingen: Universität Tübingen, 1853.
Bahnsen, Julius, 'Der Bildungswerth der Mathematik', *Schulzeitung für die Herzogtümer Schleswig-Holstein und Lauenberg*, 21, 25, 26 (21 Feb., 21 and 28 Mar. 1857).
Bahnsen, Julius, *Schiller: Eine Gedächtnisrede gehalten den 10ten November 1859 im Gymnasiums zu Anclam*. Anclam: Schillerstiftung, 1859.
Bahnsen, Julius, *Beyträge zur Charakterologie: Mit besonderer Berücksichtigungen pädagogischer Fragen*. Leipzig: Brockhaus, 1867. 2 vols.
Bahnsen, Julius, *Zum Verhältniß zwischen Wille und Motiv: Eine metaphysische Voruntersuchung zur Charakterologie*. Lauenberg: H. Eschenhagen 1870.
Bahnsen, Julius, 'Andeutungen über die Arten des Seins', *Philosophische Monatshefte*, 7 (1871), 214–44.
Bahnsen, Julius, review of 2nd edn of *Philosophie des Unbewussten*, *National-Zeitung*, 359 (4 Aug. 1871), and 361 (5 Aug. 1871). Unpaginated.
Bahnsen, Julius, 'Zur Kritik des Kriticismus', *Philosophische Monatshefte*, VI (1871), 349–66.
Bahnsen, Julius, *Zur Philosophie der Geschichte: Eine kritische Besprechung des Hegel-Hartmann'schen Evolutionismus aus Schopenhauer'schen Prinzipien*. Berlin: Duncker, 1872.
Bahnsen, Julius, 'Der Pessimismus als historische Macht', *Die Literatur*, 2 (1874), 499–500.
Bahnsen, Julius, *Landläufige Philosophie und Landflüchtige Wahrheit. Unprivilegirte Forderungen eines Nicht Subventionirten*. Leipzig: Krüger & Roskoschny, 1876.
Bahnsen, Julius, *Das Tragische als Weltgesetz und der Humor als ästhetische Gestalt des Metaphysischen*. Lauenberg: Verlag von F. Ferley, 1877.
Bahnsen, Julius, *Mosaiken und Silhouetten*. Leipzig: Wigand, 1877.
Bahnsen, Julius, review of Hartmann, *Neukantianismus, Schopenhauerismus und Hegelianismus* and *Das Unbewusste vom Standpunkt der Physiologie und Descendenztheorie*, *Jenaer Literarturzeitung*, Nr. 23 (1878), 346–8.
Bahnsen, Julius, *Pessimisten-Brevier: Von einem Geweihten*. Berlin: Theobald Grieben, 1879. 2nd edn, 1881.
Bahnsen, Julius, *Der Widerspruch im Wissen und Wesen der Welt*. Berlin: Theobald Grieben, 1880–2. 2 vols.

Bahnsen, Julius, 'Ist eine Rechtsphilosophie überhaupt möglich? Und unter welchen Bedingungen resp. Einschränkungen?', *Zeitschrift für vergleichende Rechtswissenschaft*. 3 (1882), 219–31.

Bahnsen, Julius, *Wie ich Wurde was ich Ward*, ed. Rudolf Louis. Munich: Georg Müller, 1905.

Bähr, C. G., *Die Schopenhauer'sche Philosophie in ihren Grundzügen*. Dresden: Rudolf Kuntze, 1857.

Bona Meyer, Jürgen, *Philosophische Zeitfragen*. Bonn: Adolph Marcus, 1870.

Bona Meyer, Jürgen, *Arthur Schopenhauer als Mensch und Denker*. Berlin: Carl Habel, 1872.

Bona Meyer, Jürgen, *Weltelend und Weltschmerz: Eine Rede gegen Schopenhauer's und Hartmann's Pessimismus*. Bonn: Marcus, 1872.

Bona Meyer, Jürgen, 'Weltlust und Weltleid', in *Probleme der Weltweisheit*, 253–95. Zweite Auflage. Berlin: Allgeminer Verein für deutsche Literatur, 1887.

Börries, Gottfried, *Ueber den Pessimismus als Durchgangspunkt zu universaler Weltanschauung*. Münster: E. C. Brunn, 1880.

Büchner, Ludwig, *Kraft und Stoff: Empirisch-naturphilosophische Studien*. Frankfurt: Meidiger, 1855.

Busch, Otto, *Arthur Schopenhauer: Beitrag zu einer Dogmatik der Religionslosen*. Heidelberg: Bassermann, 1877.

Carey, Henry, *Principles of Social Science*. Philadelphia: J. B. Lippincott & Co., 1858–60. 3 vols. Translation: *Prinzipien der Socialwissenschaft*. Munich: E. A. Fleischmann, 1863–4.

Christ, Paul, *Der Pessimismus und die Sittenlehre*. Haarlem: De Evren F. Bohn, 1882.

Dorguth, Friedrich, *Schopenhauer in seiner Wahrheit*. Magdeburg: Heinrichshofen'sche Buchhandlung, 1845.

Dorguth, Friedrich, *Grundkritik der Dialektik und des Identitätssystem*. Magdeburg: Heinrichshoften, 1849.

Duboc, Julius, 'Eduard von Hartmann's Berechnung des Weltelends', *Deutsche Warte*, VI (1874), 350–61.

Duboc, Julius, *Der Optimismus als Weltanschauung und seine religiös ethische Bedeutung*. Bonn: Emil Strauβ, 1881.

Duboc, Julius, *Hundert Jahre Zeitgeist in Deutschland*. Leipzig: Wigand, 1889. 2 vols.

Duboc, Julius, *Jenseits vom Wirklichen. Eine Studie aus der Gegenwart*. Dresden: Hellmuth Henkler, 1896.

Duboc, Julius, *Anti-Nietzsche*. Dresden: Hellmuth Henkler, 1897.

Dühring, Eugen, *Capital und Arbeit: Neue Antworten auf alte Fragen*. Berlin: Eichhoff, 1865.

Dühring, Eugen, *Carey's Umwälzung der Volkswirthschaft und Socialwissenschaft*. Munich: E. A. Fleischmann, 1865.

Dühring, Eugen, *Der Werth des Lebens: Eine Philosophische Betrachtung*. Breslau: Eduard Trewendt, 1865. Later editions appeared in 1881, 1894, 1902, 1916, 1922 with O. R. Reisland.

Dühring, Eugen, *Natürliche Dialektik*. Berlin: Mittler, 1865.

Dühring, Eugen, *Kritische Grundlegung der Volkswirthschaftslehre*. Berlin: Eichhoff, 1866.

Dühring, Eugen, *Die Verkleinerer Carey's und die Krisis der Nationalökonomie*. Breslau: Trewendt, 1867.

Dühring, Eugen, *Kritische Geschichte der Philosophie von ihren Anfängen bis zur Gegenwart*. Berlin: L. Heimann, 1869.

Dühring, Eugen, *Cursus der Philosophie als streng wissenschaftlicher Weltanschauung und Lebensgestaltung*. Leipzig: E. Koschny, 1875.
Dühring, Eugen, *Cursus der National und Socialökonomie*. 2nd edn. Leipzig: Fues, 1876.
Dühring, Eugen, *Der Werth des Lebens populär dargestellt*. Zweite, völlig umgearbeitete und bedeutend vermehrte Auflage. Leipzig: Fues, 1877.
Dühring, Eugen, *Logik und Wissenschaftstheorie*. Leipzig: Fues, 1878.
Dühring, Eugen, *Der Ersatz der Religion durch Vollkommeneres und die Ausscheidung alles Judäerthums durch den Modernen Völkergeist*. Karlsruhe: Reuther, 1881.
Dühring, Eugen, *Die Judenfrage als Frage der Racenschädlichkeit für Existenz, Sitte und Cultur der Völker*. Karlsruhe: Reuther, 1881.
Dühring, Eugen, *Sache, Leben und Feinde*. Leipzig: Reuther, 1882. 2nd edn, Leipzig: Thomas Verlag, 1902.
Dühring, Eugen, *Die Ueberschätzung Lessings und dessen Anwaltschaft für die Juden*. Karlsruhe: Reuther, 1883.
Dühring, Eugen, *Der Weg zur höheren Berufsbildung der Frauen und die Lehrweise der Universitäten*. Zweite Auflage. Leipzig: Fues, 1885.
Dühring, Eugen, *Der Werth des Lebens: Eine Denkerbetrachtung im Sinne heroischer Lebensauffassung*. Vierte, verbesserte Auflage. Leipzig: O. R. Reisland, 1891.
Dühring, Eugen, *Kritische Geschichte der Philosophie*. Vierte, verbesserte und vermehrte Auflage. Leipzig: O. R. Reisland, 1894.
Erdmann, Johann Eduard, *Die Entwicklung der deutschen Spekulation seit Kant*. Zweite Auflage. Leipzig: Vogel, 1853.
Fereus, Zdenko, ed., *Stimmen des Weltleids*. Leipzig: Wigand, 1887.
Feuerbach, Ludwig, *Grundsätze der Philosophie der Zukunft*. Zurich: Fröbel, 1843.
Fichte, J. G., *Sämtliche Werke*, ed. I. H. Fichte. Berlin: Veit & Comp, 1845–6. 8 vols.
Fischer, J. C., *Hartmann's Philosophie des Unbewussten: Ein Schmerzenschrei des gesunden Menschenverstandes*. Leipzig: Otto Wigand, 1872.
Fischer, Kuno, *Logik und Metaphysik oder Wissenschaftslehre*. Stuttgart: Scheitlin, 1852.
Fischer, Kuno, *Kant's Leben und die Grundlagen seiner Lehre*. Mannheim: Friedrich Bassermann, 1860.
Fischer, Kuno, *System der Logik und Metaphysik oder Wissenschaftslehre*. Heidelberg: Bassermann, 1865.
Fischer, Kuno, *Der Philosoph des Pessimismus: Ein Charakterproblem*. Heidelberg: Winter, 1897.
Fischer, Kuno, *Schopenhauers Leben, Werke und Lehre*. Zweite Auflage, Band IX of *Geschichte der neueren Philosophie*. Heidelberg: Winter, 1898.
Fortlage, Carl, *Genetische Geschichte der Philosophie seit Kant*. Leipzig: Brockhaus, 1852.
Frauenstädt, Julius, *Die Freiheit des Menschen und die Persönlichkeit Gottes*. Berlin: Hirschwald, 1838.
Frauenstädt, Julius, *Die Menschwerdung Gottes, nach ihrer Möglichkeit, Wirklichkeit und Nothwendigkeit: Mit Rücksicht auf Schaller und Göschel*. Berlin: Voß, 1839.
Frauenstädt, Julius, *Studien und Kritiken zur Theologie und Philosophie*. Berlin: Voß, 1840.
Frauenstädt, Julius, *Schellings Vorlesungen in Berlin: Darstellung und Kritik der Hauptpunkte derselben*. Berlin: Hirschwald, 1842.
Frauenstädt, Julius, *Ueber das wahre Verhältniß der Vernunft zur Offenbarung: Prolegomena zu jeder künftigen Philosophie des Christenthums*. Darmstadt: Carl Wilhelm Leske, 1848.

Frauenstädt, Julius, 'Stimmen über Arthur Schopenhauer', *Blätter für literarische Unterhaltung*, 277–81 (19–23 Nov. 1849), 1105–22.

Frauenstädt, Julius, review of *Parerga und Paralipomena*, *Blätter für literarische Unterhaltung*, 9 (28 Feb. 1852), 196–202.

Frauenstädt, Julius, *Aesthetische Fragen*. Dessau: Gebrüder Katz, 1853.

Frauenstädt, Julius, *Briefe über die Schopenhauer'sche Philosophie*. Leipzig: Brockhaus, 1854.

Frauenstädt, Julius, *Die Naturwissenschaft in ihrem Einfluß auf Poesie, Religion, Moral und Philosophie*. Leipzig: Brockhaus, 1855.

Frauenstädt, Julius, *Der Materialismus. Seine Wahrheit und sein Irrthum: Eine Erwiderung auf Dr. Louis Büchner's Kraft und Stoff*. Leipzig: Brockhaus, 1856.

Frauenstädt, Julius, *Briefe über natürliche Religion*. Leipzig: Brockhaus, 1858.

Frauenstädt, Julius, *Arthur Schopenhauer: Von ihm. Ueber ihn*. Berlin: Hayn. 1863.

Frauenstädt, Julius, *Das sittliche Leben: Ethische Studien*. Leipzig: Brockhaus, 1866.

Frauenstädt, Julius, *Schopenhauer-Lexikon: Ein philosophisches Wörterbuch, nach Schopenhauers sämmtlichen Schriften und handschriftlichen Nachlass*. Leipzig: Brockhaus, 1871.

Frauenstädt, Julius, *Neue Briefe über die Schopenhauer'sche Philosophie*. Leipzig: Brockhaus, 1876.

Garve, Christian, *Eigene Betrachtungen über die allgemeinsten Grundsätze der Sittenlehre*. Breslau: Korn, 1798.

Garve, Christian, *Uebersicht über die verschiedenen Principe der Sittenlehre von dem Zeitalter Aristotles bis auf unsere Zeiten*. Breslau: Korn, 1798.

Gass, W., *Optimismus und Pessimismus: Der Gang der christlichen Welt- und Lebensansicht*. Berlin: Reimer, 1876.

Golther, Ludwig von, *Der moderne Pessimismus*. Leipzig: Brockhaus, 1878.

Gottschalk, Rudolf, review of Hartmann *Philosophie des Unbewussten*, *Blätter für literarische Unterhaltung*, 8. (18 Feb. 1869), 113–18.

Häckel, Ernst, *Generelle Morphologie der Organismen*. Berlin: Reimer, 1866. 2 vols.

Hardenberg, Friedrich von, *Novalis: Werke, Tagebücher und Briefe Friedrich von Hardenbergs*, ed. Hans-Joachim Mähl and Richard Samuel. Munich: Hanser Verlag, 1978.

Hartmann, Alma von, *Zurück zum Idealismus. Zehn Vorträge*. Berlin: Schwetschke & Sohn, 1902.

Hartmann, Alma von, 'Chronologische Übersicht der Schriften von Eduard von Hartmann', *Kant-Studien*, 17 (1912), 501–20.

Hartmann, Eduard von, 'Erwiderung auf Herrn Professor Michelets Kritik meiner Schrift Ueber die dialektische Methode', *Philosophische Monatshefte*, 1 (1868), 502–5.

Hartmann, Eduard von, *Ueber die dialektische Methode*. Berlin: Duncker, 1868.

Hartmann, Eduard von, 'Fichte und seine Vorgänger', *Blätter für literarische Unterhaltung*, 28 (8 July 1869), 433–6.

Hartmann, Eduard von, *Philosophie des Unbewussten: Versuch einer Weltanschauung*. Berlin: Duncker, 1869.

Hartmann, Eduard von, *Schelling's positive Philosophie als Einheit von Hegel und Schopenhauer*. Berlin: Löwenstein, 1869.

Hartmann, Eduard von, *Briefe über die christliche Religion*. Stuttgart: Verlag von J. G. Kötzle, 1870. Published under the pseudonym F. A. Müller.

Hartmann, Eduard von, *Das Ding an sich und seine Beschaffenheiten: Kantische Studien zur Erkenntnistheorie und Metaphysik*. Berlin: Duncker, 1870.

Hartmann, Eduard von, 'Ist der pessimistische Monismus trostlos?', Philosophische Monatshefte, 5 (1870), 21–41.
Hartmann, Eduard von, Philosophie des Unbewussten. 2nd, revised edn. Berlin: Duncker, 1870.
Hartmann, Eduard von, review of Dühring Kritische Geschichte der Philosophie, Blätter für literarische Unterhaltung, 1 (1 Jan. 1870), 9–12.
Hartmann, Eduard von, review of Julius Bahsen Beiträge zur Charakterologie, Philosophische Monatshefte, 4 (1870), 378–408.
Hartmann, Eduard von, 'Naturforschung und Philosophie: Eine Unterhaltung in zwei Briefen', Philosophische Monatshefte, 8 (1871), 49–58, 97–105.
Hartmann, Eduard von, 'Zur Kantischen Philosophie', Blätter für literarische Unterhaltung, 10 (2 Mar. 1871), 151–4.
Hartmann, Eduard von, Das Unbewusste vom Standpunkt der Physiologie und Descendenztheorie. Berlin: Duncker, 1872.
Hartmann, Eduard von, Gesammelte philosophische Abhandlungen zur Philosophie des Unbewussten. Berlin: Duncker, 1872.
Hartmann, Eduard von, Die Selbstzersetzung des Christenthums und die Religion der Zukunft. Berlin: Duncker, 1874.
Hartmann, Eduard von, Erläuterung zur Metaphysik des Unbewussten. Berlin: Duncker 1874.
Hartmann, Eduard von, Kritische Grundlegeung des transcendentalen Realismus. Berlin: Duncker, 1875.
Hartmann, Eduard von, Wahrheit und Irrtum im Darwinismus. Berlin: Duncker, 1875.
Hartmann, Eduard von, Gesammelte Studien und Aufsätze. Berlin: Duncker, 1876.
Hartmann, Eduard von, Neukantianismus, Schopenhauerismus und Hegelianismus in ihrer Stellung zu den philosophischen Aufgaben der Gegenwart: Zweite erweiterte Auflage der Erläuterungen zur Metaphysik des Unbewussten. Berlin: Duncker, 1877.
Hartmann, Eduard von, 'Ist der Pessimismus schädlich?', Gegenwart, 16 (1879), 211–14, 233–5.
Hartmann, Eduard von, 'Ist der Pessimismus wissenschaftlich zu begründen?', Philosophische Monatshefte, 15 (1879), 589–612.
Hartmann, Eduard von, Phänomenologie des sittlichen Bewusstseins. Berlin: Duncker, 1879.
Hartmann, Eduard von, Die Krisis des Christenthums in der modernen Theologie. Berlin: Duncker, 1880.
Hartmann, Eduard von, Zur Geschichte und Begründung des Pessimismus. Berlin: Duncker, 1880.
Hartmann, Eduard von, Das religiöse Bewußtsein der Menschheit im Stufengang seiner Entwicklung. Berlin: Duncker, 1882.
Hartmann, Eduard von, Die Religion des Geistes. Berlin: Duncker, 1882.
Hartmann, Eduard von, 'Zur Pessimismusfrage', Philosophische Monatshefte, 19 (1883), 60–80.
Hartmann, Eduard von, Das Judenthum in Gegenwart und Zukunft. Leipzig: Friedrich 1884.
Hartmann, Eduard von, Moderne Probleme. Leipzig: Friedrich, 1885.
Hartmann, Eduard von, Philosophische Fragen der Gegenwart. Leipzig: Friedrich, 1885.
Hartmann, Eduard von, Das sittliche Bewusstsein. 2nd edn. Phänomenologie des sittlichen Bewusstseins. Leipzig: Friedrich, 1886.
Hartmann, Eduard von, Lotze's Philosophie. Leipzig: Friedrich, 1888.
Hartmann, Eduard von, Zwei Jahrzehnte deutscher Politik. Leipzig: Friedrich, 1889.

Hartmann, Eduard von, *Zur Geschichte und Begründung des Pessimismus*. Zweite, erweitere Auflage. Leipzig: Hermann Haacke, 1891.
Hartmann, Eduard von, *Tagesfragen*. Leipzig: Hermann Haacke, 1896.
Hartmann, Eduard von, *Ethische Studien*. Leipzig: Hermann Haacke, 1898.
Hartmann, Eduard von, *Zur Zeitgeschichte. Neue Tagesfragen*. Leipzig: Hermann Haacke, 1900.
Hartmann, Eduard von, *Die Weltanschauung der modernen Physik*. Leipzig: Hermann Haacke, 1902.
Hartmann, Eduard von, *Grundriss der Naturphilosophie*. Bad Sachsa: Hermann Haacke, 1907.
Hartmann, Eduard von, *Gedanken über Staat, Politik und Sozialismus*. Leipzig: Kröner, 1923.
Hartmann, Eduard von, *Phänomenologie des sittlichen Bewusstseins*. Berlin: Wegweiser Verlag, 1924.
Hartmann, Eduard von, *Philosophischer Briefwechsel. 1888–1906*, ed. Rudolf Mutter and Eckhart Pilick. Rohrbach: Peter Guhl, 1995.
Hartsen, F. A. von, *Die Moral des Pessimismus*. Nordhausen: F. Förstemann's Verlag, 1874.
Haym, Rudolf, *Arthur Schopenhauer*. Berlin: Reimer, 1864.
Haym, Rudolf, *Die romantische Schule*. Berlin: Gaertner, 1870.
Haym, Rudolf, 'Die Hartmann'sche Philosophie des Unbewussten', *Philosophische Jahrbücher*, 31 (1873), 41–80, 109–39, 257–311. Reprinted as: *Die Hartmann'sche Philosophie des Unbewussten*. Berlin: Reimer, 1873.
Hegel, G. W. F., *Werke in zwanzig Bänden*, eds. K. Michel and E. Moldenhauer. Frankfurt: Suhrkamp, 1970. 20 vols.
Hellenbach, Lazar, *Eine Philosophie des gesunden Menschenverstandes*. Vienna: Wilhelm Braumüller, 1876.
Hellenbach, Lazar, *Der Individualismus im Lichte der Biologie und Philosophie der Gegenwart*. Vienna: Wilhelm Braumüller, 1878.
Hellenbach, Lazar, *Die Vorurtheile der Menschheit*. Vienna: L. Rosner, 1879. 2 vols.
Herbart, Johann Friedrich, review of *Die Welt als Wille und Vorstellung*, *Hermes*, 3 (1820), 131–49.
Herbart, Johann Friedrich, *Sämtliche Werke*, ed. Karl Kehrbach and Otto Flügel. Langasalza: Hermann Beyer & Söhne, 1907. 19 vols.
Heymons, Carl, *Eduard von Hartmann: Erinnerungen aus den Jahren 1868–1881*. Berlin: Duncker, 1881.
Horwicz, Adolf, 'Die psychologische Begründung des Pessimismus', *Philosophische Monatshefte*, 16 (1880), 264–88.
Huber, Johannes, *Der Pessimismus*. Munich: Theodor Ackermann, 1876.
Jacobi, Friedrich Heinrich, *Werke*, ed. Friedrich Roth and Friedrich Köppen. Leipzig: Fleischer, 1815. 6 vols.
Kant, Immanuel, *Schriften*, ed. Prussian Academy of the Sciences. Berlin: de Gruyter, 1902. 9 vols.
Kemmer, Otto, ed. *Pessimisten Gesangbuch*. Minden: J. C. C. Brun's Verlag, 1884.
Knauer, Gustav, *Conträr und Contradictorisch (nebst convegrirenden Lehrstüken) festgestellt und Kants Kategorientafel berichtigt: eine philosophische Monographie*. Halle: Pfeffer, 1868.
Knauer, Gustav, *Das Facit aus E.v. Hartmann's Philosophie des Unbewussten*. Berlin: L. Heimann, 1873.
Leibniz, G. W. F., *Die philosophischen Schriften*, ed. C.I. Gerhardt. Berlin: Weidmann, 1875–90. 7 vols.

Liebmann, Otto, *Die Klimax der Theorieen. Eine Untersuchung aus dem Bereich der allgemeinen Wissenschaftslehre*. Straßburg: Trübner, 1884.

Lotze, Hermann, *Metaphysik*. Leipzig: Hirzel, 1841.

Mainländer, Philipp, *Die letzen Hohenstaufen. Ein dramatisches Gedicht in drei Theilen*. Leipzig: Heinrich Schmidt & Carl Günther, 1876.

Mainländer, Philipp, *Die Philosophie der Erlösung*. Berlin: Grieben, 1876.

Mainländer, Philipp, *Die Philosophie der Erlösung*, II. *Zwölf philosophischer Essays*. Frankfurt: C. Koenitzer, 1886. 2nd edn, 1894.

Mainländer, Philipp, *Schriften*, ed. Winfried H. Müller-Seyfarth. Hildesheim: Olms Verlag, 1996. 4 vols.

Maupertuis, Pierre Louis Moreau, *Essai de philosophie morale*. Berlin: Akademie der Wissenschaften, 1749.

Nietzsche, Friedrich, *Die Geburt der Tragödie aus dem Geiste der Musik*. Leipzig: Ernst Wilhelm Fritzsch, 1872.

Nietzsche, Friedrich, *Briefwechsel, Kritische Gesamtausgabe*, ed. Giorgo Colli, Renate Müller-Buck, Annemaire Pieper et al. Berlin: de Gruyter, 1975. 7 vols.

Nietzsche, Friedrich, *Sämtliche Werke, Kritische Studienausgabe*, ed. Giorgo Colli and Mazzino Montinari. Berlin: de Gruyter, 1980. 15 vols.

Paulsen, Friedrich, 'Idealismus und Positivismus', *Im neuen Reich*, 10 (1880), 735–42.

Paulsen, Friedrich, 'Gründen und Ursachen des Pessimismus', *Deutsche Rundschau*, 48 (1886), 360–81.

Pfleiderer, Edmund, *Der moderne Pessimismus*. Berlin: Carl Habel, 1875.

Plümacher, Olga, 'Die Philosophie des Unbewussten und ihre Gegner', *Unsere Zeit*, 15 (1879), 321–45.

Plümacher, Olga, 'Pessimism', *Mind*, 4 (1879), 68–89.

Plümacher, Olga, *Der Kampf um's Unbewusste*. Berlin: Duncker, 1881.

Plümacher, Olga, *Zwei Individualisten der Schopenhauer'sche Schule*. Berlin: Duncker, 1882.

Plümacher, Olga, *Der Pessimismus in Vergangheit und Gegenwart*. Heidelberg: Georg Weiss Verlag, 1883. 2nd edn, 1888.

Rehmke, Johannes, *Der Pessimismus und die Sittenlehre*. Leipzig: Verlag von Julius Klinkhardt, 1882.

Riehl, Alois, *Ueber wissenschaftliche und nichtwissenschaftliche Philosophie: Eine akademische Antrittsrede*. Tübingen: Mohr, 1883.

Riehl, Alois, 'The Vocation of Philosophy at the Present Day', in *Lectures delivered in Connection with the Dedication of the Graduate College of Princeton University*, 53–63. Princeton: Princeton University Press, 1914.

Reymond, M., *Das Buch vom bewußten und unbewußten Herrn Meyer*. Bern: Frobeen & Cie. 1879.

Schaarschmidt, Carl, 'Vom rechten und falschen Kriticismus', *Philosophische Monatshefte*, 14 (1878), 1–12.

Schelling, Friedrich Wilhelm Joseph, *Sämtliche Werke*, ed. K. F. A. Schelling. Stuttgart: Cotta, 1856–61.

Schiller, Friedrich, 'Ueber den Grund des Vergnügens an tragischen Gegenständen', *Neue Thalia*, 1 (1792), 92–125.

Schopenhauer, Arthur, *Sämtliche Werke*, ed. Julius Frauenstädt. Leipzig: Brockhaus, 1877. 6 vols.

Schopenhauer, Arthur, *Sämtliche Werke*, ed. Eduard Griesbach. Leipzig: Reclam, 1892. 6 vols.
Schopenhauer, Arthur, *Schopenhauer Briefe*, ed. Ludwig Schemann. Leipzig: Brockhaus, 1893.
Schopenhauer, Arthur, *Sämtliche Werke*, ed. Max Frisch-Eisen-Köhler. Berlin: Weichert, 1900. 8 vols.
Schopenhauer, Arthur, *Sämtliche Werke*, ed. Paul Deussen. Munich: Piper, 1911. 16 vols.
Schopenhauer, Arthur, *Sämtliche Werke*, ed. Rudolf Steiner. Stuttgart: Cotta, 1923. 12 vols.
Schopenhauer, Arthur, *Sämtliche Werke*, ed. Arthur Hübscher. Wiesbaden: Brockhaus, 1937. 7 vols.
Schopenhauer, Arthur, *Der handschriftliche Nachlaß*, ed. Arthur Hübscher. Frankfurt: Waldemar Kramer, 1966–8. 5 vols.
Schopenhauer, Arthur, *Sämtliche Werke*, ed. Wolfgang Freiherr von Löhneysen. Stuttgart: Insel, 1968. Reprint: Darmstadt: Wissenschaftliche Buchgesellschaft, 1989. 5 vols.
Schopenhauer, Arthur, *Gesammelte Briefe*, ed. Arthur Hübscher. Bonn: Bouvier, 1978.
Schulze, G. E., *Aenesidemus oder über die Fundamente der von dem Herrn Professor Reinhold in Jena gelieferten Elementarphilosophie*, ed. A. Liebert. Berlin: Reuther & Reichard, 1912.
Seiling, Max, ed., *Perlen des pessimistischen Weltanschauung*. Munich: T. Ackermann, 1886.
Sommer, Hugo, *Der Pessimismus und die Sittenlehre*. Haarlem: De Erven F. Bohn. 1882.
Sommer, Hugo, *Die Religion des Pessimismus*. Berlin: Carl Habel, 1884.
Spalding, Johann Joachim, *Die Bestimmung des Menschen*. Greifswald: Struck, 1748.
Strauss, David Friedrich, *Der alte und der neue Glaube. Ein Bekenntnis*. Leipzig: Hirzel, 1872.
Taubert, Agnes, *Philosophie gegen naturwissenschaftliche Überhebung*. Berlin: Duncker, 1872.
Taubert, Agnes, *Der Pessimismus und seine Gegner*. Berlin: Duncker, 1873.
Tautz, Theodor, *Der Pessimismus*. Karlsruhe: G. Braun'schen Hofbuchhandlung, 1876.
Trendelenburg, Adolf, *Logische Untersuchungen*. Berlin: Bethge, 1840. Zweite Ausgabe: Leipzig: Hirzel, 1862.
Trendelenburg, Adolf, 'Über den letzten Unterschied der philosophischen Systeme', *Philologische und historische Abhandlungen der königlichen Akademie der Wissenschaften zu Berlin*, 241–62. Berlin: Dümmler, 1847.
Trendelenburg, Adolf, 'Ueber eine Lücke in Kants Beweis von der ausschliessende Subjectivität des Raumes und der Zeit', in *Historische Beiträge zur Philosophie*, III. 215–76. Berlin: Bethge, 1867.
Vaihinger, Hans, *Hartmann, Dühring und Lange: Zur Geschichte der deutschen Philosophie im XIX. Jahrhundert*. Iserlohn: Baedeker, 1876.
Vischer, Friedrich Theodor, *Aesthetik oder Wissenschaft des Schönen*. Leipzig: Carl Mäcken's Verlag, 1846.
Volkelt, Johannes, 'Die Entwicklung des modernen Pessimismus', *Im neuen Reich*, 2 (1872), 287–92.
Volkelt, Johannes, review of Bahnsen *Zur Philosophie der Geschichte*, *Philosophische Monatshefte*, 8 (1872), 282–96.
Volkelt, Johannes, *Das Unbewusste und der Pessimismus*. Berlin: F. Henschel, 1873.
Volkelt, Johannes, 'Philosophische Monatshefte', *Jenaer Literaturzeitung*, 5 (1878), 95–6.
Volkelt, Johannes, *Arthur Schopenhauer; Seine Persönlichkeit, seine Lehre, seine Glaube*. Stuttgart: Frommann, 1900.
Weckesser, Albert, *Der empirische Pessimismus in seinem metaphysischen Zusammenhang im System von Eduard von Hartmann*. Bonn: Universitäts-Buchdruckerei von Carl Georgi, 1885.

Weiße, Hermann, *Über den gegenwärtigen Standpunct der philosophischen Wissenschaft.* Leipzig: Barth, 1829.
Weis, Ludwig, *Anti-Materialismus oder Kritik aller Philosophie des Unbewußten.* Berlin: F. Henschel, 1873.
Weygoldt, G. P., *Kritik der philosophischen Pessimismus der neuesten Zeit.* Leiden: Brill, 1875.
Windelband, Wilhelm, 'Pessimismus und Wissenschaft', *Der Salon*, 2 (1877), 814–21, 951–7.
Windelband, Wilhelm, *Präludien.* 9th edn. Tübingen: Mohr, 1924. 2 vols.
Zeller, Eduard, 'Ueber Bedeutung und Aufgabe der Erkennistheorie', in *Vorträge und Abhandlungen*), II. 479–96. Leipzig: Fues, 1877.

Secondary Sources

Bäckenköhler, 'Only Dreams of an Afternoon Nap? Darwin's Theory of Evolution and the Foundation of Biological Anthropology in Germany 1860-75', in Eve-Marie Engels and Thomas F. Glick, eds, *The Reception of Charles Darwin in Europe*, 98–115. London: Continuum, 2008.
Beiser, Frederick, *The German Historicist Tradition.* Oxford: Oxford University Press, 2011.
Beiser, Frederick, 'Mendelssohn versus Herder on the Vocation of Man', in Reinier Munk, ed., *Moses Mendelssohn's Metaphysics and Aesthetics*, 217–34. Dordrecht: Springer, 2011.
Beiser, Frederick, *Late German Idealism: Trendelenburg and Lotze.* Oxford: Oxford University Press, 2013.
Beiser, Frederick, *After Hegel: German Philosophy 1840–1900.* Princeton: Princeton University Press, 2014.
Beiser, Frederick, *The Genesis of Neo-Kantianism, 1796–1880.* Oxford: Oxford University Press, 2014.
Brobjer, Thomas, *Nietzsche's Philosophical Context.* Urbana, IL: University of Illinois Press, 2008.
Cartwright, David, *Schopenhauer: A Biography.* Cambridge: Cambridge University Press, 2010.
Ciracì, Fabio, with Domenico Fazio and Matthias Koßler, eds., *Schopenhauer und die Schopenhauer-Schule.* Würzburg: Königshausen & Neumann, 2009.
Copleston, Frederick, *Arthur Schopenhauer, Philosopher of Pessimism.* London: Search Press, 1975.
Daum, Andreas, *Wissenschaftspopularisierung im 19. Jahrhundert.* Munich: Oldenbourg, 2002.
Döring, Woldemar, *Schopenhauer.* 4th edn. Hamburg: Hansischer Gildenverlag, 1947.
Drews, Arthur, *Eduard von Hartmanns philosophisches System im Grundriss.* Heidelberg: Winter, 1902. Zweite Ausgabe, 1906.
Duboc, Julius, *Hundert Jahre Zeitgeist in Deutschland.* Leipzig: Wigand, 1889. 2 vols.
Engels, Eve-Marie, *Die Rezeption von Evolutionstheorien im 19. Jahrhundert.* Frankfurt: Suhrkamp, 1995.
Fazio, Domenico, 'Die "Schopenhauer-Schule": Zur Geschichte eines Begriffs', in Fabio Ciracì, Domenico Fazio and Matthias Koßler, eds, *Schopenhauer und die Schopenhauer-Schule*, 15–41. Würzburg: Königshausen & Neumann, 2009.
Fox, Michael, ed., *Schopenhauer: His Philosophical Achievement.* Totowa, NJ: Barnes & Noble, 1980.
Gardiner, Patrick, *Schopenhauer.* Harmondsworth: Penguin, 1963.

Giovanni di, George, 'The Year 1786 and *Die Bestimmung des Menschen*, or *Popularphilosophie* in Crisis', in Reinier Munk, ed., *Moses Mendelssohn's Metaphysics and Aesthetics*, 217–45. Dordrecht: Springer, 2011.

Gregario, Mario Di, 'Under Darwin's Banner: Ernst Haeckel, Carl Gegenbaur and Evolutionary Morphologoy', in Eve-Marie Engels and Thomas F. Glick, eds, *The Reception of Charles Darwin in Europe*, I. 79–97. London: Continuum, 2008.

Hamerow, Theodore, *Restoration, Revolution, Reaction: Economics and Politics in Germany, 1815–1871*. Princeton: Princeton University Press, 1958.

Hamlyn, D. W., *Schopenhauer*. London: Routledge & Kegan Paul, 1980.

Heydorn, Heinz-Joachim, *Julius Bahnsen. Eine Untersuchung zur Vorgeschichte der modernen Existenz*. Göttingen: Verlag "Öffentliches Leben", 1952.

Horkheimer, Max, 'Die Aktualität Schopenhauers', in *Sociologica II: Aufsätze und Reden*, 121–41. Frankfurt: Europäische Verlagsanstalt, 1962.

Horkheimer, Max, 'Schopenhauer und die Gesellschaft', in Werner Brede, ed., *Sozial-philosophische Studien: Aufsätze, Reden und Vorträge 1930–1972*, 68–77. Frankfurt: Fischer Taschenbuch, 1972.

Horkheimer, Max, 'Schopenhauers Denken im Verhältnis zu Wissenschaft und Religion', in Werner Brede, ed., *Sozial-philosophische Studien: Aufsätze, Reden und Vorträge 1930–1972*, 145–55. Frankfurt: Fischer Taschenbuch, 1972.

Hübscher, Arthur, 'Arthur Schopenhauer: Ein Lebensbild', in *Arthur Schopenhauer: Sämtliche Werke*, I. 81–120. Leipzig: Brockhaus, 1937.

Hübscher, Arthur, *The Philosophy of Schopenhauer in its Intellectual Context*, tr. David Cartwright. Lewiston, NY: Edwin Mellen Press, 1989.

Jackson, Francis Helen, *The Swiss Colony at Gruelti*. Gruelti-Laager: Grundy County Swiss Historical Society, 2010.

Jacquette, Dale, *The Philosophy of Schopenhauer*. Montreal: McGill-Queens University Press, 2005.

Janaway, Christopher, *Self and World in Schopenhauer's Philosophy*. Oxford: Oxford University Press, 1989.

Janaway, Christopher, *Schopenhauer: A Very Short Introduction*. Oxford: Oxford University Press, 1994.

Janaway, Christopher, ed., *The Cambridge Companion to Schopenhauer*. Cambridge: Cambridge University Press, 1999.

Janaway, Christopher, ed., *Better Consciousness: Schopenhauer's Philosophy of Value*. Chichester: Wiley-Blackwell, 2009.

Kelly, Alfred, *The Descent of Darwin: The Popularization of Darwinism in Germany 1860–1914*. Chapel Hill, NC: University of North Carolina Press, 1981.

Kieser, Rolf, *Olga Plümacher-Hünerwadel: Eine gelehrte Frau des neunzehnten Jahrhunderts*. Lenzurg: Lenzburger Ortsbürgerkommision, 1990.

Köhnke, Klaus, *Entstehung und Aufstieg des Neu-Kantianismus*. Frankfurt: Suhrkamp, 1986.

Labau, Ferdinand, *Die Schopenhauer-Literatur*. Leipzig: Brockhaus, 1880.

Lukács, Georg, *Die Zerstörung der Vernunft*. Neuwied am Rhein: Luchterhand, 1962.

Lütkehaus, Ludger, *Schopenhauer: Metaphysischer Pessimismus und "soziale Frage"*. Bonn: Bouvier Verlag, 1980.

Lütkehaus, Ludger, *Nichts*. Frankfurt: Zweitausendeins, 2003.

Magee, Bryan, *The Philosophy of Schopenhauer*. Revised and enlarged edn. Oxford: Oxford University Press, 2009.
Marcuse, Ludwig, *Philosophie des Un-Glücks*. Zurich: Diogenes, 1981.
Montgomery, William, 'Germany', in Thomas F. Glick, ed., *Comparative Reception of Darwinism*, 81–115. Austin, TX: University of Texas Press, 1972.
Müller-Seyfarth, Winfried, ed., *"Die modernen Pessimisten als décadents": Von Nietzsche zu Horstmann. Texte zur Rezeptionsgeschichte von Philipp Mainländers Philosophie der Erlösung*. Königshausen & Neumann, 1993.
Müller-Seyfarth, Winfried, ed., *Metaphysik als Entropie: Philipp Mainländers transzendentale Analyse und ihre ethisch-metaphysische Relevanz*. Berlin: van Bremen, 2000.
Müller-Seyfarth, Winfried, ed., *Was Philipp Mainländer ausmacht: Offenbacher Mainländer Symposium 2001*. Würzburg: Könisgshausen & Neumann, 2002.
Müller-Seyfarth, Winfried, ed., *Anleitung zum glücklichen Nichtsein: Offenbacher Mainländer Essaywettbewerb*. Würzburg: Königshausen & Neumann, 2006.
Müller-Seyfarth, Winfried, ed., 'Julius Bahnsen. Realdialektik und Willenshenadologie im Blick auf die "postmoderne" Moderne', in Fabio Ciracì, Domenico Fazio and Matthias Koßler, eds, *Schopenhauer und die Schopenhauer-Schule*, 231–46. Würzburg: Königshausen & Neumann, 2009.
Nyhart, Lynn, *Biology Takes Form: Animal Morphology and the German Universities 1800–1900*. Chicago: University of Chicago Press, 1995.
Pauen, Michael, *Pessimismus: Geschichtsphilosophie, Metaphysik und Moderne von Nietzsche bis Spengler*. Berlin: Akademie Verlag, 1997.
Plümacher, Olga, 'Chronologische Verzeichniss der Hartmann-Literatur von 1868–1880', in *Der Kampf um's Unbewusste*, 115–50. Berlin: Duncker, 1880.
Plümacher, Olga, *Der Pessimismus in Vergangenheit und Gegenwart*. Heidelberg: Georg Weis Verlag, 1883.
Rasch, W., 'Weltschmerz', in Joachim Ritter, Karlfried Gründer and Gottfried Gabriel, eds, *Historisches Wörterbuch der Philosophie*, XII, 514–15. Basel: Schwabe, 2004.
Rauschenberger, Walther, 'Aus der letzten Lebenszeit Philipp Mainländers: Nach ungedruckten Briefen und Aufzeichnungen des Philosophen', *Süddeutsche Monatshefte*, IX (1911/12), 117–31.
Rosenberg, Hans, *Grosse Depression und Bismarckzeit*. Berlin: de Gruyter, 1967. Veröffentlichen der Historischen Kommision zu Berlin beim Friedrich-Meinecke-Institut der freien Universität Berlin, Band 24. Publikationen zur Geschichte der Industrialiserung, Band 2.
Safranski, Rüdiger, *Schopenhauer and the Wild Years of Philosophy*, tr. Ewald Osers. Cambridge, MA: Harvard University Press, 1989.
Schmidt, Alfred, *Idee und Weltwille: Schopenhauer als Kritiker Hegels*. Munich: Karl Hanser Verlag, 1988.
Schnädelbach, Herbert, *Philosophy in Germany 1831–1933*. Cambridge: Cambridge University Press, 1984.
Siebert, Otto, *Geschichte der neueren deutschen Philosophie seit Hegel*. Göttingen: Vandenhoeck & Ruprecht, 1898.
Slochower, Henry, 'Julius Bahnsen: Philosopher of Heroic Despair', 1830–1881', *The Philosophical Review*, 41 (1932), 368–84.

Snow, Dale and James, 'Was Schopenhauer an Idealist?', *Journal of the History of Philosophy*, 29 (1991), 633–55.

Sommerlad, F., 'Aus dem Leben Philipp Mainländers: Mitteilungen aus der handschriftlichen Selbstbiographies des Philosophen', *Zeitschrift für Philosophie und philosophische Kritik*, 112 (1898), 74–101.

Stern, Fritz, *The Politics of Cultural Despair*. Berkeley, CA: University of California Press, 1961.

Stern, Fritz, *The Failure of Illiberalism: Essays on the Political Culture of Modern Germany*. New York: Knopf, 1972.

Thodoroff, C., *Julius Bahnsen und die Hauptprobleme seiner Charakterologie*. Erlangen: Junge & Sohn, 1910.

Weimer, Wolfgang, *Schopenhauer*. Darmstadt: Wissenschaftliche Buchgesellschaft, 1982.

Weindling, P. J., 'Darwinism in Germany', in David Kohn, ed., *The Darwinian Heritage*, 685–98. Princeton: Princeton University Press, 1985.

Wicks, Robert, 'Schopenhauer's Naturalization of Kant's A Priori Forms of Empirical Knowledge', *History of Philosophy Quarterly*, 10 (1993), 181–96.

Wicks, Robert, *Schopenhauer*. Oxford: Blackwell, 2008.

Wolf, Jean Claude, *Eduard von Hartmann: Ein Philosoph der Gründerzeit*. Würzburg: Königshausen & Nemann, 2006.

Wolf, Jean Claude, *Eduard von Hartmann. Zeitgenossen und Gegenspieler Nietzsches*. Würzburg: Königshausen & Nemann, 2006.

Young, Julian, *Schopenhauer*. Abingdon: Routledge, 2005.

Zint, Hans, *Schopenhauer als Erlebnis*. Munich: Ernst Reinhardt Verlag, 1954.

Index

Abbt, Thomas 17
Abendroth, Walter 12n22
aesthetic redemption:
  and Schopenhauer's theory of
    redemption 43, 52, 60–2, 242
  and value of life 184, 190–5
Asher, David 83n43
Augustine 59, 64, 208

Baader, Franz von 37
Bachmann, C. F. 70
Backenköhler, Dirk 6n14
Bacmeister, Albert 163n5
Baer, Seligman 6, 131
Bahnsen, Julius:
  and characterology 238–41, 252
  on contradictions 273–6
  his ethics 279–81
  and Hartmann 232, 244–5, 246–9, 254–7, 270
  and Hegel 230–1, 234, 254, 265, 271–2
  on idealism and realism 250–2
  on individualism 276–81
  his irrationalism 272–6
  and Kant 236–7, 250–1, 271
  life of 232–4
  and Nietzsche 229, 239, 263–4, 270, 284
  and pessimism 233, 243, 268–71, 281–4
  his real dialectic 231, 233–4, 271–6
  reasons for his neglect 230
  on redemption 243, 273–4
  relationship with Hartmann 252–3, 257–9
  and Schiller 265–6
  and Schopenhauer 230–2, 235–8, 239–43, 246, 251–2, 269–70
  on sex and love 279
  on tragedy 263–7
  on the will 229, 231, 240–3, 244–5, 252, 272–3
Batz, Philipp. *See* Mainländer, Philipp
Bauer, Bruno 6, 72, 73, 131
Becker, Johann August 14
Beneke, Friedrich 19, 21
Berkeley, George 213
Boeckh, August 30, 273
Börne, Ludwig 68
Brobjer, Thomas 182n60, 229n4
Büchner, Ludwig 6, 10, 21, 76
Busch, Otto 74n22

Calvin, John 64, 65, 130, 133
Cassirer, Ernst 123n9
Carey, Henry 111
Carnap, Rudolf 88
Cartwright, David E. 14n8, 45n4
Christ, Paul 3, 163n5, 198
Cohen, Hermann 10, 25, 123n10, 150
Comte, Auguste 23, 88, 89, 114, 118, 119
Copleston, Frederick 38n32, 43n1
Czolbe, Heinrich 21

Darwin, Charles 6n14, 128, 159
Darwinism 6, 128, 159, 160, 162, 198
Daum, Andreas 6n14
Deußen, Paul 13, 239n39
Di Giovanni, George 17n12
Di Gregorio, Mario 6n14
Dilthey, Wilhelm 24, 30, 159
Doß, Adam von 14
Dorguth, Friedrich 13n3, 14
Drews, Arthur 124n12, 168n32, 169n33, 259n81
Droysen, Johann Gustav 30, 273
Duboc, Julius 1n5, 2n6, 43, 176n49, 179, 185n64
Dühring, Eugen:
  as controversial figure 88
  his criticism of classical economics 110–11
  his criticism of radical socialism 110
  critique of neo-Kantians 114–17
  on death 104–7
  economics and the value of life 108–11
  and epicureanism 90, 99, 101
  on hypostasis 92–3
  and the infinite 92
  his influence on Nietzsche 87, 103–4
  on the intellect 97–8
  and Kant's critique of metaphysics 91–2
  his materialistic metaphysics 95–6, 111–17
  his natural dialectic 91–5; and positivism 88–90, 91, 93–4
  on the replacement of religion 118–20
  on Schopenhauer 92, 93, 96, 102–4, 107–9, 111–12
  and Spinoza 120
  on suicide 107
  his theory of value 99–100
  on the value of life 89–90, 94–5, 96–8, 100–1, 103, 107, 111, 118–19
  on the worker question 109–10

Engels, Eve-Marie 6n14
Engels, Friedrich 88, 88n6, 90, 110
Epictetus 51
Epicurus 50, 51, 106n40, 202, 208
epicureanism 49, 51, 90, 91, 101, 103, 106, 208, 236
Erdmann, Johann Eduard 14n7
Eschenmeyer, Adam Karl August von 37

Fazio, Domenico 229n3, 230n7
Fereus, Zdenko 1n3
Feuerbach, Ludwig 6, 19, 71–3, 89, 96, 108, 119, 127, 209, 234–5
Fichte, Johann Gottlieb 19, 21, 25, 26, 39, 41, 77, 142, 149, 218
Fischer, Kuno 2, 2n6, 10, 14n8, 19–21, 25, 46n9, 68n10, 143, 150–1, 251
Fortlage, Carl 14n7, 21
Fox, Michael 15n9
Frauenstädt, Julius:
 his conversion to Schopenhauer 70, 71–4
 criticism of Hegel 70, 71
 criticism of Schopenhauer's dualisms 83–4
 his critique of Schopenhauer's separation of science and philosophy 85
 his critique of Schopenhauer's theory of history 85–6
 as expositor of Schopenhauer's philosophy 68–9, 75–6, 82
 as Hegelian 70–1
 and Kant's transcendental idealism 77–8, 79
 on materialism and the materialism controversy 76–9
 his practical conception of faith 73–4
 his realistic interpretation of Schopenhauer 84
 and Schopenhauer's pessimism 80, 81–3
 on Schopenhauer's theory of redemption 80–1
 on Schopenhauer's theory of will and representation 84–5
Freud, Sigmund 14, 15, 202n7
Fries, Jakob 19, 21

Gardiner, Patrick 12n22, 38n32
Garve, Christian 81
Glick, Thomas F. 6n14
Goethe, Johann Wolfgang von 62, 190
Golther, Ludwig von 4n11
Gottschalk, Rudolf 244n52
Grabbe, C. D. 1
Grotius, Hugo 65

Haeckel, Ernst 6n14, 261
Hamerow, Theodore 3n9
Hamlyn, D. W. 28n3, 32n17, 32n18, 33n23, 38n32

Hardenberg, Friedrich von. *See* Novalis
Hartmann, Alma von 124n11, 124n13, 125n14, 137n48, 158n103
Hartmann, Eduard von:
 critique of Bahnsen's philosophy 246–9, 259–63
 critique of Christianity 131–2, 133
 and Darwin 159
 his distinction between will and representation 136–8, 139–41
 and Dühring 166–7
 his eudemonic calculus 176–7
 his evolutionary optimism 156–61
 on first principles 136
 and Hegel 142–6
 and history 159–60
 on ideal and real realms 139–41
 and idealism 123–4, 129, 147
 and Kant 148–50, 151, 166
 on love and sex 196–7, 199–200
 and neo-Kantians 146–8, 150–1, 165–6, 175–6
 and pantheism 127, 134
 and pessimism 135–6, 152–6, 163–5
 his relationship with Bahnsen 252–3, 257–9
 and religion 130–5
 and Schelling 137–8, 141–2
 and Schopenhauer 125, 128, 141, 143, 152–3, 157–8
 and suicide 165
 and the unconscious 126–9
 on work 186
Hartsen, F. A. von 168n27
Haym, Rudolf 21, 21n20, 168, 172–6, 178–9, 181, 184, 186–7, 190–3, 194
Hegel, G. W. F. 11, 14, 19, 21, 25, 26, 67, 70–4, 85–6, 116, 123, 126, 128, 129, 137–9, 142–6, 155, 157, 159, 209–10, 218, 230–1, 234, 254–7, 260–1, 265, 271, 277, 278
Heine, Heinrich 1, 134, 187
Hellenbach, Lazar 13
Helmholtz, Hermann 78, 88
Herbart, Johann Friedrich 14, 19, 21, 163n4
Herder, Johann Gottfried 17, 190
Heydorn, Heinz-Joachim 229n3, 232, 233n16, 235, 237, 238, 239n42, 239n44, 241n49, 244n53
Heymons, Carl 1n2, 122n3, 167, 168, 171
Hölderlin, Friedrich 42
Horwicz, Adolf 176n49, 183, 184
Huber, Johannes 165n11, 174
Hübscher, Arthur 14n8, 21n19, 29n6, 63n11, 67n1
Hume, David 98

identity-crisis in philosophy 8–10, 15, 18–24
Immermann, K. L. 1

Jackson, Francis Helen 169n34
Jacobi, Friedrich Heinrich 16, 149
Jacquette, Dale 12n22, 38n32
Janaway, Christopher 12n22, 13n2, 28n3, 29n11, 32n17, 32n18, 33n22, 41n35

Kant, Immanuel 6, 19, 20, 21, 25, 27–30, 33–5, 37, 39–41, 57, 60, 65, 68, 77, 79, 83, 91–5, 99n28, 142, 147, 148–51, 164, 166, 203, 205, 212–15, 218, 219, 236–7, 247, 250–1, 266, 271, 274n103, 277, 279–81
Kelly, Alfred 6n14
Kemmer, Otto 1n3
Kieser, Rolf 168n31, 169n35
Klages, Ludwig 239
Knauer, Gustav 168, 170–2, 197, 198
Kohn, David 6n14
Köhnke, Klaus Christian 22n23, 24n29

Labau, Ferdinand 162n1, 162n2
Lange, Friedrich 25, 68, 150
Lasalle, Ferdinand 223, 226
Leibniz, Gottfried Wilhelm 25, 27, 47, 129, 138, 138n50, 153, 159
Lenau, N. 1
Leopardi, Giacomo 4
Lewis, Peter 12n22
Liebmann, Otto 20, 21, 22, 25
Lindner, Ernst 13
Lotze, Hermann 19, 19n16, 123, 181
Louis, Rudolf 229n1, 229n2, 231n11, 232n14, 233n15, 233n16, 234n17, 234n18, 236n26, 265n89, 281n110
love:
  controversy over the nature of 195–200
  Dühring's theory of 103, 105–7
  and Hartmann's theory of 131–2, 196–8
  Schopenhauer's theory of 50–1, 53, 195–6
  see also sex
Löwith, Karl 10, 10n19, 11
Lukács, Georg 2n6
Luther 64, 65, 130, 133
Lütkehaus, Lüdger vi, 11n21, 122n1, 202n7, 217n35

Magee, Bryan 15n9, 28n3, 32n18, 36n31, 38n32, 46n10
Magnus, Albertus 34
Mainländer, Philipp:
  on chastity and sex 221–2
  on Christianity 202, 208–9, 210–11
  his critique of Kant 213–15
  his critique of Schopenhauer 212, 214–15, 222, 223–4
  on death 202, 206–9
  on the death of God 202, 216–19
  on egoism 219–21, 224–5

and Hegelianism 210
and immanence 211–12
his interpretation of the trinity 216–17
life of 203–7, 221–2
his metaphysics 217–19
and nominalism 212
and pessimism 227
his philosophy of redemption 206–9, 210, 211–12
his political views 202–3, 223–5, 225–8
and Schopenhauer 204–5, 207, 219–20
on space 214
on Spinoza 204
on suicide 222–3
his theory of state 223–5, 226–8
on transcendental idealism 212–15
on the will 215–16, 219, 220
Malthus, Thomas 110, 111
Mann, Thomas 14, 15
Marr, Wilhelm 88
Marx, Karl 11, 90, 110, 226
Maupertuis, Pierre Louis 183
Materialism 6, 21
  and Dühring 114–16
  and Frauenstädt 68–9, 74–9
  and Hartmann 126–7, 132, 134
  materialism controversy 75–6
  Schopenhauer's critique of 39–42, 74–5
Mendelssohn, Moses 17
Meyer, Jürgen Bona 2, 19n15, 21, 25, 150, 168, 177–8, 186–7, 190–1, 200n102
Michelet, Karl 145n72
Mill, John Stuart 110, 278
Moleschott, Jacob 6, 21
Montgomery, William 6n14
Müller, F. A. 130n33
Müller, Johannes 78
Müller, Wolfgang 17n11
Müller-Seyfarth, Winfried 201, 203n12, 204n14, 229n3, 239n41

Neill, Alex 12n22
Neiman, Susan 5n13
neo-Kantianism:
  and identity-crisis 8–10, 19–24
  and pessimism 44, 172–5
  and pessimism controversy 165–8, 170–7, 187
  and Schopenhauer 15, 25–7, 36, 43–4
  see also Knauer; Meyer; Haym; Volkelt
Nietzsche, Friedrich 4n12, 6, 7, 10, 11–12, 13, 14, 15, 24, 45, 87, 87n3, 91, 97, 103–4, 107, 122, 123, 156, 160, 182, 193–4, 195n87, 202, 203, 203n13, 221, 228, 229, 239, 254, 263, 270n97, 278, 284
Neurath, Otto 88
Noack, Ludwig 142n60

Novalis 42, 195
Nyhart, Lynn 6n14

Oken, Lorenz 37

Pauen, Michael vi, 3n10, 11n21, 122n1, 156n97
Paulsen, Friedrich 10, 20, 21, 22, 176n49
pessimism:
  legacy of 10–12
  and identity-crisis 8–10
  objections to 163–5
  origins of 1–7
  and perceived dangers of 43–4, 172–6
  and problem of evil 5–8
  as zeitgeist 1–3
  see also Bahnsen; Dühring; Frauenstädt; Hartmann; Mainländer; Plümacher; Schopenhauer; Taubert
pessimism controversy: 8–12, 123, 162,
  see also ch. 8
Pfleiderer, Edmund 4n11
Plato 242
pleasure and pain:
  debate on the nature of 176–82, 183–5
  Dühring's views on 99–102
  Hartmann's views on 152–5, 157–8, 176–82
  and pessimism 9
  Schopenhauer's views on 32, 47–51, 102
Plümacher, Olga:
  on aesthetic experience 194–5
  her defense of pessimism 182–5
  influence on Nietzsche 182
  on work 188–90
positivism 9–10, 15, 20, 22, 23, 88–9, 93, 117–18, 121

Ranke, Leopold von 30, 159
Rasch, W. 1n4
Rauff, Jakob Friedrich 234, 235
Rehmke, Johannes 163n5, 180–1, 180n57, 184, 275n104
Reichenbach, Hans 88
Reinhold, Karl Leonhard 19, 68
Reymond, M. 1n2
Ricardo, David 110, 278
Rickert, Heinrich 10
Riehl, Alois 10, 20, 21, 23, 25
Rosenberg, Hans 2n7
Rousseau, Jean-Jacques 191, 277, 279

Savigny, Friedrich Carl von 159
Schaarschmidt, Carl 22
Schelling, F.W.J. 14, 19, 21, 25, 26, 37, 42, 71, 72, 77, 114, 116, 126, 128, 129, 137, 138–42, 144, 218
Schiller, Friedrich 190, 265–6

Schleiermacher, Friedrich 120, 273
Schlegel, Friedrich 42
Schlick, Moritz 88
Schnädelbach, Herbert 18n14
Schopenhauer, Arthur:
  on aesthetic experience 60–1
  on the affirmation and denial of the will 53–6
  on asceticism 61–2
  on death 105–6
  and doctrine of salvation 56–62, 63–6
  and the identity crisis 21–4
  influence of 13–15
  influence of stoics on 56–9
  and Kant 27–8, 30, 33–5, 37–40, 41–2, 57, 60, 65
  on love and sexual desire 195–6, 199–200
  his metaphysics 25–30
  and Naturphilosophie 37–8
  and neo-Kantianism 21–3
  and original sin 63–6
  and pessimism 43–4, 45, 46–51, 64
  his reinterpretation of thing-in-itself and appearance 27–30, 31–5, 38–41
  on suicide 107n42
  and transcendental idealism 38–42
  and value of existence 16–18 (see also, Pessimism)
  and the will 27–30, 31–5, 35–8
Schulze-Delitzsch, Hermann 110
Seiling, Max 1n3
sex:
  controversy over nature of 198–9
  and Hartmann's pessimism 154, 155, 196–7
  and Mainländer 221
  Schopenhauer's views of 50–1, 53, 55, 195–6
Shaftesbury, Anthony 65
Sheehan, James 132n37
Siebert, Otto 205n15, 230n7
Simmel, Georg 24, 36n30, 264
Slochower, Harry 229n2, 231n11
Snow, Dale 38n32
Snow, James 38n32
Sommer, Hugo 163n5, 181–2, 183, 200
Sophocles 4, 45
Spalding, J. J. 17
Spinoza, Baruch 25, 27, 36, 42, 96, 113, 120, 135, 140, 204, 205, 255
Stern, Fritz 2n8
Stirner, Max 209, 210, 233, 234
Stöcker, Adolf 88
stoicism 49, 56–9, 90, 269
Strauss, David 6, 72, 73, 119, 127, 131, 132, 134
Sully, James 168n32
suicide:
  and Bahnsen 270
  Dühring's views on 107

and Hartmann 155
and Mainländer 201
and Mainländer's ethics 222–3, 227
and pessimism 16, 59, 165, 227
and Schopenhauer's pessimism and prohibition of 44–5, 62, 222

Taubert, Agnes:
on aesthetic experience 191–4
her conservatism 169
and Haym 173
and Knauer 171–2
on love and sex 197, 199
and neo-Kantian critics 175–6, 178–80, 187–8, 191, 194
on the value of work 187–8
Thodoroff, Christo 241n50
Thomasius, Christian 65
Trautz, Theodor 1n1, 3
Treitschke, Heinrich von 88
Trendelenburg, Adolf 19, 123, 147n74, 151, 236, 247, 250, 251
Trendelenburg-Fischer dispute 151, 236, 250–1, *see also* Kuno Fischer; Adolf Trendelenburg

Vaihinger, Hans 10, 20, 116n63, 167
Vandenabeele, Bart 12n22
Vischer, Friedrich 235, 265
Vogt, Karl 6, 21, 75, 76

Volkelt, Johannes 21, 22n22, 23, 168, 176n49, 180n56, 187–9, 190n77, 198–200, 275n104

Wagner, Richard 14, 232
Wagner, Rudolph 75, 76
Weber, Max 264
Weckesser, Albert 176n49
Weiße, Hermann 19
Weimer, Wolfgang 12n22, 15n9, 40n33
Weindling, P. J. 6n14
Weis, Ludwig 197, 198
weltschmerz *see* pessimism
Weygoldt, Georg Peter 1n5, 3, 168n27, 174, 175, 180, 188, 189, 198
Wicks, Robert 12n22, 38n32, 41n35
Wiesike, Carl Ferdinand 14
Windelband, Wilhelm 10, 21, 22, 23n24, 24n29, 25, 174, 175
will, *see* Bahnsen; Frauenstädt; Hartmann; Mainländer; Schopenhauer
Wittgenstein, Ludwig 14, 15
Wolf, Jean-Claude 122n1, 125n19, 134n43, 160n105
Wolff, Christian 25, 27
work: value of 186–90

Young, Julian 12n22, 28n3, 38n32

Zeller, Eduard 20
Zint, Hans 14n5

Printed and bound by CPI Group (UK) Ltd, Croydon, CR0 4YY